CW01654148

How Jesus Built His Church

A Survey of Church History

How Jesus Built His Church

A *Survey of Church* History

By Joshua Schwisow
with
Kevin Swanson *and* **Daniel Noor**

Generations
PASSING ON THE FAITH

Printed in the United States of America.
1st Printing, 2023

ISBN: 978-1-954745-44-5

Cover Design: Justin Turley
Cover Image: Whitby Abbey, iStock.com
Interior Layout Design: Sarah Lee Bryant

Images in the interior of this book are taken from Wikimedia Commons (Public Domain) and iStock.com.

Published by:
Generations
19039 Plaza Drive Ste 210
Parker, Colorado 80134
www.generations.org

For more information on this and
other titles from Generations,
visit www.generations.org or call 888-389-9080.

Contents

Unit 3: The Late Middle Ages (AD 1000-1500)

Unit 4: The Reformation (AD 1500-1600)

Unit 5: The Post-Reformation Period (AD 1600-1750)

Unit 6: The Age of Missions and the Modern Period (1750-Present)

Introduction: Why Study Church History?

Dear Parents and Teachers,

Church History is the study of the greatest project the world has ever seen: Jesus Christ building His kingdom.

Unlike the history of other kingdoms of this world, this is the story of a kingdom that never fails. Pick up a textbook on world history and the recurring theme will be the rise and fall of empires, kingdoms, and nations. This recurring pattern of human history was dramatically revealed to the once-great Babylonian ruler Nebuchadnezzar. In a startling dream, Nebuchadnezzar was given a window into the future.

Unable to make sense of the meaning of this dream, Nebuchadnezzar looked to God's prophet Daniel. It was soon revealed that the various parts of the statue in the dream were different world kingdoms. Each kingdom rose to prominence, only to be destroyed by the next. Yet, there was one kingdom, the final in the dream, that would never fail. As Daniel revealed: "the God of heaven will set up a kingdom which shall never be destroyed" (Dan. 2:44).

This is the kingdom we are focusing on when we turn our attention to church history. It is a kingdom that will never be destroyed.

During Jesus' earthly ministry, He gave His disciples a promise. It was a promise of the church's victory over the forces of evil. In Matthew 16:18, we read:

And I also say to you that you are Peter, and on this rock I will build My church, and the gates of Hades shall not prevail against it. (Matt. 16:18)

Many read this verse of Matthew and think that the church is being assaulted by the forces of hell, and the church will not fall. The church is pictured like the old Alamo (in Texas), assaulted by forces on every side and barely holding on. In the case of the Alamo, the Mexicans eventually prevailed even though the Texans fought valiantly against all odds.

But to picture the church like a victorious Alamo is to misread the verse. What the verse actually says is that the gates of hell are being assaulted by the church of Christ. The forces of Christ's kingdom are doing spiritual battle with the forces of hell, and the gates of hell will eventually fall. Satan's kingdom will come to complete ruin.

To read church history is to be a front row spectator in this grand battle of Christ's kingdom against Satan's kingdom. And even though the church faces persecution, suffering, and sometimes even a decline in numbers, the kingdom of Christ marches on. The gates of hell will not be able to prevail against the onslaught of Christ and His disciples against the forces of spiritual darkness.

Important Themes in Church History

When approaching any subject, it can sometimes be difficult to keep in focus the most important things when there are so many details, so many stories, so many people, and so many dates. Any time we study history, the big question you should ask is this: "What is God doing in history?"

This assumes, of course, that God is sovereign over the entire universe, from the empires that rise to sparrows that fall from the sky (Matt. 10:29).

There is one interpretive rule that every Christian must bring to history. Jesus Christ is the ruler of all things to the church (Eph. 1:22-23). Everything that happens in history works its way out for the benefit of His church.

For Christians, God's Word is the most important interpretive tool for historical studies. What then are some important biblical truths we should keep in mind?

Here are some of the most important themes to remember as you embark on this study of church history.

Theme #1 — The conflict between the serpent and the Seed of the woman

The Lord Jesus Christ is the promised deliverer who crushes the head of the serpent (Gen. 3:15). The ancient foe of humanity, the one the Bible calls the adversary and the accuser, is defeated by the Lord Jesus Christ. The decisive blow to the serpent's head happened when Jesus died on the cross and rose again. The devil is mortally wounded. But until Jesus returns, the devil will use all of his remaining strength to go after Jesus and Jesus' people. In fact, the Bible says that the devil knows "his time is short" (Rev. 12:12). This makes him even more enraged.

Revelation 12 describes the ongoing conflict between the serpent and God's people.

Now when the dragon saw that he had been cast to the earth, he persecuted the woman who gave birth to the male Child. But the woman was given two wings of a great eagle, that she might fly into the wilderness to her place, where she is nourished for a time and times and half a time, from the presence of the serpent. So the serpent spewed water out of his mouth like a flood after the woman, that he might cause her to be carried away by the flood. But the earth helped the woman, and the earth opened its mouth and swallowed up the flood which the dragon had spewed out of his mouth. And the dragon was enraged with the woman, and he went to make war with the rest of her offspring, who keep the commandments of God and have the testimony of Jesus Christ. (Rev. 12:13-17)

The final verse of this biblical quotation helps us understand what is taking place in church history. Satan is out to make war against the offspring of the woman (the church). Those who follow Jesus are defined as those who "keep the commandments of God and have the testimony of Jesus Christ."

Satan's warfare against Christ's followers takes several forms. The Bible teaches us that Satan is a murderer and a liar. As such, it should not surprise us that one of his strategies against the offspring of the woman is to kill them. He does this through persecutions.

Another common strategy Satan employs is to introduce lies into the church. These we call "false teaching" or "heresies." These falsehoods have the effect of confusing followers of Jesus, dividing the church, and in some cases leading some people down to hell.

Persecutions and heresies, then, are common occurrences in church history.

Theme #2 — The kingdom of God grows throughout history

A second theme the Bible instructs us to look for in history is the growth of Christ's kingdom. You will see the kingdom of God grow as the church of Jesus Christ expands around the globe. The church of Jesus Christ will include every tribe and nation by the end. Jesus' kingdom works like leaven, quietly and steadily growing. Our Lord's parable in Matthew 13 says so.

Another parable He put forth to them, saying: "The kingdom of heaven is like a mustard seed, which a man took and sowed in his field, which indeed is the least of all the seeds; but when it is grown it is greater than the herbs and becomes a tree, so that the birds of the air come and nest in its branches." Another parable He spoke to them: "The kingdom of heaven is like leaven, which a woman took and hid in three measures of meal till it was all leavened." (Matt. 13:31-33)

Most of the work done by the followers of the carpenter from Galilee does not make it to the front page of the newspapers. But when the dust settles and the history books are written, we find a church around the world. We find Christian hospitals and orphanages everywhere. We find Christian culture impacting every aspect of human life on planet earth! That is how the mustard seed and the leaven works. It is slow. It is subtle. But it does really grow.

Theme #3 — Jesus Christ builds His church through the faithful ministry of His people

Unlike human empires, Jesus does not expand His kingdom with human weapons like swords, spears, or cavalry. He does not deploy tanks or airplanes. Instead, our Lord advances His kingdom through the faithful ministry of His people. Church history is about what Jesus did through faithful men, women, boys, and girls.

In the building of Christ's church, Ephesians 4 tells us that especially important are those faithful pastors and teachers who equip the rest of the saints for ministry.

And He Himself gave some to be apostles, some prophets, some evangelists, and some pastors and teachers, for the equipping of the saints for the work of ministry, for the edifying of the body of Christ (Eph. 4:11-12)

In the pages that follow, you will learn about faithful pastors and teachers who edified the church and equipped God's people for ministry. But you will also learn about people from numerous backgrounds. These include men of renown such as kings. But they also include people who the world thought of little to no importance. A poor young lady like Blandina did not seem important to the world. But her testimony in martyrdom lives on today.

Jesus' kingdom works differently than the world's kingdoms. The world prioritizes the mighty. Jesus uses weak people to put to shame the strong. The world prioritizes the rich. Jesus' people do great things though they are poor. The world prioritizes the wise. But Jesus' people often appear foolish to the world.

The stories of church history, then, are about faithful Christians who served Jesus. Through them, Jesus builds His church.

Theme #4 — The importance of preaching and teaching the Word of God

The dying words of the Apostle Paul to Timothy provide for us the mandate for the Christian Church:

I charge you therefore before God and the Lord Jesus Christ, who will judge the living and the dead at His appearing and His kingdom: Preach the word! Be ready in season and out of season. Convince, rebuke, exhort, with all longsuffering and teaching. For the time will come when they will not endure

sound doctrine, but according to their own desires, because they have itching ears, they will heap up for themselves teachers; and they will turn their ears away from the truth, and be turned aside to fables. But you be watchful in all things, endure afflictions, do the work of an evangelist, fulfill your ministry. (2 Tim. 4:1-5)

Preach the Word! That is the mandate. Wherever the Word of God is preached, clearly, truthfully, and sincerely, the work of the kingdom progresses. Where the church becomes slothful, where human ritual displaces the people's interest in the Word, where the sacraments play a stronger role than the Word, where the Word is read and preached in a language unfamiliar to the people listening, the church wilts and dies.

Jesus told us to disciple the nations by baptizing and teaching them all things Jesus commanded (Matt. 28:18-20). Therefore, the preaching and teaching of the Word of God is vital for the growth of the church.

Applying What You Learn

Faith without works is dead (Jas. 2:17). And learning about church history should change the way you live. How can you apply what you learn in this course?

First, the goal of studying church history should be to give praise to God for what He has done. As Psalm 78 says, "We will not hide them from their children, telling to the generation to come the praises of the Lord, and His strength and His wonderful works that He has done" (Ps. 78:4). As you read of God's wonderful works through the lives of men and women, give praise to God!

Second, you can apply what you learn by learning from those who came before you. How did these men and women stand fast for Christ in adversity? How did these men and women teach the faith to others? How did these men and women influence future generations? Paul once said, "follow me as I follow Christ" (1 Cor. 11:1). You should do the same for the men and women covered in this course. Insofar as they faithfully followed the Lord Jesus Christ, you should follow in their footsteps.

Third, this course should help you love Christ's church more. The Lord Jesus died for His bride, the church. He nourishes and cares for it. If we love what Christ loves, then we too must love His church. Our Lord said, "By this all will know that you are My disciples, if you have love for one another" (John 13:35).

It is our prayer that this resource will be used by our Lord to instruct, edify, and equip you to seek the kingdom of God and His righteousness (Matt. 6:33) and to dedicate your life to the most important project on planet earth: discipling the nations for Jesus.

The Church shall never perish!
Her dear Lord to defend,
To guide, sustain, and cherish,
Is with her to the end:
Though there be those who hate her,
And false sons in her pale,
Against or foe or traitor
She ever shall prevail.

(From Samuel J. Stone, "The Church's One Foundation")

— Joshua Schwisow

The Generations Curriculum Team

March 2023

BC 250
Old Testament Septuagint Produced

BC 4/AD 1
Jesus is Born

AD 33
Jesus' Death, Burial, and Resurrection

AD 44
Martyrdom of James

AD 54-68
Reign of Nero

AD 64-67
Persecution under Nero

AD 67 or 68
Martyrdom of Peter and Paul

AD 383-404
Latin Vulgate translation of the Bible is Produced

AD 397-400
Confessions by Augustine is Written

AD 410
The Sack of Rome

AD 417
Pelagian Controversy

AD 426
Augustine completes *The City of God*

AD 430
Death of Augustine of Hippo

AD 451
Council of Chalcedon

Unit 1

The Early Church (AD 30-500)

AD 81-96
Persecution under Domitian

AD 155
Martyrdom of Polycarp

AD 177
Martyrdom of Blandina

AD 202
Persecution under Septimius Severus

AD 303-311
The Great Persecution under Diocletian

AD 312
Battle of Milvian Bridge

AD 319
On the Incarnation of the Word by Athanasius is Written

AD 325
Council of Nicaea

AD 325-326
Eusebius' *Church History* is Written

AD 328
Athanasius Becomes Bishop of Alexandria

AD 354
Augustine of Hippo Born

AD 369
First Hospital Established

AD 381
Council of Constantinople

THE OLD CITY OF JERUSALEM

In the Fullness of Time

But when the fullness of the time had come, God sent forth His Son, born of a woman, born under the law, to redeem those who were under the law, that we might receive the adoption as sons. (Gal. 4:4-5)

The Bible describes Christ's church as a building and as a household. All buildings have different components including walls, a roof, and a foundation. If we are to learn about the history of Christ's church, we need to begin by looking at the foundation. The foundation, according to the Bible, is the apostles and prophets. But even more important than them is the cornerstone: our Lord Jesus Christ.

Ephesians 2 says:

Now, therefore, you are no longer strangers and foreigners, but fellow citizens with the saints and members of the household of God, having been built on the foundation of the apostles and prophets, Jesus Christ Himself being the chief cornerstone, (Eph. 2:19-20)

Let's look at the cornerstone first: our Lord Jesus; who He is, and what He did. Secondly, we must also look at the foundation of the apostles and prophets. Before we look at more of this glorious structure that is the church, we need to first look at the cornerstone and the foundation. Without the foundation, a structure cannot stand.

Who Jesus Is, and What He Came to Do

The cornerstone of the church is the Lord Jesus Christ. He is the most important person in all of human history. There is good reason that calendars in the Western world have been divided between **BC** and **AD**:

BC ▪ Before Christ

AD ▪ Anno Domini (Latin for "in the year of our Lord")

This division of history into two sections is a recognition of the Lordship of Jesus Christ. To say that we are living in the year AD 2023 (the date of this publication) is to say this: we are living in the year 2023, in which Jesus Christ continues to reign over all things. Of course, not everyone

THERE WAS NO ROOM AT THE INN FOR JOSEPH AND MARY, OR FOR THE LORD JESUS

acknowledges that Jesus Christ is Lord over all things. But one day, they will (Phil. 2:10-11).

Why is Jesus so central to human history?

Ever since Adam and Eve fell into sin in the Garden of Eden, the creation has been groaning for redemption. Mankind has experienced the terrible effects of sin. Sin has many destructive effects. But the final consequence of sin is death and eternal judgment. Even though mankind fell in the garden, the Lord God was merciful to make a promise: a promise that one day a Redeemer would come and destroy sin, Satan, and death (Gen. 3:15). The rest of the Old Testament contains promises, pictures, and prophecies about that coming Redeemer. By promises, God told His people that He would be merciful to them and forgive their sins. By pictures, such as animal sacrifices, the Lord showed His people that they needed covering for their sins. By prophecies, the Lord gave some shadowy details about who the Messiah would be and what He would do when He came.

All of the Old Testament and the entire BC period of history was a waiting period. Mankind was waiting for the Redeemer to come.

God had planned the exact timing to send His Son into the world. Paul tells us that Jesus, the Son of God, was born of a woman, "in the fullness of time." This means, when the appointed time came, Jesus came, just at the right time.

The King of kings came in a rather unexpected way. The great rulers of the kingdoms such as Augustus Caesar or Herod the Great were in their lavish palaces. But the one who was to be King over all the nations was born in a manger, among animals, in a small village. The news concerning His birth went out, not to the exalted rulers of the earth, but to lowly shepherds one night. **Luke** the physician recounts these events in His carefully written and researched Gospel:

Now there were in the same country shepherds living out in the fields, keeping watch over their flock by night. And behold, an angel of the Lord stood before them, and the glory of the Lord shone around them, and they were greatly afraid. Then the angel said to them, "Do not be afraid, for behold, I bring you good tidings of great joy which will be to all people. For there is born to you this day in the city of David a Savior, who is Christ the Lord. And this will be the sign to you: You will find a Babe wrapped in swaddling cloths, lying in a manger." And suddenly there was with the angel a multitude of the heavenly host praising God and saying: "Glory to God in the highest, and on earth peace, goodwill toward men!" (Luke 2:8-14)

The angels announced to the shepherds who this child was. He was the Savior who would deliver God's people from their sins. He was the Christ (the Messiah), the anointed one who would fulfill all of God's promises, pictures, and prophecies.

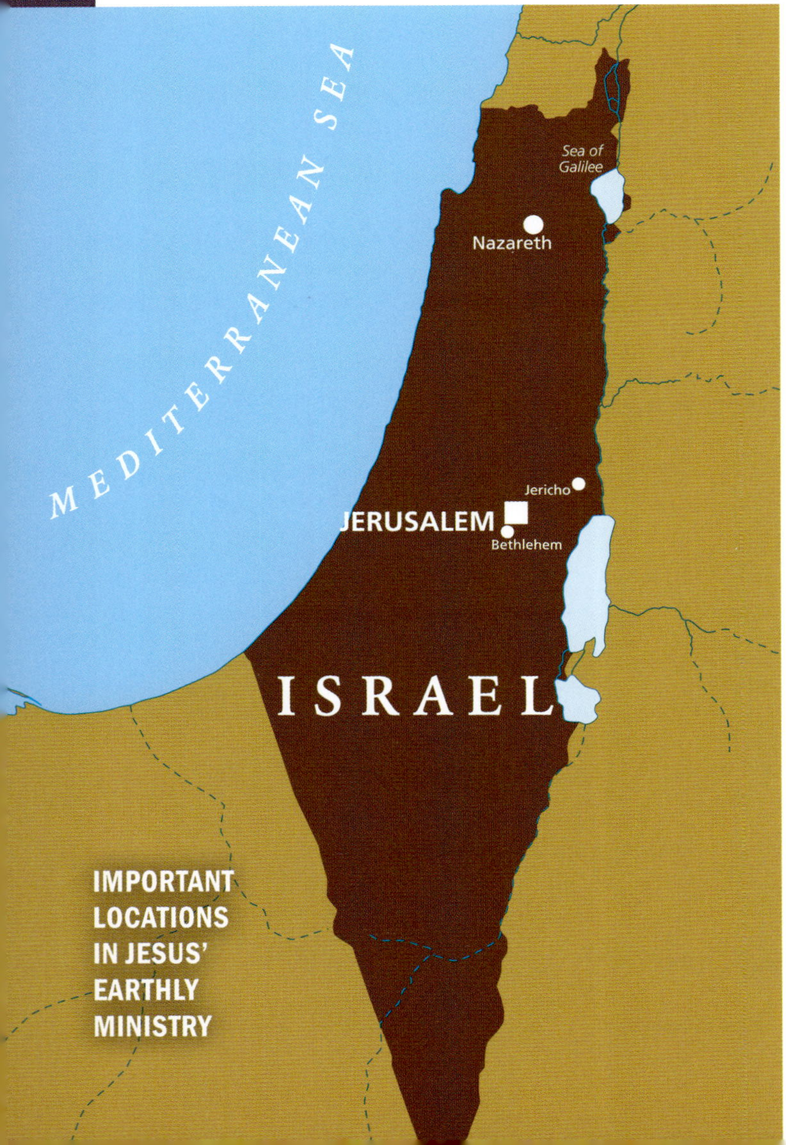

IMPORTANT LOCATIONS IN JESUS' EARTHLY MINISTRY

And He was (and is) Lord over all!

Many years passed as Jesus grew up in Nazareth. During that time, Jesus did not exercise a public ministry. But around thirty years of age, our Lord entered into His public ministry when He was baptized by John the Baptist. By His baptism, identifying with a sinful people, and by His temptation, Jesus demonstrated that He came to do what the first Adam failed to do. Jesus would obey the Lord. Jesus would defeat Satan. Jesus would accomplish a redemption through His atoning death on the cross. And He would destroy death through His resurrection.

Each of the four Gospels (Matthew, Mark, Luke, John) culminate with the central events of our Lord's death and resurrection. Before the cross, Jesus' disciples failed to understand why it was necessary for Him to die. But following His resurrection, they began to understand why He had to die and rise again. Our Lord explained from the Old Testament how He came to fulfill all that was written:

Then He said to them, "O foolish ones, and slow of heart to believe in all that the prophets have spoken! Ought not the Christ to have suffered these things and to enter into His glory?" And beginning at Moses and all the Prophets, He expounded to them in all the Scriptures the things concerning Himself. (Luke 24:25-27)

After a period of forty days, the Lord Jesus ascended to the right hand of the Father, where He remains at the present, ruling over all things. Before His ascension, our Lord gave His disciples the Great Commission. The commission was great because it involved an enormous task: discipling all the peoples of the earth by baptizing and teaching them Christ's commands. It is a project that continues today. The Gospel of Matthew records Jesus' words in the **Great Commission**:

And Jesus came and spoke to them, saying, "All authority has been given to Me in heaven and on earth. Go therefore and make disciples of all the nations, baptizing them in the name of the Father and of the Son and of the Holy Spirit, teaching them to observe all things that I have commanded you; and lo, I am with you always, even to the end of the age." Amen. (Matt. 28:18-20)

This is a monumental mission. It would be impossible if it relied on man's strength alone. But the risen Lord Jesus Christ has all authority in heaven and on earth. For this reason, we know that the commission will be accomplished. The church of Jesus Christ will prevail!

DAY OF PENTECOST

They were given the ability to proclaim "the wonderful works of God" in different languages.

Early in human history, the peoples of the earth had been divided at the Tower of Babel (Gen. 11). To keep mankind from banding together against God, the Lord divided the languages of the peoples and scattered them throughout the earth. But the Day of Pentecost was the day on which the reunion of all mankind began. From then on, and to the present, peoples from every tribe, nation, and tongue are redeemed by the Lamb of God (Rev. 5:9-10). The church is the manifestation of what the Bible calls "one new man," which refers to all peoples being united into one (Eph. 2:15-16).

At Pentecost, the worldwide gospel mission had begun. From Jerusalem the message would spread to Judea. From Judea the message would spread to Samaria. Eventually, the message would reach the heart of the Roman Empire: the city of Rome. After the gospel reached Rome, it would continue to spread throughout the earth.

The Meaning of Pentecost

Before His ascension, the Lord Jesus promised to pour out the Holy Spirit on His disciples. Our Lord told His disciples to wait for the promise of the Spirit. Luke records Jesus' parting words to His disciples in Acts 1.

Therefore, when they had come together, they asked Him, saying, "Lord, will You at this time restore the kingdom to Israel?" And He said to them, "It is not for you to know times or seasons which the Father has put in His own authority. But you shall receive power when the Holy Spirit has come upon you; and you shall be witnesses to Me in Jerusalem, and in all Judea and Samaria, and to the end of the earth." (Acts 1:6-8)

Such a worldwide mission effort would require power. That is why the Holy Spirit came on the **Day of Pentecost**. The powerful Holy Spirit of God gave His disciples power to preach the gospel to all nations and fulfill the Great Commission.

About forty days after Jesus rose from the dead, the Day of Pentecost came. Worshipers of God from different lands gathered in Jerusalem for this festival each year. On that day, the Holy Spirit descended upon the Christian disciples.

The Spread of the Early Church

One of the earliest and best documents to learn about the early history of the church is the **Book of Acts**. Not only is this book early and detailed; it is also inspired by the Holy Spirit. Acts is an infallible record of what the Lord Jesus did, through the Holy Spirit and through the apostles, to establish the foundation of the church.

Acts is especially focused upon the spread of God's Word and the growth of Christ's church. A good summary of what happens in Acts is found in chapter 9.

Then the churches throughout all Judea, Galilee, and Samaria had peace and were edified. And

walking in the fear of the Lord and in the comfort of the Holy Spirit, they were multiplied. (Acts 9:31)

The church multiplies in Acts, finally culminating in Paul's arrival at Rome (Acts 28).

Much of Acts focuses on the missionary efforts of the **Apostle Peter** and the **Apostle Paul**. Peter served as an apostle to the Jews. Paul was called by Jesus Christ to be an apostle to the Gentiles. After His resurrection, the Lord Jesus told Peter in John 21:18 that he would face martyrdom. Peter began ministering primarily to the Jews in Jerusalem, in Joppa (by the Mediterranean Sea), and Antioch (in Syria). Peter's ministry included Asia Minor (modern-day Turkey) and Rome. Peter finished the work God had for him. His earthly life ended when he was killed in Rome. By order of the evil **Emperor Nero** (reigned AD 54-68), Peter was executed around AD 67 or 68. We learn from a Christian writer named **Origen** (c. AD 185-253) that Peter was crucified upside down. This was by Peter's own request. Peter did not see himself as worthy to die in the same way Jesus had been crucified.

The conversion of Paul to faith in Christ is one of the most dramatic events in Acts. At first, we read that Paul (first called Saul) is responsible for the execution of some of the first Christians. Paul oversaw the execution of **Stephen**, the first witness to die in Acts (Acts 7-8). But on the road to Damascus, on his way to imprison and kill more Christians, Jesus stopped Paul. Paul was blinded by the light of Christ's glory. Jesus then commanded Paul to go to Damascus and wait. The Lord then sent His servant Ananias to minister to Paul. The Lord Jesus told Ananias:

EMPEROR NERO (R. AD 54-68)

Go, for he is a chosen vessel of Mine to bear My name before Gentiles, kings, and the children of Israel. For I will show him how many things he must suffer for My name's sake. (Acts 9:15-16)

Paul was baptized and was then sent by Jesus to bear witness to all the nations. In many ways, Paul was an ideal evangelist. The Lord Jesus used Paul's natural gifts for God's glory. Paul was an educated man. Paul understood Greek philosophy, having been raised in Tarsus. He was also one of the most committed Pharisees. Paul was a former disciple of one of the leading Jewish teachers, a man named Gamaliel. Paul would use this training in His preaching and teaching. But the most important factor in Paul's ministry was the Holy Spirit's empowering.

One notable example of Paul's preaching is found in Acts 17, when he confronts the pagan philosopher on Mars Hill in the ancient city of Athens. Atop Mars Hill, Paul proclaimed the truth of the gospel. When Paul saw in the city a statue to an "unknown God," he saw an opportunity to make known the one true and living God to the people of Athens who had so long lived in ignorance of the one true God.

Here is a portion of the sermon Luke the physician recorded in Acts:

Truly, these times of ignorance God overlooked, but now commands all men everywhere to repent, because He has appointed a day on which He will judge the world in righteousness by the Man whom

He has ordained. He has given assurance of this to all by raising Him from the dead. (Acts 17:30-31)

The truth of Christ's resurrection was a central topic of gospel proclamation in Acts. It was a central point in Peter's sermon in Pentecost. And it appears many other times in Acts, including in Paul's sermon on Mars Hill. The resurrection of Christ changed everything. Now, every creature on the earth needed to hear this good news (Mark 16:15).

Paul's life as an apostle wasn't easy, however. Few missionaries have ever suffered as much as Paul did. Paul tells us that he suffered the loss of all things in order to gain Jesus Christ (Phil. 3:7-11). Paul's first missionary journey covered 1,400 miles (covering Cyprus and modern-day Turkey). His second missionary journey was twice as long. It spanned about 2,800 miles. He traveled through Syria, Turkey, Greece, and Jerusalem, mostly on foot. On his third missionary journey, Paul visited Turkey, Greece, Lebanon, and Israel. On this third journey, Paul logged another 2,700 miles. The Apostle Paul also wrote a large portion of the New Testament. In his letters, Paul wrote to churches and individuals (Timothy, Titus, Philemon). On Paul's fourth missionary journey, he sailed to Rome. On this fourth journey, Paul was under arrest by the Romans, as he went to have an audience with Caesar. Sometime after this fourth journey, Paul was put to death in Rome. Historical records tell us Paul was executed by the Emperor Nero. A likely date for Paul's execution is AD 67.

Paul's final written testimony was sent to his

PAUL ON THE DAMASCUS ROAD

son in the faith, Timothy. Paul wrote:

I have fought the good fight, I have finished the race, I have kept the faith. Finally, there is laid up for me the crown of righteousness, which the Lord, the righteous Judge, will give to me on that Day, and not to me only but also to all who have loved His appearing. (2 Tim. 4:7-8)

After Peter and Paul's deaths, the Apostle John's ministry went on. John's ministry was active particularly in Asia Minor. It is believed that John spent much of his time in Ephesus (modern-day Turkey). He wrote five New Testament books in all, including three letters (1, 2, 3 John) and the Gospel of John. He penned his fifth work, the Book of Revelation, while exiled on the island of Patmos. After his exile, John died somewhere between AD 80 and AD 100 and was buried at Ephesus.

The missionary labors of the other apostles are not all recorded in the New Testament. However, early church documents tell us that the other apostles took the gospel into Egypt, Syria, Greece, Africa, and India. The apostles were faithful in carrying out Jesus' commission.

The Romans did not intend for the gospel to spread throughout the world. But in God's perfect providence, the Romans and Greeks prepared the way to make it happen. The Christian faith spread rapidly. This was due in part to the peace of Rome (the ***Pax Romana***), which provided for safer travel. A ship could cross the Mediterranean without encountering a single pirate. Also, a vast network of well-built roads throughout the Roman Empire gave the apostles a solid path upon which they would wear out their sandals. They did exactly that as they spread the good news all over the world.

Our Lord Jesus Christ is the cornerstone of the Christian church. Upon that stone was built the foundational ministry and teaching of the apostles and prophets. That foundation having been laid, the church of Jesus Christ continues to be built to the present day. ■

THE COLISEUM IN ROME

The Church Faces Opposition

2

If the world hates you, you know that it hated Me before it hated you. If you were of the world, the world would love its own. Yet because you are not of the world, but I chose you out of the world, therefore the world hates you. Remember the word that I said to you, "A servant is not greater than his master." If they persecuted Me, they will also persecute you. If they kept My word, they will keep yours also. (John 15:18-20)

Before our Lord's crucifixion, He told His disciples that they would also suffer persecution. To be a disciple, Jesus said, was to take up a cross and follow in His footsteps. A servant is not above his master. It was no surprise then that the first Christians immediately met with opposition and persecution.

Christianity is considered by many the largest religion in the world today. It should be no surprise then that persecution of Christians today is more extensive than it has ever been. Wherever the gospel advances, the defeated dragon, with the assistance of his demonic hordes, fights back (Rev. 12:17). The dragon makes war with those who keep the commandments of God and hold the testimony concerning Jesus Christ.

It is important for us to learn how the early Christians responded to the opposition of the dragon. By recounting the stories of those faithful witnesses who went before us, we too can be strengthened to stand for Jesus Christ.

It was not long before opposition against the gospel mission occurred. The early chapters of Acts record the Apostles' courage in the face of violent opposition. Suffering for the name of Jesus became a common experience for those early disciples.

The Bible records that **Peter** and **John** were imprisoned for their preaching of the gospel (Acts 5:17-18). **Stephen** suffered a martyr's death (Acts 7:54-60). **James** also died at the hands of Herod (Acts 12:1-2).

Gospel advance and church growth is evident throughout the Book of Acts. But with that church growth came suffering. It was necessary for the apostles to strengthen the hearts of the disciples. They were not to be surprised by this suffering. One example of that kind of exhortation is found in Acts 14.

And when they had preached the gospel to that city and made many disciples, they returned to Lystra, Iconium, and Antioch, strengthening the souls of the disciples, exhorting them to continue in the faith, and saying, "We must through many tribulations enter the kingdom of God." (Acts 14:21-22)

Entering the kingdom of God *through* tribulation was a necessity, Paul and Barnabas proclaimed. Such tribulation was not wasted. As the Apostle Peter wrote, the sufferings they experienced refined their faith in the furnace. As a result of such refining fires, their faith came out shining even more brightly. Such faith was more valuable than gold or silver.

In this you greatly rejoice, though now for a little while, if need be, you have been grieved by various trials, that the genuineness of your faith, being much more precious than gold that perishes, though it is tested by fire, may be found to praise, honor, and glory at the revelation of Jesus Christ, (1 Pet. 1:6-7)

Many of the early chapters of Acts detail these persecutions. Acts records some of the challenges the apostles faced, including a riot in the city of Ephesus (Acts 19). In Acts 17, the Christians are described as those who "are turning the

THE APOSTLE PAUL PREACHING ON MARS HILL

world upside down." This is an apt description of the effect that Christ has upon the world. Where the saving work of Christ takes effect, people are changed, and then cultures are changed.

One of the earliest and most severe persecutions of the early church occurred during the reign of the Roman emperor **Nero** (AD 54-68). Nero is considered by many to be one of the most wicked men who ever lived. Nero was a murderer and a despot who lived according to his own pleasures. Many of the Roman emperors had practically unbounded power. They often used their authority to secure their own selfish interests. Such was the case with Nero.

The Persecution under Nero

Do not marvel, my brethren, if the world hates you. (1 John 3:13)

When a fire broke out in Rome in AD 64, Nero blamed the Christians for the catastrophe. Many suspected that Nero himself had ordered the fire. But who would hold the emperor accountable for such a thing? The Christians proved an easy target to blame. They were a minority in the empire. Few Romans understood the claims of Christianity. Many slanderous misrepresentations of Christi-

CHRISTIAN MARTYRS IN THE COLISEUM

anity passed around the empire. Lies told about the Christians made many citizens of the empire hostile to this new and strange group of people.

What were some of the lies? They seem strange to us today. But they were believed by many. Christians were accused of cannibalism because they spoke about eating the body and blood of Christ. This was a reference to the practice of the Lord's Supper. But it confused many Romans. Christians were also accused of being **atheists**. The word "atheist" means someone who does not believe in God. It seems odd then, that Christians would be accused of atheism. But they were accused of this because the Christians rejected all the false gods of Rome. Christians were also accused of incest/immorality because they called each other brother and sister. Christians used these names because they were part of the same spiritual family. But some Romans were confused and believed false accusations. False charges like these made many Romans wary of the Christians.

THE FIRE IN ROME

ROMAN HISTORIAN TACITUS (C. AD 56-120)

It also happened to be the case that the area of Rome that most Christians resided in was largely untouched by the fire. To the superstitious Roman, this suggested that the Christians were to blame for such destruction. Nero cast blame upon the Christians and their dangerous religion. The Roman historian **Tacitus** (c. AD 56-120), in his *Annals*, records how this occurred:

> In spite of every human effort, of the emperor's largesse, and of the sacrifices made to the gods, nothing sufficed to allay suspicion nor to destroy the opinion that the fire had been ordered. Therefore, in order to destroy this rumor, Nero blamed the Christians, who are hated for their abominations, and punished them with refined cruelty. Christ, from whom they take their name, was executed by Pontius Pilate during the reign of Tiberius. Stopped for a moment, this evil superstition reappeared, not only in Judea, where was the root of the evil, but also in Rome, where all things sordid and abominable from every corner of the world come together. Thus, first those who confessed (that they were Christians) were arrested, and on the basis of their testimony a great number were condemned, although not so much for the fire itself as for their hatred of humankind.[1]

It is clear from this quotation that Tacitus is no friend to Christianity. But Tacitus also recognized that it was not actually the Christians who had caused this disaster. Tacitus believed that the Christians were hand-picked by Nero as a target for the catastrophe. Tacitus went on to record how the Christians were persecuted:

> Before killing the Christians, Nero used them to amuse the people. Some were dressed in furs, to be killed by dogs. Others were crucified. Still others were set on fire early in the night, so that they might illumine it. Nero opened his own gardens for

> these shows, and in the circus he himself became a spectacle, for he mingled with the people dressed as a charioteer, or he rode around in his chariot. All of this aroused the mercy of the people, even against these culprits who deserved an exemplary punishment, for it was clear that they were not being destroyed for the common good, but rather to satisfy the cruelty of one person.[2]

This kind of cruelty was common during the persecution of Nero which lasted until about AD 67. According to church historian **Eusebius**, Peter and Paul were also martyred in Rome during this persecution.

When Christianity first began to spread in the Roman Empire, many thought that Christianity was just a sect of the Jews. It appeared to be a variation on the religion of the Jews rather than a new religion altogether. It is true that Christianity is the fulfillment of the Old Testament Scriptures. But for those Jews who rejected Christ, they saw Christianity as a dangerous heresy. But for the average citizen of the Roman Empire with little knowledge of the Old Testament or Judaism, it was difficult to distinguish Judaism and Christianity.

One example of this attitude is found in the words of Gallio, the pronconsul of Achaia recorded in Acts 18.

And when Paul was about to open his mouth, Gallio said to the Jews, "If it were a matter of wrongdoing or wicked crimes, O Jews, there would be reason why I should bear with you. But if it is a question of words and names and your own law, look to it yourselves; for I do not want to be a judge of such matters." (Acts 18:14-15)

For Gallio, and for many other citizens of the empire, the claims of Christ were just a Jewish dispute about words and names. In time, however, this perception would change.

For centuries, the Jews had dispersed across the Roman Empire and had freely practiced their religion. While pagan Romans thought the Jews strange, there was an allowance for Jews to practice their religion unhindered in the empire. Judaism gained the status of *religio licita* (lawful religion).

But as Christianity became more widely known, and as people in the Roman Empire became familiar with Christians, they learned that

RUINS OF THE TEMPLE OF APOLLO IN CORINTH

real differences existed between Judaism and Christianity. As a "new sect," Christianity did not enjoy the legal protections that were afforded the Jews. As such, at different times in the early centuries of the church, Christianity was considered *religio illicita* (unlawful religion). Nero's persecution was evidence of how Christianity was beginning to be perceived in Rome and elsewhere.

A DENARIUS DEPICTING DOMITIAN

The Persecution under Domitian

After the death of Nero, widespread persecution abated for a time. But it resumed during the reign of **Domitian** (AD 81-96). Domitian unleashed another wave of persecution. It is not known for sure what Domitian's motive was in harming the Christians. However, Domitian did intend to "restore" the glory of the Roman Empire. In his mind, this included the restoration of Roman religion. If Rome would be restored to a former state of glory, the gods of Rome would be glorified. This was an obvious problem for the Christians. The lordship of Christ demanded that no rival god could take His place. Christians obeyed the first command. "You shall have no other gods before me" (Ex. 20:3).

After the reign of Domitian, persecution was sporadic and localized. One historical record of note is a series of letters between **Pliny the Younger** (c. AD 61-113) and the Emperor **Trajan** (r. AD 98-117). Pliny, governor of Bithynia, wrote to the Emperor Trajan for guidance. Pliny was unsure how to handle Christians in his region.

Trajan told Pliny not to go on the hunt for Christians to arrest them. But if a Christian was exposed and would not submit to the worship of the Roman gods, then they were to be arrested, tried, and executed. By Trajan's calculation, it was not worth the resources and effort to seek out Christians. But when a Christian defied the laws of the empire, they were to be punished. It was this policy outlined by Trajan that was followed for periods in the 2nd and 3rd centuries. As a result, persecution was not constant or universal. However, during the reign of **Marcus Aurelius** (r. AD 161-180), a severe persecution occurred in AD 177 in the south of France. We will learn more about this persecution below.

The Persecution under Decius

Yes, and all who desire to live godly in Christ Jesus will suffer persecution. (2 Tim. 3:12)

Near the beginning of the 3rd century, persecution once again increased during the reigns of **Septimius Severus** (r. AD 193-211) and **Decius** (r. AD 249-251). However, it was the "great perse-

EXTENT OF THE ROMAN EMPIRE IN AD 117

cution" under **Diocletian** (r. AD 284-305) and his successors that was the worst and most widespread persecution of the early church. It lasted for eight years from 303-311. This persecution is recorded with eyewitness accounts by the Christian historians **Eusebius** (c. 260-339) and **Lactantius** (c. 250-325). These narratives and eyewitness accounts are gruesome and heartbreaking. Yet they also serve as remarkable examples of tremendous faith in Christ.

The title **martyr** began to be applied to those Christians who gave their life for Christ. Originally derived from the Greek word "witness," the martyrs were those witnesses for Christ who "did not love their lives to the death" (Rev. 12:11), but overcame by the blood of the lamb and by the word of their testimony.

What follows in this chapter are a few brief accounts of well-known martyrs of the early church.

The Martyrdom of Ignatius

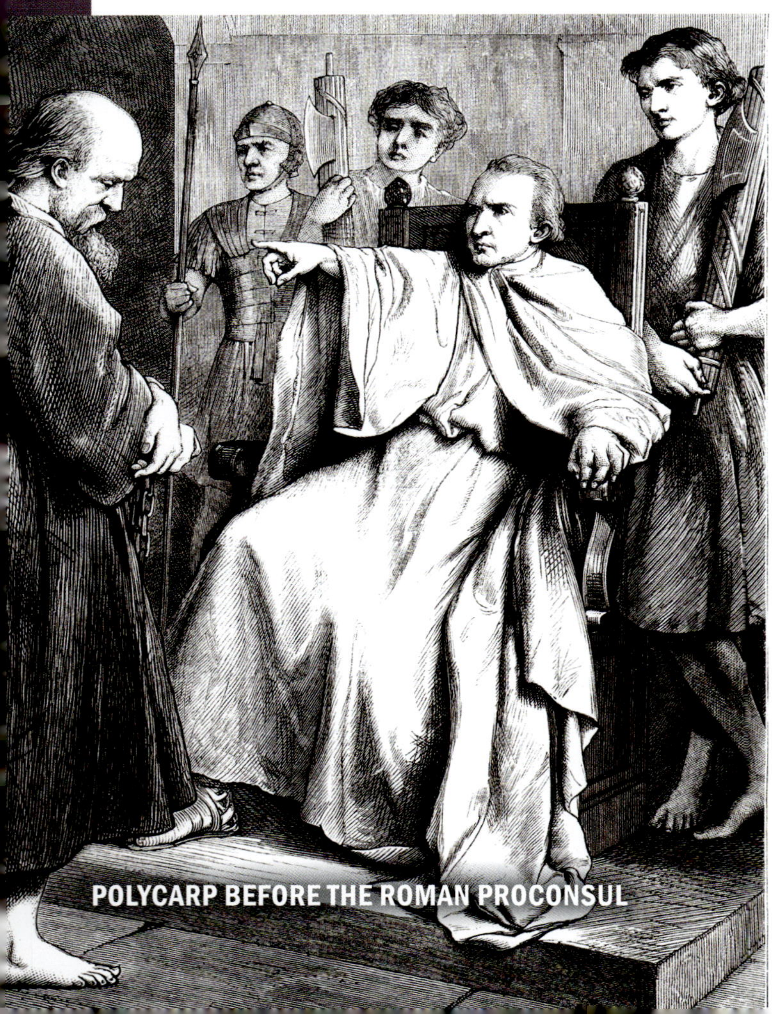

POLYCARP BEFORE THE ROMAN PROCONSUL

Ignatius (died c. 108) of Antioch wrote many letters to various churches which we still have today. In the next chapter, we will learn more about Ignatius and his writings. He is among the earliest of all Christian writers to whose writings we have access.

Ignatius was arrested by the emperor and was sentenced to be thrown to the wild beasts in Rome. He longed to give honor to Jesus his Savior, saying:

> May the wild beasts be eager to rush upon me. If they be unwilling, I will compel them. Come, crowds of wild beasts; come, tearings and manglings, wracking of bones and hacking of limbs; come, cruel tortures of the devil; only let me attain unto Christ.[3]

Ignatius' commitment to Christ was evident by his willingness to undergo such suffering. According to early church testimony, that is what Ignatius did. He gave his life for the Lord Jesus.

The Martyrdom of Polycarp

Polycarp (c. AD 69-155) was another early church leader who gave his life for Christ. Polycarp had the unique privilege of being discipled by one of the apostles (John). The story of Polycarp's martyrdom is recorded in the early church document, ***The Martyrdom of Polycarp***.

Polycarp was arrested and brought into the amphitheater in Smyrna. Since there were no images of gods in the churches of the Christians, the pagan Romans concluded that the Christians did not believe in the existence of gods.

The proconsul commanded Polycarp to join with the cries of the multitude gathered and say, "Away with the atheists!" Polycarp joined the cry and said, "Away with the atheists!" but he pointed at the crowds instead, proclaiming that they were the real atheists since they did not believe in the one true God.

The proconsul asked Polycarp to "revile Christ." He promised to release Polycarp if he would reject Jesus. Polycarp replied, "Eighty and six years have I served Him, and He has never done me wrong; how can I blaspheme Him, my King, who has saved me? I am a Christian." The crowds then cried, "Let him be burned!"

Wood was then collected and made into a pile. The woodpile was lighted, and as the flames surrounded him, Polycarp prayed to God one last time with these words:

> Lord God Almighty, Father of our Lord Jesus Christ, I praise You that You have judged me worthy of this day and of this hour, to participate in the number of Your witnesses, and in the cup of Your Christ.[4]

This was the witness of Polycarp, pastor of the church in Smyrna.

The Martyrdom of Blandina

As noted above, a significant persecution took place in AD 177. There is no indication that Marcus Aurelius was directly responsible for the persecution. However, it took place during his reign. A noteworthy example of steadfast faith is the young woman named Blandina. She gave her life for Christ in the town of Lyons (pronounced "lee-own"). Eusebius, the church historian, quotes from an eyewitness account of Blandina's testimony in Lyons.

> Blandina was filled with such power as to be delivered and raised above those who were torturing her by turns from morning till evening in every manner, so that they acknowledged that they were conquered, and could do nothing more to her. And they were astonished at her endurance, as her entire body was mangled and broken; and they testified that one of these forms of torture was sufficient to destroy life, not to speak of so many and so great sufferings. But the blessed woman, like a noble athlete, renewed her strength in her confession; and her comfort and . . . relief from the pain of her sufferings was in exclaiming, "I am a Christian, and there is nothing vile done by us."[5]

Despite the numerous tortures inflicted upon her, Blandina prevailed. She was stronger than her persecutors. Not that she did this in her own strength, but the Spirit of God enabled her to stand fast for Jesus.

> And, after the scourging, after the wild beasts . . . she was finally enclosed in a net, and thrown before a bull. And having been tossed about by the animal, but feeling none of the things which were happening to her, on account of her hope and firm hold upon what had been entrusted to her, and her communion with Christ, she also was sacrificed. And the heathen themselves confessed that never among them had a woman endured so many and such terrible tortures.[6]

Blandina was just one of many other women who "did not love their lives to death" but gave all for their Blessed Redeemer.

ANCIENT AGORA (A PUBLIC SPACE FOR ASSEMBLY AND MARKETS) IN SMYRNA

Precious in the sight of the LORD
Is the death of His saints. (Ps. 116:15)

The Conversion of Constantine

In God's providence, a pivotal event occurred near the beginning of the 4th century. After Diocletian's death, **Galerius** (r. AD 305-311) continued persecuting Christians. But in 311, he brought an end to the persecution while on his deathbed. He issued an edict allowing Christians to assemble for worship. He even asked for prayers to be made on his behalf by the Christians.

Prior to Galerius' reign, the Roman Empire was divided into four administrative regions. Different emperors ruled over each region. This occurred during Diocletian's rule. This provided a degree of stability for such a large empire. But eventually, power struggles occurred. Civil war between the various co-emperors broke out. In 312, a battle occurred that dramatically altered the direction of Western history. It is known as the **Battle of Milvian Bridge**. In that battle, Emperor Constantine defeated Emperor Maxentius on the outskirts of Rome.

The defeat of Maxentius enabled Constantine to take control of Rome. After Maxentius' defeat, Constantine took control of the Western portion of the empire. Constantine made an agreement with Licinius (who had control of the East). This agreement afforded additional protections for Christians. It granted toleration of both Christianity and Roman religion throughout the Roman Empire. Additionally, it called for the restoration of property that was confiscated from Christians in previous years. For a time, the empire was divided between Constantine and Licinius, but in 322, Constantine attacked Licinius' territory and eventually defeated him. This made Constantine the sole emperor of the entire Roman Empire.

Constantine's rise to power also played a significant role in church history. Before Constantine's battle with Maxentius, Constantine claimed to see a vision where he was told to use the sign of the cross as he went into battle. Constantine was told in the vision, "By this sign, conquer." The form of this sign was reported to be the first two Greek letters of Christ's name (Chi and Rho). Put together, these two letters form a cross symbol.

The day after Constantine received the vision, he had the Chi-Rho cross symbol painted upon the shields of his soldiers. He prayed to God for victory. And by God's sovereign determination, Constantine did win the battle.

Constantine interpreted the victory as God's favor upon him. As a result, Constantine became a friend of and protector of Christians. Constantine himself claimed a Christian profession. He attended Christian worship regularly. He often made speeches in his court condemning pagan idolatry. Additionally, Constantine enacted laws in the empire favorable toward Christianity. In a later chapter, we will also learn how Constantine participated in the development of church doctrine.

Constantine did enact a law prohibiting pagan sacrifice. While those who still performed sacrifice were not prosecuted, this nevertheless demonstrated Constantine's commitment

THE MILVIAN BRIDGE IN ROME

to the worship of the one true God. Peter Leithart wrote that "by the 350s sacrifice was rare enough that it took some daring to perform."[7] Legislation under Constantine took an increasingly biblical direction. He made Sunday a day of rest and exempted churches from taxation. Prior to this, Sunday had been a working day in the Roman Empire.

The gladiatorial games began to be restricted and would eventually be prohibited. New laws against various forms of sexual immorality were enacted. He banned crucifixion as a form of punishment. His legislation even extended to the humane treatment of animals. Constantine had his flaws. He may have wrongly executed people. One of the most tragic events in Constantine's life was the execution of his son Crispus and his wife Fausta. We don't know why Constantine executed them or whether he carefully investigated the charges against them before doing so.

Regardless of Constantine's heart condition, we can see that Constantine's allegiance to Christianity changed the direction of church history. Once a forbidden and persecuted religion, under Constantine's reign, Christianity became not only tolerated but embraced by many. From that point on, Christianity would have a much larger influence on the development of culture in Europe.

After Constantine's death, both Christianity and paganism continued their existence side-by-side in the Roman Empire, but paganism gradually declined. But the struggle between the dragon and Christ's followers did not end with the rise of Constantine. Wherever Christ's gospel goes forth, the dragon strikes back. However, we need not fear the attacks of the evil one. Our Lord Jesus is the victorious King. He is greater than the prince of this world. ■

You are of God, little children, and have overcome them, because He who is in you is greater than he who is in the world. (1 John 4:4)

ONE OF PAUL'S LETTERS BEING READ TO THE EARLY CHRISTIANS

Writings from the Early Church

3

Bring the cloak that I left with Carpus at Troas when you come—and the books, especially the parchments. (2 Tim. 4:13)

Much of what we know about the early Christians we learn from the writings they left behind. Letters and books still exist today that were written as far back as the 1st century AD. Of course, the Bible is always the most important source of truth for the Christian. It is God's Word. It is inspired by God. It is without error. All that it teaches is true. Our beliefs and our practices must be based on the supreme authority of God's Word.

Other writings outside of the Bible may be useful. But they can never equal the authority of God's Word. We must remember this when we look at the writings of early Christians.

Though these writings are not as important as the Bible, they are quite helpful in a number of ways. How are they helpful?

First, writings from the early Christians are *edifying*. Many of them contain valuable teaching and application. We can still be instructed and encouraged by reading them.

Second, writings from the early Christians are *important historical sources*. These writings give us a window into what the earliest Christians believed. They detail how early Christians worshiped. They show us how the first Christians lived for the Lord Jesus Christ. In these early writings, we learn how the faith was transferred from the apostles to the generations that followed.

The earliest writings we have are often printed together in a collection called "The Apostolic Fathers." These writers are called "Apostolic Fathers" because most of them wrote shortly after the time of the apostles. We believe that some of them (such as Polycarp) were directly discipled by the apostles.

Some documents in the Apostolic Fathers are more biblical than others. Let's look together at a few examples from this early collection. We will not be able to learn about all of them. However, the reader may still pick up a copy of the Apostolic Fathers and read them on their own.[1]

First Clement

The first of the documents we will look at is the letter known as ***First Clement***. It was written by a pastor named **Clement** who was known as a pastor (or bishop) in Rome. It is believed that the letter was written around AD 96. The letter was written to the church in Corinth. When

DEPICTION OF CLEMENT OF ROME

Paul wrote to the church in Corinth, he exhorted them toward unity (1 Cor. 1-2). Clement had similar exhortations for the brethren in Corinth. Throughout his letter, he quotes frequently from both the Old Testament and the New Testament. Here is one section that is similar to Paul's teaching on love from 1 Corinthians 13.

> Who can describe the bond of God's love? Who is able to explain the majesty of its beauty? The height to which love leads is indescribable. Love unites us with God; love covers a multitude of sins; love endures all things, is patient in all things. There is nothing coarse, nothing arrogant in love. Love knows nothing of schisms, love leads no rebellions, love does everything in harmony . . . in love the Master received us. Because of the love that he had for us, Jesus Christ our Lord, in accordance with God's will, gave his blood for us, and his flesh for our flesh, and his life for our lives.[2]

The Letters of Ignatius

Ignatius wrote seven letters that are now a part of the Apostolic Fathers. While on his way to Rome, Ignatius wrote to various churches and individuals, giving them various exhortations. It appears that all of his letters were written in the last few weeks of his life. The letters then, come with an urgency, from a man preparing to face his death. Some of the major emphases of his letters include (1) the unity of the church, (2) opposing false teachers, and (3) his impending martyrdom.

To preserve church unity, Ignatius especially emphasized obedience to the bishop. It is in Ignatius' letters that we first observe a new distinction in church government. The New Testament presents two offices in the church (bishop/elder and deacons, Phil. 1:1). But in Ignatius' letters, he presents three distinct offices: bishop, elders, and deacons. Throughout his letters, Ignatius urges obedience to the bishop of each particular church. Here is one example from Ignatius' letter to Smyrna.

> Flee from divisions as the beginning of evils. You must all follow the bishop as Jesus Christ followed the Father, and follow the council of presbyters [elders] as you would the apostles; respect the deacons as the commandment of God. Let no one do anything that has to do with the church without the bishop. Only that Eucharist [Lord's Supper] which is under the authority of the bishop (or whomever he himself designates) is to be considered valid.[3]

Over time, this distinction between the bishops and elders would become quite common in church government. However, it was not a view of church government consistent with the Bible. It is true that the Bible teaches us to "obey those who rule over you, and be submissive" (Heb. 13:17). However, the Bible does not distinguish the office of bishop from the office of elder.

ICONOGRAPHY OF IGNATIUS OF ANTIOCH

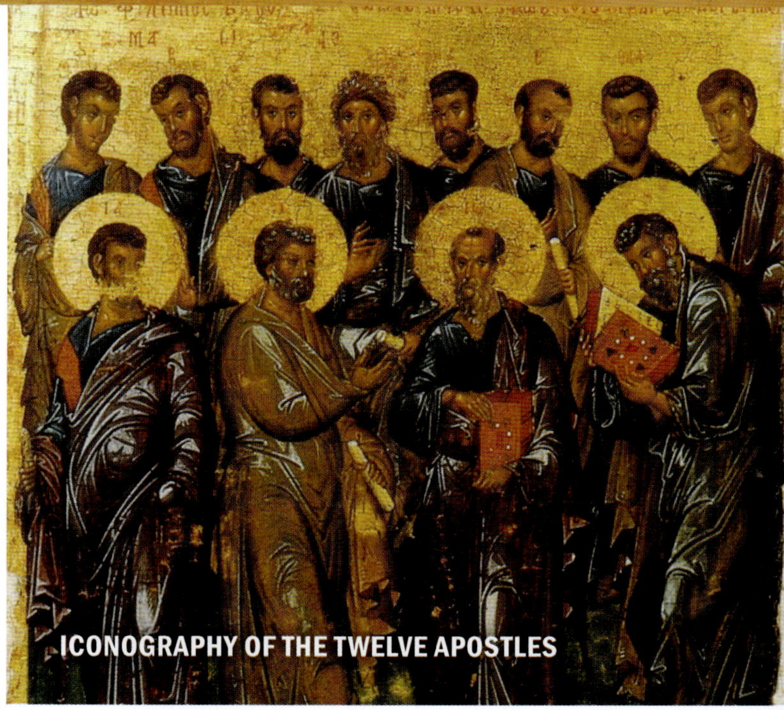

ICONOGRAPHY OF THE TWELVE APOSTLES

The two words are used for the same office in Scripture (see Acts 20:17 and Acts 20:28).

Ignatius also warned against false teaching which would surely have a deadly effect upon Christ's disciples. He uses vivid language to warn against such false teaching.

> I urge you, therefore—yet not I, but the love of Jesus Christ—partake only of Christian food, and keep away from every strange plant, which is heresy. These people, while pretending to be trustworthy, mix Jesus Christ with themselves—like those who administer a deadly drug with honeyed wine, which the unsuspecting victim accepts without fear, and so with fatal pleasure drinks down death.[4]

Ignatius' letters contain frequent references to his impending death in Rome. The Apostolic Fathers also contains one of the earliest documents concerning Christian persecution. It is known as ***The Martyrdom of Polycarp*** (referenced in the previous chapter).

The Didache

The Apostolic Fathers includes a unique document known as ***The Didache***. The word *didache* in Greek means "teaching." The document is a manual of church doctrine and practice. While it is quite short, the *Didache* gives us a window into early Christian worship and practice. Notably, the *Didache* refers to only two offices: bishops and deacons. It also speaks of how baptism was to be performed.

> Now concerning baptism, baptize as follows: after you have reviewed all these things, baptize in the name of the Father and of the Son and of the Holy Spirit in running water. But if you have no running water, then baptize in some other water; and if you are not able to baptize in cold water, then do so in warm. But if you have neither, then pour water on the head three times in the name of the Father and Son and Holy Spirit. And before the baptism let the one baptizing and the one who is to be baptized fast, as well as any others who are able. Also, you must instruct the one who is to be baptized to fast for one or two days beforehand.[5]

We learn here that baptism was performed in the name of the Triune God (as Jesus commanded in Matthew 28). We also see that there was a preference for running water and cold water. This may have involved an immersion baptism in water. But pouring on the head was also considered a valid application of baptism. We also see that fasting was practiced to prepare for baptism.

The Shepherd of Hermas

One of the strangest documents in the collection of the Apostolic Fathers is called the ***Shepherd of Hermas***. It is a mixture of visions and parables written by a Christian named Hermas. It addresses the question of whether sins committed after baptism can be forgiven. The answer given in the book is that sins can be forgiven after baptism, but only once. There are no references to the

Lord Jesus Christ in the book. The emphasis is upon strict obedience to a moral code following baptism. The teaching of the *Shepherd of Hermas* is contrary to Scripture's teaching that after baptism Christians continue to be sinners who need God's grace (1 John 1:8-2:2).

Interestingly, the *Shepherd of Hermas* was quite popular in the early centuries of the church. Many of the early church fathers commended the book as edifying. Some even considered that it might be Scripture. But in time, the shortcomings of this work became evident, and it was not considered part of the canon of Scripture.

The Letter to Diognetus

One of the most valuable documents in the Apostolic Fathers is called the ***Letter to Diognetus***. We do not know the author's name. We only know to whom the letter was addressed. It is an example of an early Christian defense (or apologetic) for the Christian faith. In a later chapter, we will learn more about the early Christian apologists.

An apologist was one who gave a defense of the faith. The word comes from the Greek word *apologeo*, which means "to give an answer" or "to give a defense." The *Letter to Diognetus* is an example of Christian apologetics. From a biblical standpoint, it is among the most faithful of all the Apostolic Fathers.

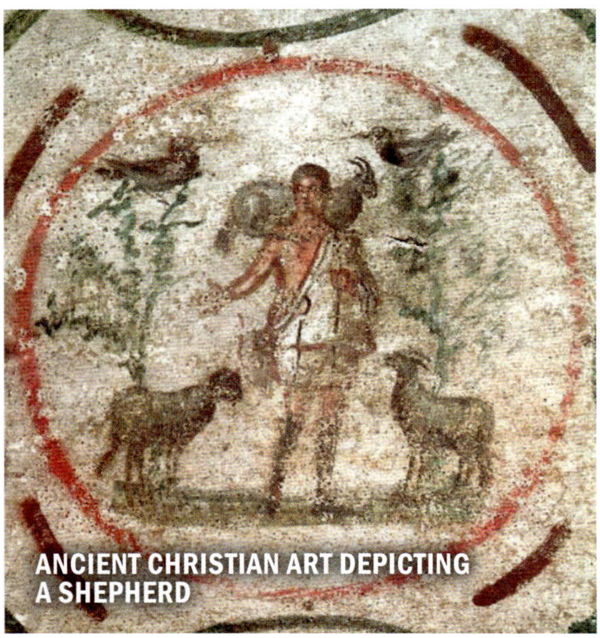

ANCIENT CHRISTIAN ART DEPICTING A SHEPHERD

In the letter, the author explains what Christians believe. He contrasts those beliefs with paganism and Judaism. And in one particularly beautiful section, the author explains the gospel of Jesus Christ. Here is what the author says about our Lord:

> But when our unrighteousness was fulfilled, and it had been made perfectly clear that its wages—punishment and death—were to be expected, then the season arrived during which God had decided to reveal at last his goodness and power (oh, the surpassing kindness and love of God!). He did not hate us, or reject us, or bear a grudge against us; instead he was patient and forbearing; in his mercy he took upon himself our sins; he himself gave up his own Son as a ransom for us, the holy one for the lawless, the guiltless for the guilty, the just for the unjust, the incorruptible for the corruptible, the immortal for the mortal. For what else but his righteousness could have covered our sins? In whom was it possible for us, the lawless and ungodly, to be justified, except in the Son of God alone? O the sweet exchange, O the incomprehensible work of God, O the unexpected blessings, that the sinfulness of many should be hidden in one righteous person, while the righteousness of one should justify many sinners![6]

This is one of the most accurate summaries of the biblical gospel, with an emphasis upon the saving work of Christ for sinners. *The Letter to Diognetus* is a valuable testimony to the faith convictions of the early Christians.

The Teaching of the Apostles (*Didascalia Apostolorum*)

The *Didache* mentioned above, was the earliest example of a manual on church doctrine, worship, and life. The church produced other manuals like it in the centuries that followed. A notable example of such a manual is the document known as the ***Didascalia Apostolorum*** (Teaching of the Apostles). The exact date of this document is unknown. But many believe it was composed sometime in the 3rd century (perhaps AD 230 or 250). In God's providence, this particular document did not survive in the original Greek. But we do have access to it through a Syriac translation.

Syriac was the language spoken in ancient Syria, particularly in the early Christian community of Antioch. In fact, it was in Antioch that the disciples were first called Christians (Acts 11:26). Somewhere in this region the *Didascalia* emerged as a manual on church life. We can learn something of what the early Christians believed and how they lived by looking at this document. Here are a few examples of what you will find in the *Didascalia*.

First, there is much about the government of Christ's church and the role of overseers and deacons in the church. As part of that government, the manual also speaks of how to handle matters of sin and church discipline. Bishops (or overseers) were instructed to reprove those who continued in patterns of sin. In this portion of the document, we read:

> If then the Bishop does not keep silence before them that sin, but reproves and censures them, and corrects and admonishes and punishes him that has sinned, he also throws fear on others; for it is required of the Bishop that by means of his doctrine he should be a preventer of sins unto death, and an exhorter to righteousness, and by the admonition of his doctrine a guide to good works, a glorifier and exalter of good things to come, that are promised by God in the place of eternal life; and a preacher also of future wrath by the judgment of God, by the threat of cruel fire, quenchless and unbearable.[7]

This summary explains how a faithful pastor will preach and shepherd. He will admonish those who go on sinning. He will seek to rescue those committing sin from danger. He will exhort others to righteousness. He will remind them of the gospel and the way to eternal life. He will also warn about the wrath to come.

However, even in rebuking those who go on in sin, the bishop was to be merciful, just as God is merciful. In another portion, we read this:

> He [God] requires from those who have sinned that they repent. And in many places He speaks about these things, and gives no place to the opinion of those who are hard-hearted, and who wish to judge sharply and without mercy, and to cast completely away those who have sinned, as if there were no repentance for them. But God is not thus, but He calls even sinners to repentance, and gives them hope.[8]

The reader is instructed to be merciful and tell sinners that by repenting, God will be merciful to those who sin.

The *Didascalia* also urges its readers to value the assembly of the church and not to neglect its worship.

> When you teach, command and remind the people, that they be constant in the assembly of the Church. So that you be not hindered, but that they be constantly assembled, that no one diminish the Church by not assembling, and make smaller by a member the body of Christ.... As, therefore, you are members of the Christ, scatter not yourselves from the Church by not assembling yourselves, for you have a head, that is the Christ.... Do not mangle and scatter His body, do not have more respect to the affairs of the world than to the Word of God, but leave everything on the Lord's day and run eagerly toward your Church, for this is your glory.[9]

This is an early testimony to the Christian practice of assembling for worship on the Lord's Day. The manual instructs Christians to forsake all the affairs of the world and to prioritize gathering with Christ's body each Lord's Day.

Eusebius' *Church History*

In the early 4th century, a Christian pastor named **Eusebius** (c. 260-339) authored a very important book. It was the first church history book ever written. He served as bishop in the city of Caesarea. This was a city located on the coast of Palestine. He wrote numerous books. His most well-known work is ***Church History*** (sometimes titled ***Ecclesiastical History***). He also wrote a biography of Constantine. Eusebius' *Church History* is important because it is the first work of its kind. In it, Eusebius chronologically details the major events of the church's history up until his time. Eusebius also collected numerous early sources and quotations for the book.

Some of the major topics included in *Church History* include a history of various Christian teachers, heresies, church documents, and martyrdoms. Without Eusebius' work, we would know far less about what happened in the first centuries of Christ's church. For example, we learn in Eusebius' history how Peter and Paul died during Nero's persecution. Here is a portion of what Eusebius wrote:

EUSEBIUS OF CAESAREA (C. 260-339)

> So it happened that this man [Nero], the first to be announced publicly as a fighter against God, was led on to slaughter the apostles. It is related that in his reign Paul was beheaded in Rome itself and that Peter was also crucified, and the cemeteries there still called by the names of Peter and Paul confirm the record.[10]

Eusebius is also an early witness to how Christians viewed the books of the New Testament. What books were included in the **canon** of inspired Scripture was a topic on which there was much unity in the early church. However, there were disputes about some books. Eusebius, writing in the early 300s, said this about the New Testament books:

> At this point it may be appropriate to list the New Testament writings already referred to. The holy quartet of the Gospels [Matthew, Mark, Luke, John] are first, followed by the Acts of the Apostles. Next are Paul's epistles, 1 John, and 1 Peter. The Revelation of John may be added, the arguments regarding which I shall discuss at the proper time. These are the recognized books. Those that are disputed yet known to most are the epistles called James, Jude, 2 Peter, and the so-named 2 and 3 John.[11]

All the New Testament books are listed here, with the exception of James, Jude, 2 Peter, and 2 and 3 John. Hebrews was usually considered a letter written by Paul.

Later in the same section, Eusebius explains that other books were considered not apostolic and not part of Scripture. These include the *Shepherd of Hermas*, the *Epistle of Barnabas*, and the *Didache*, among others.

This shows us that there was significant unity on what books were included in the New Testament. But there was debate over some books in the early centuries of the church. This was eventually resolved as the 4th century progressed.

The final chapters of Eusebius' *Church History* focus on Constantine. Eusebius saw Constantine's rise to power as a great deliverance from persecution. Eusebius begins the final section of his history with these words:

> Thanks be to God, the almighty King of the universe, and to Jesus Christ, the Savior and Redeemer of our souls, through whom we pray that peace from troubles external and internal may be preserved for us intact and undisturbed.[12]

After quoting from the Psalms, Eusebius described this new period the church entered as a period of joyful restoration.

> From now on, a cloudless day, radiant with rays of heavenly light, shined down on the churches of Christ throughout the world, and there was no reluctance to share even with those outside our society the enjoyment, if not of equal divine blessings, at least of their effects.[13]

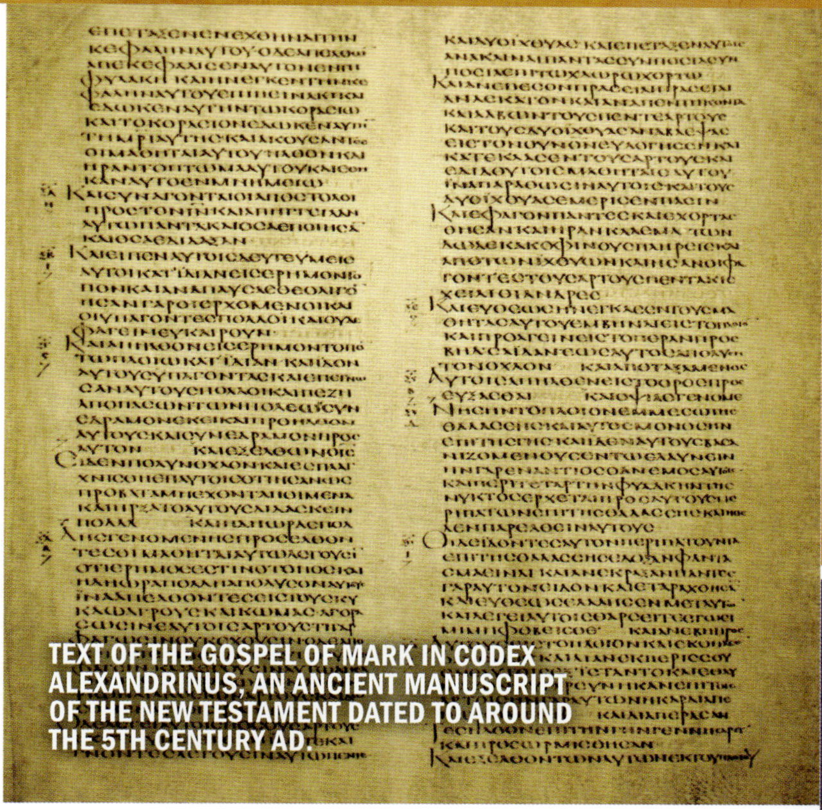

TEXT OF THE GOSPEL OF MARK IN CODEX ALEXANDRINUS, AN ANCIENT MANUSCRIPT OF THE NEW TESTAMENT DATED TO AROUND THE 5TH CENTURY AD.

Some readers think that Eusebius was too optimistic about Constantine. However, it is important to remember that Eusebius and others of his day had witnessed the terrible persecutions under Diocletian and Galerius. For Constantine to declare freedom and peace for Christians was certainly cause for rejoicing. Eusebius' experience with persecution surely influenced how he viewed Constantine's rise to power.

Summary

The Lord has preserved for us numerous documents from the early centuries of His church. These are a blessing to us, because from them we can learn more about how Christ built His church. We can also be edified by the wisdom of these writings. Of course, as we have seen, they are not perfect like God's Word, the Bible. But they remain helpful as we mature in the faith once for all delivered to the saints (Jude 3). ■

RUINS OF ANCIENT CAESAREA

CHRISTIAN MOSAIC OF BREAD AND FISH

Christian Worship and Doctrinal Development

Then those who gladly received his word were baptized; and that day about three thousand souls were added to them. And they continued steadfastly in the apostles' doctrine and fellowship, in the breaking of bread, and in prayers. (Acts 2:41-42)

On the Day of Pentecost, thousands received the gospel preached through Peter. Those that received the Word were baptized and were "added." What were they added to? The next verse tells us that they were added to the believing and worshiping community. They were added to the church of the Lord Jesus Christ. The Bible teaches us that those who believe in Christ and are baptized are members of the body of Christ (1 Cor. 12:13-14, Eph. 4:4-6). This church, which is found all over the world, is a worshiping community.

How a church worships is a reflection of what it believes. Each element of worship is an expression of faith. While there is much we do not know about early Christian worship, we do have various documents that shed light on what worship in the early church looked like.

What the New Testament Says About Worship

Rejoice always, pray without ceasing, in everything

ANCIENT BAPTISMAL

give thanks; for this is the will of God in Christ Jesus for you. (1 Thess. 5:16-18)

We learn about the worship of the early church first from the New Testament. Acts is the inspired account penned by Luke the physician. In addition to Acts, many of the other New Testament books teach us about early Christian worship.

We know that the church gathered on the first day of the week (Acts 20:7). They did so because it was the day that Jesus rose from the dead. It was known as the Lord's Day (Rev. 1:10). We also observe that the early Christians gathered for common meals. But they also frequently celebrated the Lord's Supper together (1 Cor. 10-11). Baptism was a fundamental identity marker for those who were disciples of Jesus Christ (Rom. 6:1-4, Gal. 3:27, Eph. 4:5).

From the New Testament, we learn that the proclamation of God's Word was a central aspect of Christian worship (2 Tim. 4:1-2). In addition to preaching the Word, the public reading of Scripture and prayer were commanded (1 Tim. 2:1-2, 4:13). The singing of psalms, hymns, and spiritual songs was also commanded in both Christian worship and in daily Christian life (Eph. 5:18-20, Col. 3:16-17). We also find that there were collections of offerings made for the saints on certain occasions (1 Cor. 16:1-4).

JUSTIN MARTYR (100-165)

The Worship of the Early Church

These things I write to you, though I hope to come to you shortly; but if I am delayed, I write so that you may know how you ought to conduct yourself in the house of God, which is the church of the living God, the pillar and ground of the truth. (1 Tim. 3:14-15)

Turning now from the inspired biblical record to early written sources, we get glimpses into how the early church worshiped the Lord. We have an important firsthand account of the worship of the early church from **Justin Martyr** (100-165). Justin was an important church father from the 2nd century. He records this testimony in his *First Apology*:

> And on the day called Sunday, all who live in cities or in the country gather together to one place, and the memoirs of the apostles or the writings of the prophets are read, as long as time permits; then, when the reader has ceased, the president verbally instructs, and exhorts to the imitation of these good things. Then we all rise together and pray, and, as we before said, when our prayer is ended, bread and wine and water are brought, and the president in like manner offers prayers and thanksgivings, according to his ability, and the people assent, saying Amen; and there is a distribution to each, and a participation of that over which thanks have been given, and to those who are absent a portion is sent by the deacons. And they who are well to do, and willing, give what each thinks fit; and what is collected is deposited with the president, who succours the orphans and

> widows and those who, through sickness or any other cause, are in want, and those who are in bonds and the strangers sojourning among us, and in a word takes care of all who are in need. But Sunday is the day on which we all hold our common assembly, because it is the first day on which God, having wrought a change in the darkness and matter, made the world; and Jesus Christ our Saviour on the same day rose from the dead.[1]

Justin tells us that the church would gather on the first day of the week. They would read the "memoirs of the apostles or the writings of the prophets," and then the "president" or pastor/elder would instruct the congregation on the text of Scripture. Then they would take communion. The church would give thanks to God as they partook of the communion meal. Then an offering would be taken for those in need. This pattern of worship described by Justin looks very similar to what the New Testament records.

Baptism was considered an essential rite for disciples. A document written by **Hippolytus** (AD 170-235) called *Apostolic Tradition* includes information about how baptism was practiced. Those converts who were to be baptized often went through an extended period of instruction. This was called "catechesis," a word that means "instruction" or "teaching." Hippolytus writes that this period could last up to three years. Not only were the converts instructed, but their conduct was observed. For those who had practiced various kinds of sinful pagan behaviors, it was important that those ungodly practices would cease before baptism.

When the day of baptism came, the disciple was to renounce all the works of the devil and declare their repentance. Some early church documents indicate that the baptismal candidate was sometimes baptized naked (men and women being separated).

The bishop or elder presiding would ask the disciple if they believed in the Father, the Son, and the Holy Spirit. Following the baptism, the baptized would be dried off and clothed (sometimes with a white robe). This was to symbolize putting off the old sinful nature and putting on Christ (Eph. 4:22-24, Gal. 3:27). The bishop would then pray over the baptized disciple, for the work of the Holy Spirit. The newly baptized person would partake of the Lord's Supper. In some cases, there was the tradition of giving the baptized milk and honey (signifying their entrance into the "Promised Land").

TERTULLIAN (155-220)

Baptismal practices varied depending on the particular date and location. Hippolytus' summary is just one example from the early church. There are other documents that attest to this pattern as well.

Some Christians believe that the practice of household baptism (including infants) is a biblical practice taught in the New Testament. Anglicans, Lutherans, Presbyterians, and Reformed are examples of those who hold this view. Baptists disagree with this perspective and believe that infant baptism was a practice that arose after the time of the apostles.

The earliest church records that describe infant baptism come from the 2nd or 3rd century. Early writers from these centuries mention the practice and advocate for it. Examples of those who advocated for the practice include Hippolytus and **Cyprian** (210-258). Tertullian (155-220) mentions the practice but was against it. In later centuries, the practice of baptizing infants and small children became the dominant practice of the church.

The Government of the Early Church

For this reason I left you in Crete, that you should set in order the things that are lacking, and appoint elders in every city as I commanded you. (Tit. 1:5)

When we learned about Ignatius, we observed how the New Testament speaks about two church offices: elder and deacon. The government of the early church was organized around these two main church offices, in addition to the apostles. There was the office of pastor/elder. These men were responsible for preaching and teaching, for the ministry of prayer, and for shepherding the flock. Secondly, the office of deacon existed to care for those in need, particularly widows and orphans (see Acts 6).

After the New Testament period, we begin to see different perspectives on church government. Some believed that the proper organization of the church consisted of only elders and deacons. Others argued that bishops should be appointed to succeed the apostles. The first view saw only two offices in the church (elder and deacon). The second view believed that the bishop was a separate office from the elder and deacon.

This second position became very common and by the 3rd and 4th century, the office of bishop in addition to elder and deacon was firmly established in most of the church. However, this structure of church government is not taught in the New Testament (Acts 20:17, 28-29, Phil. 1:1). Ignatius, whom we learned about in the previous chapter, believed in three separate offices. But other early documents witness to the two-office perspective.

This distinction of bishop from elder would play a significant role in the development of church government in the centuries that followed. Church government would become increasingly complex in later centuries. To that topic, we will return in later chapters.

Early Christian Art

So far, we have learned about early Christian worship from written documents. Yet we are not limited to written documents. There is visual art from the early church that still exists. This art shows us what was important to the early Christians. We know that the celebration of the Lord's Supper was very important in early church worship. Much early Christian art depicts the bread and wine of communion. Another common symbol in early Christian art was fish and bread. This, of course, came from Jesus' miraculous feeding of the five thousand

ANCIENT CHRISTIAN FRESCO DEPICTING THE LORD'S SUPPER

(John 6:1-14).

The fish was also a common symbol used by the early church. The Greek word for fish is *ichthus*. Each letter of the Greek word for fish referred to part of Jesus' title.

Translated from the Greek, each letter stood for the following title:

English ▪ "Jesus Christ, Son of God, Savior"

Greek ▪ "Isous Christos, Theou Huios, Soter" (ICHTHUS)

The fish, then, was code for "Jesus Christ." As you might have seen, the fish is still in use by Christians today (sometimes on the bumper of cars).

There were also examples in early Christian art of various biblical events such as Noah's Ark, Daniel in the Lion's Den, the raising of Lazarus from the dead, and other events. This artwork often is quite simple and not very realistic. If you compare the detail of paintings by the Dutch painter Rembrandt (1606-1669) with these ancient Christian paintings, there is a significant gap in detail and quality. We are looking at this Christian art not mainly for its excellence and detail. Rather, we want to see what the early Christians created because it helps us better understand what was important to them.

CIRCUS MAXIMUS IN ROME, WHERE CHARIOT RACES OCCURRED

Christians in a Pagan World

Therefore, since Christ suffered for us in the flesh, arm yourselves also with the same mind, for he who has suffered in the flesh has ceased from sin, that he no longer should live the rest of his time in the flesh for the lusts of men, but for the will of God. For we have spent enough of our past lifetime in doing the will of the Gentiles—when we walked in lewdness, lusts, drunkenness, revelries, drinking parties, and abominable idolatries. In regard to these, they think it strange that you do not run with them in the same flood of dissipation, speaking evil of you. They will give an account to Him who is ready to judge the living and the dead. (1 Pet. 4:1-5)

Christians faced many challenges living in pagan Greco-Roman society. Sexual immorality, including homosexuality, was rampant. Abortion was widespread. Clement of Alexandria rebuked the Romans for spending so much time and

MOSAIC DEPICTING GLADIATORS FIGHTING A LION

money on their pets while exposing their own children to die, and not caring for the elderly.[2]

Abortion methods were more primitive back then. So instead of killing their children in the womb, many people abandoned them to die right after they were born. Christians rescued and adopted many of these abandoned infants. Abortion was universally condemned as murder by the early church. The *Didache* says: "Do not murder a child by abortion or kill a new-born infant."[3]

All across the Roman Empire, gladiatorial games took place in amphitheaters. Gladiators, usually slaves, criminals, or captives taken in war, would fight with each other and with wild beasts for the entertainment of the spectators. These contests were violent. If a gladiator lost a contest, whether with another gladiator or with a wild beast, the crowd would decide his fate. If they gave a thumbs up, he would be allowed to live. If they gave a thumbs down, he would be killed. Many Christians were killed by wild beasts and gladiators in the arena. The church fathers condemned these violent games and discouraged Christians from watching them.

Private charity was not widely practiced by the Greco-Romans. Rome was a welfare state. People in the city of Rome were given bread and circuses. The Christians had a very different view of charity. They took care of their own. They cared for widows and orphans, adopted abandoned children, helped the poor, and took care of the elderly. They also took care of the sick and founded hospitals.

Like many non-Christian societies, the Greco-Romans had a low view of women. But Christians valued and honored women, treating them with dignity and respect. Many of the abandoned babies adopted by Christians were girls. Many godly women (some married to pagan husbands) like Nonna, Anthusa, and Monica faithfully reared their children in the faith. The pagan orator Libanius confessed: "What women these Christians have!"

Slaves were also despised in Greco-Roman society. But Christians treated them with dignity as spiritual equals. They recognized that all believers are members of the household of God and spiritual brothers and sisters (1 Tim. 3:15). Callistus, a former slave, even became bishop of Rome (c. 220). The early Christians honored those whom the Roman upper classes despised. They lived lives that were different from their pagan neighbors.

Development of Church Doctrine

Hold fast the pattern of sound words which you have heard from me, in faith and love which are in Christ Jesus. (2 Tim. 1:13)

Even in the New Testament, we read that there were false teachers who perverted God's truth. The Apostles frequently warned us about false teaching (Rom. 16:17-18, 2 Tim. 4:3-4, 2 Pet. 2:1-2, 1 John 4:1-3). It is no surprise then, that from the beginning of the church, the dragon has been busy trying to pervert the truth of God's Word. The devil cannot defeat the Lord Jesus Christ. But he can lie about who Jesus is and what Jesus did to save us.

In different parts of the church, false teachers arose and tried to lead Christ's disciples astray. Godly pastors rose to the occasion and defended God's Word. A good example of such a faithful pastor is **Irenaeus of Lyons** (AD 130-202). He wrote a massive book we call *Against Heresies.* In this book, Irenaeus uses his vast knowledge of Scripture to defend God's truth against false teachers prevalent in his day. In the next chapter, we will learn more about Irenaeus and other pastors like him.

Two Pivotal Early Church Councils

God's truth was also defended through assemblies of church leaders called church councils. These councils met to refute error and give clarity and definition to the truth. Such gatherings of church leaders took place in the first few centuries of the church. But they were often localized to one region. Some of the early church persecutions prevented the church from holding a larger council.

But that changed with Constantine's rise to power. One of the most important church councils that ever met was convened by Constantine himself. This council is called the **Council of Nicaea**. The assembly occurred in AD 325 in the town of Nicaea. An invitation to the council went out all over the empire. And some 300 bishops answered the summons and appeared. Some of these bishops bore the marks of the recent Diocletian persecution. Scars and wounds were visible on their bodies. Now, these church leaders were gathered under the authority and with the support of a Christian emperor. This was a new day for the church.

The council settled a variety of issues including matters of church government and the date of Easter. However, the most important matter settled at Nicaea was a dispute concerning the nature of the Lord Jesus Christ. The council met to resolve the **Arian controversy**.

The controversy takes its name from a church leader named **Arius** (c. 256-336). This man was a presbyter (or elder) who lived in Alexandria, Egypt. Arius taught that Jesus was not the eternally begotten Son of God. Instead, Arius believed Jesus was the first and highest of God's created beings. Arius' view was sometimes described this way: "there was a time when the Son was not."

Some church leaders agreed with and supported Arius. But others firmly opposed Arius and believed his teaching was contrary to the plain teaching of Scripture. These included Arius' own bishop Alexander and a young deacon named **Athanasius** (c. 298-373). The debate spread throughout the empire and became a matter of great concern. So well known was the dispute that the streets of Alexandria rang with theological songs and rhymes by followers and opponents of Arius.

The Council of Nicaea met to debate the issue and decided in favor of the view that Jesus Christ, the Son of God, has eternally existed with the Father. The council's conclusions are in harmony with what the Word of God teaches. Jesus Christ is eternally God (John 1:1, 17:5, Rom. 9:5, Col. 1:15-17). The Son of God is equal in power and glory with the Father. The council then taught the deity of Christ.

The Council produced the **Nicene formula**, the original version of which reads as follows:

> We believe in one God, the Father Almighty, maker of all things visible and invisible; and in one Lord Jesus Christ, the Son of God, the only-begotten of his Father, of the substance of the Father, God of God, Light of Light, very God of very God, begotten, not made, being of one substance (ὁμοούσιον) with the Father, by whom all things were made, both which be in heaven and in earth. Who for us men and for our salvation came down from heaven

THE COUNCIL OF NICAEA (325)

> and was incarnate and was made man. He suffered and the third day he rose again, and ascended into heaven. And he shall come again to judge both the living and the dead. And we believe in the Holy Ghost. And whosoever shall say that there was a time when the Son of God was not, or that before he was begotten he was not, or that he was made of things that were not, or that he is of a different substance or essence from the Father or that he is a creature, or subject to change or conversion — all that so say, the Catholic and Apostolic Church anathematizes them.

The word catholic means "universal." The use of the term "apostolic" simply means the church continues faithfully in accord with what the apostles taught. The term "anathematize" means to "condemn." This means that the Council of Nicaea took the position that to deny the truth of the Son's eternal nature was a grave heresy that struck at the heart of the Christian faith. The council's condemnation of the Arian heresy was firm. But despite the decision of the council, this heresy continued to afflict the church for the next few centuries. Some emperors even supported the Arians and persecuted the orthodox, but eventually the truth prevailed.

The Council of Nicaea focused on the nature of Christ, the Son of God. But it did not address the deity of the Holy Spirit. Since there were continuing doctrinal struggles in the church, eventually a second council was called in 381 AD. This council (called the **Council of Constantinople**) reaffirmed the Nicene formula quoted above. It also affirmed that the Holy Spirit was also God. The Council produced a new version of the creed that clearly taught the doctrine of the Trinity.

Here is the form of the Nicene Creed which combines the Nicene formula with the wording adopted at the Council of Constantinople. This is called the **Niceno-Constantinopolitan Creed**, but this is often shortened to the **Nicene Creed** for simplicity.

> I believe in one God, the Father Almighty,
> Maker of heaven and earth, and of all things visible and invisible.
> And in one Lord Jesus Christ, the only begotten Son of God,
> begotten of the Father before all worlds;
> God of God, Light of Light, very God of very God;
> begotten, not made, being of one substance with the Father,
> by whom all things were made.
> Who, for us men and for our salvation, came down from heaven
> and was incarnate by the Holy Spirit of the virgin Mary,
> and was made man;
> and was crucified also for us under Pontius Pilate;
> he suffered and was buried;
> and the third day he rose again, according to the Scriptures;
> and ascended into heaven,
> and sits on the right hand of the Father;
> and he shall come again, with glory, to judge the living and the dead;
> whose kingdom shall have no end.
> And I believe in the Holy Spirit, the Lord and Giver of life;
> who proceeds from the

Father and the Son;
who with the Father and the Son together
is worshiped and glorified;
who spoke by the prophets.
And I believe in one holy catholic and
apostolic church.
I acknowledge one baptism for the remission of sins;
and I look for the resurrection of the dead,
and the life of the world to come. Amen.

Alongside the Apostles Creed, the Nicene Creed is the most widely adopted statement of faith by Christians all over the world.

The Council of Chalcedon

Nicaea and Constantinople brought greater clarity to what the Bible taught about the Trinity. Additional disputes arose concerning the nature of our Lord. If Jesus was God, then how did His deity relate to His humanity? What is the relationship between these two natures? Some said that Jesus only appeared to be man but that He was not truly human. Others said that Jesus only became God at His baptism, and that He was not the eternally begotten divine Son. There were many differences of opinion and some dangerous heresies about how Jesus could be both God and man.

Sometimes what the Bible teaches is difficult for our finite human minds to understand. Our God has revealed Himself in His Word. But we cannot fully understand God. It is for us to humbly receive His revelation. It would be prideful for us to reject God's revelation because it does not make sense to us. It is wisest for us to humbly receive what God reveals about Himself, even when it is beyond our understanding. The doctrine of the Trinity and the doctrine of Christ's two natures are difficult to understand. But they are taught in the Word of God.

To resolve some of these disputes, another church council convened in Chalcedon in AD 451. Approximately six hundred bishops were present. The council discussed how Christ's deity and humanity related. The council reached a conclusion that was faithful to the teaching of Scripture. The council stated that Jesus has two natures, God and man, and that these two natures are not mixed or separated, but they exist together in one person, Jesus Christ.

The **Council of Chalcedon** produced a definition in the following words:

> Therefore, following the holy fathers, we all with one accord teach men to acknowledge one and the same Son, our Lord Jesus

THE COUNCIL OF CHALCEDON

PELAGIUS (C. 354-418)

AUGUSTINE OF HIPPO (354-430)

> Christ, at once complete in Godhead and complete in manhood, truly God and truly man, consisting also of a reasonable soul and body; of one substance with the Father as regards his Godhead, and at the same time of one substance with us as regards his manhood; like us in all respects, apart from sin; as regards his Godhead, begotten of the Father before the ages, but yet as regards his manhood begotten, for us men and for our salvation, of Mary the Virgin, the God-bearer; one and the same Christ, Son, Lord, Only-begotten, recognized in two natures, without confusion, without change, without division, without separation; the distinction of natures being in no way annulled by the union, but rather the characteristics of each nature being preserved and coming together to form one person and subsistence, not as parted or separated into two persons, but one and the same Son and Only-begotten God the Word, Lord Jesus Christ; even as the prophets from earliest times spoke of him, and our Lord Jesus Christ himself taught us, and the creed of the fathers has handed down to us.

This definition carefully preserved the teaching of the Bible, guarding the mystery of Christ's person while rejecting false doctrines that were dividing the church.

The Pelagian Controversy

Therefore, just as through one man sin entered the world, and death through sin, and thus death spread to all men, because all sinned. (Rom. 5:12)

Another important doctrinal controversy in the early church is known as the **Pelagian** controversy. Like the Arian controversy, the Pelagian controversy is named after a church leader. **Pelagius** (c. 354–418) was a monk born in Great Britain. He taught that mankind did not fall into sin with Adam when Adam ate the forbidden fruit. Pelagius argued that men are not born corrupt. All people are born innocent, but they become sinners by imitating sinners around them. This was a denial of the doctrine of **original sin**.

A church leader named **Augustine** (354-430) argued against Pelagius' teachings. Augustine explained that the Scriptures teach that all mankind fell into sin with Adam (Rom. 5:12-21). Augustine taught that we are all born with a corrupt sin nature (Ps. 51:5). He explained that it is only by the grace of God, giving us spiritual life and granting us faith to believe, that any one of us can be saved (Eph. 2:8-9). At the heart of the debate between Augustine and Pelagius is the question "How is man saved?" Augustine affirmed what the Bible clearly teaches. We can't save ourselves. We are born into sin. And we need a redeemer who will save us from our sins. This is why Jesus came (Matt. 1:21).

These are just a few of the major doctrinal developments of the early church. By God's preserving grace, the truth of God's Word was maintained by faithful and godly Christians. Of course, the church in these early centuries was not perfect. There are examples of teachings or practices that are not fully in accord with Scripture. Nevertheless, Jesus Christ was and is building His church. The attempts of the dragon with his demonic hordes to thwart Christ's truth will not succeed. ■

RUINS OF ANCIENT CHURCH IN EPHESUS

OLD STONE CHAPEL OF ST. ALBANS, FRANCE

Leaders of the Early Church

Coming to Him as to a living stone, rejected indeed by men, but chosen by God and precious, you also, as living stones, are being built up a spiritual house, a holy priesthood, to offer up spiritual sacrifices acceptable to God through Jesus Christ. (1 Pet. 2:4-5)

The church of Jesus Christ is not a physical building. However, the Word of God often uses the imagery of a building or structure to describe the spiritual constitution of the church. As Peter writes in the verses quoted above, the church is a "spiritual house" made up not of physical bricks and stones but instead constructed with "living stones." Those living stones are men, women, boys, and girls who are all members of the same body.

To study the history of Christ's church is to study the lives of Christ's people. How has this spiritual house been built? What are the contributions of the various living stones that constitute the church?

It is noteworthy that in the list of faithful in Hebrews 11, while many figures are named, there are many who are not named and yet are still given as examples of faith (Heb. 11:35-40). Even though we do not know their names, they are described as ones of whom "the world was not worthy" (Heb. 11:38). This reminds us that there are many members of Christ's church whose names are lost to us. On this side of eternity, we will not know the influence of all past members of Christ's church. But we know that every true member of Christ's body has an important function (1 Cor. 12:4-11).

Even though we cannot know about the influence of every past member of Christ's church, we do know about some of those in the cloud of witnesses who came before us. In this chapter, we will learn about a few selected pastors and leaders from the early church. These are some of the men whose writings exist today. By getting a brief glimpse of their life and work, we will come away with a better understanding of what Christ's church was like in these early centuries.

In the brief survey that follows, we will find that some of these teachers and writers were more faithful to God's Word than others. They are included in this chapter because of the influence they had on future generations, whether that influence was positive or negative.

Irenaeus of Lyons

O Timothy! Guard what was committed to your trust, avoiding the profane and idle babblings and contradictions of what is falsely called knowledge—by professing it some have strayed concerning the faith. (1 Tim. 6:20-21)

We begin our brief survey of these men with **Irenaeus** (AD 130-202). He lived in the region of Gaul (ancient France). He served as a bishop in the city of Lyons. Irenaeus was originally born in Smyrna. There he was taught by Polycarp, whom we learned about earlier. You may recall that Polycarp was discipled by the Apostle John. So Irenaeus was discipled by a man who was discipled by one of the apostles. This does not mean that everything Irenaeus wrote is correct. But it does mean he is one of the earliest witnesses to the teaching of Christ's church after the time of the apostles.

Irenaeus was one of the earliest defenders of biblical doctrine. In his book *Against Heresies*, Irenaeus set out to defend the church against poisonous false teaching.

A number of people split off from the church and wandered into false teaching. This false teaching was known as **Gnosticism**. The meaning of this word comes from the Greek word for knowledge (*gnosis*). It was called Gnosticism because its followers claimed to have a secret, special knowledge that others did not have. Only those with this secret knowledge could attain the greatest heights of salvation.

STAINED-GLASS DEPICTION OF IRENAEUS

Gnostics despised the physical creation. They believed that physical things like the ocean, plants, dirt, and animals were created by a lower god. They called this god the **demiurge**. They believed Jesus came to give us the knowledge necessary to escape this physical creation and become "pure spirits." Gnostics believed that a person's body was a "prison house" from which we need to escape.

This is contrary to what the Bible teaches. God calls His creation "good." God is redeeming all things through Jesus Christ. As human beings, we have both a body and soul. One day, when Jesus returns, there will be a resurrection of the dead. Physical things are not evil. It is the fall into sin that damaged the creation. But God will restore all things.

Because of their unbiblical beliefs, the Gnostics also lived in ungodly ways. Some Gnostics abstained from many foods and drinks. They believed the body and its pleasures were evil. They would abstain from marriage and certain foods. Paul warned that false teachers like them would come to deceive the church (1 Tim. 4:1-3). Other Gnostics didn't think it mattered what they did with their bodies. They reasoned, "We are leaving these bodies behind anyway." These Gnostics thought they could do whatever they wanted. As a result, they broke God's commandments by sinning with their bodies.

Irenaeus was deeply concerned about this false teaching. He began studying what the Gnostics were saying. Over many years, he wrote several books against the Gnostics. These books were collected into one larger work called ***Against Heresies***.

In this very large work, Irenaeus explains and refutes the strange, silly, and unbiblical teachings of the Gnostics. Irenaeus did more than simply expose false teaching. He also taught people the truth. He compared the Gnostic teaching with what the Bible teaches. He argued that the Gnostics were separating from the faith delivered by the

RUINS OF THE ROMAN AMPHITHEATER IN LYONS, FRANCE

CLEMENT OF ALEXANDRIA (150-215)

Apostles. Irenaeus also showed how all the Christian churches in different places held to the same basic core convictions. The churches held to what was called the **Rule of Faith**. There were different written summaries of early Christian beliefs. One of the earliest Christian creeds is called the **Apostles Creed**. The creed was probably not written by the twelve apostles, but it states what the apostles believed. It is a good summary of what the New Testament teaches.

Irenaeus' writings provide a good example of defending the true faith against counterfeits in the early centuries of the church.

Clement of Alexandria

Beware lest anyone cheat you through philosophy and empty deceit, according to the tradition of men, according to the basic principles of the world, and not according to Christ. For in Him dwells all the fullness of the Godhead bodily; and you are complete in Him, who is the head of all principality and power. (Col. 2:8-10)

Next, we turn our attention to a church leader who lived in the port city of Alexandria, Egypt. His name was Clement of Alexandria (150-215). He was likely born in the city of Athens. Clement's parents were pagan. They did not know the Lord Jesus Christ. We don't know the exact story, but apparently young Clement converted to the Christian faith sometime during his youth. After his conversion, Clement traveled to find others who could give him deeper instruction in the Christian faith.

It was in Alexandria that he found a teacher to instruct him in the deeper matters of the faith. Clement's teacher was **Pantenus**, of whom we know very little. After Pantenus died, Clement became the primary pastor and teacher in Alexandria. In AD 202, persecution occurred under **Septimius Severus** (AD 193-211). To avoid execution, Clement fled Alexandria for a time. He then traveled on and off until his death in AD 215.

Why is Clement important? To understand his importance, we need to know about the city Clement lived and taught in. Alexandria was one of the most important intellectual centers of the ancient world. It was the second largest city in the Roman Empire, and it housed one of the largest libraries of the ancient world. The port of Alexandria also made it a crucial trading center in the Mediterranean. Many influential people and ideas passed to and from Alexandria to the rest of the Roman Empire.

It was in this environment where Clement was discipled and where he taught others. Because it was such a significant intellectual center, Clement was very knowledgeable about Greek philosophy. His tendency was to demonstrate where unity existed between Greek philosophy and Christianity. Clement's intention was to defend the faith by doing this. He devoted much of his preaching and writing to convincing unbelievers that Christianity was not absurd, as many of them thought. Clement sought to demonstrate that Christianity was a religion that did not contradict reason, rightly understood. To do this, Clement made generous use of Greek philosophy. His approach to theology was heavily indebted to the thought of the Greek philosophers.

For Clement, there is ultimately only one truth. According to Clement, philosophy was given to the Greeks by God just as the Law was given to the Jews. Both have the purpose of leading to truth, which has now been revealed in Jesus Christ. Clement then sought to show the consistency between these two sources. For Clement, the thought of the Greeks and the teachings of Scripture were not in contradiction with one another. Rather, they supported each other.

One example of this approach is found in Clement's work *Exhortation to the Pagans*. He contends that Christian doctrine is consistent with much of what the Greek philosopher Plato wrote. He asks the following question:

> I seek to know God, and not only the works of God. Who will aid me in my quest? ... How then, oh Plato, is one to

ALEXANDRIA, EGYPT

RUINS OF ANCIENT CARTHAGE

seek after God?[1]

Many other Christian leaders have since seen Clement's quest as misguided. This is not to say that everything in Greek philosophy is untrue. But it was not sourced in the fear of the Lord (Prov. 1:7) or the knowledge of the true God. It is important to know something about Clement because his attempt to harmonize pagan philosophy with biblical truth would continue to appear in later centuries of the church.

Tertullian of Carthage

We turn our attention now to someone who was in many ways the polar opposite of Clement. It was **Tertullian of Carthage** (155-220) who rendered a different judgment on Greek philosophy.

Tertullian was likely a native of the North African city of **Carthage**. Although he spent most of his life in that city, it was in Rome where Tertullian was converted to Christianity. Once Tertullian returned to Carthage, he began to write various books defending Christianity. He wrote against the pagans and their denial of the faith and against heretics who perverted the truth. Tertullian is known by many as the father of Western theology because he was the first church father to write exclusively in Latin. Latin would become the main language of the church in the West, whereas Greek continued to predominate in the Eastern churches.

Unlike Clement, Tertullian had an antipathy toward philosophical speculation. For example, Tertullian once said this of Aristotle:

> Miserable Aristotle, who gave them dialectics! He gave them the art of building in order to tear down, an art of slippery speech and crude arguments ... which rejects everything and deals with nothing.[2]

Tertullian is also the source of a memorable phrase in church history. He once asked, "What has Athens to do with Jerusalem?"[3] Implied in the question is the idea that these two cities, representing different religions, are not to be harmonized. Rather, they represent conflicting worldviews.

Tertullian wrote numerous works on a variety of topics including theology, apologetics, church practice, and moral questions. His works have a legal and logical flavor to them. Tertullian used logic in his favor to demolish the arguments of his opponents. He was also known to use sarcasm and humor to make his points.

A good example of Tertullian's logic, sarcasm, and humor is found in *Against Marcion*. Marcion taught that the god who created this world was an evil god (like Gnosticism), not the God and Father of our Lord Jesus Christ. Marcion believed that the God of the Old Testament was not the same God as is found in the New Testament. Marcion rejected all the Old Testament and most of the New Testament. His Bible consisted of ten of Paul's epistles and a heavily edited version of the Gospel of Luke, from which he removed all Old Testament references to Jesus. In Marcion's view, Jesus taught love and mercy rather than judgment. For his mutilation of the canon, Tertullian called Marcion "that Pontic mouse who has gnawed the Gospels to pieces."[4]

Marcion's "god" was not a creator. Tertullian parodied this. Tertullian pointed out that the true God of the Bible had made the entire universe with all its wonders. In contrast, Marcion's "god" had not created a single vegetable.

Although he defended the faith, Tertullian was not free from error. In AD 207, Tertullian joined a strange schismatic movement known as the **Montanists**. Montanism is named after its founder Montanus. This man was a pagan until his conversion to Christianity in AD 155. Montanus began to prophesy, declaring that he was possessed by the Holy Spirit. Two women named Priscilla and Maximilla joined Montanus and began prophesying as well. They believed that their movement was the beginning of a new age. The Montanist movement especially emphasized moral purity. This appealed to Tertullian, who was concerned about moral laxity in the church. The rest of the church opposed Montanism due to its fanaticism, erroneous views of prophecy, and divisiveness. Montanists were divisive and separated themselves from other brothers and sisters in Christ.

Even after Tertullian became a Montanist, he continued writing against heretics. He wrote some valuable works during this time such as ***Against Praxeas***. In this work, written against a false teacher named Praxeas, Tertullian gives careful definition to the doctrine of the Trinity. In fact, Tertullian coined the word "Trinity" as a combination of "tri" (three) and "unity" (one). The word expressed well the biblical truth that there is one God eternally existing in three persons. Tertullian's terms and distinctions would be used in later debates about Trinitarian doctrine.

Tertullian is an unusual character in the history of the church. He was a champion of many orthodox teachings, yet he joined a schismatic sect. He was right on many things yet fell into some serious errors. Nevertheless, his writings remain an enduring contribution to the church.

Origen of Alexandria

The next figure we will learn about is **Origen of Alexandria** (185-253). Clement's most significant student in Alexandria was Origen. He was the son of Christian parents. During the persecution of Septimius Severus, Origen's father was executed for his faith in Christ. Origen was eager to follow in his father's footsteps and sought to offer himself for martyrdom. But his mother, who didn't want her son to be killed, hid his clothes so that he could not leave the house. This quick measure by a concerned mother may have saved Origen's life.

During Origen's teens, Bishop Demetrius of Alexandria gave Origen the task of training catechumens for baptism. This was a very important responsibility. A catechumen was a disciple in training, preparing for baptism. Soon Origen was known for his theological and philosophical learning. Eventually, he founded a school of philosophy in Alexandria very similar to some of the schools founded by the classical philosophers. It was there that Origen lectured to many, both Christians and non-Christians.

During the persecution of Decius, Origen had the opportunity to show the strength of his faith. Though Origen was not martyred, he was severely tortured, almost to the point of death. Shortly after being released, he died of his wounds at age seventy.

Origen left behind many commentaries on the Bible. He also wrote a large and influential work of theology known as *On First Principles*. The spirit of Origen's theology is very similar to that of his mentor Clement. Origen attempted to reconcile Christianity with neo-Platonism. This was a philosophy based on Plato's writings. This Greek influence led him to interpret Scripture allegorically and speculatively.

Origen was one of the most speculative of the church fathers. This meant that Origen was willing to suggest ideas that were not plainly taught in Scripture. Because of his speculation, he was often not faithful to what Scripture taught. His speculation extended into areas like the doctrine of creation (were there two creations?), the preexistence of the soul, and universalism (the doctrine that teaches that everyone will be saved). So controversial were some of Origen's teachings that the Second Council of Constantinople condemned Origen as a heretic in 553. ■

ORIGEN TEACHING HIS STUDENTS

ROMAN AMPHITHEATER IN CARTHAGE

More Leaders of the Early Church

6

And He Himself gave some to be apostles, some prophets, some evangelists, and some pastors and teachers, for the equipping of the saints for the work of ministry, for the edifying of the body of Christ. (Eph. 4:11-12)

In this chapter, we continue with brief sketches of some of the most influential pastors and theologians of the early church. These are some of the "living stones" that constitute the church of the Lord Jesus Christ.

Athanasius of Alexandria

Beloved, while I was very diligent to write to you concerning our common salvation, I found it necessary to write to you exhorting you to contend earnestly for the faith which was once for all delivered to the saints. (Jude 3)

One of the most important early defenders of the biblical faith was a man named **Athanasius** (298-373). Athanasius was born in Egypt, and it was here he spent most of his life. During the terrible persecution of Diocletian, Athanasius was just a boy. What he saw must have affected him deeply.

After the persecution ended, a man named **Alexander** became bishop of Alexandria. He succeeded bishop Peter who lost his life during the persecution. Alexander met Athanasius as a boy and began to disciple him in the faith. Alexander taught Athanasius the Bible and prepared him to be a leader in the church. Around 319, Athanasius became a deacon. Until Alexander's death, Athanasius served as an assistant to the bishop. Under Alexander's discipleship, Athanasius was prepared for future ministry. Soon Athanasius would be called to lead the church in Alexandria through hard times.

While Alexander was bishop in Alexandria, a presbyter named **Arius** began teaching false doctrine. In a previous chapter, we learned about the Arian controversy. Arius declared that Jesus must have had a beginning since He is the Son of God. He did not believe that the Son of God had existed eternally with the Father. This meant that Jesus the Son was not equal with the Father in His divine nature. In Arius' view, Jesus was actually a creature, not God. Arius could not understand how Jesus could both be equal with the Father and yet be the Son of God. Arius believed the Bible taught that Jesus had a beginning. But other Christians ably showed that the Bible teaches that the Son of God is not created. The Son of God is eternal. All things were created through Him (Col. 1:16).

The Council of Nicaea rejected Arius' teaching. As a result, Arius and his

ATHANASIUS (298-373)

ARIUS

followers were exiled because they did not accept the definition of the council. Even though the council set forth a definition that was biblical, this did not bring peace to the church. The Arians and those who held to the Nicene definition continued to argue.

Bishop Alexander died in 328. Athanasius seemed an obvious choice to replace him. But the Arians didn't want Athanasius to become bishop. They fought against his election and ordination. But in June 328, Athanasius became bishop of Alexandria. He would serve in that office for the next forty-five years. However, he would be exiled from his church and city of Alexandria four times for his faithfulness. Athanasius was unwilling to give up the Nicene definition of Christ's nature. He knew that much was at stake in understanding who Jesus Christ is. For this reason, he would never compromise what the Bible taught about Jesus.

Emperor **Constantine** had banished Arius and many of his followers from their posts in the church. But later Constantine relented and allowed Arius to return to Alexandria. In 330, Arius and some of his followers entered the city. Because Athanasius saw Arius' teaching as heretical and dangerous, he refused to allow Arius to enter the church. Athanasius wrote to Constantine, telling him about his decision to refuse Arius. Constantine was not happy about Athanasius' decision. Constantine threatened Athanasius with exile if Athanasius did not obey his orders.

It is important to remember that the authority of the church and the authority of the state are separate. Rulers in the state cannot tell the church what to do. Church leaders cannot force the state to change its laws. The Lord Jesus Christ is the only head of the church. Pastors in the church must obey the Lord and protect the peace and unity of the church. For this reason, Athanasius would not submit to Constantine's orders. He refused to allow Arius into the church.

The Arians wanted to see Athanasius gone. Various plots were made to get rid of Athanasius. Slander and false accusations were brought against the bishop. One false accusation was that Athanasius had stopped the grain shipments from Alexandria to Constantinople. (Alexandria was a port city that supplied much food to Constantinople.) This was a lie. But once Constantine heard about it, he ordered Athanasius into exile. By order of the emperor, he was sent to Treves in February 335. (Treves was located in modern-day Germany.) For the next two years, Athanasius lived in Treves. Though he was in exile, he was still the bishop of Alexandria. He continued to write letters to the church there and shepherd his people from a distance. Each year, Athanasius would write a festal letter on Easter. In these letters, he would instruct the church on matters of Christian faith and practice.

Although he had not repented of his heresy,

POMPEY PILLAR AND SPHINX IN ALEXANDRIA, EGYPT

Arius was to be restored to the church and admitted to communion in Constantinople. But the day before this was to take place, Arius died of a sudden illness. Many believed Arius' death was an act of divine judgment. Even though Arius was dead, his teaching continued to divide the church. Another death also occurred while Athanasius was in exile. Emperor Constantine died on May 22, 337. The empire was divided among his sons Constantine II, Constantius, and Constans. The Arian doctrine even divided Constantine's sons. Constantine II held to the Nicene view of Christ. He allowed Athanasius to return to Alexandria in 337. The people of Alexandria received their beloved pastor back with great joy and celebration. But the Arians did not want to see Athanasius return. The city and much of the empire was still bitterly divided over the Arian controversy.

Even though Constantine II was favorable to Athanasius, Constantius was in control of the region in which Alexandria was located. The enemies of Athanasius convinced Constantius that Athanasius was a troublemaker. They blamed the local violence and division on the bishop. Constantius decided to send a new bishop to Alexandria. This man hoped to take over the church by force. Gregory, a man who held Arian views, was sent to the city. A host of troops were sent with him. In order to save his life, Athanasius fled to Rome. From 340-346, he lived in Rome, teaching and preaching. In Rome, Athanasius was well-received by the Christians. The bishop of Rome, **Julius I** (337-352), also agreed with the Nicene Creed.

Constantine II died in AD 430. His brother Constans then took control of the Western portion of the empire. He threatened war against Constantius if he would not allow Athanasius to return to Alexandria. In order to avoid conflict, Constantius agreed to allow Athanasius to return. The bishop was once again welcomed back to Alexandria in 346. The people of Alexandria celebrated his return. They even came to meet him a hundred miles outside of the city. For the next few years, Athanasius enjoyed a time of peace while serving the church.

But the challenges were not over. In 350, Constans died. This made Constantius the only emperor of the empire. Constantius was always hostile to Athanasius. He forced many church leaders in the western part of the empire to reject the Nicene Creed. Anyone who would not submit to his authority was banished or imprisoned. Many leaders refused. They suffered for their decision, but they remained faithful to the truth. Athanasius also refused to submit to this decree. He would not give up the truth in order to protect himself.

In February 356, Constantius sent soldiers to the church to arrest Athanasius. Thousands of soldiers surrounded the church as Athanasius led an evening service. The people were frightened. But Athanasius led the people in reading Psalm 136. Together they recited the repeated phrase "For His mercy endures forever." Once the soldiers broke into the church, Athanasius' friends smuggled him out of the church. He later escaped into the Egyptian desert, where he was sheltered by friendly monks.

Athanasius was no stranger to trials and persecutions. Even though he suffered much, he knew that God would remain faithful. He was convinced by the Word of God that "nothing can separate us from the love of Christ" (Rom. 8:35-39). From 356 to 362, Athanasius lived in the desert of Egypt with other Christians. We believe that during this time he wrote many important books. Athanasius' writings are still read by Christians today. His book ***On the Incarnation of the Word*** explained why it was necessary for Jesus the Son of God to become man. The Son of God became man in order to save us through His sacrificial death and resurrection. Athanasius also wrote a book on the Holy Spirit. In this book, he argued that the Holy Spirit was also equal in nature with the Father. Athanasius helped Christians to better understand the biblical doctrine of the Trinity.

In 361, Constantius died. He was succeeded by the Emperor **Julian** (r. 361-363). Julian was the nephew of Constantius. The Christian church eventually called Julian "the Apostate" because he rejected Christianity. He became a promoter of the old Roman gods. He didn't set out to destroy the church. But he did persecute Christians in some ways. He did not want to see the church's influence grow. Athanasius returned to Alexandria in 362. Once he returned to the church, he resumed his preaching ministry. Influential citizens in the city began to convert to Christianity. This angered Julian, and he ordered Athanasius to leave. Soldiers were sent to find the bold pastor.

Thus began Athanasius' fourth exile from his beloved home. He once again fled to the Egyptian desert for refuge. Soldiers roamed through Egypt trying to find Athanasius. But he was able to escape. One day he was traveling in a boat down the Nile with his companions. Roman soldiers in another boat called out to Athanasius, "Have you seen Athanasius?" Athanasius replied, "He is not far from here." This was true. Athanasius was right in front of them. But the soldiers didn't know what Athanasius looked like. They continued on without capturing the bishop.

Once again, Athanasius was protected by the Lord. Soon Julian's reign came to an end. In 363, while Julian was fighting the Persians, he died in battle. Jovian, the next emperor (363-364), was a Christian. He was favorable towards Athanasius. But Jovian only reigned for eight months before he died. The empire was then divided. Valentinian ruled in the West and Valens ruled in the East. Since Alexandria was in the eastern part of the empire, Valens ruled it. Valens was an Arian and did not agree with Athanasius. He affirmed Constantius' decision to expel any bishops who did not agree with Arianism. For a time, Athanasius went back into hiding. But soon Valens became busy with other matters. Athanasius was able to continue his work as bishop.

Athanasius' last years were spent in peace in Alexandria. He returned to the city in 364 and served the church until his death in 373. Athanasius pastored the church and wrote commentaries on Scripture and letters to the church. One of his most important letters was his festal letter written in 367. This letter is known as *Festal Letter* 39. The reason this is an important letter is because Athanasius lists the books of the New Testament canon within it. The list of books in the letter is the same twenty-seven books of the New Testament we have today. The church did not create the canon. Instead the church recognized the books inspired by God that make up the canon. Athanasius' letter is an important early witness to the New Testament canon.

After Athanasius' death, the church still struggled with the Arian controversy. But in 381, a council in Constantinople reaffirmed the teaching of the Council of Nicaea. This council also affirmed that the Holy Spirit was equal with the Father as God. This helped to bring greater unity around the truth. The church now saw that the Father, Son, and Holy Spirit are the three persons in the Godhead.

Ambrose of Milan

The elders who are among you I exhort, I who am a fellow elder and a witness of the sufferings of Christ, and also a partaker of the glory that

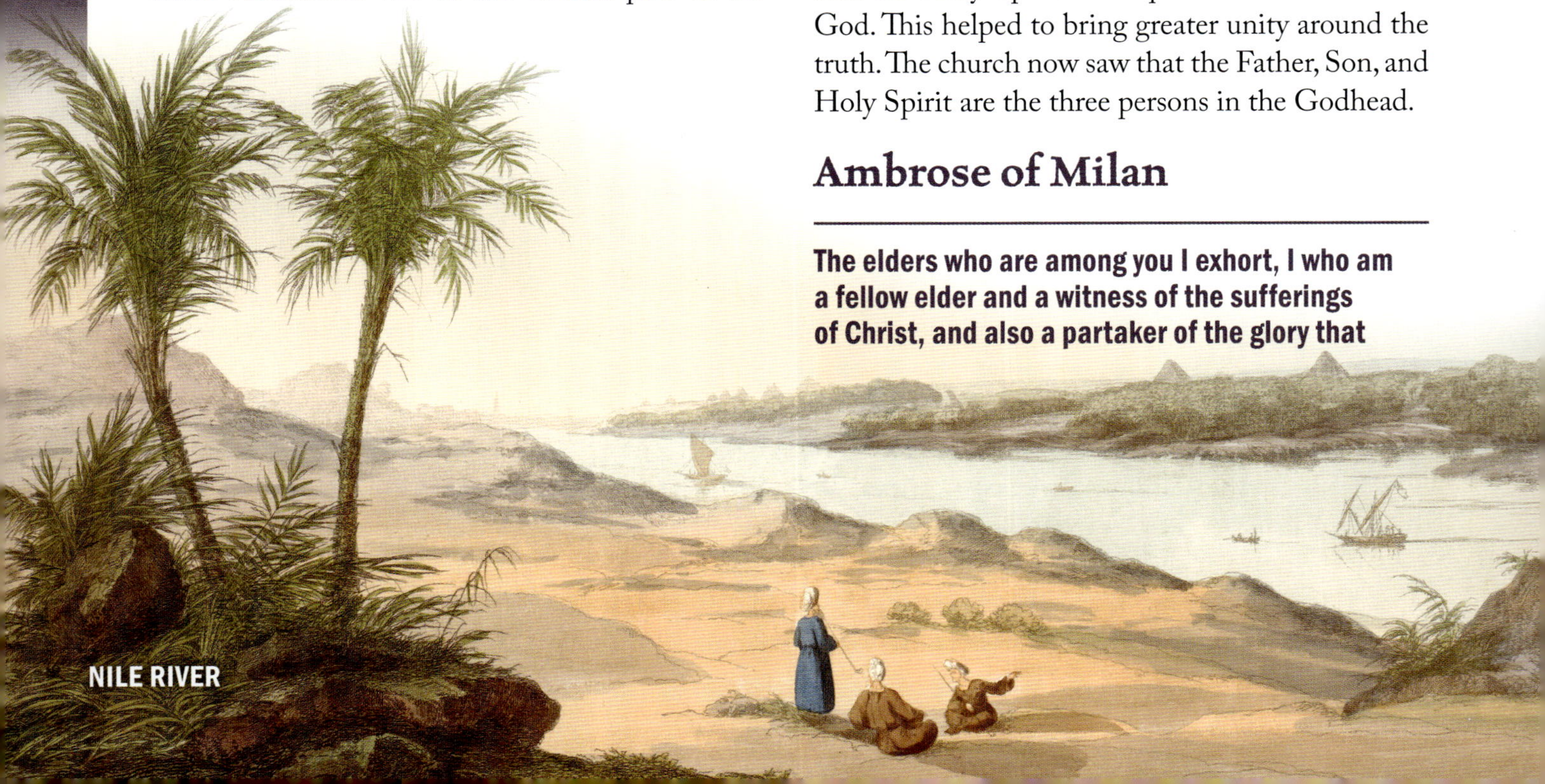

NILE RIVER

will be revealed: Shepherd the flock of God which is among you, serving as overseers, not by compulsion but willingly, not for dishonest gain but eagerly; nor as being lords over those entrusted to you, but being examples to the flock; and when the Chief Shepherd appears, you will receive the crown of glory that does not fade away. (1 Pet. 5:1-4)

Ambrose (c. 339-397) was a pastor who led God's people in the city of Milan. In the year 373 the bishop of Milan died. This left the city divided between two factions. Each group wanted to appoint a bishop consistent with their views. The first group were the Arians, who rejected the Nicene Creed's teaching on Jesus Christ as eternally God. The second group were those who held to the Nicene definition. The question was, who would become bishop? And which teaching in Milan would prevail?

At this time, Ambrose was the governor of the city. He was a civil ruler, and he did not hold any church office. During some of the arguments and conflicts that broke out, Ambrose came to the church to seek to calm the situation as governor of the city. Ambrose exercised wise peacemaking skills to bring some calm to a tense situation.

Suddenly, a young boy in the crowd started chanting "Ambrose, bishop, Ambrose, bishop!" Everybody else began repeating the same words. Ambrose was surprised and had no desire to become bishop. When it became apparent that the people did want to appoint Ambrose to this role, he made plans to escape. He tried to flee the city several times, but the people would not allow it. They were determined to make Ambrose their bishop.

The emperor agreed that Ambrose would be the right person to fill that role. But there was a problem. Ambrose was a catechumen and therefore he was not yet even baptized. The church leaders of Milan had to raise him through the various ministerial orders to make him bishop. In the period of eight days, Ambrose was baptized, became a deacon, became a presbyter, and finally became the bishop of Milan on December 1st, AD 373.

Ambrose did not want this job. But once he was ordained, Ambrose took his new role quite seriously. He devoted himself to the study of the Bible and theology. In time, he became known as a great preacher. Ambrose would also be responsible for discipling another influential early church leader: Augustine. Ambrose also wrote a number of important books and hymns and defended the orthodox doctrine of the Trinity. His defense of the Nicene Creed's teaching further cemented the biblical doctrine concerning Christ's nature in the church.

MOSAIC OF AMBROSE

Ambrose was not afraid to stand up to civil rulers. In 390, there was a riot in the city of Thessaloniki. The townspeople killed some imperial officials and soldiers. The Emperor **Theodosius** was furious. He retaliated by sending his troops against the city, and the soldiers massacred about 7,000 people. When Ambrose learned of this, he excommunicated Theodosius. Theodosius attempted to enter the church in Milan where Ambrose was about to celebrate communion. Ambrose stopped Theodosius at the door, rebuked him for what he had done, and urged him to repent. After several months during which Theodosius was mourning his sin, the emperor publicly repented and made a law to prevent further bloodshed. Ambrose then restored Theodosius to the fellowship of the church.

THE BASILICA OF ST. AMBROSE IN MILAN

Augustine of Hippo

But put on the Lord Jesus Christ, and make no provision for the flesh, to fulfill its lusts. (Rom. 13:14)

Augustine of Hippo (354-430) was a rebellious sinner who became a lover of God, by God's grace. He was born in North Africa in the city of Thagaste. Augustine was born on November 13th in the year of our Lord 354. He had a pagan father and a godly mother named Monica. In later years, he recounted his childhood, youth, and eventual conversion to the Christian Faith in his ***Confessions***. In this important book, Augustine confessed that he was a sinner committed to pride, lust, and fame. For many years, he lived a life of paganism and immorality.

Monica wept and prayed often, asking God to save her son from his sins. On one occasion, a pastor encouraged Monica to keep on praying. "It is not possible that the son of so many tears should perish," he said. Then Augustine moved to Milan. There he was influenced by the teaching and life of Ambrose. In 386, thirty-one-year-old Augustine was sitting in a garden. He heard a child's voice cry, "Take up and read!" Augustine opened the Bible and read Romans 13:14. The Lord used that Scripture to sovereignly convert Augustine that day. Monica sowed in tears, but she reaped in joy (Ps. 126:5-6) when Augustine became a Christian.

AMBROSE STOPPING THEODOSIUS

Following his conversion, Augustine became a bishop of the church in Hippo. From this small town in North Africa, Augustine wrote works that changed the course of church history. His partial autobiography *Confessions*, along with ***The City of God***, are two of the most important works of Western literature.

In 410, the Visigothic King **Alaric** captured and sacked the city of Rome. This was a shock to the Roman world. Many pagan Romans attributed the collapse of the empire to the rise of Christianity. Augustine wrote *The City of God* to answer these attacks. In doing so, he set forth a biblical philosophy of history.

Augustine said there are two cities made up of two kinds of citizens: the City of God and the City of Man. The citizens of the City of God are those who love God and live for Him. The citizens of the City of Man are those who love and live for themselves. Augustine traced the origin and progress of these two cities throughout history from the Fall to the Last Judgment at the end of time.

Shortly after Augustine's death in 430, the Vandals captured Hippo. Thankfully, Augustine's friends were able to save his writings from being destroyed. They survived to profoundly influence Christians in the West in a variety of traditions. Along with his contributions as a theologian and pastor, Augustine is highly regarded as a great philosopher.

John Chrysostom

I charge you therefore before God and the Lord Jesus Christ, who will judge the living and the dead at His appearing and His kingdom: Preach the word! Be ready in season and out of season. Convince, rebuke, exhort, with all longsuffering and teaching. (2 Tim. 4:1-2)

John Chrysostom (347-407) is one of the most well-known preachers in all of Christian history. Many of his sermons are still available to read today. They are some of the most powerful and valuable sermons still in existence from the early church. The name "Chrysostom" means "golden-mouthed," and this name was given to John because of his gifts as a preacher and teacher.

Originally, John was trained as a lawyer. Later he became a monk and lived a monastic life, far different from the life of a lawyer. After some time, others urged him to enter the Christian ministry. John began his work of public ministry in the city of Antioch. He was first ordained a deacon, then a presbyter (elder). In 397, the bishopric in Constantinople became vacant and the emperor called

RUINS OF HIPPO WITH CHURCH IN THE BACKGROUND

JOHN CHRYSOSTOM (347-407)

John to fill that role as bishop of Constantinople. Constantinople was the capital of the Byzantine Empire, and this was an important post.

John understood that his office was a weighty responsibility. He committed himself to faithfully shepherd the church in Constantinople. He sought to reform the church leaders in the city, many of whom were openly practicing immorality. Additionally, John sought to declare the whole counsel of God, including saying the needful but hard words that God's people needed to hear. This sometimes meant that John had to openly rebuke the sins of the people.

He preached through whole books of the Bible with great eloquence. Listeners hung on every word John preached, with rapt attention. Yet, Chrysostom lamented that people came to church not to hear the Word of God but to be entertained. They would loudly applaud his sermons as if they were concerts or plays. Once, Chrysostom preached a sermon against this practice of clapping. At the end of the sermon, the people enthusiastically applauded.

John made powerful enemies by fearlessly preaching against sin. He was banished by the emperor and died in exile. This happened because he was a faithful and courageous preacher. He did not "tickle ears" but preached God's Word. John's sermons rightly emphasize the historical and grammatical meaning of the biblical text rather than arbitrarily allegorizing like many of his contemporaries.

HAGIA SOPHIA (CHURCH OF THE HOLY WISDOM), ONE OF THE OLDEST CHURCHES IN CONSTANTINOPLE. HOWEVER, IT WAS NOT YET BUILT IN THE YEARS THAT JOHN CHRYSOSTOM MINISTERED IN CONSTANTINOPLE.

Jerome

Jerome (347-420) was born in the region of northern Italy. It was said by some that Jerome was "born an old man" because of his maturity at a young age. This maturity helped him in the work that he would do for the church.

As Jerome grew up, he found pleasure in reading non-Christian literature. However, once Jerome became a Christian, he believed that his love for pagan literature was sinful. Justo L. Gonzalez recounts an important event in the life of Jerome:

> Jerome once dreamed that he was at the final judgment and the judge asked him, "Who are you?" "I am a Christian," Jerome answered. But the judge retorted: "You lie. You are a Ciceronian" [referring to the writer Cicero]. After that experience, Jerome resolved to devote himself fully to the study of Scripture and of Christian literature, but he never ceased reading and imitating the style of the classical pagan authors.[1]

Following his conversion, Jerome made the study of the Bible his chief pursuit. He learned Greek and Hebrew even though his native language was Latin. Eventually Jerome decided to go to Palestine and leave Rome. It was, as he said, "leaving Babylon and going to Jerusalem." There he founded a monastic house where he devoted himself to the study of the Scriptures. His most important legacy and gift to the church would be the **Latin Vulgate**, the Latin translation of the entire Bible from the original Hebrew and Greek. The Latin Vulgate translation would influence the Western church for centuries all the way until the time of the Protestant Reformation (1500s). Jerome produced the translation to make the Scriptures accessible to the Latin-speaking Western church. Knowledge of the Greek language was diminishing in the West. Latin was becoming the common language. For this reason, the Latin translation of the Bible was important for passing on God's revelation to His people.

Jerome spent twenty-three years working on his new translation. He completed the work in AD 404. It became known as the Vulgate. The word "vulgate" comes from the Latin word for "common." Jerome's version did become the common version in use throughout the Western church. However, when it was first completed, Jerome's translation was poorly received. Many early church figures had concerns about it. One concern was due to Jerome's use of the Hebrew Old Testament. The main version of the Old Testament used by the church at that time was the Greek **Septuagint**. The Septuagint was the Greek translation of the Old Testament from Hebrew produced around 250 BC. It is called the "Septuagint" (Greek for "seventy") because it was allegedly the work of seventy Jewish elders. It became evident to Jerome, in translating from the Hebrew Old Testament, that the canon of the Old Testament did not contain certain books from the Greek translation of the Old Testament.

JEROME IN HIS STUDY

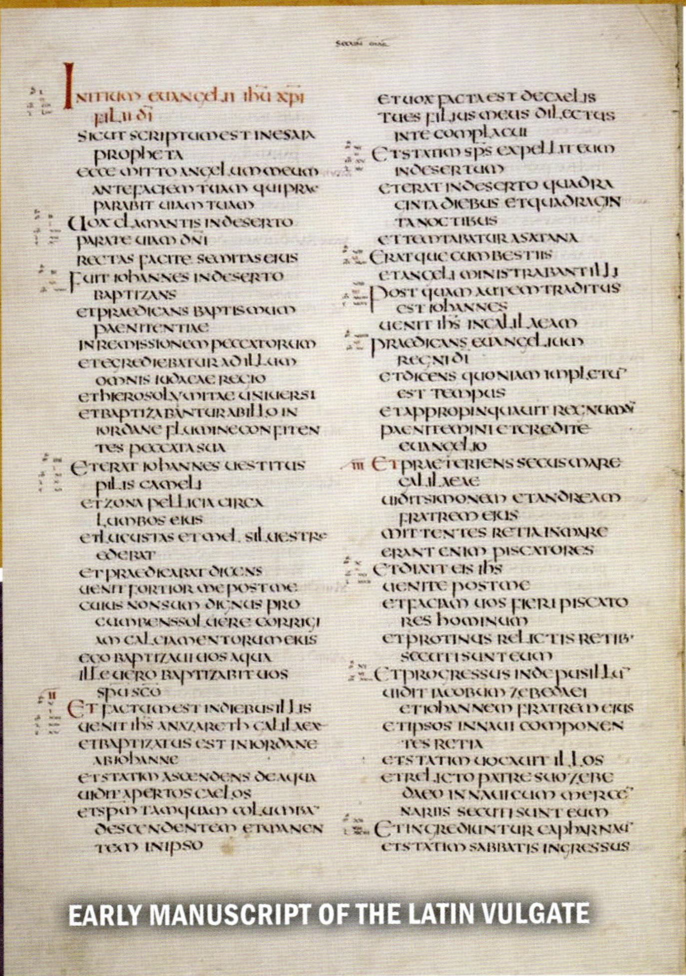

EARLY MANUSCRIPT OF THE LATIN VULGATE

In particular, the Greek Old Testament contained various writings that were written in the inter-testamental period. This refers to the period of time between the last of the Old Testament prophetic writings (Malachi) around 400 BC to the time of Christ (the beginning of the AD period). These writings were not originally written in Hebrew, and the Jews did not consider them Scripture. Jerome agreed with this and believed that these additional writings were not to be considered Scripture. These writings are often called the Apocrypha (a word that means "hidden"). Even though Jerome translated some of these apocryphal works into Latin, he did not believe them to be Scripture. This is noteworthy because Jerome argued for the same Old Testament canon (consisting of 39 books of the Hebrew Old Testament) that Protestants hold to today. However, in the 1500s, the Roman Catholic Church declared the apocryphal books to be Holy Scripture.

Eventually, the Latin Vulgate would become the standard Bible translation of the Western church. Ironically, centuries later, the Reformers would be criticized by Roman Catholics for doing what Jerome had done — translating the Bible from the original Hebrew and Greek into the common vernacular languages of Europe. The Roman Catholic Church became so committed to the Latin Vulgate that they eventually declared it to be the authoritative version of Scripture. This declaration was made at the Council of Trent (1540s-1560s).

The Cappadocians: Basil, Gregory, and Gregory

For through Him we both have access by one Spirit to the Father. (Eph. 2:18)

As noted in a previous chapter, the battle over Arianism raged for decades after the Council of Nicaea. Not only was the Arian controversy a major matter of dispute. There were other disputes and questions about the doctrine of the Trinity. It would take another generation of faithful theologians and pastors to clarify and defend the truth about God. Among the most important defenders of Trinitarian doctrine were the **Cappadocian Fathers**. These three men are called this because they each came from the region of Cappadocia. Their names were **Basil of Caesarea** (330-379), **Gregory of Nyssa** (335-394), and **Gregory of Nazianzus** (330-390). Each of these three men had the benefit of growing up in Christian homes.

As a young man, Basil lived in Caesarea, the capital city of Cappadocia. There he met Gregory of Nazianzus. Together, these men studied the Scriptures and other writings. After his season of study, Basil became a presbyter in the church of Caesarea and then succeeded Eusebius as bishop. Basil was known as a gifted administrator and eloquent preacher. He contributed an influential work to our understanding of the Trinity when he wrote *On the Holy Spirit* in AD 375. In this book, Basil demonstrated from the Scriptures that the Holy

Spirit was a divine person. Basil's careful biblical reasoning brought further clarification to the doctrine of the Trinity.

For example, in a letter to Gregory of Nyssa, Basil explained both the unity and the distinction between the persons in the Godhead. He wrote:

> There can be no room in our minds for any idea of separation or division, as if the Son could be conceived apart from the Father, or the Spirit separated from the Son. In a way that we cannot describe or imagine, the three persons share a oneness with each other, and yet are distinct. The difference between the persons never tears apart the unity of their nature; and the oneness of their essence does not destroy their proper marks of distinction.[2]

Gregory of Nazianzus became a presbyter in his hometown of Nazianzus. Later, he became bishop in Constantinople. While there, he penned a book called *Five Theological Orations*. It was a valuable summary of the Nicene doctrine of the Trinity. Gregory used the Scriptures to refute Arianism and win many over to the biblical view of the Trinity.

Gregory of Nyssa was the younger brother of Basil. He also became an influential leader of the church when he became bishop in the town of Nyssa. This was a town just outside of Caesarea, where his brother Basil served. He also contributed numerous important writings that defended the doctrine of the Trinity. When the Council of Constantinople convened in AD 381, Gregory of Nyssa was tasked with giving the opening address.

Basil and his brother Gregory of Nyssa are also known for their works of charity. Basil was responsible for building some of the first orphanages in human history. He also assisted in the establishment of one of the earliest hospitals. The hospital was built in AD 369. It included a number of dwellings for doctors, nurses, and patients. Gregory of Nyssa argued against the long-entrenched institution of slavery. He wrote that to own slaves was "to set one's power above God's."[3] He also said that no price in the universe "would constitute an adequate payment for the soul of a mortal."[4] Gregory's perspective on slavery was not adopted widely. But it showed his concern for those afflicted by the institution. Basil and Gregory showed themselves to be both faithful teachers and loving men who cared for the needs of others.

Through the faithful ministry and writings of the three Cappadocians, the church matured further in its understanding of who our great God is. ■

PROVINCE OF CAPPADOCIA

"FAIRY CHIMNEYS" FORMATION IN CAPPADOCIA

AD 381
Council of Constantinople

AD 385
Patrick of Ireland Born

AD 410
Sack of Rome

AD 516
Rule of St. Benedict Written by St. Benedict of Nursia

AD 570
Muhammad Born in Mecca

AD 589
Synod of Toledo

AD 610
Muhammad Claims Revelations From God

AD 1095
Council of Clermont

AD 1096-1099
The First Crusade

AD 1147-1149
The Second Crusade

AD 1198-1216
Papacy of Pope Innocent III

AD 1291
Siege of Acre

AD 1453
Fall of Constantinople

Unit 2

The Early Middle Ages (AD 500-1000)

AD 672
Venerable Bede Born

AD 717
Siege of Constantinople

AD 723
Boniface Cuts Down the Sacred Oak

AD 731
Bede's *Ecclesiastical History of the English People* written

AD 732
Battle of Tours

AD 754
Martyrdom of Boniface

AD 787
Second Council of Nicaea

AD 863
Cyril and Methodius Translates the Bible into Slavonic

AD 871-899
Reign of Alfred the Great

AD 1054
The Great Schism

AD 1059
Lateran Synod

AD 1073-1085
Papacy of Hildebrand/ Gregory VII

AD 1076
Synod of Worms

WHITBY ABBEY, NORTH YORKSHIRE, ENGLAND

Missionary Expansion

7

Arise, shine;
For your light has come!
And the glory of the LORD is risen upon you.
For behold, the darkness shall cover the earth,
And deep darkness the people;
But the LORD will arise over you,
And His glory will be seen upon you.
The Gentiles shall come to your light,
And kings to the brightness of your rising.
(Isa. 60:1-3)

By now it should be clear to all readers of this book that the church of Jesus Christ has not been a perfect church since its founding. The church does not advance without opposition. That opposition may arise within the church by false teaching and scandal. Or it may arise outside the church through slander and persecution. Either way, the church advances despite the opposition.

We move to a new period of church history, sometimes called the Middle Ages. As we do so, we must approach our survey of these centuries with the right faith convictions. One important conviction is the promise our Lord Jesus gave to His disciples in Matthew 16. Our Lord promised that the gates of hell would not prevail against His church (Matt. 16:18). We know that Christ's kingdom project will continue.

What does the term **Middle Ages** refer to? One prior church historian, Philip Schaff, defined the period of the Middle Ages this way:

> The Middle Age, as the term implies, is the period which intervenes between ancient and modern times, and connects them, by continuing the one, and preparing for the other.[1]

Schaff suggests that this period be dated from about the 6th century to the 16th century (the period of the Reformation). We will follow a similar division as we survey this fascinating period of church history.

Some historians have used the term Dark Ages to refer to this period. The first person to characterize this period as a time of darkness was **Petrarch** (1304-1374), the father of the Italian Renaissance. The Renaissance period saw a rebirth of interest in Greek and Roman literature, philosophy, and architecture. It was tempting for some to characterize this period of the church's dominance as a time of darkness. Petrarch called this period "the time of darkness." Christians cannot adopt this perspective of the Middle Ages. Far from being a period of darkness, this was a period in which our Lord Jesus was fulfilling His purposes and building His church. The development of Western civilization during this period is remarkable to behold. The influence of the Christian faith can be seen in every area of life. It is important that we appreciate the work of God as we survey this period.

Therefore, we must approach the period of the Middle Ages with both gratitude for and appreciation of God's works in history. Yet it is true that we will encounter negative things like heresy, division, and moral scandal. In our survey, we will witness both good and bad. On the one hand, topics such as the Roman papacy and the Inquisition will be cause for lament. But on the other hand, we will find topics of great encouragement and edification. These include the faithful men and women who stood for truth, even when it might cost them their lives. We will rejoice in seeing how the Christian faith had a transformative effect upon Western society in numerous ways.

We begin our survey with an event that was monumental in church history: the fall of Rome.

The Fall of Rome

If a trumpet is blown in a city, will not the people be afraid?
If there is calamity in a city, will not the LORD have done it? (Amos 3:6)

In the late 300s and early 400s, signs of weakness in the Roman Empire were apparent. The empire was massive in size, but the Roman government was not able to maintain control over such a vast territory. North of Italy, various Germanic tribes were gaining strength and furthering their territorial holdings through battle. Interestingly, some of these tribes converted from their pagan religion to a form of Arian Christianity. A bishop named **Ulfilas** (311-381) evangelized some of the tribes and translated the Bible into the Gothic language. It was the Visigoths who first converted to Arian Christianity. Other Germanic tribes such as the Angles, Saxons, and Jutes continued in pagan religion. They worshiped false gods such as Wodin, Thor, and others.

The Visigoths, mighty in battle, expanded their territory. **King Alaric** (395-410) of the Visigoths entered northern Italy with his armies. After several years of battle, Alaric successfully besieged Rome itself. That great capital of the greatest empire at the time was captured and pillaged. The Visigoths set fire to much of the city and massacred people throughout. The shocking news of Rome's fall reverberated throughout the empire. Jerome, living in Bethlehem at the time, wrote, "My voice is choked, broken with sobs as I dictate this letter. The city that conquered the entire world has now itself been conquered."[2]

KING ALARIC ENTERING ATHENS

So it is with the empires of men. They rise, and then they fall. They gain strength, and then they become weak. But thanks be to God, the kingdom of Jesus Christ marches onward!

Along with the Visigoths, another Germanic tribe, the Vandals pillaged and burned their way across the empire. Eventually, as Augustine of Hippo lay dying, the Vandals besieged his city in AD 430. Here was a sign of how much the empire had declined. By AD 476, the Roman Empire had very little political power in the Western world. The breakup of the Roman Empire was a pivotal point of transition in the West.

The Expansion of the Church into the British Isles

God be merciful to us and bless us,
And cause His face to shine upon us, Selah
That Your way may be known on earth,
Your salvation among all nations. (Ps. 67:1-2)

Rome was built on the foundation of human pride, wisdom, and power. It is no surprise then that it eventually crumbled. But the kingdom of Jesus Christ, built on the foundation of the death, resurrection, ascension, and reign of God's Son, cannot fail. Following the fall of Rome, we begin to see the church of Christ expand into new frontiers. These were no dark ages. Instead, we see significant missionary efforts advanced during this period. Some historians have called this time the **Frontier Age** because Christianity expanded

MAP OF THE ROMAN EMPIRE AT ITS GREATEST EXTENT

into the frontier of Europe. This growth of Christianity stretched as far as Britain and Ireland in the West and Russia in the East.

The British Isles consist of the islands of Great Britain and Ireland. To the Romans, these islands represented the western extremity of the known world. The Romans conquered and ruled the southern and central parts of Britain from AD 43-410. Christianity came to Roman Britain during this time and won many converts. Some British bishops took part in early church councils, and the heretic Pelagius was from Britain. When the Romans withdrew from Britain, the pagan Angles and Saxons from mainland Europe conquered much of the island from the native Britons. The Britons were enslaved or driven into Wales. The Anglo-Saxon territory eventually became known as England after the Angles. Christianity declined there for a time.

The Christian faith came to Ireland in the 5th century through the work of a man named **Patrick** (385-461). Patrick was a native of western Britain. When Patrick was about sixteen, he was kidnapped by Irish raiders and taken to Ireland. Patrick was a slave for years in Ireland, herding sheep for his Irish masters. Patrick had been raised in a Christian home but only came to true faith in captivity. After about six years, Patrick was able to escape from Ireland and return to his home in Britain. But he was called by God in a dream to

CLIFFS OF MOHER, IRELAND

return and help the Irish. So Patrick left his home and family to preach the Gospel to the very people who had kidnapped and enslaved him. His story is told in his autobiographical ***Confessions***.

Patrick faced tremendous opposition from druids, kings, hostile men, and the demonic forces behind them. But trusting in the power of God he went forth in the strong name of the Trinity. And his labors were blessed by the Lord. He baptized thousands of converts and planted hundreds of churches. Eventually all of Ireland was Christianized. Thus while Britain was falling back into paganism, Ireland was becoming a new center of Christianity. The Celtic Christians of Ireland preserved much learning that would have been lost. Celtic Christians went as missionaries to Scotland, northern England, and beyond the sea to the European continent.

AUGUSTINE OF CANTERBURY

The Christian faith came back to much of England through **Augustine of Canterbury** (not to be confused with Augustine of Hippo) who was sent there as head of a missionary team by **Gregory I** (often called **Gregory the Great**) around 597. King Ethelbert of Kent, whose wife Bertha was a Christian, allowed them to stay and gave them freedom to evangelize. Eventually, King Ethelbert himself converted to Christ, and the faith spread through Anglo-Saxon England. Churches were established there through the work of Augustine and other Christian missionaries. The main local seat of the Church of England became the city of Canterbury in Kent. Even today, Canterbury is considered the center of the English church and the archbishop of Canterbury is the most important Anglican church leader.

ST. MARTIN'S CHURCH IN CANTERBURY, ENGLAND, THE OLDEST CHURCH BUILDING IN ENGLAND STILL IN USE.

The small Scottish island of **Iona** is also an important part of the story of Christianity in the British Isles. This tiny island would have great influence on the British Isles and Europe. The Celtic Christian Columba and twelve other companions founded a monastery on Iona around 563. It became a missionary training and sending center for many generations.

The Venerable Bede (c. 672-735) was an English scholar and monk. He wrote about many of the most important events in the Christianization of Britain in his ***Ecclesiastical History of the English People***. Bede also translated portions of the New

IONA ABBEY

THE VENERABLE BEDE

Testament into Anglo-Saxon, finishing the last chapter of the Gospel of John on his deathbed. Bede also popularized the BC-AD dating system that we use today. It's a testimony to the difference the Lord Jesus Christ has made in history that most people today all over the world date their years from His coming!

Gregory the Great

I have coveted no one's silver or gold or apparel. Yes, you yourselves know that these hands have provided for my necessities, and for those who were with me. I have shown you in every way, by laboring like this, that you must support the weak. And remember the words of the Lord Jesus, that He said, "It is more blessed to give than to receive." (Paul's words to the Ephesian elders in Acts 20:33-35)

Before we survey additional missionary efforts in Europe, let's look at a central figure of this period. Gregory I, the bishop of Rome (590-604), was responsible for the first major missionary enterprise to England. As we have seen, he sent Augustine of Canterbury and others to preach the gospel to the Angles and Saxons, Germanic tribes living in England.

In addition to these mission efforts, Gregory left behind an important legacy in other ways. Gregory was the bishop of Rome and was also known as the "Pope" of Rome. The word "pope" means "father." Originally, this became a word applied to numerous bishops. But over time, the word took on a special meaning and began to refer only to the bishop of Rome. In a later chapter, we will investigate the origins and the development of the papacy. For now, however, we will look at how Gregory held this office.

Under Gregory, the office of the pope grew in its role of political leadership. At this time, the bishop of Rome held significant swaths of land in Italy. As such, the pope was more than just a church leader. He had significant land interests. Gregory was a pastor, but he was also a leader whom many looked to for guidance. When the Lombards threatened portions of Italy, it was Gregory who stepped into the gap and sought peace with the Lombards. He established an agreement with the king of the Franks. Gregory also used his lands to care for those who had been displaced by the Lombards' advances. By taking these actions, Gregory helped transform the office of bishop of Rome into more than a church leadership post.

DEPICTION OF GREGORY I

Under Gregory, the power of the Roman bishop expanded. But unlike later popes, Gregory did not seek power and prominence. Throughout his life, Gregory spoke in humble ways about how his office should be viewed. In fact, Gregory spoke of his office in ways quite contrary to later popes. Gregory once said, "Whoever calls himself universal priest, or desires that title, is by his pride the forerunner of Antichrist."[3] Despite Gregory's strong words, his successor Boniface III (607) claimed the title of "universal bishop." Instead of claiming universal supremacy as later popes would, Gregory's favorite title for himself was "servant of the servants of God."

One of Gregory's enduring contributions to church literature was his book on pastoral ministry. The work is titled **Pastoral Care**. In this book, Gregory explained what a faithful pastor should be and how he should minister. Gregory's book became a classic that continues to be read today. Gregory taught that the pastor should be a godly example to the flock and practice what he preaches. Here is a portion of Gregory's *Pastoral Care*:

> The pastor must keep careful watch over himself, in case the craving to be popular assaults him. As he studies to understand spiritual things and as he ministers to his people, he must beware that he does not try to make the congregation love him more than they love the truth. He must take care in case his self-love puts him at a distance from His Creator, even if his good life seems to show that he does not belong to this world. For a man becomes an enemy of the Redeemer, if by his good works he covets being loved by the church instead of by Christ.[4]

Gregory warns pastors against the ungodly desire to be popular. If pastors are motivated by love of self, it will damage their ministry. A pastor may even become an "enemy" to Christ by taking the glory and honor for himself!

Gregory also counseled pastors to be faithful in delivering rebuke, but do so with gentleness. He wrote:

> But others, whom the pastor sees have no power against him, he keeps down with the roughness of harsh rebuke, never warning them gently, but (forgetting all pastoral kindness) terrifying them with the power of domination. Such pastors God rightly condemns through the prophet, saying, "You have not strengthened the weak, nor have you healed the sick, nor have you bound up the broken, nor brought back those driven away, nor sought the lost; but you have ruled over them with violence and with cruelty" (Ezek. 34:4). Loving themselves more than their Creator, these pastors exalt themselves proudly over those who are under them . . . They have no fear of future judgment, but arrogantly glory in worldly power.[5]

Pastors should deliver warnings with gentleness. They should not use their authority to dominate the flock for their own selfish interests. Instead, out of love, they must seek to shepherd with love. These quotes from Gregory's *Pastoral Care* demonstrate the biblical wisdom with which Gregory guided his fellow pastors.

Missionary Efforts in Continental Europe

Enlarge the place of your tent,
And let them stretch out the curtains of your dwellings;
Do not spare;
Lengthen your cords,
And strengthen your stakes.
For you shall expand to the right and to the left,
And your descendants will inherit the nations,
And make the desolate cities inhabited. (Isa. 54:2-3)

BONIFACE FELLING THE OAK OF THOR

During the Frontier Age, the Christian faith spread far and wide throughout continental Europe. The Franks in modern-day France embraced Christianity during the reign of **King Clovis** (c. 466-511). Echoes of Constantine's conversion story appear with Clovis. In a dream before battle, Clovis saw a sign of the cross in the sky. Clovis vowed to become a Christian if he was victorious in the battle.

After winning the victory, as promised, Clovis was baptized on Christmas Day AD 496 along with 3,000 of his warriors. As mentioned above, many of the Germanic tribes had already embraced an Arian form of Christianity. But Clovis and the Franks adopted the orthodox faith (as expressed in the Nicene Creed). From this point on, Christianity was the predominant religion of the Franks.

Courageous missionaries also brought the faith to Germany and the Netherlands. One of the most important of these missionaries was a man from England named **Boniface** (c. 675-754). Boniface journeyed across the sea to evangelize the Germanic tribes. One of the tribes Boniface encountered was the Hessians. Boniface confronted them with the truth of the gospel, calling them to believe in Jesus and repent of their idolatry.

BASILICA OF SAINT-PIERRE-AUX-NONNAINS IN METZ, FRANCE, ONE OF THE OLDEST CHURCHES IN FRANCE

Among the most revered deities of the Germanic tribes was the false god Thor, a fierce god of power, known for thunder and lightning. The Hessians worshiped Thor at a sacred oak tree atop Mt. Gudenberg. The enormous oak was the center of pagan worship in the region. Much like Elijah atop Mt. Carmel, Boniface challenged the Hessians to a contest of the gods. Which was the true God? The God of Christianity, or the god Thor?

Boniface boldly marched to the sacred oak accompanied by a great crowd. Boniface said he would cut down the great tree to show the power of the one true God. The pagan Hessians warned

Boniface, "Thor will strike you dead!" Unfazed, Boniface took an axe and began to cut down the oak. His biographer Willibald records that as soon as he had cut a notch in the oak, the Lord sent a great blast of wind which knocked over the great tree, splitting it into four pieces.

The awestruck crowd expected Boniface to be struck dead by a thunderbolt from Thor. But nothing happened. Thor's sacred oak lay in pieces, and Boniface was still standing. Many Hessians saw that the Lord was greater than Thor and all the pagan gods they had worshiped. They asked Boniface to tell them about his God. Boniface preached the gospel and many believed in the Lord. Boniface used the wood of the oak to build a church in that place. This event proved to be a decisive turning point. Through Boniface's courageous labors, the Germanic tribes began to accept Jesus Christ as Lord and Savior. Christian churches were established throughout Germany, and Boniface appointed pastors in the surrounding churches. He then moved north and west to take the gospel to other unreached people groups. He was martyred by a pagan tribe of Frisians in 754.

Missionaries also brought the faith to central and eastern Europe. **Cyril** (826-869) and **Methodius** (815-885) were two brothers who came from Byzantium to work as missionaries among the Slavs there in the 9th century. They translated the Bible into Slavonic and created the Cyrillic Alphabet which is still used in Slavic countries today. They also wrote the first Slavic law code. During this time, there was a growing division between Christians in the east and west. Some central and eastern European countries such as Poland, Hungary, and the Czech lands converted to western Christianity and looked to Rome. Others, such as Romania, Bulgaria, and Russia, adopted eastern Christianity and looked to Constantinople.

STATUE OF CYRIL AND METHODIUS IN RADHOST, CZECH REPUBLIC

The Conversion of the Vikings

While much of Europe was converting to Christ, the people of Scandinavia (modern Denmark, Norway, Sweden, and Finland) remained pagan. They were fierce warriors known as Vikings. Beginning in the late 700s, the Vikings began raiding the coasts of Europe. At first, they just came to raid. They would sail in their longboats, land, burn, kill, and steal. They often targeted churches and monasteries. After securing their plunder, they would sail back to their homeland. But eventually, the Vikings came to stay and conquer. Would Christian Europe fall to these fierce pagans?

The Vikings invaded England. One by one, the Anglo-Saxon kingdoms fell. The last one standing was Wessex. Wessex was ruled by a wise Christian king named **Alfred the Great** (r. 871-899). The Vikings overran nearly all of Wessex. But Alfred rallied his men and fought back. He defeated the Vikings in several battles. He spared their leader Guthrum's life but required him to be baptized. Despite the unusual circumstances, Guthrum's conversion seems to have been genuine. Alfred successfully fortified his kingdom, establishing walled towns and training an army and navy to defend it from Viking attacks. The Vikings continued to rule northern and eastern England, but under Alfred southern and western England was secure.

Alfred was a godly king who wanted his people to know the Lord. He gathered scholars

BAPTISM OF GUTHRUM

KING CANUTE LISTENING TO THE MONKS OF ELY

and encouraged schools to teach the people to read and write. With the help of these scholars, Alfred translated several books into Anglo-Saxon. They included fifty of the Psalms, Gregory the Great's *Pastoral Care*, Bede's *Ecclesiastical History*, some of Augustine of Hippo's writings, and other Christian literature.

King Alfred also reformed English law, seeking to provide liberty and justice. He began his law code with the Ten Commandments and based his laws on the Bible. These laws would become the foundation for English Common Law. Common Law has formed the basis of law in Britain and her former colonies, including the United States, Canada, Australia, and parts of Africa and Asia.

Eventually, the Vikings in England converted to Christianity. Missionaries also took the gospel to the Viking's homelands in Scandinavia. A monk from Picardy named **Ansgar** (801-865) became the first missionary to Denmark and Sweden. Known as the "Apostle to the North," he began his work in 826 and continued until his death in AD 865. Outside of a few converts in Sweden and a single church plant at Schleswig, Denmark, it was an uphill battle in those initial years. Nevertheless, Ansgar's work would not be in vain. The gospel did take root among the peoples of northern Europe.

In the early 900s, a tyrannical and wicked king named Gorm the Old (r. 936-958) unleashed a severe persecution on the few churches in Denmark, killing priests and destroying church buildings. In the providence of God, however, Gorm's son Harald Bluetooth (r. 958-986) turned to Jesus Christ. He sought to make the Danes Christians.

Sixty years later, Harald's grandson, **Canute** (king of Denmark from 1018-1035), took an estimated 200 Viking longships and 10,000 troops across the sea to England. He was made king of England in 1017 while his brother Harald served as king of Denmark. A year later, his brother died, and Canute ascended to the throne of Denmark as well. This was a key moment for the Christian church's influence in Denmark. Canute had gained himself an empire in the nations surrounding the North Sea, with Denmark, Norway, England, and parts of Sweden under his rule.

STATUE OF ANSGAR IN COPENHAGEN, DENMARK

NORWAY, SWEDEN, FINLAND, AND DENMARK

But the Lord Jesus Christ would have this powerful king serve Him instead. In his later years, Canute turned his attention to spiritual things, and he brought the Danish church for a time under the archbishop of Canterbury until a new governing archbishopric for the Danes was established in Lund, Sweden. This further cemented a Christian witness in this northern land. By the end of the 11th century, pagan burial customs had all but ceased in Denmark. This was a clear sign that Christian discipleship of the nation had borne lasting fruit.

At about the same time that God was working with Harald and Canute, another swashbuckling man of war from Norway felt the call. **Olaf Tryggvason** (reigned 995-1000) came upon a hermit in the Scilly Islands off the coast of Britain, and the Lord used an obscure Christian hermit on a remote island to baptize the Viking warrior. Olaf eventually became king of Norway in 995. For the next five years, Olaf did what he could to bring the gospel to Norway until he was killed at the Battle of Svolder in AD 1000. His successor, Olaf II Harraldsson (r. 1015-1028), continued this work. Most of the mission work in Norway was done by missionaries whom these kings brought from England. Eventually, Christianity would take root throughout Scandinavia and northern Europe.

Missionary Efforts in Asia and Africa

Christian missionary efforts were not limited to Europe. Christianity spread in Asia. An Armenian noble named **Gregory the Illuminator** (c. 257–331) brought the gospel to his people. At first, King Tiridates III tortured and imprisoned Gregory for refusing to offer sacrifices to pagan gods. Gregory spent more than ten years in prison. But the Lord softened King Tiridates' heart. He released Gregory and allowed him to preach to him. King Tiridates and many of his people were converted. Armenia became the first Christian nation around 301, several years before Constantine's conversion.

Christianity also spread in Persia (Iran) and India. There is a tradition that the Apostle **Thomas** took the gospel to India. India has had a community of "Saint Thomas" Christians in Kerala since at least the 4th century AD.

Christianity was taken to China by

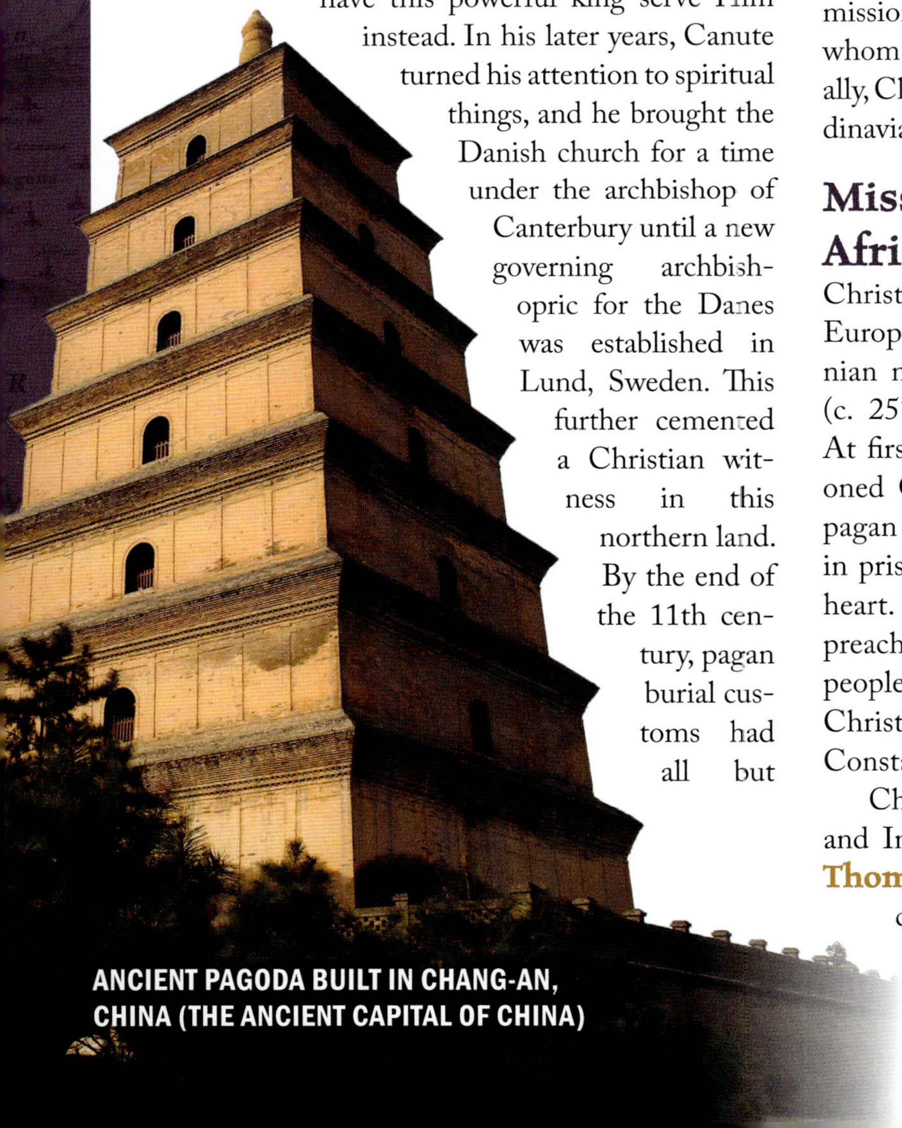
ANCIENT PAGODA BUILT IN CHANG-AN, CHINA (THE ANCIENT CAPITAL OF CHINA)

Christians in Syria and Persia (Iran). In 635, the monk **Alopen** traveled to China on the Old Silk Road and reached the Chinese capital, Chang-an, one of the largest and most technologically advanced cities of that time. Alopen was able to speak to the Chinese Emperor Taitsung (598–649), who listened favorably. Alopen planted churches in China, and his fellow missionaries translated the New Testament and parts of the Old Testament into Chinese. Some Chinese emperors gave Christians freedom, and Christianity spread in China. But other Chinese emperors severely persecuted Christians, and their numbers dwindled. Ultimately, the faith did not take deep root in China at this time.

Christianity also spread in Africa. In the early 4th century, two young Christian brothers from Tyre, **Frumentius** and **Edesius**, were sailing off the Horn of Africa with their uncle. The two boys were kidnapped and sold as slaves to the king of Ethiopia. They gained favor with the king and queen who promoted them to positions of influence, and they used their influence to spread the gospel there. After the king died, the queen persuaded the brothers to stay in Ethiopia to help govern the kingdom and educate her son, the boy king Ezana (c. 325–360). When King Ezana reached adulthood, the brothers traveled back north to Egypt. Frumentius was sent back to Ethiopia by Athanasius as a missionary. He baptized King Ezana and many other Ethiopians. Ethiopia became a Christian nation. The Ethiopian church maintained close ties with its mother church in Egypt. On many occasions, the Ethiopians protected Egyptian Christians from oppression by Muslims.

A pattern stands out in these conversions. In the New Testament, when the head of a household believed and was baptized, his whole family followed him into the faith (Acts 16:14-15, 30-34). This biblical pattern continued in the Middle Ages. It was also common that when a ruler embraced Christianity, his people would join him in following the faith. Eventually, the entire nation would become Christian. In this way, Christians sought to make disciples of all nations (Matt. 28:19).

By the power of Jesus Christ, who has all authority in heaven and earth, the borders of the church and the kingdom greatly expanded during the early Middle Ages. Although Christian missions were not limited to Europe, they took deepest root there. Christ's influence in Europe would be felt at every level of culture in the centuries to follow. Even today, though much of Europe has embraced a secular identity, the influence of Christianity is still quite evident. Let us praise the Lord Jesus Christ who is King of kings and Lord of lords, the Lamb of God who takes away the sin of the world! ■

A STELE FROM KING EZANA'S REIGN IN AKSUM, ETHIOPIA

THE ABBEY OF CLUNY, FRANCE

Christian Monasticism

8

Then Jesus said to His disciples, "If anyone desires to come after Me, let him deny himself, and take up his cross, and follow Me. For whoever desires to save his life will lose it, but whoever loses his life for My sake will find it. For what profit is it to a man if he gains the whole world, and loses his own soul? Or what will a man give in exchange for his soul?" (Matt. 16:24-26)

Monasticism became influential among Christians in the early 4th century. A man named Antony moved to the Egyptian desert to live the Christian life in solitude. Antony began a movement that would have great influence on the church. The word monasticism derives from a Greek word which means "to live alone." In its original form, this is an accurate description of the movement. Antony, the original monk, lived alone. As we will see, however, later forms of monasticism were communal in nature (monks living together).

Before we explore early forms of monasticism, let us answer an important question: why did monasticism arise within the Christian church? What provoked the creation of this influential way of life?

The Formation of Monasticism

Antony of Egypt (c. 251-356) made his trek into the desert around 270. But monasticism as a movement did not become widespread until after the early church persecutions came to an end in 313. Those early centuries were characterized by conflict and hostility between the church and civil authorities. Christianity was a minority religion, often persecuted. The conflict between the church and a hostile world was felt acutely.

But following the reign of Constantine, the Christian church began to enjoy various privileges. As the state and church began to influence one another more directly, some were concerned for the purity of the church. Would this newfound status of accepted religion threaten the purity of Christian living? The monastic movement appears on the scene as a reaction. Monastics were responding to moral decline in the church. Philip Schaff points out that with the loss of martyrdom by the Roman authorities, monastics put "self-martyrdom" in its place.

For monastics this meant radical self-denial by punishing the body. Self-denial could take the form of denying oneself food or water for a time by fasting. Or a monk might not sleep for varying

ST ANTHONY'S MONASTERY IN EGYPT

ANTONY OF EGYPT

lengths of time. Monks would also deny themselves other pleasures enjoyed by ordinary people. This practice of severe self-discipline is called **asceticism**. How should Christians view asceticism?

The Bible does teach fasting as a spiritual discipline (Matt. 6:16-18). The Scriptures do call us to discipline our bodies in the pursuit of holiness (1 Cor. 9:27). However, the Bible also warns against externalistic rules and regulations that do not address the heart. Paul says the following in Colossians and 1 Timothy:

Therefore, if you died with Christ from the basic principles of the world, why, as though living in the world, do you subject yourselves to regulations—"Do not touch, do not taste, do not handle," which all concern things which perish with the using—according to the commandments and doctrines of men? These things indeed have an appearance of wisdom in self-imposed religion, false humility, and neglect of the body, but are of no value against the indulgence of the flesh. (Col. 2:20-23)

Now the Spirit expressly says that in latter times some will depart from the faith, giving heed to deceiving spirits and doctrines of demons, speaking lies in hypocrisy, having their own conscience seared with a hot iron, forbidding to marry, and commanding to abstain from foods which God created to be received with thanksgiving by those who believe and know the truth. For every creature of God is good, and nothing is to be refused if it is received with thanksgiving; for it is sanctified by the word of God and prayer. (1 Tim. 4:1-5)

As we will see, monasticism in certain forms produced good fruit. The good fruit included missionary expansion, a God-centered piety and worship, and the production and preservation of biblical manuscripts and Christian literature. But monasticism also had harmful effects. These harmful effects included human traditions not in accord with God's Word, such as the elevation of poverty and celibacy and the depreciation of marriage. Additionally, monasticism, by its tendency to withdraw from the world, also depreciated the goodness of other Christian callings. It tended to produce a division in the church between the "spiritual" (those in monastic orders) and the "non-spiritual" (all other Christians engaged in regular life-callings).

In the chapters that follow, we will encounter various forms of monasticism. If we would be thoughtful Christians, we should seek to discern both the fruitful and unfruitful aspects of monasticism. We may thereby benefit by learning from monasticism while rejecting its unbiblical and unfruitful characteristics.

Various Forms of Monasticism

As mentioned above, Antony of Egypt is known as the first Christian monk. Antony interacted with others but lived alone. Due to Antony's example, the earliest monks lived solitary lives. This form of monasticism has come to be known as **eremitic** monasticism (from the Greek word for desert or wilderness). This earlier form of monasticism emphasized individual and solitary life as a hermit secluded from society.

Eventually however, monasticism developed into a more communal approach. This form of monasticism was called **cenobitic** monasticism (from the words *koinos bios* in Greek, meaning "common life"). This communal monasticism was popularized in the early church through the work of **Pachomius** (290-346). Pachomius founded a community of monks in Egypt. Together, they worked, prayed, and ate together. They also shared all property in common. In order to set standards for the community, Pachomius wrote a "rule" or code of conduct that all monks were required to follow.

Another characteristic of monasticism is submission and obedience to a spiritual leader. Many monastic rules required the monks to obey the head monk in all things. The leader of a monastery became known as the abbot (from the Aramaic word for father). It is from this word that "abbey" came into use to describe a monastery. At first, monastic orders were made up of men. But eventually, female monastic orders arose as well.

The Rule of St. Benedict

Christian history is filled with a variety of monastic orders. One of the most influential of these orders was the Benedictine. Their monastic rule, known as the ***Rule of St. Benedict***, shaped much of the Western monasticism that would follow. The founder of this order was **Benedict of Nursia** (480-547).

Benedict grew up in the village of Nursia in

ST. CATHERINE'S MONASTERY AT MT. SINAI

BENEDICT OF NURSIA (480-547)

central Italy. As a young man, Benedict was sent to Rome by his parents to pursue an education. While living in Rome, Benedict was repulsed by the immoral behavior of the populace. He decided to pursue the life of a hermit and dwelt alone to the east of Rome. Then, in 529, Benedict founded a monastery in Monte Cassino.

He produced his own monastic rule (based on some previous examples available to him) to regulate the life and work pattern of his new community. Benedict's *Rule* would serve as the foundation for much of Western monasticism.

Because Benedict's *Rule* was so influential, it gives us an understanding of the patterns of monasticism common in the Western church. Of course, each order had its own unique rules and emphases. But Benedict's *Rule* was the foundation of much monastic practice. For this reason, we will read portions of Benedict's classic work.

The opening words of the *Rule of St. Benedict* are as follows:

> Listen, O my son, to the precepts of your master, and incline the ear of your heart, and cheerfully receive and faithfully execute the admonitions of your loving Father, that by the toil of obedience you may return to Him from whom by the sloth of disobedience you have gone away. To you, therefore, my speech is now directed, who, giving up your own will, take up the strong and most excellent arms of obedience, to do battle for Christ the Lord, the true King. In the first place, beg of Him by most earnest prayer, that He perfect whatever good you begin, in order that He who has been pleased to count us in the number of His children, need never be grieved at our evil deeds. For we ought at all times so to serve Him with the good things which He has given us, that He may not, like an angry father, disinherit his children, nor, like a dread lord, enraged

ABBEY AT MONTE CASSINO

> at our evil deeds, hand us over to everlasting punishment as most wicked servants, who would not follow Him to glory.[1]

Benedict then goes on to explain the character needed for a godly abbot as well as the spiritual characteristics of faithful disciples. The abbot of the community was to be a man faithful in word and deed. His teaching and his life must be consistent. Hypocrisy in a leader is deadly for the community, as Benedict wisely understood.

> When, therefore, anyone takes the name of Abbot he should govern his disciples by a twofold teaching; namely, he should show them all that is good and holy by his deeds more than by his words; explain the commandments of God to intelligent disciples by words, but show the divine precepts to the dull and simple by his works.[2]

Disciples in the community were to be characterized by humility. Benedict gives numerous examples of humility. But first and foremost, Benedict taught that humility begins with the fear of the Lord. He wrote:

> The first degree of humility, then, is that a man always have the fear of God before his eyes shunning all forgetfulness and that he be ever mindful of all that God has commanded, that he always considers in his mind how those who despise God will burn in hell for their sins, and that life everlasting is prepared for those who fear God. And while he guards himself evermore against sin and vices of thought, word, deed, and self-will, let him also hasten to cut off the desires of the flesh. Let a man consider that God always sees him from Heaven, that the eye of God beholds his works everywhere, and that the angels report them to Him every hour.[3]

Benedict's *Rule* also regulated the daily hours of the community. First of all, the monks would spend three to four hours in worship together. Second, there was to be about six or seven hours of manual labor. Third, the monks would dedicate themselves to the study of the Scriptures and other Christian literature for three to five hours. Monks were given some seven to eight hours to sleep. As you can see, there was no time for leisure built into Benedict's schedule!

Benedict believed that this threefold pattern was essential for the community to be fruitful. Concerning manual labor, Benedict wrote:

> Idleness is the enemy of the soul; and therefore the brethren ought to be employed in manual labor at certain times, at others, in devout reading. On Sunday also let all devote themselves to reading, except those who are appointed to the various functions. But if anyone should be so careless and slothful that he will not or cannot meditate or read, let some work be given him to do, that he may not be idle.[4]

The pattern of worship consisted of Scripture readings, prayer, and the singing of the entire Book of Psalms. When instructing the disciples on how to approach prayer, Benedict urged humility and reverence.

> If we do not venture to approach men who are in power, except with humility and reverence, when we wish to ask a favor, how much more must we beseech the Lord God of all things with all humility and purity of devotion? And let us be assured that it is not in many words, but in the purity of heart and tears of compunction [remorse] that we are heard. For this reason prayer ought to be short and pure, unless, perhaps it is lengthened by the inspiration of divine grace. At the community exercises, however, let the prayer always be short, and the sign having been given by the Superior, let all rise together.[5]

Benedict required monks to live a simple life, content with the basics of food and clothing. But his rule was not so severe as to inflict harm upon the body. In this regard, Benedict's Rule better reflected the teaching of Scripture. We are to be content with food and clothing (1 Tim. 6:8). But inflicting harm upon the body is not taught in Scripture. For example, Benedict said the following about clothing:

> Let clothing be given to the brethren according to the circumstances of the place and the nature of the climate in which they live, because in cold regions more is needed, while in warm regions less. This consideration, therefore, rests with the Abbot.[6]

The pattern of meals was also modest, but the abbot, taking into account especially strenuous labor, could provide additional food to the monks.

> Making allowance for the infirmities of different persons, we believe that for the daily meal, both at the sixth and the ninth hour, two kinds of cooked food are sufficient at all meals; so that he who perchance cannot eat of one, may make his meal of the other. Let two kinds of cooked food, therefore, be sufficient for all the brethren. And if there be fruit or fresh vegetables, a third may be added. Let a pound of bread be sufficient for the day, whether there be only one meal or both dinner and supper. If they are to eat supper, let a third part of the pound be reserved by the Cellarer and be given at supper. If, however, the work has been especially hard, it is left to the discretion and power of the Abbot to add something, if he think fit, barring above all things every excess, that a monk be not overtaken by indigestion.[7]

Benedict's *Rule* provides a helpful introduction to some of the common characteristics of monasticism in the Western church. The quotes provided above demonstrate Benedict's thoughtful approach to Christian community.

The later Middle Ages saw the rise of many additional monastic orders including the Augustinians, Cluniacs, Cistercians, Franciscans, Dominicans, and Carmelites. Each of these orders was formed with different emphases, driven by the personal interests and convictions of its founder. In later chapters, we will learn more about some of these orders.

Monasticism grew in dominance as a church institution until the time of the Protestant Reformation. It took until the 16th century for monasticism as an institution to be evaluated on a biblical basis. The Protestant Reformers, while seeking to

ILLUSTRATION DEPICTING THE VARIOUS "HABITS" (DRESS) OF MONASTIC ORDERS

retain some of the benefits of monasticism, rejected the institution as a whole. The Reformers recovered a biblical view of life calling and work. They saw that all lawful work is holy when done to the glory of God.

As Paul taught in 1 Corinthians:

Was anyone called while circumcised? Let him not become uncircumcised. Was anyone called while uncircumcised? Let him not be circumcised. Circumcision is nothing and uncircumcision is nothing, but keeping the commandments of God is what matters. Let each one remain in the same calling in which he was called. Were you called while a slave? Do not be concerned about it; but if you can be made free, rather use it. For he who is called in the Lord while a slave is the Lord's freedman. Likewise he who is called while free is Christ's slave. You were bought at a price; do not become slaves of men. Brethren, let each one remain with God in that state in which he was called. (1 Cor. 7:18-24)

Therefore, whether you eat or drink, or whatever you do, do all to the glory of God. (1 Cor. 10:31)

MUSLIM MOSQUE IN ORTAKOY, TURKEY

The Rise of Islam

9

For though we walk in the flesh, we do not war according to the flesh. For the weapons of our warfare are not carnal but mighty in God for pulling down strongholds, casting down arguments and every high thing that exalts itself against the knowledge of God, bringing every thought into captivity to the obedience of Christ. (2 Cor. 10:3-5)

The ancient serpent, Satan, is a defeated foe. But until our Lord Jesus returns, Satan continues to unleash his fury against the children of Adam. He is particularly enraged by King Jesus' victory and still seeks to do harm to Christ's people (Rev. 12:17). In the early 7th century AD, Satan devised a new strategy to combat the kingdom of Christ. That strategy was the creation and propagation of a false religion known as **Islam**.

In the modern day, Islam stands as one of Christianity's largest rivals. It is debated which religion has more adherents: Christianity or Islam. Of course, we cannot know the exact number for sure. But it is clear that Islam is a powerful rival to the Christian faith around the world. Thankfully, we already know how the story ends. Jesus wins. But that triumph often comes through suffering, persecution, and martyrdom.

The rise of Islam is a crucial part of the church's story. The conflict between Islam and Christ has continued unabated since Islam's beginning in the 600s. Islam was once confined to North Africa, the Middle East, and Asia. But today, Islam has spread to all different parts of the globe. The Western world (Europe and North America) is increasingly experiencing the effects of Islam's spread. For this reason, it is important that Christians know about the origins and beliefs of Islam.

The Beginning of Islam

But there were also false prophets among the people, even as there will be false teachers among you, who will secretly bring in destructive heresies, even denying the Lord who bought them, and bring on themselves swift destruction. (2 Pet. 2:1)

The story of Islam begins with a man named **Muhammad** (c. 570-632). He was born in the city of Mecca around 570. Muhammad grew to be a successful merchant and traveled widely in the regions of Arabia and Syria. During his travels, Muhammad came into contact with both Jews and Christians. Muhammad learned some of what these two rival religions taught. At this time, the primary religion in Arabia was a mixture of tribal

A DEPICTION OF MUHAMMAD RECEIVING REVELATION FROM THE ANGEL GABRIEL

pagan religions. In general, the people of Arabia were **polytheists**. They worshiped many gods. The **monotheism** of Christianity and Judaism was much different than the tribal religions Muhammad grew up with.

In 610, Muhammad claimed to receive revelation from Allah (the Arabic word for "god"). Allah revealed himself as the one true god who had been worshiped by the Jews and by the Christians. But now, through this revelation to Muhammad, the true religion was being revealed. Muhammad believed that he was the final prophet of Allah. Allah had spoken previously in the Scriptures of the Jews and Christians, but he was now speaking to Muhammad. Muhammad's series of visions were collected in the holy book of Islam, the **Qur'an**. The Qur'an is divided into 114 chapters called surahs.

The new faith of Islam was a call to the Arabic people to renounce polytheism and to worship the one god Allah. The new religion began to grow and gather converts, who became known as Muslims. Due to Muhammad's radical beliefs, he was expelled from the city of Mecca in 622. Muhammad and his followers moved to Medina and propagated Islamic beliefs there. After Muhammad's followers grew to a larger number, he returned to Mecca with a significant military force. He successfully conquered Mecca and claimed an ancient building in Mecca called the "Ka'ba." According to Islamic tradition, the Ka'ba was believed to have been built by Abraham and his son Ishmael. Since Muhammad's time, the Ka'ba has been a site of religious devotion for Muslim pilgrims to Mecca.

Islam (Arabic for "submission") maintains belief in the unity and oneness of god. The divine attribute that was most emphasized by Muhammad was the attribute of power. This belief in the absolute oneness of god brought Muhammad into conflict with the Christian belief that there is one God in three persons. The Qur'an's statements show a misunderstanding of this doctrine of the Trinity. For example, in Surah 4 of the Qur'an, we read:

> O People of the Scripture, do not commit excess in your religion or say about Allah except the truth. The Messiah, Jesus, the son of Mary, was but a messenger of Allah and His word which He directed to Mary and a soul [created at a command] from Him. So believe in Allah and His messengers. And do not say, "Three"; desist—it is better for

THE KA'BA IN MECCA

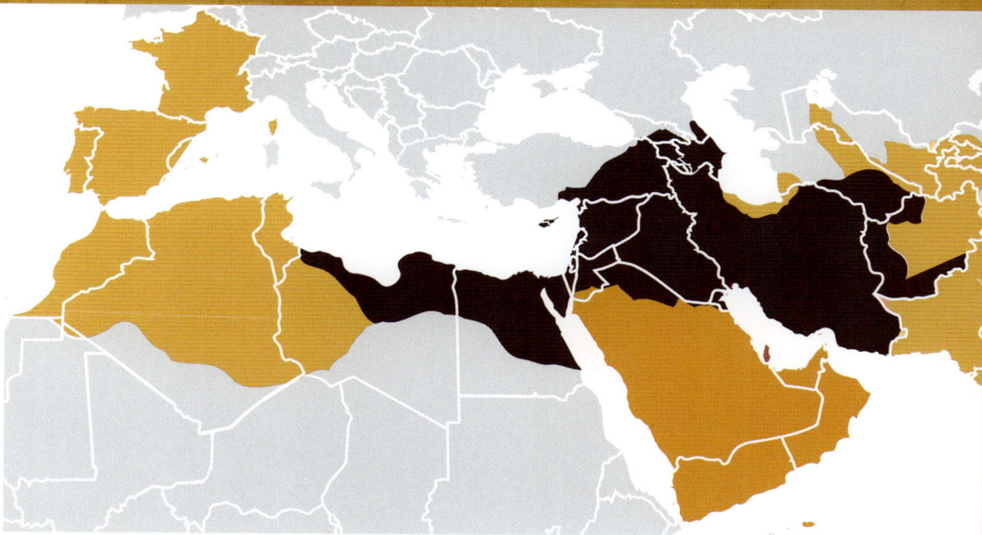

EXPANSION UNDER MUHAMMAD, 622–632
EXPANSION UNDER THE RASHIDUN CALIPHATE, 632–661
EXPANSION UNDER THE UMAYYAD CALIPHATE, 661–750

> you. Indeed, Allah is but one God. Exalted is He above having a son. To Him belongs whatever is in the heavens and whatever is on the earth. And sufficient is Allah as Disposer of affairs. (Surah 4)

In another section (Surah 5), it appears that a claim is made that Jesus, Mary, and God are three gods. It is possible that Muhammad believed that Christians claimed Mary as part of the Trinity. Of course, this was never the case at any time in church history. And Christians do not believe there are three gods. They believe there is one God in three persons, the Father, the Son, and the Holy Spirit.

The Qur'an also denies the crucifixion of Christ, though it claims Jesus was one of the true prophets. Of course, this also means that the resurrection of Christ is denied as well.

> And for their saying, "We have killed the Messiah, Jesus, the son of Mary, the Messenger of God." In fact, they did not kill him, nor did they crucify him, but it appeared to them as if they did. Indeed, those who differ about him are in doubt about it. They have no knowledge of it, except the following of assumptions. Certainly, they did not kill him. (Surah 4)

By denying the Triune nature of God and the central facts of the gospel, Islam showed itself to be a heresy of the most dangerous kind.

Despite the Qur'an's attack upon central Christian beliefs, it does have some positive things to say about Jews and Christians. It calls Jews and Christians "people of the book." They are so called because both Jews and Christians received revelation from Allah (in the Old Testament and the Gospels), but the claim was eventually made that prior revelation had been corrupted. For Muslims, the Qur'an alone is without error.

The new religion of Islam is summarized in five basic beliefs and duties known as the **five pillars**.

1. The *Shahadah*, the basic creed of Islam, "There is no God but Allah, and Muhammad is his prophet."
2. The *Salah*, prayer five times a day facing Mecca.
3. The *Zakah*, giving to the poor.
4. *Sawm*, fasting during the holy month of Ramadan.
5. *Hajj*, the pilgrimage to Mecca to be made at least once in a lifetime.

Armed with these beliefs and practices, the new faith of Islam spread rapidly. By Muhammad's death in 632, all Arabia had been conquered for Islam. Most of its growth came by the sword. The early Muslims were highly successful in their campaigns of **jihad** or "holy war." They conquered large sections of land stretching from North Africa and Spain in the West to the land of Persia (Iran) and eventually portions of India in the East. Weakened by internal divisions, Christian lands in the Middle East and North Africa rapidly fell to Islam.

THE BATTLE OF TOURS

The Arab Muslim advance took them to the gates of Constantinople. In 717, they laid siege to the city and nearly conquered it. But the Byzantines repulsed the Muslims and drove them back, retaking Asia Minor (Turkey). In the West, the Muslims conquered Spain, which they would rule for centuries. Then they invaded France. But there they were stopped and decisively defeated by **Charles Martel** at the **Battle of Tours** in 732. In God's providence, these two victories spared most of Europe from Islam for centuries, and Christianity took root there. The Byzantine Empire survived and would stand as a bulwark against the advance of Islam into Europe for the next 700 years until the fall of Constantinople in 1453.

As Islam spread into regions dominated by Christianity, Muslims had to determine how to treat the Christians they had conquered. Likewise, Christians had to count the cost of discipleship and decide whether they would follow Jesus or take the easier way by adopting the religion of their conquerors. In general, Muslims allowed Christians to continue the practice of their religion as long as they did not proselytize or publicly challenge Islam. However, they suffered discrimination, oppression, and sporadic persecution. Additionally, Christians and Jews often had to pay tribute (in the form of additional taxes) to their Muslim rulers. In some regions however, Christian scholars were employed in Muslim courts because of their wisdom and knowledge.

But there are some examples of Muslims executing Christians for their beliefs. It was unlawful to renounce Islam, so any Muslim who converted to Christianity would be punished with death. In 850-851, approximately fifty Christians were executed in Cordoba, Spain. Over the centuries, many in the Middle East and North Africa converted to Islam. But a steadfast minority remained Christian.

The Crusades

Even after the Battle of Tours, the Muslim threat against Europe was always on the horizon. Christians were concerned about Muslim expansion. Likewise, it brought sorrow and grief to many to see once Christian lands now dominated by a false religion. Islam had made its conquests through "holy war." And in self-defense, some of the Christian rulers of Europe had fought back (such as Charles Martel). An offensive war against Islam had not yet been waged.

The **Crusades** marked a new epoch in Muslim-Christian relations. The word "crusade" comes from a number of related terms such as *crucere* (French) or *crux* (Latin for "cross"). The French word means "to take up the cross." Therefore, to "crusade" was to take up "one's cross." Jesus Himself commanded us to take up our cross daily and follow Him (Luke 9:23). But how did one take up the cross by going into military battle? Is this what Jesus meant when He commanded us to take up the cross? Jesus was not referring to military conquest in this passage but was commanding His disciples to humbly follow Him in the path of self-denial and suffering.

With the advent of the Crusades, the conception of what it meant to "take up the cross" would take on a new meaning.

The Crusades were a series of military expeditions fought over several centuries. Their purpose was to defend the Byzantine Empire from Muslim attack and to retake the former Christian lands of the Middle East that had been conquered by the Muslims.

For many centuries, Christians went on pilgrimages to visit the Holy Land. It was considered a great act of devotion to visit the Holy Land and to see the Biblical sites. Persecution and mistreatment of Christian pilgrims had been sporadic under the Arabs. But it greatly increased when the Seljuk Turks conquered Palestine in the 11th century. The Turks were also defeating and driving back the Byzantines. This was a serious threat, and Byzantine emperors appealed to their Christian brothers in the West for help.

In 1095, at the **Council of Clermont, Pope Urban II** (1088-1099) called for a campaign to retake the Holy Land. The crowd present heartily received Urban's call and they began to chant *Deus vult*. This means "God wills it." By saying this, the people proclaimed the call to "holy war" as the very will of God. If God willed it, then the call could not be ignored or denied.

Here is a portion of the speech Urban II gave, recorded by one of the eyewitnesses at the council:

> Most beloved brethren: Urged by necessity, I, Urban, by the permission of God chief bishop and prelate over the whole world, have come into these parts as an ambassador with a divine admonition to you, the servants of God.
>
> Although, O sons of God, you have promised more firmly than ever to keep the peace among yourselves and to preserve the rights of the church, there remains still an important work for you to do. Freshly quickened by the divine correction, you must apply the strength of your righteousness to another matter which concerns you as well as God. For your brethren who live in the east are in urgent need of your help, and you must hasten to give them the aid which has often been promised them. For, as the most of you have heard, the Turks and Arabs have attacked them and have conquered the territory of Romania [the Greek empire] as far west as the shore of the Mediterranean and the Hellespont, which is called the Arm of St. George. They have occupied more and more of the lands of those Christians, and have overcome them in seven battles. They have killed and captured many, and have destroyed the churches and devastated the empire. If you permit them to continue thus for awhile with impurity, the faithful of God will be much more widely attacked by them.
>
> On this account I, or rather the Lord, beseech you as Christ's heralds to publish this everywhere and to persuade all people of whatever rank, foot-soldiers and knights, poor and rich, to carry aid promptly to those Christians and to destroy that vile race from the lands of our friends. I say this to those who are present, it is meant also for those who are absent. Moreover, Christ commands it.
>
> All who die by the way, whether by land or by sea, or in battle against the pagans, shall have immediate remission of sins. This I grant them through the power of God with which I am invested. O what a disgrace if such a despised and base race, which worships demons, should conquer a people which has the faith of omnipotent God and is made glorious with the name of Christ! With what reproaches will the Lord overwhelm us if you do not aid those who, with us, profess the Christian reli-

POPE URBAN II AT THE COUNCIL OF CLERMONT

> gion! Let those who have been accustomed unjustly to wage private warfare against the faithful now go against the infidels and end with victory this war which should have been begun long ago. Let those who for a long time have been robbers, now become knights. Let those who have been fighting against their brothers and relatives now fight in a proper way against the barbarians. Let those who have been serving as mercenaries for small pay now obtain the eternal reward. Let those who have been wearing themselves out in both body and soul now work for a double honor. Behold! on this side will be the sorrowful and poor, on that, the rich; on this side, the enemies of the Lord, on that, his friends. Let those who go not put off the journey, but rent their lands and collect money for their expenses; and as soon as winter is over and spring comes, let them eagerly set out on the way with God as their guide.[1]

Pope Urban II promised forgiveness of sins for those who would go on this great crusade to retake the holy land. It happened to be a difficult time in Western Europe where famine had struck and disease was rampant. The call of Urban and other preachers to go to a foreign land as soldiers of Christ was received with enthusiasm by many.

Following's Urban's original proclamation in 1095, a series of crusades took place over several centuries. Historians come up with different numbers of distinct crusades due to the variety that took place. By most counts, there were eight major crusades. The First Crusade was the most successful militarily. Jerusalem and a large part of the Holy Land were retaken by the crusaders from the Muslims in 1099. For almost one hundred years, crusader rule was established in Jerusalem and much of Palestine. But the Muslim ruler Saladin took Jerusalem from the crusaders in 1187.

Perhaps the most well-known crusade was the Third Crusade (1189-1192). It was led by three important monarchs of Western Europe: **Richard the Lionhearted** of England, **Frederick Barbarossa** of the Holy Roman Empire, and **Philip II** of France. It was an attempt to retake Jerusalem. But the Third Crusade and those that followed generally ended in failure and defeat. The Crusades were ultimately unsuccessful. The last crusader city of **Acre** fell to the Muslims in 1291.

Effects of the Crusades

What were some of the residual effects of the Crusades?

1. The Crusades were part of an ongoing conflict between Christians and Muslims. This conflict in some ways continues to the present day.
2. The Crusades increased the divisions between the Eastern and Western churches. The relationship between East and West had already been ruptured due to

the **Great Schism** that occurred in 1054 (discussed in a later chapter). The relationship was further strained during the Crusades. In the Fourth Crusade in 1204, crusaders actually captured Constantinople from the Byzantines and set up a kingdom there for a time.

3. The Crusades opened additional trade between Europe and Asia. There was also increased access to learning, technology, science, mathematics, literature, and philosophy between East and West.

How should Christians view the Crusades? First, the unjust shedding of blood, wherever it occurred, must be condemned. Second, the union of the Cross and the Sword led to confusion about how the Christian gospel was to be propagated among Muslims. Sadly, Muslims were often viewed as enemies to be killed rather than a mission field. Third, despite some of the unjust circumstances and actions of the Crusades, it nevertheless was an important part of the defense of Europe and may have protected the church from further destruction by the Muslims.

At points, Europe did face real threats of Muslim invasion. And it was lawful for European Christians to defend their nations militarily from Muslim attack. But sadly, it seems that very few thought of taking the gospel to the Muslims. Instead of the sword of God's Word, many in Europe took the physical sword against the Muslims.

But the missionary **Raymond Lull** (1232-1315) did make a real effort to convert Muslims to Christ. He wrote:

> I see many knights going to the Holy Land beyond the seas and thinking that they can acquire it by force of arms. But in the end all are destroyed before they attain that which they think to have. It seems to me that the conquest of the Holy Land ought not to be attempted except in the way in which the Apostles acquired it, namely by love and prayers, and the pouring out of tears and blood.[2]

Raymond Lull founded a missionary training center where Christians could learn Arabic and study Islam and apologetics. In 1315, Lull poured out his blood on Muslim soil as a martyr. He gave

THE SIEGE OF ACRE

his life for Jesus Christ. He longed to see Muslims come to faith in the Savior.

John of Damascus

And who is he who will harm you if you become followers of what is good? But even if you should suffer for righteousness' sake, you are blessed. "And do not be afraid of their threats, nor be troubled." But sanctify the Lord God in your hearts, and always be ready to give a defense to everyone who asks you a reason for the hope that is in you, with meekness and fear. (1 Pet. 3:13-15)

As mentioned above, Christians in Muslim-conquered lands were often still able to practice their faith. But they faced restrictions and persecution because of their convictions. One notable example of a Christian living, teaching, and writing in Muslim society is the theologian **John of Damascus** (675-749).

During the caliphate of 'Abd al-Malik (685-705), John of Damascus, a Christian, worked as a government official in al-Malik's court. He was a learned man who was fluent in both Arabic and Greek, and had an extensive knowledge of the Qur'an. John became al-Malik's secretary giving him direct influence upon the caliph (leader of the Muslims). In 726, he left civil service and dedicated time to writing theological and apologetic works defending Christian doctrine. His most famous book is titled ***The Orthodox Faith***, which is a summary of Christian theology. He also wrote a book titled *On Heresies*, in which he assaults the teachings of Islam head on.

John is one of the first Christian theologians to directly confront the claims of Islam in written form. In his book, he calls the Muslims "Ishmaelites" since they claimed to be descended from Abraham's son Ishmael. John is direct in rejecting the claims of Islam. He called Muhammad a false prophet and rejected the Qur'an as a false book. John goes on to contrast the Christian doctrine of God as Trinity with the Muslim claim of God's absolute oneness. John's book was most likely written to strengthen Christians in their stand against Islam rather than to convince Muslims to reject their faith. Since Christians were being confronted with the claims of this new religion, it was important for disciples of Christ to take a stand for truth. ■

JOHN OF DAMASCUS (675-749)

UMAYYAD GRAND MOSQUE IN DAMASCUS, SYRIA

THE VATICAN IN ROME VIEWED FROM THE TIBER RIVER

The Development of the Papacy

But Jesus called them to Himself and said to them, "You know that those who are considered rulers over the Gentiles lord it over them, and their great ones exercise authority over them. Yet it shall not be so among you; but whoever desires to become great among you shall be your servant. And whoever of you desires to be first shall be slave of all. For even the Son of Man did not come to be served, but to serve, and to give His life a ransom for many." (Mark 10:42-45)

INNOCENT III

In 1199, **Pope Innocent III** (r. 1198-1216) wrote to the patriarch of Constantinople and expressed his views on the role and power of the papacy. Historian Philip Schaff summarized Innocent's views of his office this way:

> The pope is the vicar of Christ, yea of God himself. Not only is he entrusted with the dominion of the Church, but also with the rule of the whole world. Like Melchizedek, he is at once king and priest. All things in heaven and earth and in hell are subject to Christ. So are they also to his vicar. He can depose princes and absolve subjects from the oath of allegiance. He may enforce submission by placing whole nations under the interdict.[1]

Pope Innocent III represents the height of papal pretensions. So extensive was this one man's power that Philip Schaff suggested that no other person in human history "before or since wielded such extensive power."[2] The word "vicar" means "to stand in the place of." Hence, to be the vicar of Christ is to stand in place of Christ as His earthly representative. To be the vicar of God is to be the direct representative of God on earth.

How is it that a man claiming to be the most important leader of Christ's church on earth could come to say such things? How did the papacy develop into such a massive institution with such extensive power over earthly affairs? Is this what the Lord Jesus Christ intended for the shepherds of His church? The words of Innocent III are far removed from the humble exhortations of the Apostle Peter, who calls himself a fellow elder and instructs the shepherds of the church to not domineer over those in their charge, but to be examples to the flock (1 Pet. 5:3).

How did the institution of the papacy develop into what it was under Innocent III and popes after him? The purpose of this chapter is to gain some understanding of the history of this institution and how it affected the church.

SAINT PETER'S SQUARE, VATICAN, ROME

Early Beginnings

Let nothing be done through selfish ambition or conceit, but in lowliness of mind let each esteem others better than himself. Let each of you look out not only for his own interests, but also for the interests of others. (Phil. 2:3-4)

In an earlier chapter on government in the early church, we learned that a division occurred in the early centuries of the church between the office of bishop and presbyter (or elder). Bishops were appointed to oversee various towns or regions. Thus, within the first few centuries of the church, major cities such as Rome had their own bishop who functioned as the pastor who oversaw the various churches in that city. For the first two centuries of church history, we have no evidence that any bishop claimed greater power than another bishop.

The earliest evidence we have for the bishop of Rome claiming power over others is found in the writings of **Stephen I**, the bishop of Rome (r. 254-257). Stephen argued that his authority came from his succession to the Apostle Peter. He believed that since Christ said that Peter was the rock upon which the church would be built (Matt. 16:18), the successor of Peter was to be the supreme leader of the church. Stephen's claim would be further clarified and expanded by later bishops of Rome.

Stephen's interpretation of Matthew 16 grew in popularity. But even with later church fathers, such as Ambrose, Jerome, and Augustine there is a variety of opinions about Peter's role and the meaning of Matthew 16. Some church fathers did believe that the bishop of Rome succeeded Peter. But even this did not mean that the bishop of Rome had primacy over all other bishops. Additionally, the word "pope" (a word that comes from the Latin term for "father") was commonly used for many of the bishops, not just the bishop of Rome.

The idea of Roman papal supremacy developed further with **Pope Leo I** (r. 440-461). Many historians consider Leo I to be the first "pope" in the proper sense of the word. Leo believed himself to be the successor of Peter, and as such the supreme bishop entrusted with the care of the whole church. In a special manner, Leo believed that Christ had entrusted the Roman bishop with the "keys of the kingdom of heaven." Leo also taught that resistance to his authority was a manifestation of pride and would lead to hell. Thus Leo made obedience to him a necessity for salvation. Leo claimed that when he spoke, Peter was speaking directly through him. We find then in Leo I a significant development of the papacy as an institution.

The Papacy's Development in the Middle Ages

Then He came to Capernaum. And when He was in the house He asked them, "What was it you disputed among yourselves on the road?" But they kept silent, for on the road they had disputed among themselves who would be the greatest. And He sat down, called the twelve, and said to them, "If anyone desires to be first, he shall be last of all and servant of all." (Mark 9:33-35)

In a previous chapter, Gregory the Great was discussed. Though he was bishop of Rome, and is thus known as **Pope Gregory I** (r. 590-604), Gregory was among the most humble holders of the office. He somewhat reluctantly involved himself in political affairs. Gregory saw himself primarily as a pastor. Gregory was known to use the phrase for himself: "servant of the servants of God," and he protested the title of "universal bishop" for his office. Gregory objected to the patriarch of Constantinople adopting the terminology of universal bishop. In a letter to the patriarch John, he wrote:

> What will you say at the last judgment to Him who is the Head of the universal Church, when by your title of "universal" you wish to bring all His members under your power? I ask you, whom are you imitating by this perverse title of yours? You are following Satan who despised his fellow legions of angels and tried to ascend to the highest place, that he might be subject to none and exalted alone above all others . . . Let your Holiness then consider how much you are puffed up when you claim a title that none of them [the apostles] had the arrogance to assume.[3]

Gregory wrote in another letter that "whosoever calls himself universal priest, or desires to be called so, was the forerunner of Antichrist."[4] Though Gregory rejected such titles, he did exercise a great degree of authority over the church in the West, much like popes after him.

One wishes that later popes had heeded the advice of Gregory. Sadly, however, the papacy drifted further into universal pretensions and tyrannical control in many cases.

Significant developments occurred in the papacy of **Nicholas I** (r. 858-867). A collection of important documents reinforced Nicholas' authority as pope. They are known as the **Pseudo-Isidorian Decretals**. These documents purported to be a series of papal decrees granting the popes certain authority. The documents contained some sixty spurious decretals from various bishops of Rome going all the way back to the 2nd century. The content of the decretals ranges from doctrinal matters to church government and the power of the papacy over church and civil affairs.

For a long time, the decretals were considered to be authentic. But today, both Roman Catholic and Protestant historians reject the decretals as forgeries. Evidence of their forged nature is evident in a number of ways. For example, decretals claiming to be from the 2nd and 3rd centuries are written in Frankish Latin from the 9th century. Some of the decretals quote the Bible as it was known in the Latin translation after the 800s. There are other historical inaccuracies contained in them as well.

Within this collection is another important document known as **The Donation of Constantine**. The document claims that in 324, when Pope Sylvester baptized the Emperor Constantine, the emperor granted the pope the Lateran

FRESCO DEPICTING CONSTANTINE GIVING THE DONATION TO POPE SYLVESTER

Palace in Rome as well as all Roman and Italian territory. The goal of this forged document was apparently to reinforce the power of the pope over these regions by making it look as if Constantine had granted them to the papacy. The authenticity of this document was doubted for centuries. But in 1440, **Lorenzo Valla** (c. 1407-1457) skillfully demonstrated it to be a forgery. The "Donation" would contribute greatly towards centralizing power in the papacy. And with that increasing power came further corruption.

Following Nicholas I, the papacy continued to degenerate. Many of the popes that followed became known for their avarice, sexual immorality, and in some cases, murderous behavior. The papacy had ascended to newfound heights of power and influence. It is no surprise then that its office-holders were corrupted by the allure of such power. Many popes could be listed here who contributed to the corruption of the church in the 10th and 11th centuries. However, just to give one example, **Pope Benedict IX** (1032-1048) was among the most disreputable and criminal of all the popes.

At the time of his election, he was one of the youngest popes at age twenty. His election was obtained through bribery. Benedict IX entered this office fully intent upon wicked conduct from the start. Popes of this era rivaled some of the cruelest and most corrupt Roman emperors. Benedict IX was known for his openly adulterous behavior and for numerous murders. He would rob the pilgrims who came to the graves of the martyrs. It was rumored that Benedict IX also engaged in homosexual sin. A later pope, **Victor III** (r. 1086-1087), said of Benedict IX, "his life as a pope was so vile, so foul, so execrable, that I shudder to think of it."

Not every pope of this era equaled Benedict IX in descending into the cesspool of debased and godless behavior. Nevertheless, Benedict's tenure as pope was an indication of just how degraded and corrupt the papacy had become. It should also come as no surprise that when the church moves beyond God's institution and creates its own man-made positions (such as the office of pope), it is sure to corrupt the purity of Christ's church.

Henry III and the Reforms of Hildebrand

Now the works of the flesh are evident, which are: adultery, fornication, uncleanness, lewdness, idolatry, sorcery, hatred, contentions, jealousies, outbursts of wrath, selfish ambitions, dissensions, heresies, envy, murders, drunkenness, revelries, and the like; of which I tell you beforehand, just as I also told you in time past, that those who practice such things will not inherit the kingdom of God. (Gal. 5:19-21)

By the mid-11th century, the papacy was in dire need of cleansing. One is reminded of the cycles of "good" and "evil" in the books of Kings and Chronicles. Like the kings of Israel and Judah, some popes lived wickedly, and others lived relatively faithful lives (despite holding an unbiblical office).

A significant turning point in the papacy occurred in 1046. The emperor of the Holy Roman Empire, **Henry III** (1039-1056), arrived in Rome. Henry journeyed to Rome in order to be formally crowned as emperor by the pope. But due to the intrigue, bribery, and corruption, Henry found that there were three competing rivals all claiming the title of pope.[5] Such confusion illustrated the dire need for church reform.

Henry III happened to be a beneficiary of another pivotal movement of this time. A movement of reform in the monasteries was occurring called the **Cluniac Revival**. From a monastery in Cluny, reform and purification of the monasteries had spread throughout Europe. One of the goals of the Cluniac Revival was to bring back the discipline and purity of the Rule of St. Benedict (studied in an earlier chapter). Those engaged in this reform work began to train the sons of those in authority, including such men as Henry III. Because of this discipleship Henry received, he was committed to the reform of the church and purity of life.

Henry III called for a church assembly (known as a synod) to address the confusion caused by three rival popes. The Synod of Sutri deposed all three claimants to the papal office. Henry III then appointed a German bishop, **Clement II** (r. 1046-1047), to the office of pope. Like Henry, Clement II was a committed reformer. This act of the synod put the papacy on a path of moral reform.

Another reformer who left an indelible mark on the papacy was **Hildebrand**. He became pope in 1073. His papal name was **Gregory VII** (r. 1073-1085). However, before Hildebrand became pope, he assisted in a number of reform efforts.

Hildebrand, assisted by other like-minded reformers, began a series of reforms to the papacy and church government in general. To achieve them, Hildebrand wanted to ensure that the papacy was free from political control. It was especially important to Hildebrand that the popes

POPE GREGORY VII (HILDEBRAND)

not be under the political sway of the aristocracy in Rome. Where bribery and political intrigue reigned, the pope could not be an independent spiritual leader of the church. As part of achieving this papal independence, Hildebrand elevated the authority of the papacy. Hildebrand taught that the pope was the successor of Peter. This meant he had apostolic authority over all other church leaders and over civil rulers as well.

Hildebrand and other reformers also sought to purify the church of **simony**. The word simony refers to the selling of church offices. The term is derived from Simon the Magician's request in Acts 8 to purchase the power of the Holy Spirit (Acts 8:18-19). Church offices were not to be sold to the highest bidder. Simony put church office and authority in the hands of the wealthy and powerful rather than those who were biblically qualified.

Hildebrand also wanted to purge sexual immorality from the clergy, including the papacy, and enforce clerical celibacy. Many in church office were guilty of committing sexual sin outside of marriage. But other church leaders were happily married with wives and families. A synod was held in 1059 at the Lateran in Rome. The synod re-asserted the necessity of celibacy for all members of the clergy. Married clergy had to give up their wives. Sadly, this attempt at reform overturned the biblical standards for church office (1 Tim. 3:1-7). The Scriptures teach that ordinarily a man who holds the office of "overseer" should be the husband of one wife. The requirement of celibacy was imposed with the goal of purity for Christ's shepherds. But because it was contrary to God's Word, purity was often not achieved (see 1 Tim. 4:1-3). In fact, enforcing this unbiblical requirement made matters worse.[6]

When Hildebrand became pope in 1073, he published a papal decree. In this decree, Hildebrand (now Pope Gregory VII) set forth his lofty views of the papal office. Here are some of the more notable points from Hildebrand's decree:

HENRY IV AT CANOSSA

- The Roman pope alone is universal bishop.
- The pope alone can depose and reinstate bishops.
- The pope may be judged by no one.
- The Roman Church has never erred and will never err.
- The pope may depose emperors.

This elevation of papal authority by Hildebrand further cemented the pope's role in the Western church and in Europe in general.

After Hildebrand became pope, he continued his efforts to free the papacy and other church offices from secular control. This led to conflict in 1075 when Hildebrand clashed with Emperor Henry IV (r. 1054-1106). For some time, the emperors of the Holy Roman Empire had claimed authority to appoint men to some church offices. A synod held in 1075 forbade the emperor or any other layperson from appointing bishops to church office. This matter is known as the **Investiture Controversy**.

Bishops partial to Henry IV held a council in Worms in 1076. There they condemned Hildebrand and rejected him as pope. Henry sent a letter following the meeting condemning Hildebrand. Henry urged Hildebrand to step down from being pope. The letter did not come with soft words of entreaty. It was direct and confrontational. Henry wrote this to Hildebrand:

> To Hildebrand, not a pope but a false monk. How dare you, who have won your power by deceit, flattery, bribery, and force, stretch forth your hand against the Lord's anointed, despising the command of the true pope, Saint Peter 'Fear God, honour the king' (1 Pet. 2:17)? You do not fear God, and you dishonour me whom He has appointed. Condemned by the voice of all our bishops, leave the apostolic throne and let someone else sit there, someone who will preach the healthy doctrine of Saint Peter and not exploit religion as a cloak for violence. I, Henry, by the grace of God, with all my bishops, say to you come down,

come down from the papal throne, and be damned through all ages![7]

Not surprisingly, Hildebrand did not follow Henry's heated exhortation. Instead, Hildebrand excommunicated Henry IV. Hildebrand also released all bishops from any obligation to obey Henry IV as emperor. Hildebrand then made plans to appoint a new emperor in Henry's place. The German nobles joined Hildebrand and suspended Henry from his office as emperor.

With his title and power at risk, Henry IV humbled himself. In 1077, he journeyed south to Italy and begged Hildebrand for mercy. Hildebrand had taken refuge in a castle in Canossa because he feared military action from Henry. But instead, Henry came without an army. He came only with his wife and children and a few loyal supporters. For three days outside the castle walls, in the freezing snow, Henry cried out to Hildebrand for mercy. After three days, Hildebrand allowed Henry inside and received his confession. Henry, prostrate before the pope, wept and repented of his practice of lay-investiture. Hildebrand accepted Henry's repentance and restored him to his office as emperor. But this did not settle the matter. Additional conflicts would follow after Henry's restoration. But this moment dramatically illustrated how powerful the pope had become.

In these conflicts, the kings and emperors were fighting for the state to be over the church while the popes were fighting for the church to be over the state. This struggle between church and state did not happen in the East. There the state pretty much ruled over the church. Neither the church nor the state should rule over the other. Rather, both have their own separate spheres of authority under God and His Word.

We will return to the ongoing saga of the papacy in a later chapter. For now, we see something of how Innocent III was able to make such pretentious claims. The story of the papacy's development is a cautionary tale. It is a reminder of how giving such extensive power to any sinful human being comes with grave consequences. It is also a valuable reminder that God opposes the proud, but He gives grace to the humble (Jas. 4:6). The popes often lorded their authority over others. But this is not the way of Christ. Every Christian is called to a life of humble servanthood. He who would be first, Jesus says, must be last of all and servant of all (Mark 9:35). ■

RUINS OF THE CASTLE CANOSSA

INTERIOR OF THE HAGIA SOPHIA (CHURCH OF THE HOLY WISDOM) IN CONSTANTINOPLE (NOW ISTANBUL). HAGIA SOPHIA IS NOW A MUSLIM MOSQUE.

Schism in the Church

I, therefore, the prisoner of the Lord, beseech you to walk worthy of the calling with which you were called, with all lowliness and gentleness, with longsuffering, bearing with one another in love, endeavoring to keep the unity of the Spirit in the bond of peace. (Eph. 4:1-3)

Since our Lord's ascension, the church of Christ has faced challenges to its unity. Until our Lord returns, the church will be imperfect in its purity and unity. The church will face false teaching, scandals, and division. It is true that we hold to Jesus' promise: the gates of hell will not prevail against Christ's church. But the conquest of Christ's church over the gates of hell is not without its dangers and challenges. The evil one, who hates Christ and His people, deceives and accuses, thus dividing the church.

However, the Lord also has His own sovereign purposes in church division. The Apostle Paul in 1 Corinthians explains that factions and divisions occur in Christ's church to show who really is with Jesus Christ.

For, in the first place, when you come together as a church, I hear that there are divisions [Greek *schisma*] among you. And I believe it in part, for there must be factions among you in order that those who are genuine among you may be recognized. (1 Cor. 11:18-19 ESV)

Division in the church, though painful and heartbreaking, is still used by our Sovereign Lord to purify and build His church.

It is also important to remember another fact. Today, there may be many different types of churches in the world who claim the name of Jesus Christ. Yet there is still only one universal church in the world. Local congregations and various denominations are just parts of that one church Jesus established. Jesus' church is found all over the world, in many different cultures speaking different languages. But wherever Jesus' true disciples are gathered for worship and service, there His church is found.

In this chapter, we will learn more about one of the most significant divisions in church history. Sometimes such divisions are described with the word *schism*. This word comes from a Greek word appearing in the New Testament that describes divisions or factions. A schism, then, is a tearing apart of something that once was together. The division between the Eastern and Western branches of the church changed church history forever.

Many centuries of growing distance contributed to this division. However, many historians use the date AD 1054 to mark the division between the Eastern and Western church. This is called the **Great Schism**. How did this division occur? And what were the factors that contributed to the separation?

For centuries, differences between the Eastern and Western branches of the church were evident. Over time, these differences in doctrine and worship grew and became more evident.

Differences between East and West

Some of the key differences between the East and the West include:

- The Western church affirmed that the pope was the universal head of the church. The East did not.
- The Western church taught that the Holy Spirit proceeded from the Father and the Son. The East argued that the Holy Spirit

proceeded *only* from the Father.

- The Western church came to affirm the doctrine of **purgatory**, a place of purging after death. The Eastern church did not.
- The Western church did not allow priests to marry. But the Eastern church would allow priests to be married prior to ordination (bishops could not marry, however).
- The Western church practiced baptism in different ways, including by immersion but also by pouring. The Eastern church practiced threefold immersion.
- The Western church used unleavened bread in communion. The East used leavened bread.

Some of these differences are of a minor nature. But they, along with other differences, were part of the growing division between East and West. There were also cultural and political issues at play. For one, the two branches of the church used two different languages. Greek was the primary language in the Eastern church. Latin was the primary language in the Western church. These language differences sometimes contributed to confusion about doctrine between East and West.

There was also controversy over the use of images and icons (mosaics and paintings) in the worship of the church. For the first four hundred years after Christ, most Christians were opposed to the use of images in worship. But then this attitude gradually began to change. People began to venerate icons by bowing to them, kissing them, burning candles before them, etc. In the 700s, there was a fierce controversy in the East between those who venerated icons (iconodules) and those who opposed their use (iconoclasts). The question had to do with how to apply the Second Commandment.

You shall not make for yourself a carved image—any likeness of anything that is in heaven above, or that is in the earth beneath, or that is in the water under the earth; you shall not bow down to them nor serve them. For I, the Lord your God, am a jealous God, visiting the iniquity of the fathers upon the children to the third and fourth generations of those who hate Me, but showing mercy to thousands, to those who love Me and keep My commandments. (Ex. 20:4-6)

INTERIOR OF A GREEK ORTHODOX CHURCH IN CYPRUS

THE SECOND COUNCIL OF NICAEA

The iconodules eventually won and the Eastern church affirmed the veneration of icons at the **Second Council of Nicaea** in 787. But much of the Western church rejected the council's decision and continued to oppose the **veneration** of icons. Over time, however, the Western church changed. Statues of saints and other figures became common in Western churches. The Eastern church rejected statues and only used flat paintings. But both venerated images. Sadly, this disregard for the Second Commandment led to much idolatry in the worship of God.

A Divisive Phrase in the Nicene Creed

But when the Helper comes, whom I shall send to you from the Father, the Spirit of truth who proceeds from the Father, He will testify of Me. (John 15:26)

One of the most consequential theological disagreements was over a clause contained in the Nicene Creed. As we learned earlier, the First Council of Nicaea in 325 was the first universal church council since the Council of Jerusalem in the 1st century AD (Acts 15). Nicaea condemned the false doctrine of Arianism and produced a doctrinal statement later called the Nicene formula. In 381, at the Council of Constantinople, this formula was shaped into a creed that we call the **Nicene Creed** today.

Here is the form of the Nicene Creed as confessed in the Western churches:

> I believe in one God, the Father Almighty,
> Maker of heaven and earth, and of all things visible and invisible.
> And in one Lord Jesus Christ, the only begotten Son of God,
> begotten of the Father before all worlds;
> God of God, Light of Light, very God of very God;
> begotten, not made, being of one substance with the Father,
> by whom all things were made.
> Who, for us men and for our salvation,
> came down from heaven
> and was incarnate by the Holy Spirit of the virgin Mary,
> and was made man;
> and was crucified also for us under Pontius Pilate;
> he suffered and was buried;
> and the third day he rose again, according to the Scriptures;
> and ascended into heaven, and sits on the right hand of the Father;
> and he shall come again, with glory, to judge the living and the dead;
> whose kingdom shall have no end.
> And I believe in the Holy Spirit, the Lord and Giver of life;
> **who proceeds from the Father and the Son;**
> who with the Father and the Son together is worshiped and glorified;
> who spoke by the prophets.
> And I believe in one holy catholic and

apostolic church.
I acknowledge one baptism for the remission of sins;
and I look for the resurrection of the dead,
and the life of the world to come. Amen.

The line bolded above is where controversy erupted between the East and West. The original form of this creed said this of the Holy Spirit: "who proceeds from the Father." The phrase "and the Son" was not in the original form of the creed. The Western church, with the goal of stamping out Arianism, expanded this part of the creed to include the words "and the Son" (Latin: ***filioque***). The first appearance of this line in the creed came from the **Synod of Toledo** (589) in Spain. In the centuries that followed, the change to the creed became popular, though it took some time before it was widely accepted in the West.

Debate and controversy arose over the insertion between two influential church leaders: **Pope Nicholas I** (r. 858-867) and the Patriarch of Constantinople, **Photius** (r. 858-867, 877-886). Photius, representing the Eastern view, believed the phrase affected how the persons of the Trinity were viewed. To change an ancient creed that united Christians for so long was viewed as a serious matter by those in the East. Photius went so far as to call the insertion of the phrase "and the Son" heresy and blasphemy. Strong language like this had the effect of making fruitful discussion about the matter difficult. Disagreement over this phrase had only become more heated when the schism finally occurred in 1054.

CARDINAL HUMBERT AND MICHAEL CERULARIUS

The Schism

For where envy and self-seeking exist, confusion and every evil thing are there. (Jas. 3:16)

In addition to doctrinal disagreements, there were matters of authority and power at play as well. This is what occurred. The Byzantine emperor Constantine IX (r. 1042-1055) allied himself with the emperor of the Holy Roman Empire Henry III (r. 1039-1056). Constantine also allied himself with **Pope Leo IX** (r. 1049-1054) against the Normans (residing in northern France). The Normans were threatening military action against land in the south (including papal lands). To secure this alliance, Emperor Constantine IX demanded that the patriarch of Constantinople recognize the authority of the Roman bishop over Constantinople.

This was one of the key matters of debate between East and West: whether the pope of Rome was the supreme head of the church, or whether the various bishops such as the patriarch of Constantinople had equal authority.

The patriarch of Constantinople who was faced with these questions was a man named **Michael Cerularius** (r. 1043-1058). Cerularius had no interest in subjecting Constantinople to Roman authority. In fact, Cerularius, as with other Eastern leaders, had grave concerns about errors propagated in the Western church. In 1053, he wrote a letter detailing the various errors of the Western church.

As these controversies with other disagreements grew, Pope Leo IX sent an ambassador to Constantinople (the leading city in the Eastern church) to deal with the controversies. Unfortunately, Leo IX did not wisely choose his ambassador. He sent **Cardinal Humbert**, a man who knew no Greek, to represent the Western church.

Cardinal Humbert was zealous for the views of the Western church and had no sympathy for the views of the Eastern church. He exchanged insults with Cerularius upon his arrival. Finally, on a momentous day, June 16, 1054, Cardinal Humbert appeared at the church of St. Sophia, walked to the high altar, and placed on it a sentence of excommunication against the patriarch and any who agreed with him. The document classed these Easterners with heretics such as Arians, Manichees, and others. Not surprisingly, Cerularius in turn excommunicated Humbert and the other papal ambassadors.

This proved to be the breaking point between the Eastern and Western church. From that time on, the two branches of the church would be viewed as separate communions. Five hundred years later, the Western church would divide into Protestants and Roman Catholics. The Eastern church would become known as the **Eastern Orthodox Church**.

Since the Great Schism, the church has faced other divisions. However, the prayer of Jesus will eventually come to pass. There will come a day when the church is perfected in unity.

I do not pray for these alone, but also for those who will believe in Me through their word; that they all may be one, as You, Father, are in Me, and I in You; that they also may be one in Us, that the world may believe that You sent Me. And the glory which You gave Me I have given them, that they may be one just as We are one: I in them, and You in Me; that they may be made perfect in one, and that the world may know that You have sent Me, and have loved them as You have loved Me. (John 17:20-23)

Eastern Orthodoxy and Its Differences from the West

The Eastern church continues today in various parts of the world. By some estimates, there are some 200 million Eastern Orthodox Christians in the world today. There are a variety of branches to this Eastern church, including Greek Orthodox and Russian Orthodox churches. For the Christian reader who holds Protestant convictions, Eastern Orthodoxy and Roman Catholicism may look very similar. However, it is important to identify some of the differences between the Roman Church and the Eastern Orthodox Church.

Below is a list of some of the differences between Roman Catholicism and Eastern Orthodoxy.

1. Roman Catholicism recognizes the pope (the bishop of Rome) as the universal head of the church, as the successor of the Apostle Peter. Eastern Orthodoxy, in contrast, has a head bishop (known as a patriarch) for each of the major countries or regions where the Eastern Orthodox church has a presence.
2. Roman Catholicism teaches the doctrine of purgatory. Eastern Orthodoxy does not.
3. Roman Catholicism does not allow any of its priests to marry. Eastern Orthodoxy allows marriage for priests prior to ordination. Bishops, however, are not allowed to marry.
4. Roman Catholicism teaches that Mary, the mother of Jesus, was free from original sin (called the **immaculate conception**). Eastern Orthodoxy teaches that Mary was a sinner like any other human being.
5. Roman Catholicism venerates the saints, including by the use of statues. Eastern Orthodoxy expresses this devotion to the saints by the use of icons (flat imagery).
6. Roman Catholicism requires those who partake of the Lord's Supper (most often called the Eucharist) to reach a certain age to be confirmed. Eastern Orthodoxy practices infant communion, allowing the youngest of children to partake.
7. Roman Catholicism receives the added clause to the Nicene Creed ("and the Son"). Eastern Orthodoxy rejects this addition.

What are some of the differences between Protestant churches and Eastern Orthodoxy? Of course, there are also differences between various Protestant groups. But we can summarize some general areas of disagreement.

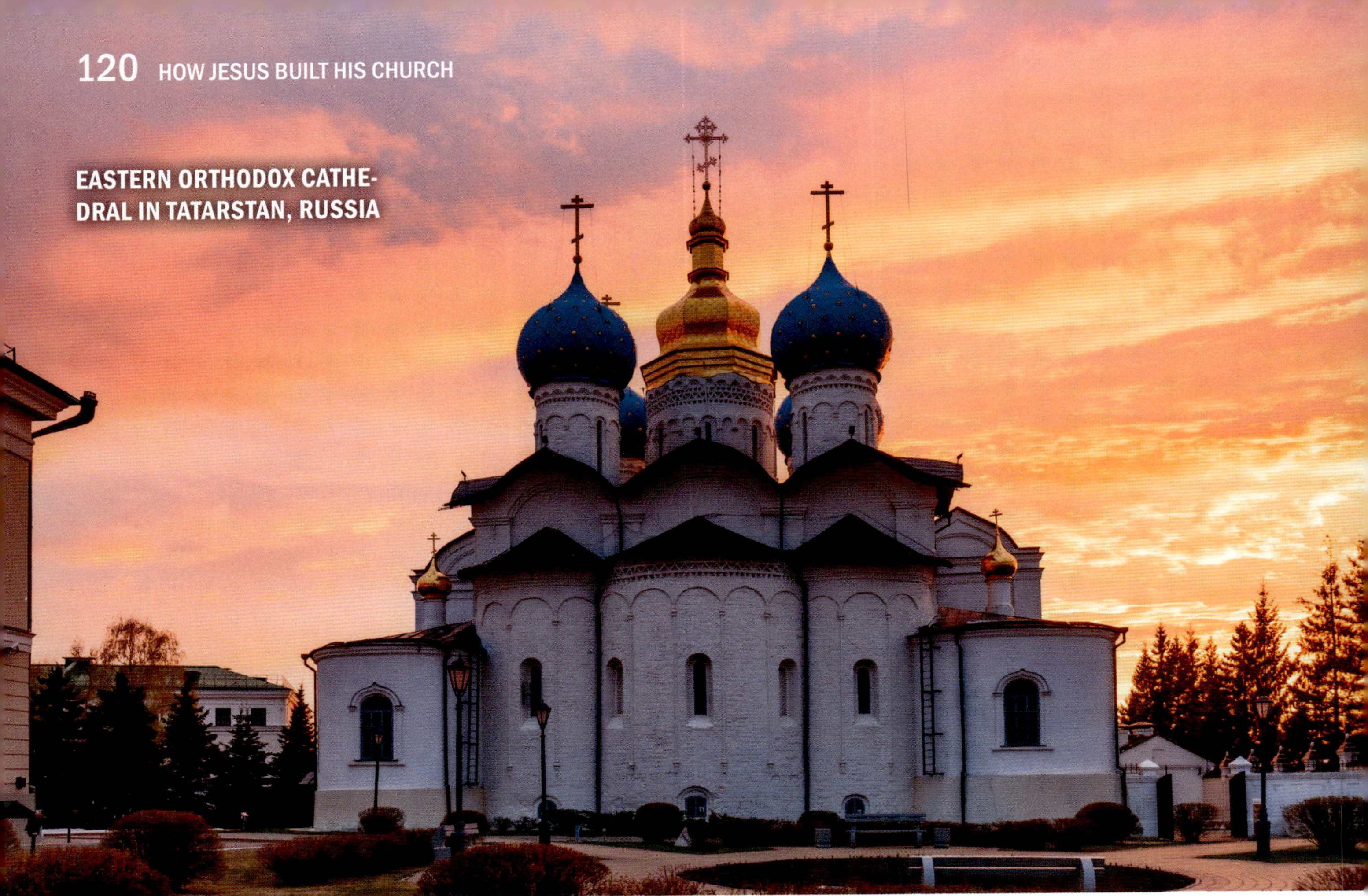

EASTERN ORTHODOX CATHEDRAL IN TATARSTAN, RUSSIA

1. Protestants believe in the supreme authority of Scripture. In Eastern Orthodoxy, Scripture, tradition, and the ecumenical councils are given equal weight in determining faith and practice.
2. Protestants believe in two sacraments or ordinances (baptism and the Lord's supper). Eastern Orthodoxy affirms seven sacraments (baptism, communion, chrismation, confession, unction, marriage, and ordination).
3. Protestants in most cases receive the addition of the clause "And the Son" in the Nicene Creed. Eastern Orthodoxy does not.
4. Protestants generally do not use icons or statues in their worship. Eastern Orthodoxy makes extensive use of icons.
5. Protestants believe in salvation by grace, through faith alone for all who trust in Jesus Christ. Eastern Orthodoxy teaches salvation as a process of **theosis** or **deification**. We must participate in this process. This does not mean we actually become gods, but we become like God in His divine nature (purified, resurrected, and living eternally with God).
6. Protestants maintain that the Old Testament canon consists of 39 books. Eastern Orthodoxy receives an additional ten books (known as the Apocrypha or deuterocanonical books) alongside the Old Testament canon.

Additional differences could be listed. However, the purpose of the above list is to introduce the student to some of the key differences and debates between these groups of professing Christians in the world.

Even though there are differences between Protestants and Eastern Orthodox, there are also points of unity. Here are a few topics upon which Protestants and Eastern Orthodox agree.

1. Protestants and Eastern Orthodox both agree that God is Triune: Father, Son, and Holy Spirit.

2. Protestants and Eastern Orthodox both reject the claims of the pope.
3. Protestants and Eastern Orthodox both reject the doctrine of purgatory.
4. Protestants and Eastern Orthodox both believe in baptism and the Lord's Supper. But they view the meaning of these sacraments differently, and they practice them in a different manner.
5. Protestants and Eastern Orthodox both believe that Jesus is both God and man (in line with the Council of Chalcedon).

Praying for Unity in Christ's Church

The Lord Jesus Christ has His sovereign purposes even in the present divisions among Christians throughout the world. Nevertheless, the day will come when all true Christians will be united just as God the Father and God the Son are in perfect unity and harmony. It is for us as followers of Jesus Christ to pray for unity in the truth. Not only should we pray for unity, but we should make every effort to preserve unity with our brothers and sisters in Christ. To be in unity with our brothers and sisters in Christ, walking in love, brings honor to Jesus Christ.

But this requires humility, longsuffering, forgiveness, and fervent love which covers a multitude of sins (1 Pet. 4:8). If we desire to see more unity in Jesus' church, it can start with us. It can start with how we treat our brothers and sisters in our local church.

Let us also pray in confidence, because we know that the church will prevail against the gates of hell. Come, Lord Jesus!

Though with a scornful wonder
Men see her sore oppressed,
By schisms rent asunder,
By heresies distressed,
Yet saints their watch are keeping,
Their cry goes up, "How long?"
And soon the night of weeping
Shall be the morn of song.

The church shall never perish!
Her dear Lord to defend,
To guide, sustain and cherish
Is with her to the end;
Though there be those that hate her,
And false sons in her pale,
Against or foe or traitor
She ever shall prevail. ■

("The Church's One Foundation," Samuel J. Stone)

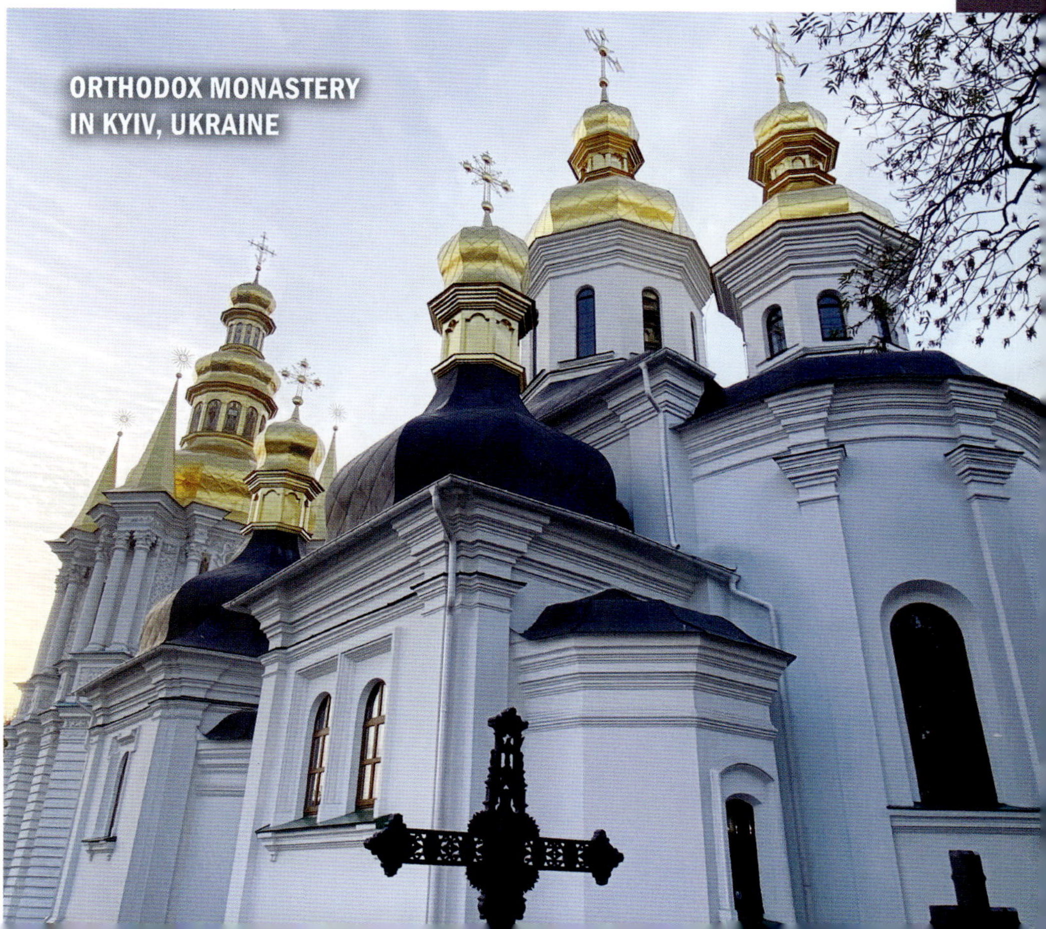

ORTHODOX MONASTERY IN KYIV, UKRAINE

AD 1033
Anselm of Canterbury Born

AD 1088
University of Bologna Founded

AD 1090
Bernard of Clairvaux Born

AD 1098
New order of Cistercian Monasteries founded

AD 1146-1149
The Second Crusade

AD 1170
Beginning of the Waldensian Movement

AD 1182
Francis of Assis Born

AD 1378
Great Papal Schism

AD 1391
Bethlehem Chapel established

AD 1409
Council of Pisa

AD 1414-1418
Council of Constance

AD 1415
Martyrdom of John Huss

AD 1431
Council of Basel

Unit 3

The Late Middle Ages (AD 1000-1500)

AD 1184
Council of Verona

AD 1198-1216
Papacy of Pope Innocent III

AD 1215
Fourth Lateran Council

AD 1215
Dominican Order Founded

AD 1218-1221
The Fifth Crusade

AD 1265-1274
Thomas Aquinas writes the *Summa Theologica*

AD 1285-134
Reign of King Philip IV

AD 1294-1303
Papacy of Pope Boniface VIII

AD 1301
Papal Bull of Boniface *Unam Sanctam*

AD 1309-1377
The Avignonese Captivity of the Papacy

AD 1328
John Wycliffe Born

AD 1347
The Black Death

AD 1370
John Huss Born

ALL SOULS COLLEGE, OXFORD, ENGLAND

Universities and Scholasticism

Now concerning things offered to idols: We know that we all have knowledge. Knowledge puffs up, but love edifies. And if anyone thinks that he knows anything, he knows nothing yet as he ought to know. But if anyone loves God, this one is known by Him. (1 Cor. 8:1-3)

Today, if you visit any major city in the Western world, you will find several universities or colleges. Where did these institutions come from? And how long have they been around?

The university can be traced back to the 11th century with the founding of the University of Bologna in Italy founded in 1088. After the University of Bologna was founded, many other universities were established throughout Europe. By the end of the 15th century, there were around eighty universities in Europe. This educational movement made a significant impact upon theology in the church and upon education in society in general.

As we will see, the theology that developed in these new schools impacted church and society in important ways. Theology as it was developed in these universities became known as **Scholasticism**. As universities grew, the primary center of discipleship and education shifted from the monasteries to the universities.

Before the rise of universities, education was provided in some churches through what was known as the cathedral school. There, young men could seek a free education from the church and learn some basic subjects. It is important to remember that at this time, knowledge of reading and writing was not widespread in European society.

The various universities that were established in the 11th, 12th, and 13th centuries varied in their curriculum. But over time, they were standardized around several subjects including grammar, rhetoric, dialectic (or the art of debate), arithmetic, geometry, astronomy, and music. In all of these subjects, theology played some role as well. Lectures in European universities were given in Latin since it remained the common language of learning throughout Europe. Additionally, Latin was the language of the church's Bible and liturgy.

Teaching in the universities took two primary forms: the **lecture** and the **disputation**. Lectures were given by a teacher who would read out of a key text and then make comments on it. Students would take extensive notes on what the teacher said about the text. Since books were rare in the Middle Ages, many students would not have direct access to books. Because of this, they relied on the teacher's comments. The lecture format was also complemented by disputations. A disputation involved a statement or question that would then be debated by students. This approach to learning trained students in how to use logic to

STUDENTS IN A MEDIEVAL COLLEGE

MEETING OF DOCTORS (PROFESSORS) AT THE UNIVERSITY OF PARIS

resolve various debated matters.

Students in these early universities were boys or very young men. Often, they traveled a long distance from home to participate in university studies. At this time, there was no easy and quick means of communication for parents to check on how their boys were doing. As a result, discipline was lax in many universities. Grouping large numbers of young men together without sufficient oversight was a recipe for foolish and ungodly behavior. For example, a complaint was made at the University of Paris in 1218 because a group of young students broke into nearby houses and carried off young women. In 1269, a public proclamation was made denouncing gangs of students who broke into houses, committing robberies and "many other enormities hateful to God." In other cases, some universities established rules to guard students against temptation. For example, rules established at the University of Bologna in 1367 forbade students from dancing, stating that "the devil easily tempts men to evil through this amusement." While the kind of behavior described at the University of Paris likely did not occur everywhere, each university faced the challenge of how to maintain discipline among so many young men without their parents present.

As the number of universities increased, their influence in church and society multiplied. For example, the University of Paris became known as the chief center of theological learning in Europe until the time of the Protestant Reformation. Certain universities gained a reputation for excellence in certain subjects, and to become a student of such a university was a way of gaining prestige before others.

The shift from learning in the monasteries to learning in the universities made a considerable impact on how the Bible and theology was taught and learned. Now, theology was studied as an academic discipline. In the monastery, theology was studied in the context of worship and monastic disciplines. But these same components did not exist in the universities. Over time, this created a division between knowledge and spiritual growth in the context of church life.

The Development of Scholastic Theology

Scholasticism is the term given to describe theology as it was taught in the universities of the Middle Ages. The scholastic theologians built on the foundation of teaching from the early church fathers. Many of their writings quote frequently from the pastors and writers of the early church. The scholastics were also interested in the relationship between faith and reason. They attempted to explain that Christian truth was not contrary to reason. They also attempted to bring together the various doctrines of the faith into a systematic whole and explain how these truths relate to one another.

The scholastics made some valuable contributions to our understanding of certain Chris-

OXFORD, ENGLAND, WITH THE UNIVERSITY OF OXFORD IN THE BACKGROUND

tian doctrines. But there were also theologians who moved far away from what Scripture teaches. Some of them submitted God's truth to fallible human reason and arrived at wrong conclusions. When the Protestant Reformation began, the Reformers rejected much the scholastics taught. The Reformers made it their aim to return to Scripture as the authority for Christian faith and life.

Another problem with scholastic theology was the elevation of the philosophy of **Aristotle** (c. 384-322 BC). Many theologians became interested in Aristotle's writings and methods. Aristotle's works were not widely available at the beginning of the 11th century. But Muslim scholars translated Aristotle's works from Greek into Arabic. Then Christian scholars took the Arabic translations and brought them into Latin.

Increasingly, Aristotle's writings were studied even though Aristotle was a pagan who lived before the time of Christ. Aristotle and Greek philosophy began to exercise influence over the church's theology. This mixture of pagan and Christian teaching had the effect of corrupting the church's doctrine. Although there was some resistance to introducing Aristotle into the university curriculum, in 1366, Pope Urban V made Aristotle required reading for university students. The purpose of this mandate: "Aristotle shall be the universal teacher."

Scholasticism had some valuable aspects, but it also had weaknesses. The precision of the scholastic method did at times bring a greater precision of understanding to some doctrines. But scholasticism also tended to be speculative in nature. Many scholastic theologians suggested ideas that could not be found in Scripture but may have seemed reasonable to the human mind. In some cases, theologians exalted human reason above the teaching of Scripture.

Additionally, scholastics sometimes spent far too much time discussing questions of little importance. In many cases, Scripture did not answer these questions, and to answer them often had little value. Here are a few examples of the complex questions some of the scholastics asked. Albertus Magnus asked, "Was it harder for God to create the universe or to create man?" Anselm and Hugo de St. Victor asked, "Who sinned most, Adam or Eve?" Alexander of Hales wanted to answer the question, "Which hour of the day did Adam sin?" Robert Pullen asked the question, "Will man in the resurrection receive back his rib which was lost in Eden?"[1]

As the universities grew in their influence, the theologians who studied and taught in those universities began to produce writings that influenced how Christians thought about the truths of the faith. To better understand this movement in Christian thought, let's look at a few scholastic theologians.

Anselm of Canterbury

**For with You is the fountain of life;
In Your light we see light.
(Ps. 36:9)**

One of the earliest theologians known as a scholastic is **Anselm of Canterbury** (c. 1033-1109). Anselm's writings were produced before the rise of the universities. But his method was followed by later scholastics. For this reason, Anselm is considered by most to be the first scholastic theologian. Anselm was a native of Italy who became archbishop of Canterbury, England.

SEAL OF ANSELM OF CANTERBURY

Anselm's reputation is one of deep reverence, love for God, and a commitment to knowing God. Anselm left behind many prayers that continue to inspire Christians today. One of Anselm's quotes sums up his approach to the study of the things of God: "I do not seek to understand so that I may believe; I believe so that I may understand."[2] This meant that, for Anselm, faith comes before reason. It is in believing God's truth as foundational that we are then able to see and understand. Or as the Psalmist wrote in Psalm 36, "in God's light we see light."

This devotion to seeking understanding is found in the opening words of one of Anselm's books. Here is what Anselm wrote:

> Now, my whole heart, say to God,
> "I seek your face;
> Lord, it is Your face I am seeking" …
> So that I can remember You,
> Think of You,
> And love You.
> But Your image in me is so worn away,
> So blotted out by faults,
> So darkened by the smoke of sin,
> That it cannot do the thing it was made for,
> Unless You renew it and remake it.
> Lord, I am not trying to climb up to Your height;
> My understanding is simply not equal to that.
> But I do want to understand a little of Your truth
> Which my heart already believes and loves.
> I do not seek to understand so that I may believe;
> I believe so that I may understand.
> More than that,
> I believe that unless I do believe
> I will not understand.[3]

Anselm sought to show the reasonableness of Christian truth. He wrote a number of important books applying reason to matters of faith. His three most well-known books are called *Monologion*, *Proslogion*, and *Cur Deus Homo* (Why the God Man?). In the first two books, Anselm set out to prove God's existence by reason. His argument for God's existence is called the **ontological argument**.

Nick Needham explains Anselm's argument for God's existence in this way:

> We can sum up Anselm's argument for God's existence in the *Monologion* and *Proslogion* as follows. By definition, God is the most perfect of all possible beings. But if God does not exist, He would not be the most perfect of all possible beings; for a God who does exist would be more perfect than a God who does not exist. Therefore, if God is by definition the most perfect of all beings, He *must* exist.[4]

Whether Anselm's argument really makes sense is still debated today.

Anselm's other book, ***Cur Deus Homo*** (*Why

the God Man?) was an important book that gave explanation to Jesus Christ's atonement. Anselm wanted to answer the question: why did God the Son come in the flesh, and why did He have to die on the cross? Many early church fathers thought that Jesus' death on the cross was a ransom paid to Satan to set sinners free from Satan's control. This is sometimes called the **ransom theory** of the atonement. To this view, Anselm rightly explained that Satan has no rights over the human race. Ransom is not to be paid to Satan. Instead, the ransom price is paid to God because sin creates a debt. We must either suffer punishment for our sins, or the price must be paid to set us free from that curse. For this reason, Jesus Christ came and offered Himself as a sacrifice in place of sinners.

Anselm's explanation of the atonement was more accurate to what the Bible teaches than the ransom theory popular among some in the early church. It fit well with passages like 1 Peter 3:

For Christ also suffered once for sins, the just for the unjust, that He might bring us to God, being put to death in the flesh but made alive by the Spirit. (1 Pet. 3:18)

Many of Anselm's prayers are consistent with God's Word and are edifying. However, we do find that by Anselm's time, devotion and prayer to Mary was becoming more common. This is reflected in some of Anselm's prayers which are directed to Mary. It would take the Protestant Reformation to bring correction to this veneration and prayer to Mary, which the Reformers would reject.

Peter Lombard

Peter Lombard (c. 1096-1160) was responsible for creating the most-used theology textbook of the Middle Ages. His work was entitled ***The Sentences***. This four-volume work was a compilation of Biblical passages and quotations from theologians of the Church organized under various topics and headings. This work became a foundational work in theology for centuries. *The Sentences*

PETER LOMBARD (C. 1096-1160)

became the standard book read by all theological students thereafter. If a student wanted to obtain a doctorate in theology, they would often write a commentary on Lombard's work.

The method Lombard followed was in these steps:

1. Summarize what the church taught about a topic
2. Quote Scripture to prove it
3. Quote the church fathers showing their opinion on the topic
4. Resolve any difficulties by the use of logic

Lombard was the first theologian to officially list the sacraments as seven in number. His list would become the standard view in Roman Catholic theology. The seven sacraments became the official teaching of the church at the Council of Florence in 1439.

Thomas Aquinas

The next of the scholastics we should give our attention to is **Thomas Aquinas** (1225-1274). Thomas was born in Italy, near Aquino (from which his name "Aquinas" is derived). He joined the Dominican order in 1244 against the wishes of his family. He then went to study in various universities including Naples, Paris, and Cologne. It was in Cologne, under the tutelage of a teacher named **Albertus Magnus** (c. 1193-1280), that Thomas was introduced to the writings of Aristotle. Albertus studied and wrote commentaries on all of Aristotle's works. This, in turn, influenced Thomas to study Aristotle's philosophy. Among the scholastics, Thomas was most responsible for adapting Aristotle's philosophy for use in the church. Aquinas reintroduced Aristotle to the church and sought to show how the foundations of Greek philosophy could be used to bolster and demonstrate the truth of the church. Thomas' attempt to mix biblical teaching with Aristotle's philosophy introduced further doctrinal error into the church's teaching.

The two most important and influential works of Thomas Aquinas were his *Summa Contra Gentiles* (*Against the Gentiles*) and **Summa Theologica**. The second work is a massive treatment of Christian theology and ethics. This work would become highly influential in the late Middle Ages and remains an important and influential work of theology. Today, it is still read by many students of theology.

THOMAS AQUINAS (1225-1274)

Here are a few key points about Thomas' theology that are important to remember. These are important because later teachers and councils of the church would be built upon the foundation of Thomas' teaching.

- Thomas taught that the existence of God could be proved by human experience and reason.
- Thomas taught the doctrine of transubstantiation, the view that the elements of bread and wine in the Lord's Supper, when consecrated by the priest, are turned into the body and blood of Christ. However, Thomas used Aristotle's philosophy to explain how the outward form of something (like bread and wine) could still appear to be the same while the inward substance was changed (into Christ's body and blood).
- Thomas distinguished between two types of sins: mortal sins and venial sins. Mortal sins were more serious sins (such as blasphemy or murder) that had the effect of killing the soul. Venial sins were lesser sins (like speaking a careless word, or a sin done in ignorance) and these "damage" the soul, but they do not "kill" the soul.

These teachings, among others, would shape later Roman Catholic theology to the present day. ■

UNIVERSITY OF BOLOGNA

MONT SAINT-MICHEL, NORMANDY, FRANCE

13 Monasticism in the Middle Ages

Now godliness with contentment is great gain. For we brought nothing into this world, and it is certain we can carry nothing out. And having food and clothing, with these we shall be content. (1 Tim. 6:6-8)

As the Middle Ages progressed, monasticism as a Christian movement continued to increase in size and influence. The later Middle Ages witnessed the rise of an abundance of new orders with their own distinctive practices. In fact, the proliferation of monastic orders became so profuse that the **Fourth Lateran Council** of 1215 put a stop to any new orders being formed. Canon 13 of the Fourth Lateran Council stated the following:

> Lest too great a diversity of religious orders lead to grave confusion in the Church of God, we strictly forbid anyone in the future to found a new order, but whoever should wish to enter an order, let him choose one already approved. Similarly, he who would wish to found a new monastery, must accept a rule already proved. We forbid also anyone to presume to be a monk in different monasteries (that is, belong to different monasteries), or that one abbot preside over several monasteries.

This rule did have the effect of slowing the creation of new orders. But it certainly did not slow down the growth of monasticism in general. Various orders of the Middle Ages exercised a significant impact upon church life and society in general. It is our purpose in this chapter to look at a few of the significant developments in monasticism and how they affected Christ's church.

The Cistercian Order and Bernard of Clairvaux

Jesus said to him, " 'You shall love the Lord your God with all your heart, with all your soul, and with all your mind.' This is the first and great commandment. And the second is like it: 'You shall love your neighbor as yourself.' On these two commandments hang all the Law and the Prophets." (Matt. 22:37-40)

Because there was such diversity in monasticism, it is not possible in this chapter to survey every known monastic order of the Middle Ages. However, we will focus on some of the more important orders and key leaders in those orders. First, we will learn about the Cistercian order, which continues in existence today.

In the spring of 1098, a group of Benedictine monks founded a monastery in Cîteaux in the region of Burgundy (located in modern-day France). This new order, which became known as the **Cistercians**, made it their aim to observe the *Rule of St. Benedict* strictly. They purged any elements that had been added on to Benedict's original rule in later centuries, and restored Benedict's original rule as they saw it. These "additions" included things like comfortable clothes, unnecessary meals, and income not allowed in Benedict's *Rule*.

The Cistercian order expanded rapidly. They established their monasteries on uncultivated land, away from towns. This enabled the monks to withdraw from regular society. But it also meant they could cultivate the surrounding land, providing resources for the monastery. The Cistercians aimed to keep the purity of Benedict's *Rule*. To guard against compromise, when a new Cis-

THE MODERN CLAIRVAUX ABBEY

BERNARD OF CLAIRVAUX (1090-1153)

tercian monastery was founded, a nearby abbot from another monastery would visit once a year to make sure the *Rule* was carefully observed. By the year 1200, just one hundred years after their founding, there were over 500 Cistercian monasteries throughout Europe.

One of the most influential men of the Middle Ages was a Cistercian monk named **Bernard of Clairvaux** (1090-1153). He founded a Cistercian monastery in 1115 in what was known as the "Valley of Wormwood." There the brothers built structures on the land and renamed it "Clairvaux," which means "clear valley." For the next thirty-eight years, Bernard served as the abbot of Clairvaux.

In most cases, monks lived quiet, secluded lives that were of little influence on wider society. But that was not the case with Bernard. Bernard traveled widely, preached, counseled kings and popes, and influenced the scholastic theologians. Some 500 letters exist today of Bernard's correspondence to men in positions of church and state authority. He preached many sermons and wrote hymns which are still read and sung today. The Protestant Reformers Martin Luther and John Calvin both loved Bernard's writings. They found support for the doctrine of justification by faith alone in them.

Bernard's hymn "Jesus, Thou Joy of Loving Hearts" expresses his love for Jesus Christ. Here are the lines of Bernard's hymn in English translation:

O Jesus, joy of loving hearts,
thou fount of life, thou light of men,
from fullest bliss that earth imparts
we turn unfilled to thee again,
we turn unfilled to thee again.

Thy truth unchanged has ever stood,
thou savest those that on thee call;
to them that seek thee, thou art good,
to them that find thee, all in all,
to them that find thee, all in all.

We taste thee, O thou living bread,
and long to feast upon thee still;
we drink of thee, the fountainhead,
and thirst our souls from thee to fill,
and thirst our souls from thee to fill.

Our restless spirits yearn for thee,
where'er our changeful lot is cast,
glad that thy gracious smile we see,
blest that our faith can hold thee fast,
blest that our faith can hold thee fast.

O Jesus, ever with us stay,
make all our moments calm and bright;
chase the dark night of sin away,
shed o'er the world thy holy light,

Like other church leaders of his time, Bernard was a supporter of the Crusades. He was instrumental in raising popular support for the Second Crusade (1146-1149). Bernard preached a famous

RUINS OF CARCASSONNE, A SITE WHERE THE ALBIGENSIAN CRUSADE WAS CARRIED OUT

sermon in Vézelay urging Christians to defend the Holy Land against the Muslim invaders. Bernard preached to a massive audience in 1146, promising indulgences to those who participated in the crusade. Not only did Bernard preach in Vézelay, but he journeyed to nearby regions, raising support for the crusade.

Tragically, some saw this as an opportunity to turn their swords on Jews residing in Europe. A German monk named Rudolf in his preaching urged people to rid Europe of the Jews before they set out on the crusade. As a result, hundreds of Jews in Germany were killed. Once Bernard heard the news about this, he intervened and urged people to defend the Holy Land but not to kill the Jews. Bernard desired the conversion of the Jews and rightly saw it was wrong to harm them.

The Dominican Order

In the late 1100s, a new movement originated in southern France. The people involved in it were called the **Albigenses** because many of them came from the town of Albi, France. They were also called the **Cathars** (a Greek word meaning "pure ones"). Though the Cathars pursued moral purity, their doctrine and practice were not biblically pure. Their beliefs were heretical and dangerous.

The Cathars held to an unbiblical view of God. They claimed that the physical world was not created by a good God. Instead, they taught that the world was created by an evil force. Because of this, they viewed physical things (like the human body, trees, or animals) as corrupt. The Cathars weren't very concerned about being saved from sin and death. Instead, they wanted to be saved from a physical existence. This is quite different from the teaching of the Bible. In biblical teaching, Jesus destroys all death (spiritual and physical) through His death and resurrection. And, according to 1 Corinthians 15, we look forward to the resurrection of our physical bodies.

The Cathars did not see it this way. They taught that the soul had been kidnapped by Satan. The physical body was just Satan's prison house. They also taught that Christ did not have a physical body and that He never died on the cross. This rejection of the biblical doctrine of Christ comes under the direct condemnation of Scripture. For example, in 1 John, we read:

By this you know the Spirit of God: Every spirit that confesses that Jesus Christ has come in the flesh is of God, and every spirit that does not confess that Jesus Christ has come in the flesh is not of God. And this is the spirit of the Antichrist, which you have heard was coming, and is now already in the world. (1 John 4:2-3)

Because they viewed the physical world as evil, the Cathars would frequently fast. They would avoid certain foods like eggs, milk, and cheese. They believed these foods were particularly tainted with corruption. However, because the Cathars were still in physical bodies, they had to eat something. In between frequent fasts, they would eat foods like wine and fish. Paul warned about such false and dangerous doctrines in 1 Timothy 4:

Now the Spirit expressly says that in latter times some will depart from the faith, giving heed to deceiving spirits and doctrines of demons, speaking lies in hypocrisy, having their own conscience seared with a hot iron, forbidding to marry, and commanding to abstain from foods which God created to be received with thanksgiving by those who believe and know the truth. (1 Tim. 4:1-3)

The Cathars also rejected the sacraments of the church. They isolated themselves from the church and avoided all public worship. The people within this heretical movement believed that they alone were the true disciples of Christ. They thought no one could be saved unless they believed everything the Cathars did.

To suppress this new movement, Pope Innocent III authorized violent force against the Cathars. Numerous violent massacres occurred, wiping out most of the Cathar movement. In the midst of this conflict, the **Dominican Order** was founded in 1215 by **Dominic of Caleruega** (1170-1221).

DOMINIC OF CALERUEGA (1170-1221)

Dominic was born in Castile, Spain. This was a region once occupied by Muslims and often threatened by Muslim invasion. In this environment, Dominic became committed to the defense of the Catholic faith against Islam. But he was also zealous in defending the church's teaching against other heretics such as the Cathars.

Following some of the violent suppression of the Cathars, Dominic received a plot of land in Toulouse. He organized a group of preachers who would preach against heresy but also instruct God's people in Christian doctrine. The Dominicans became known as the "order of preachers" because they were characterized by their preaching ministry.

Dominic's order was founded right around the same time that the canons of the Fourth Lateran Council required that any new order use a monastic rule already approved. Because of this, Dominic chose the popular ***Rule of St. Augustine*** for the Dominican Order. The Dominican Order was also noteworthy as one of the **Mendicant** orders of the Middle Ages. The Mendicant orders practiced begging because members of the order were forbidden from owning any personal property.

Unlike monastic orders which primarily focused upon personal spiritual development and solitary contemplation, the Dominicans were an order devoted to teaching and preaching. Dominic made it his aim to see preachers sent all over Europe. The purpose of this order was the "health of souls," and the Dominicans directed themselves to be "useful to the souls of our neighbors." The Dominicans also established many monasteries near universities. This enabled the Dominicans to exercise an influence in education, something they were very interested in.

As was the case with the Cistercians, the Dominican Order grew rapidly. By the middle of the 14th century, there were some 13,000 Dominicans scattered throughout Europe.

The Dominican friars[1] often chose to preach in cities because there they could speak to larger groups. One Dominican leader, Humbert of Romans (1200-1277), explained the reason for this: "There preaching is more efficacious because there are more people, and the need is greater, for in the city there are more sins."

Dominican monasteries were unique in having classrooms where lectures were regularly held. Study and teaching were central disciplines in the life of a Dominican. Many hours per day were given to study to enable the Dominican friars to be well equipped for their task of preaching. The Dominicans not only lectured in their monasteries. They also hosted public services in various cities and towns where locals were invited to hear the friars preach.

Due to their zeal for orthodoxy, the Dominicans also supported the efforts of the Inquisition. They became known as the "hounds of the Lord" because they made efforts to persuade heretics to return to the church's teaching. Otherwise, such heretics were turned over to the Inquisition to be tried and in some cases executed. These activities in support of the Inquisition, made the Dominicans unpleasant to many. They became viewed as the "spiritual police" who were on the hunt for heresy.

The Dominicans were also partially responsible for the introduction of Aristotle's works into the universities. Thomas Aquinas, himself a Dominican, is the primary example of a Dominican theologian making use of Aristotle's philosophy in his theological works.

The Franciscan Order

Go your way; behold, I send you out as lambs among wolves. Carry neither money bag, knapsack, nor sandals; and greet no one along the road. (Luke 10:3-4)

Another influential mendicant order of the Middle Ages is the **Franciscan Order**. Along with Bernard of Clairvaux, **Francis of Assisi** (1182-1226), the founder of the Franciscans, was among the most influential Christians of the Middle Ages. The Franciscan Order grew rapidly. By 1250, there were some 30,000 Franciscans.

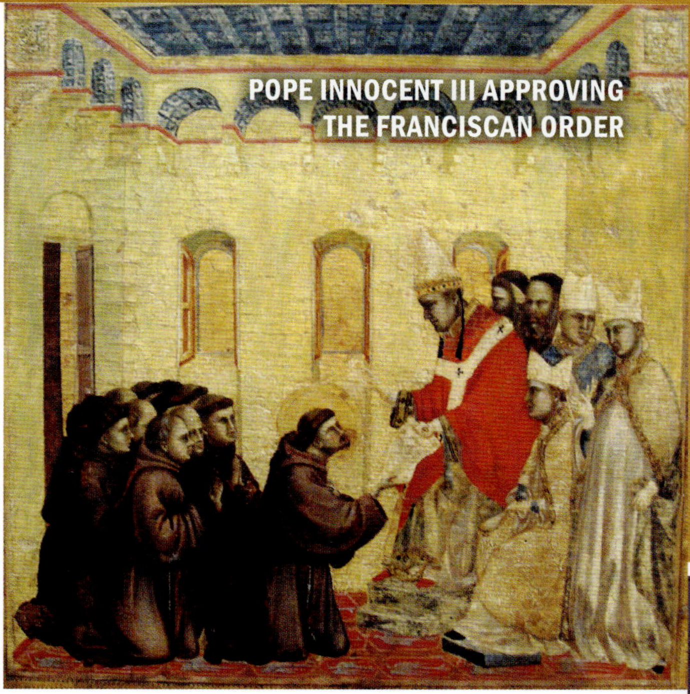
POPE INNOCENT III APPROVING THE FRANCISCAN ORDER

Francis was born in 1182 in Assisi (in modern-day Italy). Francis' father Pietro was a wealthy cloth merchant. It was Pietro's desire that Francis would follow in his footsteps and become a merchant. As a young man, a military conflict between Assisi and Perugia broke out. Francis went into battle with many others from his town. The men of Assisi were defeated. As a result, Francis was imprisoned for a year. Pietro only secured Francis' release by paying a large ransom. Francis' time in prison made him contemplate matters of eternity and the state of his soul.

After his release, Francis was in church one day hearing the Scripture reading. It was from Matthew 10:

These twelve Jesus sent out and commanded them, saying: "Do not go into the way of the Gentiles, and do not enter a city of the Samaritans. But go rather to the lost sheep of the house of Israel. And as you go, preach, saying, 'The kingdom of heaven is at hand.' Heal the sick, cleanse the lepers, raise the dead, cast out demons. Freely you have

received, freely give. Provide neither gold nor silver nor copper in your money belts, nor bag for your journey, nor two tunics, nor sandals, nor staffs; for a worker is worthy of his food. Now whatever city or town you enter, inquire who in it is worthy, and stay there till you go out. And when you go into a household, greet it. If the household is worthy, let your peace come upon it. But if it is not worthy, let your peace return to you. And whoever will not receive you nor hear your words, when you depart from that house or city, shake off the dust from your feet." (Matt. 10:5-14)

Francis was struck by the Lord's words. He took them as a direct command to him. He forsook his former life and made it his aim to live a life of poverty in service to Jesus Christ. Francis wrote, "No one showed me what I should do ... but the Most High revealed to me that I should live according to the form of the holy gospel."[2]

Francis began a ministry of preaching and acquired all his food by begging. Soon, others joined Francis in this work. As the Franciscans traveled around preaching, they would find shelter overnight in abandoned barns or caves. One unique aspect of the Franciscan Order was the requirement of corporate destitution. This meant that the Franciscans would not even share any possessions in common. In Francis' rule, he required:

> The brothers shall appropriate nothing to themselves, neither a place nor anything; but as pilgrims and strangers in this world, serving God in poverty and humility, they shall with confidence go seeking alms.[3]

Francis was also known for his missionary zeal. While the Crusades were still occurring, Francis decided to leave Italy and travel to Muslim lands to seek the conversion of the Muslims. Francis made a number of attempted trips with this aim. In 1219, Francis set out for Egypt by sea. He eventually entered the court of a Muslim ruler in Egypt and spoke with him about the things of God. Francis urged this Muslim ruler to forsake Islam and be baptized as a Christian. But the sultan refused. Francis made this journey while the Fifth Crusade (1218-1221) was occurring. Francis was one of the first Christians to embark on such a missionary endeavor to the Muslims. A hundred years later, another Christian named **Raymond Lull** (1232-1315) would make a similar effort to reach the Muslims.

Francis of Assisi is often remembered for his love of God's creation. In 1919, a man named William Henry Draper took the words of one of Francis' poems on creation and turned it into a hymn titled *All Creatures of Our God and King*. This hymn clearly expresses Francis' appreciation for God's glory in creation. Here is a portion of that beautiful hymn:

All creatures of our God and King,
lift up your voice and with us sing,
alleluia, alleluia!
Thou burning sun with golden beam,
thou silver moon with softer gleam,
O sing ye, O sing ye, alleluia, alleluia,
alleluia!

Thou rushing wind that art so strong,
ye clouds that sail in heav'n along,
alleluia, alleluia!
Thou rising morn in praise rejoice,
ye lights of evening, find a voice,

FRANCIS OF ASSISI (1182-1226)

O sing ye, O sing ye, alleluia, alleluia, alleluia!

Thou flowing water, pure and clear,
make music for thy God to hear,
alleluia, alleluia!
Thou fire so masterful and bright,
that givest all both warmth and light,
O sing ye, O sing ye, alleluia, alleluia, alleluia!

And ev'ryone, with tender heart,
forgiving others, take your part,
alleluia, alleluia!
Ye who long pain and sorrow bear,
sing praise and cast on God your care,
O sing ye, O sing ye, alleluia, alleluia, alleluia!

Evaluating Monasticism in the Middle Ages

The aim of our charge is love that issues from a pure heart and a good conscience and a sincere faith. (1 Tim. 1:5 ESV)

Philip Schaff, the church historian suggests that the monasteries of the Middle Ages were both the "chief centre of true religion as well as of dark superstition."[4] On one hand, we can see how the monastic orders promoted love for God, genuine commitment to discipleship, and acts of loving service to others. Yet monastic orders also placed unbiblical requirements upon their adherents. The traditions of men, in the form of various monastic "rules," were imposed as absolute requirements upon men and women living in monasteries. Increasingly, this meant that holiness was measured by a man-made rule, rather than by the standard of God's Law.

Monasticism also contributed to a radical divide between the "sacred life" (lived by monks and nuns) and the "secular life" (lived by ordinary laborers, the lay-people). Many in the Middle Ages thought the higher way to devoutly serve God was to join one of the monastic orders. And many monks spoke of this way of life as the surest way of salvation. For example, Bernard of Clairvaux was not at peace until all of his brothers and sisters had joined monastic orders. Anselm in many of his letters urged others to become monks. Anselm did not believe it was a requirement for salvation, but he did believe it was the safest way to salvation. He wrote, [who] "can attain to it in a safer or nobler way, he who seeks to love God alone or he who joins the love of the world with the love of God?"[5]

As with every period of church history, it is important that we keep our eyes focused on how the Lord Jesus built His church. In God's providential care and purposes for His church, the development of monasticism in the Middle Ages was another important chapter in the unfolding story of Christ's church. ■

ASSISI, ITALY

AVIGNON, FRANCE

The Papal Schism and the Conciliar Movement

The elders who are among you I exhort, I who am a fellow elder and a witness of the sufferings of Christ, and also a partaker of the glory that will be revealed: Shepherd the flock of God which is among you, serving as overseers, not by compulsion but willingly, not for dishonest gain but eagerly; nor as being lords over those entrusted to you, but being examples to the flock; and when the Chief Shepherd appears, you will receive the crown of glory that does not fade away. (1 Pet. 5:1-4)

We learned in a previous chapter how the papacy reached the apex of its power during the time of Innocent III (1198-1216). The popes who followed Innocent III did not exercise the same degree of power. Nevertheless, the papacy remained an influential institution in the West. But the popes became mired in various disputes with monarchs in Europe. Eventually, the papacy became fractured. Not only was the church divided, but all of European society was divided as well.

In this chapter, we will learn about how the papacy was torn in two in the **Papal Schism** or the **Western Schism**. For a time, two or three men in different parts of Europe each claimed to be the pope. How did such division and confusion occur?

Division, conflict, and confusion occur when people set out to fulfill their selfish ambitions (Jas. 3:16). It is no surprise then that conflict occurred when competing powers each asserted their supremacy over the other. Though claiming to be the successor of the Apostle Peter, the popes of the Middle Ages were nothing like the humble fisherman who led Christ's church as a faithful apostle and elder.

Conflict between the French Monarchy and the Papacy

For where envy and self-seeking exist, confusion and every evil thing are there. (Jas. 3:16)

We begin our retelling of this period with a conflict that developed between the French monarchy and the papacy. Under **King Philip IV** (r. 1285-1314), the French monarchy grew to new heights of power. In 1295, King Philip sought to tax the clergy to finance his war with England. The clergy

KING PHILIP IV (1285-1314)

BONIFACE VIII

of the French church did not agree with this tax. They appealed to **Pope Boniface VIII** (r. 1294-1303) for relief. In response, the pope threatened to excommunicate anyone who imposed taxes on the church without the pope's approval. Philip did not appreciate the pope's intervention in this matter. In response, he forbade all exports of gold and silver from France. This decision negatively impacted Rome's economy.

Conflict continued to increase between King Philip and Pope Boniface. In 1301, Boniface sent a papal representative named Bernard of Saisset to Philip's courts, complaining of some of the king's actions against the church, including the seizure of church property. But Philip had no respect for the pope or his messenger. He imprisoned Bernard. Philip then called a national assembly of French authorities who supported him in defying the pope.

In 1301, Boniface responded with a papal bull titled *Unam Sanctam*. The bull set forth colossal claims regarding the authority of the papacy. Part of the bull read as follows:

> We are forced by the faith to believe and hold, and we do indeed firmly believe and sincerely confess, that there is one holy Catholic and apostolic Church, and that outside this church there is no salvation or forgiveness of sins.... There is one body and one head of this one and only Church—not two heads, like a monster—and that is Christ, and Christ's vicar is Peter and the successor of Peter.... Both the spiritual and civil sword are in the power of the church. The civil sword is to be used for the church, the spiritual sword by the church: the spiritual sword is to be used by the priest, the civil sword by kings and captains, but only at the will of the priest and by priestly permission.... We declare, state, define and pronounce that it is absolutely necessary to salvation for every human being to be subject to the Roman pope.[1]

The final line quoted is important: Boniface taught that for a person to be saved, it was *absolutely necessary* to submit to the authority of the pope of Rome. But Boniface did not succeed in bringing Philip to submit. The papal bull only escalated the conflict. Philip declared Boniface to be unfit to hold the papal office. With the agreement of the French Parliament and the University of Paris, Philip summoned the pope to appear before a church council. Boniface refused and prepared to excommunicate Philip.

Tired of the verbal disputes, Philip simplified the situation by kidnapping and imprisoning Boniface. Philip demanded that Pope Boniface resign from his office, but the pope refused. Eventually, Boniface was rescued from prison, but he died within a month of his rescue. Though Boniface was out of the picture, disagreement continued between the French and supporters of the pope in Rome.

Pope Benedict XI (r. 1303-1304) succeeded Boniface but only reigned eight months. The French cardinals, who had a role in selecting the next pope, wanted a French pope that would act in submission to King Philip. Clement V (r. 1305-1314) was elected, but he never lived in Rome. Instead, Clement V established the papal court in a French town called **Avignon**. From 1309 to

THE PAPAL PALACE IN AVIGNON

1377, the papacy resided in Avignon. This period is sometimes called the **Babylonian Captivity of the Papacy** or the **Avignonese Captivity**. Seven popes reigned at the papal court in Avignon, all of whom were French.

God's Judgments in Europe: The Black Death

For the time has come for judgment to begin at the house of God; and if it begins with us first, what will be the end of those who do not obey the gospel of God? (1 Pet. 4:17)

While the papacy resided in Avignon, the Lord's terrible judgments fell upon Europe in the mid-1300s. The horrific plague of this period is known in history as the **Black Death**. In God's providence, traders imported more than just treasures from the East. They unknowingly carried to European ports rats infested with plague-ridden fleas. The Black Death began its march of destruction through Europe in 1347. The plague killed tens of millions of people. Historians are divided on what percentage of Europe's population died during the epidemic. Estimates vary from between one third and one half of the entire European population. There is no way to know the exact number. But firsthand accounts from this period certainly reinforce a very high percentage. No war has ever claimed so many lives as the Black Death. This plague was among the deadliest epidemics in world history.

The plague may have spread as the Mongols expanded their trade routes across Asia to the city of Constantinople. In addition, European traders brought disease into the docks of Genoa, Naples, Venice in Italy, Marseilles in France, and other Mediterranean port cities. Merchants from these cities unknowingly took the plague home with them and infected their families. For people in northern Europe such as England, the plague remained far away for a time. News reports came from southern Europe about the terrible plague, but people hoped it would not reach the shores of Great Britain. Eventually, however, it did. There was almost no part of Europe that was untouched by the deadly pestilence.

The Black Death was the bubonic plague, a disease that gets its name from the swelling of the lymph nodes or buboes. It was called the "black death" because of the black blotches which appeared on the skin. The disease was initially transmitted to humans by fleas from infected rats, not from human contact. The Black Plague later affected the lungs and changed to "pneumonic plague," spreading rapidly from person to

BURYING VICTIMS OF THE BLACK DEATH

person without the need of fleas as carriers. The death rate was so high that at times there weren't enough people left alive to bury all the dead. Half the population died in Avignon, France, where the pope lived. The pope consecrated the Rhine River to permit corpses to be thrown into it for a mass burial. One chronicler in one of the English monasteries described his experience this way:

> This plague slew Jew, Christian, and Muslim alike. It filled the whole world with terror. So great an epidemic has never been seen nor heard of before this time, for it is believed that even the waters of the flood which happened in the days of Noah did not carry off so vast a multitude.[2]

The Black Death did not kill nearly the percentage of people that Noah's flood did (100% except for Noah and his family). However, this contemporary account does give us a sense of how dire the times were. After 1350, the plague in Europe began to abate. Nevertheless, outbreaks of the bubonic plague would continue to appear occasionally in the centuries that followed. The Black Death was a world-changing calamity to the peoples of the Western church. It is noteworthy that it took place at a time when the church was bitterly divided and when the highest ranks of leadership in the church were so corrupt.

The Papal Schism

For you are still carnal. For where there are envy, strife, and divisions among you, are you not carnal and behaving like mere men? For when one says, "I am of Paul," and another, "I am of Apollos," are you not carnal? (1 Cor. 3:3-4)

In 1377, the papacy returned to Rome during the papacy of **Gregory XI** (r. 1370-1378). But within a year of the return to Rome, Gregory XI died. The French cardinals wanted the papacy returned to Avignon. But the people of Rome wanted an Italian pope. Pope Urban VI (r. 1378-1389) was then elected. Urban desired to free the papacy from French control. Shortly after Urban became pope, many cardinals contested Urban's election, and they then chose another Frenchman as pope, Clement VII (r. 1378-1394). The French cardinals condemned Urban VI with the strongest words imaginable, calling him "apostate, anathema, Antichrist, and the mocker and destroyer of Christianity." Words like these did not help in restoring unity.

Clement returned to Avignon to establish his papal court there. Urban VI stayed in Rome and continued to claim the title of pope. Now there was a division between those who followed Clement and those who followed Urban. There were two popes who claimed universal supremacy over the church. Each pope denied the claim of the other, and they each excommunicated one another. As a result, Europe was split in two. This division continued for some forty years.

Corruption at the papal court of Avignon was well known. For example, the Italian poet **Dante** (1265-1321) said of Clement V and his successor John XXII in Avignon, "In garb of pastors ravening wolves are seen from here above in all the pastures." Another Italian poet, Petrarch (1304-1374), called Avignon the sewer of the earth.[3]

The Avignon popes were in many ways captive to French interests and did not leave a reputation of faithful leadership.

The Conciliar Movement

The Papal Schism produced a crisis for the church. With no higher authority to resolve the dispute between the Avignon and Roman popes, the church remained divided. Leaders and thinkers now proposed a way forward to resolve the division. At the University of Paris, theologians such as **Peter d'Ailly** (1350-1420) and **John Gerson** (1363-1429), among others, proposed that a whole church council (known as an ecumenical council) be held to resolve the matter. These men believed that the pope was not infallible. Instead they argued that the church as a whole, gathered in council, would act infallibly. The pope was accountable to the church as a whole instead of the whole church being accountable to the pope.

As you can see, the teaching of these theologians was in direct contradiction to the claim of the papal bull where Boniface stated, "We declare, state, define and pronounce that it is absolutely necessary to salvation for every human being to be subject to the Roman pope."[4] Instead, these theologians argued that the pope was subject to the church as a whole. This movement, begun at the University of Paris, became known as the **conciliar movement**. It is known as the conciliar movement because it prioritized the authority of church councils.

Three major councils would assemble to solve the fracture. Those three councils are the **Council of Pisa** (1409), the **Council of Constance** (1414), and the **Council of Basel** (1431). The first counsel was held in 1409 in the town of Pisa. The Council of Pisa was assembled by the authority of the cardinals alone. The result was the deposition (or removal) of both existing popes in Avignon and Rome. Then the council elected a new pope, Alexander V (r. 1409-1410). But rather than solving the division, now there were three men who claimed the office of pope! England and France received the council's decision and supported Alexander V. But other countries remained allied with the existing Avignon and Roman popes. The schism that had divided Europe into two parts now fractured further into three.

The next council was held in the town of Constance (on the modern-day border of Germany and Switzerland). Another attempt to heal the divisions was made. For four years (1414-1418),

CATHEDRAL OF PISA

LAKE CONSTANCE, GERMANY. THE COUNCIL OF CONSTANCE WAS HELD NEAR THE LAKE.

the council met and deliberated. It was a massive undertaking. Contemporary records preserved for us by a man named Ulrich von Richental describe the scope of this meeting. Richental listed the following attendees for the Council of Constance:

- 38 cardinals and patriarchs
- 285 bishops and archbishops
- 1,978 teachers of theology and law
- 530 priests and scholars

In addition to these clergymen, a few monarchs and other key civil leaders attended the council as well. Richental estimated that in the course of the council's meetings, some 70,000 people came and went from the town of Constance to participate in the council.

A key statement of the conciliar movement view is found in the council's own words explaining its authority.

> This sacred synod of Constance declares, in the first place, that it forms a general council, legitimately assembled in the Holy Spirit and representing the Catholic Church Militant, that it has its power immediately from Christ, and that all men, of every rank and position including even the pope himself, are bound to obey it in those matters that pertain to the faith, the extirpation of the said schism, and the reformation of the said church in head and members.[5]

The council's attempt to heal the division was successful. The council persuaded the Roman pope (Gregory XII) to resign. Then the council deposed the Avignon pope (Benedict XIII). Then, once again, a new pope was chosen to replace the existing ones. Pope Martin V (r. 1417-1431) was elected. The various nations of Europe decided to back the decision of the council, and the division was healed.

Even though it was through the councils that the new pope was elected, Pope Martin V began to assert his authority against the councils. His successor, Pope Eugenius IV (r. 1431-1447), attempted to stop the Council of Basel (1431) from doing its work, but it refused to submit to the pope. The council continued to meet in different locations from 1431 to 1449, attempting to bring reform to the church.

Pope Eugenius continued to oppose the

council, and eventually the council attempted to depose Pope Eugenius IV and replace him with a new pope, Felix VI (r. 1439-1449). But by this time, the council had lost credibility with many in Europe, and their decision to replace Pope Eugenius was not widely accepted. One of the reasons Pope Eugenius prevailed is because he had established a reunion with the Eastern Greek church in 1439. The Greek church made this agreement not because they were truly doctrinally in agreement with the Roman Church. Rather, it seems that some leaders of the Greek church and the ailing Byzantine Empire made this agreement, known as the **Union of Florence**, out of expediency. They needed military support to resist the advances of the Muslim Turks in the East. This agreement only lasted for a few years. The Turks captured Constantinople in 1453, putting an end to the Byzantine Empire. The Greeks then rejected the Union of Florence. It did not ultimately heal the schism of 1054 between the Eastern and Western churches.

PARTICIPANTS IN THE COUNCIL OF CONSTANCE

After the Council of Basel was disbanded in 1449, the conciliar movement lost strength. And the papacy continued in Rome, now no longer with any competing claims. The conciliar movement, though it was short-lived, brought some balance to the claims of the pope. However, there was a glaring omission in the authority disputes of the 1300s and 1400s. Supporters of the conciliar movement claimed supreme authority for church councils. Popes claimed supreme authority for their office. But where were those Christians who held to the supreme authority of God's Holy Word?

There were only a few voices calling the church back to the supreme authority of Holy Scripture. One of them was **John Huss** (c. 1370-1415). He was executed at the Council of Constance. Another voice calling the church to return to Scripture was **John Wycliffe** (c. 1328-1384). Though Wycliffe had already died in 1384, the Council of Constance declared him to be a heretic. An order was made to exhume Wycliffe's remains from church grounds and have them burned and scattered into the River Swift in Lutterworth, England. The conciliar movement was no friend to these early reformers. It would take another generation of reformers, during the Protestant Reformation, to recover and proclaim God's Word as the supreme authority in Christ's church. ▪

JOHN HUSS (C. 1370-1415)

NOTRE DAME CATHEDRAL, LYONS, FRANCE

Reform Efforts in the Middle Ages

15

Your testimonies are wonderful;
Therefore my soul keeps them.
The entrance of Your words gives light;
It gives understanding to the simple.
(Ps. 119:129-130)

There were numerous attempts to reform and purify the church during the Middle Ages. For example, in a previous chapter we saw how Hildebrand and the Cluniac movement in general sought to purify the church of corruption. In the centuries leading up to the Protestant Reformation of the 1500s, several reform-minded leaders arose who established movements that made a considerable impact on certain regions of Europe.

The Cathars, studied in a previous chapter, sought purity, but they did so by embracing heresy and departing from the faith once for all delivered to the saints. However, there were other leaders and movements that moved the church in the direction of biblical reformation. In this chapter, we will look at three major reform events begun by three men: Peter Waldo, John Wycliffe, and John Huss. In each of these three movements, the recovery of the Bible as God's authoritative Word was a central issue.

Peter Waldo and the Waldensian Movement

The Waldensian movement began in the city of Lyons (pronounced "Lee-own"). In 1170, a wealthy merchant named Pierre Valdes lived in Lyons. Pierre's name is often written in English as **Peter Waldo** (c. 1140-1205). Little is known about this man. But there is a traditional story concerning Peter Waldo's spiritual awakening.

One day, one of the leading men of Lyons died unexpectedly. This sudden passing awakened Waldo. It reminded him that life is short and that he could die at any time. He consulted a priest. "What should I do to follow Christ?" he asked. The priest read to Waldo the account of the rich young ruler in the Bible. In that story, the Lord Jesus told the rich young ruler to sell all that he had and to follow Him.

Jesus said to him, "If you want to be perfect, go, sell what you have and give to the poor, and you will have treasure in heaven; and come, follow Me." (Matt. 19:21)

Waldo followed the priest's counsel. He distributed his goods to the poor. He began to read the Bible. He commissioned a few men to translate parts of the Gospels into the common tongue spoken in Lyons. He was burdened to share the word of Christ with others. Waldo began preaching in the streets of Lyons. Soon, others joined him in a life of poverty and preaching. The movement grew rapidly.

From the beginning, the Waldensian movement had three common characteristics: poverty, preaching, and obedience to the word of Christ. Those following

STATUE OF PETER WALDO

Waldo became known as "the poor of Lyons." The Waldensians retained this title for centuries. Others called them "Waldensians." However, it took a few hundred years before the Waldensians used this name themselves. They did not wish to be called by the name of one man.

The Waldensians were considered strange and dangerous by many. Authorities in Lyons and in the surrounding region began to oppose them. During that time, men who were part of the priesthood were the only ones who were allowed to preach. It was not lawful for anyone else to proclaim the Bible in a public place. Additionally, the church considered it inappropriate for laypeople to read and interpret the Bible for themselves. The Waldensians did not submit to these rules. Both Waldensian men and women proclaimed the Bible in the streets. They also translated and shared portions of the Bible with the common people.

Eventually, local authorities commanded Peter Waldo to stop preaching. But he refused to submit. He, with his other followers, believed it to be their obligation to keep on preaching. Because he refused to submit, Peter Waldo was excommunicated from the church in 1182. Then, at the **Council of Verona** in 1184, all Waldensians were declared to be heretics. In the church's eyes, the Waldensians were just as bad as the Cathars. After the declaration of 1184, things became more difficult and dangerous for the Waldensians.

Waldensian Beliefs and Practices

What did the Waldensians believe? Were they true Christians? Or did they reject the true faith like the Cathars?

The Waldensians loved to read and memorize the Bible. Peter Waldo and his followers believed the Bible was the final and only infallible authority. Because of this, their beliefs and practices were often faithful to Scripture. But they did have some wrong beliefs too. They tended to emphasize the New Testament more than the Old Testament. Women preached, at least at first. Also, the Waldensians did not always have access to the entirety of the Bible in their native language. Because of this, they sometimes were wrong about certain doctrines. The Protestant Reformation (in the 1500s) brought further progress in understanding the Bible.

The Waldensians did see that many Roman Catholic beliefs were in error. They rejected many Roman Catholic teachings, including the authority of the pope, purgatory, prayers for the dead, and indulgences.

The Waldensians also held other unique views. They refused to take oaths of any kind. They believed that Jesus forbids Christians to take oaths when He said:

Again you have heard that it was said to those of old, "You shall not swear falsely, but shall perform your oaths to the Lord." But I say to you, do not swear at all. (Matt. 5:33-34)

Some of the things the Waldensians believed were not correct. Not all of their practices and doctrines had firm, Biblical rooting. However, their respect for Scripture was noteworthy

ENTRANCE TO WALDENSIAN CHURCH IN ROME

PIEDMONT, ITALY

and commendable in its time. In many ways, the Waldensian movement was a precursor to the Protestant Reformation.

Persecution and Dispersion of the Waldensians

Waldensian teaching spread far and wide from Lyons. It spread to Languedoc, Spain, Austria, and Germany. After the Cathars, the Waldensian movement was the second-largest movement to separate from the Roman Church.

The Roman Church did not see much difference between the Waldensians and the Cathars. They saw them as equally dangerous. Both Cathars and Waldensians were a threat to the pope's authority. During crusades against the Cathars, many Waldensians were caught up in the bloodbath and executed. Eventually, the Cathars were mostly wiped out. But by God's sovereign protection, the Waldensians still exist to this day.

After most of the Cathars were wiped out, church leaders turned their attention to the Waldensians. They were now the primary target. As persecution increased, the Waldensians fled for safety. If the Waldensians were to survive, they needed a place of refuge. Many of them hid in the rocky crags of the Alps in northern Italy. The region of northern Italy known as **Piedmont** became the center of the Waldensian community. To this day, there are many Waldensians still living in the Piedmont region.

For over three hundred years, the Waldensians faced persecution from the Roman Church and state authorities. Sometimes they were ignored, and they would increase for a generation or so. But eventually, they were to face another assault. In 1487, another pope named Innocent VIII (pope from 1484-1492) planned to wipe them out. Inspired by his predecessor Innocent III (pope from 1198-1216), he called for another attack on the Waldensians living in Piedmont. Again, a great many were killed. Waldensians were scattered as far as the Netherlands, Germany, Poland, Bohemia (modern-day Czech Republic), and England. Eventually, reformation would occur in these same areas in the 1500s. The Waldensians themselves would come to embrace the teachings of the Reformation and unite with the Protestants in the 1500s.

John Wycliffe

Oh, send out Your light and Your truth!
Let them lead me;
Let them bring me to Your holy hill
And to Your tabernacle. (Ps. 43:3)

In the mid-1300s, a sliver of light dawned in England. In the university town of Oxford, a man named **John Wycliffe** (c. 1328-1384) called God's people to read the Bible, preach the Bible, practice the Bible, and love the Bible. Wycliffe believed the church had gone astray on many matters of faith and practice. In order to equip the church to know the Bible, he labored to translate the Scriptures into English. Through writing, preaching, and translating, Wycliffe became known as "the morning star of the Reformation." He is known by this title because he prepared the way for the Protestant Reformation of the 1500s.

At age fifteen, Wycliffe attended Oxford to study. This was around the year 1345. He spent many years at Oxford. However, his studies were interrupted by the repeated waves of the Black Death. From 1349 to 1353, Oxford lost many of its residents to the dreaded plague. After graduating as a theology student, Wycliffe remained at Oxford. He spent his time teaching, writing, and preaching. He was also ordained a priest.

JOHN WYCLIFFE (C. 1328-1384)

As Wycliffe taught and preached, his views became increasingly different from the church of that age. Some considered what he was teaching to be heresy. Wycliffe was repeatedly summoned by civil and church authorities to answer for his doctrine. In February 1377, **Bishop Courtney** summoned Wycliffe to London. Courtney demanded Wycliffe give an answer for his views. But Wycliffe had many who supported him. Among those supporters was **John of Gaunt** (c. 1340-1399). This man was the son of King Edward III. John of Gaunt protected Wycliffe from any harm.

Only months later, in May 1377, **Pope Gregory XI** (pope from 1370-1378) commanded Wycliffe to appear in Rome. Wycliffe was charged with teaching false doctrine. But Wycliffe did not believe he had to obey the pope's demands. He refused to go. Even though he refused, the English authorities did not do anything about this. God protected Wycliffe.

A third attempt was made to stop Wycliffe. In January 1378, the archbishop of Canterbury sought to hold a trial to condemn Wycliffe. But a large mob supporting Wycliffe put a stop to the meeting. Wycliffe frequently condemned immoral leaders. This gained him popular support from English citizens. He became a national hero of sorts.

Wycliffe's Teachings

What was it that made John Wycliffe so controversial? Why did popes and other church leaders condemn him? The answer can be found by examining Wycliffe's teachings. Wycliffe's sermons and writings taught the truth of the Scriptures even when this truth contradicted what the church of his day was teaching. Much of what he taught would make its appearance again during the Protestant Reformation.

As we learned in the previous chapter, in 1378

JOHN WYCLIFFE READING HIS BIBLE TRANSLATION TO JOHN OF GAUNT

a significant event in church history occurred. Today it is called the **Papal Schism** or the **Western Schism**. The word "schism" means a "division." In that momentous year, Pope Gregory XI died. To replace Gregory, two different popes were elected. Urban VI was one of them. He resided in Rome. The second man who claimed to be pope was Clement VII. He resided in Avignon, France. Thus, for a time, there were two men claiming the single office of pope. Kings and nations took sides and chose whomever they believed to be the true pope. Some followed Urban VI. Others followed Clement VII.

Such division and confusion gave Wycliffe a unique opportunity. Soon after Gregory died, Wycliffe wrote a book called *The Truth of Holy Scripture*. In this book, he argued that the Bible was the only infallible source of truth for Christian faith and practice. Since the Bible is God's Word, it should judge the teachings of popes and councils. Popes shouldn't decide what is right; the Bible should decide this. In the Medieval church, this order was often reversed. Often, popes and councils trumped Scripture in practice.

Since Wycliffe so revered God's Word, it is natural that he wanted to translate the Bible into English. At the time, portions of the Bible were available in English, but no complete translation existed. To remedy this, Wycliffe began translating the Latin version of the Bible into English. (This Latin Bible is known as the **Latin Vulgate**.) Wycliffe did not finish translating the entire Bible. But his followers, called **Lollards**, continued the translation work. The most important of these translations was completed by Wycliffe's secretary John Purvey in 1395. Below are a few verses from Wycliffe's Bible. On the left is the 1395 English translation. On the right is a modern English translation of the same verses.

Can you spot the similarities in these translations? What words are the same? What words are different? As you can see, English has changed

Matthew 5:3-6	
Wycliffe Bible (1395)	**New King James Version (1982)**
Blessed ben pore men in spirit, for the kyngdom of hevenes is herne.	Blessed are the poor in spirit, For theirs is the kingdom of heaven.
Blessid ben thei that mornen, for thei schulen be coumfortid.	Blessed are those who mourn, For they shall be comforted.
Blessid ben mylde men, for thei schulen welde the erthe.	Blessed are the meek, For they shall inherit the earth.
Blessid ben thei that hungren and thristen riytwisnesse, for thei schulen be fulfillid.	Blessed are those who hunger and thirst for righteousness, For they shall be filled.

since 1395. However, the foundational translation work of Wycliffe was a steppingstone for future translations. During the Reformation period, English Bible translation would be furthered by **William Tyndale** (1494-1536).

By making the Bible more available to English citizens, Wycliffe's translation enabled ordinary Christians to examine the church's teachings and practices. Were those teachings and practices consistent with God's Word? Or was the church in error? As God's Word began to be read by more people, many concluded with Wycliffe that the church was in grave error.

The Lollards

Whatever I tell you in the dark, speak in the light; and what you hear in the ear, preach on the housetops. And do not fear those who kill the body but cannot kill the soul. But rather fear Him who is able to destroy both soul and body in hell. (Matt. 10:27-28)

THE BURNING OF JOHN OLDCASTLE

After Wycliffe went to be with the Lord, his followers were scattered throughout England. They took with them portions of Scripture in English, and they sometimes had short tracts written by Wycliffe. Over time, they became known as **Lollards**. The exact meaning of this word is debated, but most believe it means something like "mumbler" or someone who "lolled." The name was not meant as a compliment. Many would have rejected the open-air preaching of the Lollards as just a bunch of "mumbling."

For decades after Wycliffe's death, the Lollards kept on with their "mumbling." Wycliffe's teaching and his translations of the Bible touched every part of England to some degree or another. Lollards preached in the open and gained many followers. Sometimes local church leaders would have Lollards arrested and punished. But for many years, the Lollards got away with much of their activity. By the early 1400s, more opposition against the Lollards arose. Open-air preaching was more often suppressed. Some Lollards were executed. One particular English nobleman named **Sir John Oldcastle** (1378-1417) was a leader among the Lollards. When Oldcastle staged a rebellion against the king in 1414, he gave the Lollards a bad reputation. Oldcastle was executed in 1417. After that time, the Lollard movement largely went underground.

From 1417 until the time of the Reformation, "Lollardy" continued as a quiet but always present movement in England. Most Lollards passed on their teaching in private house meetings. Lollard teaching was also passed on from generation to generation by parents who taught their children. They were a people dedicated to knowing and applying the Bible. When the Reformation took England by storm, many of the Lollards joined the reformation efforts.

John Huss

And when they say to you, "Seek those who are mediums and wizards, who whisper and mutter," should not a people seek their God? Should they seek the dead on behalf of the living? To the law and to the testimony! If they do not speak according to this word, it is because there is no light in them. (Isa. 8:19-20)

JOHN HUSS (C. 1370-1415)

On June 10, 1415, the Czech preacher John Huss (c. 1370-1415) wrote a letter to his own people. Huss was in prison in the city of Constance awaiting trial. The Council of Constance was being held there. The council was examining Huss' teaching. Huss had been charged with numerous heresies, and he knew his life was in danger.

Writing on June 10, Huss exhorted his people:

> Faithful and beloved of God, lords and ladies, rich and poor! I entreat you and exhort you to love God, to spread abroad His word, and to hear and observe it more willingly. I entreat you to hold fast the truth of God, which I have written and preached to you from the Holy Scriptures and the utterances of His saints. I entreat you also, if any have heard in my preaching or private conversation that which is opposed to God's truth, or if I have ever written anything of that kind—I trust God that it is not so—not to hold to it. I entreat you, if any have noticed frivolity in my words or actions, not to imitate it, but to pray God that it may please Him to pardon me. . . . I write this letter to you in prison, bound with chains and expecting on the morrow the sentence of death, yet fully trusting in God that I shall not swerve from His truth nor swear denial of the errors whereof I have been charged by false witnesses. What grace God has shown me, and how He helps me in the midst of strange temptations, you will know when by His mercy we meet in joy in His presence.[1]

Huss' final letters from prison tell us much about this man's faith. Huss was a man committed to the truth of God's Word. He was a man of principle. He was a man of courage. And he was a humble man.

About one month later, on July 6, 1415, John Huss was condemned to death by the **Council of Constance**. He was burned at the stake for

BETHLEHEM CHAPEL, PRAGUE

his refusal to renounce his belief in the truth of the Word of God. By his death, Huss left behind an impactful testimony that has created ripple effects in the history of Christ's church ever since.

To understand why it was that Huss gave up his life on July 6, 1415, we must review the rest of his story. We must journey from Constance back to the Bohemian capital of Prague (today the capital of the Czech Republic). There in **Prague**, at the university and in the **Bethlehem Chapel**, Huss became a leader among his people.

The Ministry of Huss in Prague

It was through a royal marriage that a unique tie between England and Bohemia was formed. **King Richard II** of England married **Anne of Luxembourg**. Anne happened to be the sister of the king of Bohemia. (Today, the region of Bohemia is known as the Czech Republic.) After this marriage, students from Bohemia made the journey to England to study in the universities of England. This took place in the mid-1300s.

ENGLAND, BOHEMIA, AND FRANCE, LOCATIONS OF MAJOR REFORM MOVEMENTS DURING THE MIDDLE AGES

At this time, **John Wycliffe** was a professor in the University of Oxford. As we've seen, Wycliffe was a controversial figure in his time. Many of his teachings were similar to the teachings of the Protestant Reformers of the 1500s.

As Bohemian students returned to their native land, many brought Wycliffe's teachings back with them. Soon, Wycliffe's controversial writings were in Bohemia as well. In the early 1400s, John Huss began to read Wycliffe's writings and was influenced by them. Starting in 1402, Huss was appointed preacher in the Bethlehem Chapel in Prague.

The Bethlehem Chapel was established in 1391 by two men who were passionate for preaching God's Word in the Czech language. It was called Bethlehem Chapel because it was to be a place where the Bohemians were fed with the bread of God's Word. "Bethlehem" in Hebrew means "house of bread."

For over a decade, Huss preached God's Word in the Bethlehem Chapel. The effect of his teaching and preaching was monumental. Huss became a beloved leader among the people of Prague. As Huss studied the Bible and read the writings of Wycliffe, his views began to change. Wycliffe's commitment to the supreme authority of the Bible deeply influenced Huss. In time, Huss developed the same commitment. He became a man who submitted his life to the authority of God's Book.

The doctrine of transubstantiation taught that the bread and wine of the Lord's Supper become the physical body and blood of Christ. When transubstantiation became the predominant view of the Western church in the 1200s, the people were no longer allowed to drink the communion wine for fear of spilling Christ's blood. They were only allowed to eat the bread. Huss insisted that the people partake of communion in both kinds.

The time for reform in the church

JOHN HUSS AT THE COUNCIL OF CONSTANCE

was ripe. The unity of the church in Europe was being torn asunder. The Papal Schism led to a strange situation. For a time, then, three rival popes all claimed to be the head of the Roman Catholic Church. This conflict and division made it clear that the church needed reform. Besides this division, the church was also filled with moral corruption. Ungodly priests, bishops, and popes brought reproach upon the name of Christ because of their wicked lives.

Huss' zeal for reform resonated with the Bohemian people. Huss' bold preaching and godly character won the hearts of the Bohemians. Even **King Wenceslas** (reigned 1378-1419) supported Huss' leadership in Prague. Huss became a national leader of sorts for the Bohemian people.

The Council of Constance

In 1414, Huss was summoned to the Council of Constance. He knew that traveling to Constance could result in his death. But he was promised a safe conduct. This meant that no one would harm him at the council. The brother of King Wenceslas, **Emperor Sigismund** (r. 1410-1437), promised Huss safe conduct. Before departing Bohemia, Huss prepared his will in case he didn't return.

Upon arriving in Constance, the emperor's promise was shown to be empty. Huss was quickly imprisoned. For over half a year, Huss suffered in various prisons in Constance, awaiting trial. While in prison, he suffered numerous physical maladies and almost died several times due to illness. However, he did what he could to continue his ministry through letter writing.

In June and July 1415, Huss was brought before church and civil authorities repeatedly. He was pressured to renounce his teachings. He was also falsely accused. Just what was it that Huss was accused of?

On some matters, Huss was indeed "guilty" of teaching certain doctrines that were considered heresy. Huss taught that immoral and wicked clergy should not be followed if they lead God's people astray. In this way, Huss challenged the authority of the church. He even argued that the pope could be disobeyed if the pope was not following God's Word. The authorities at the council believed it was heresy to submit the authority of the church to the rule of God's Word. For Huss to elevate the Scriptures to the role of supreme authority was a central issue.

Huss was also accused of being a "Wycliffite." This meant that he was accused of following the teachings of John Wycliffe, who was seen as a heretic. To make Huss appear heretical, false witnesses were brought in. Some accused Huss of teaching that there were more than three persons in the Godhead. Huss was accused of adding to the Trinity a fourth person. And the false witnesses claimed that fourth person was Huss himself! To this charge, Huss protested vigorously. He argued he had never taught such a blasphemous doctrine. He explained he had always taught that there is one God eternally existing in three persons.

A verdict was soon reached. Huss was declared guilty of heretical teaching. He was also declared guilty of refusing to submit to the church's authority. The sentence was death. When the verdict was read, Huss fell to his knees and prayed to God. He prayed that Christ, out of His great mercy, would pardon his enemies. As Huss prayed, the council sneered at him.

The bishops surrounded Huss and stripped him of his priestly robes. They also took a chalice they had put in his hands and said, "O cursed Judas, who has spurned the counsels of peace and have taken counsel with the Jews, we take from you this cup of redemption." Symbolically, they were saying that Christ's blood would not save Huss.

Huss was not silent. He replied, "My trust is in the Lord God Almighty, for whose name I patiently suffer this blasphemy, for He will not take away from me the cup of His redemption. And I firmly hope that today I shall drink it in His kingdom."

Then, a paper cap of eighteen inches height was placed upon Huss' head. The cap had three demons pictured on it. Each of the three demons were tugging at a man's soul. The word "heresiarch" was also written on the cap. This word means "founder of a heresy." The bishops then proclaimed, "We commit your soul to the devil."

Huss raised his hands to heaven and said, "And I commit it to my most gracious Lord, Jesus Christ. The crown my Savior wore on His most sacred head was heavy and irksome. The one I wear is easy and light. He wore a crown of thorns even to the most awful death. And I will wear this much lighter one humbly for the sake of His name and the truth."

Huss was led to the stake where he would be burned. Kneeling before his execution, he prayed, "Lord Jesus Christ, I wish to bear most patiently and humbly for Your Gospel's sake and the preaching of Your Word, this dire, ignominious, and cruel death."

Huss was bound to the stake with chains as the wood was placed underneath him. Looking at the executioners, Huss spoke, "The Lord Jesus Christ, my Redeemer, was bound with a harder chain, and I, a miserable sinner, am not afraid to bear this one, bound as I am for His name's sake." Having said these words, Huss died in the flames as he commended his soul to God.[2]

The Moravians

John Huss' earthly life ended at the Council of Constance in 1415. But his legacy lived on. He left behind him many committed disciples in Bohemia called Hussites. When news of Huss' death reached Bohemia, there was great indignation. In 1419, Emperor Sigismund, the man who had broken his safe conduct to kill Huss, tried to become king of Bohemia and suppress the Hussites. Many of the Czech nobles and people joined the Hussites and fought against Sigismund. The Hussites were attacked

by the forces of surrounding countries, and the pope even called for a crusade against them. But, led by their brilliant general Jan Zizka, the Hussites successfully defended themselves and defeated their enemies over and over again.

Unable to defeat the Hussites, the Roman Catholic authorities agreed to compromise with them. The Council of Basel in 1433 allowed the Hussites to restore the communion cup to the people and conduct worship services in the Czech language rather than in Latin. Some of the Hussites became known as the **Bohemian Brethren** or the **Moravian Brethren**. Like the Waldenses and Lollards, the Hussites joined the Protestant Reformation in the 1500s. Later, the Moravians would become a missionary-sending movement. ■

JOHN HUSS MEMORIAL IN PRAGUE

AD 1453
Fall of Constantinople

AD 1455
The Gutenberg Bible Printed

AD 1484
Martin Luther Born

AD 1492
Expulsion of Jews from Spain

AD 1516
Erasusmus' *Novum Instrumentum* Published

AD 1517
The Protestant Reformation Begins

AD 1556
Martyrdom of Thomas Cranmer

AD 1558
Death of Bloody Mary

AD 1559
Pope Paul IV Issues the *Index Librorum Prohibitorum*

AD 1560
First Edition of the *Geneva Bible* Published

AD 1560
Treaty of Edinburgh

AD 1572
St. Bartholomew's Day Massacre

Unit 4

The Reformation (AD 1500-1600)

AD 1519
Zwingli Begins to Preach Reform in the Grossmünster Church

AD 1521
The Diet of Worms

AD 1523
Zwingli Releases His 67 Articles

AD 1531
War Between the Swiss Cantons

AD 1533
Thomas Cranmer Appointed as Archbishop of Canterbury

AD 1534
Tyndale Translates and Prints the English New Testament

AD 1536
Martyrdom of William Tyndale

AD 1538
Authorization of Reading the Bible in English By King Henry VIII

AD 1540
Jesuits Founded by Ignatius Loyola

AD 1545-1563
Council of Trent

AD 1555-1558
Persecution Under Bloody Mary

AD 1555
Martyrdom of Nicholas Ridley and Hugh Latimer

THE CHURCH OF ST. MICHAEL DE RUPE, DARTMOOR

The Dawn of Reformation

16

Then Jesus spoke to them again, saying, "I am the light of the world. He who follows Me shall not walk in darkness, but have the light of life." (John 8:12)

In the previous chapter, we discussed some forerunners to the Protestant Reformation including the Waldensians, Wycliffe and the Lollards, and John Huss and the Moravians who followed after him. All of these reform movements in the late Middle Ages showed that the church was in serious need of change.

The conciliar movement also saw the need to reform the church. The Council of Constance did heal some division in the church, but it did not address the underlying spiritual needs of the church. The papacy was restored to its dominance, but it continued its corrupting influence. The corruption of covetousness, sexual immorality, and violence appeared often in the leaders of both church and state. The councils attempted reformation but made little progress. It was also the aim of monastic orders to seek reform and purity for the church. The earlier Cluniac reforms were one example of this.

Nevertheless, the church in the West was still in dire need of widespread reformation. The Waldensians, Lollards, and Moravians had each in their own way, laid foundations for the Protestant Reformation. Reformers like **Martin Luther**, **Ulrich Zwingli**, **John Calvin**, and others would build on these foundations as they began to preach and teach the Bible anew.

The Reformation is one of the most exciting periods of church history. Here in this period, we see much of God's wonderful works on display. The Lord made His face shine upon the church. The grace of God, as revealed in the gospel, was once again made known to the people of God. The Lord graciously provided greater access to His Word through faithful translations into the common languages of Europe.

However, times of revival in Christ's church do not come without controversy or conflict. Such was the case during the Reformation as well. The division between Protestants and Roman Catholics was intense. Additionally, various heretical movements also sprang up. Some, believing that the Reformation was not going far enough, established what became known as the **Anabaptist** movement. As the various kingdoms of Europe took their stand for Romanism or Protestantism, armed conflicts in some cases ensued.

Despite the many challenges of this period, the Lord brought abundant blessings to the church through it. The Protestant Reformers recovered and relaid biblical foundations for the church. The recovery of Scriptural teaching and the return to the teachings of the apostolic and early church strengthened Christ's church. Not only did the Reformation dramatically impact the church in the West, but it continues to impact the world today. Protestant churches of various denominations have sent missionaries all over the world. The Bible has been distributed throughout the world more than ever before.

Before turning to the story of Martin Luther and the beginning of the Reformation in 1517, it is important for us to understand some important historical background of this period.

Efforts at Reform during the Middle Ages

Let's review what we learned about reform efforts during the Middle Ages. One of the earliest movements of reform was led by the Waldensians. The Waldensians held many teachings in common with the later Protestant Reformers. They believed

JOHANN GUTENBERG (C. 1393-1468)

PRINTING PRESS

that God's Word should be accessible to every Christian. They also preached the Bible in many European towns until they were persecuted and isolated. However, the Waldensians, due to their emphasis upon the New Testament primarily (to the neglect of the Old Testament), sometimes lacked a fuller biblical understanding.

In the 14th and 15th centuries, John Wycliffe and John Huss made an impact upon England and Bohemia. Both men inspired a following. The Lollards continued Wycliffe's work. The Hussites or Moravians maintained Huss' teachings. Wycliffe and Huss were even closer in their perspectives to the later Protestant Reformers. But the progress of their followers was limited, even though both the Lollards and Hussites continued as small and sometimes covert movements.

The desire for a purer church was not limited to these reform movements. The average person in Europe was aware of the church's corruption to some degree or another. But for many people, the issue was a *moral* issue. Most people did not see the doctrine of the church as being in error.

But the Waldensians, Lollards, and Hussites pointed out numerous doctrinal errors needing correction. They sought to correct these problems by returning to the Scriptures. This attempt to ground Christian doctrine and practice in the Scriptures led to the rejection of certain doctrines. These false doctrines included the papacy, veneration of the virgin Mary, purgatory, indulgences, and pilgrimages.

The Movable-Type Printing Press

An important invention was created in 1439. **Johann Gutenberg** (c. 1393-1468), a German printer, created a **movable-type printing press**. Compared to previous methods of printing, the movable-type format enabled Gutenberg and other printers who adopted this new technology to create books at a much faster and more efficient rate. Gutenberg's invention led to a printing revolution that swept across Europe. Literature became much more widely available. The invention of the printing press made it much easier for the Protestant Reformers to broadcast their message to the people of Europe.

In 1455, the **Gutenberg Bible** was printed. Around 180 copies were produced. Gutenberg's Bible was a printed edition of the common Latin version known as the Latin Vulgate. Gutenberg's beautiful production demonstrated how the new printing press could be used for the distribution of the Bible and other literature.

THE *GUTENBERG BIBLE*

Renaissance Humanism and the Recovery of Ancient Texts

The events surrounding the **Renaissance** (the French word for "rebirth") in Europe are important because they had an influence on the Protestant Reformation. The Renaissance and the Reformation were very different movements with different beliefs and goals. By and large, leaders of the Renaissance in Italy, France, and elsewhere were interested in recovering ancient art, literature, and philosophy from Greek and Roman times. Those engaged in the study of ancient literature and philosophy became known as **humanists**. This term was used because advocates of the Renaissance were studying the humanities or ancient productions of humans from earlier periods of Europe's history.

Humanist scholars devoted their attention to learning the Greek language to read classic Greek works such as the writings of Plato. Knowledge of Greek had faded in the West, though it was still a commonly used language in portions of the Eastern church. In addition to a study of the ancient Greek and Roman classics, humanist scholars were also interested in reading the Scriptures in their original languages. This meant a return to the study of the Hebrew Old Testament and the Greek New Testament. Humanists also devoted their attention to the writings of the early church fathers.

This renewed interest in ancient texts would be used for both good and ill. For the Reformers, this renewed access and interest in both the Scriptures and the church fathers provided them with tools to reform the church. For humanist scholars who elevated human learning and reason, it became a tool for apostasy from the Christian faith. In later chapters, we will learn about how some of the ideals of the Renaissance were continued in the so-called **Enlightenment** of the 17th and 18th centuries.

A slogan used by the humanist scholars was the Latin phrase *ad fontes*. This means "back to the sources." Humanist scholars wanted to return to the original sources that gave birth to Western Civilization. This goal of returning to the sources could be either helpful or harmful. It depended on the sources *that you went back to*. Would you return to the pagan writings of the Greeks and the Romans and their ideas? Or would you return to the earliest literature of the Christian church? The humanist movement of the Renaissance included a spectrum that included Christian "humanist" scholars (who devoted most of their study to the Scrip-

FLORENCE, ITALY, CONSIDERED THE BIRTHPLACE OF THE RENAISSANCE

tures and the early church fathers) and those that aligned more with a "secular humanist" approach by returning to the Greeks and Romans. In some cases, those humanist scholars sought to undermine the very foundations of the Christian faith.

But the recovery of the knowledge of the Hebrew and Greek languages in Europe would be key to the success of the Reformation. The Protestant Reformers would now have access to the Scriptures in the original languages in which they were written by God's inspiration. Several providential events made this possible.

DESIDERIUS ERASMUS (1466-1536)

In 1453, Constantinople fell to the Muslim Turks. The fall of the city caused many Greek scholars to flee west into Europe. They brought their knowledge of the Greek language and their Greek manuscripts west with them. In 1492, the same year that Christopher Columbus reached America, King Ferdinand and Queen Isabella expelled many Jews from Spain. The expelled Jews moved to other parts of Europe. They brought with them copies of the Hebrew Old Testament. This contributed to a revival of the study of Hebrew.

A man named **Johannes Reuchlin** (1455-1522) was especially significant in reviving the study of Hebrew, which he learned from the Jews. Reuchlin published both a Greek grammar and a Hebrew grammar. Many future Reformers studied under him. Reuchlin was the great uncle of the Reformer Philip Melanchthon. Sadly, Reuchlin fell into a type of occultic Jewish study called Kaballism. Despite this, Reuchlin's Hebrew studies played an important role in paving the way for the Reformation.

Another humanist scholar who was influential in giving birth to the Reformation was a man named **Desiderius Erasmus** (1466-1536). His publication of an edition of the Greek New Testament provided the Reformers with an important tool for reformation. Though Erasmus never fully joined the Reformation cause, he did agree with some of the concerns of the Reformers. Erasmus wrote against the immorality and corruption of the church by writing several important books. These works often got Erasmus into trouble with the church hierarchy, though he was never excommunicated. A good example of Erasmus' critiques can be seen in his work *Pope Julius Excluded from Heaven*. In this book, a fictional dialogue occurs between the warlike and immoral Pope Julius II (1503-1513) and Peter the Apostle at the gates of Heaven. Pope Julius II, who was claimed to be the successor of Peter the Apostle, as a pope, is in the story excluded from heaven due to his immorality. Here is a portion of Erasmus' satirical writing against Pope Julius II:

POPE JULIUS II (R. 1503-1513)

> **Julius:** What the devil is this? The doors don't open? Somebody must have changed the lock or broken it. Now I'm really getting mad; I'll knock the doors down. Ho! Ho! Somebody come and open this door right away! What's the hangup? nobody home? What's the matter with the doorman? He's asleep, I guess, or else drunk.
>
> **Peter:** A good thing our gates are of adamant, otherwise this one, whoever he is, would have kicked them in. He must be a giant of some sort, a general of the armies, a stormer of cities. But, what a sewer-stench is this! I certainly won't open the gates right away, but take a seat up here by a grated window where I can look out and keep an eye on the scene. Who are you and what do you want?
>
> **Julius:** Open the door, will you? at least, if you can. And if you were really doing your job, it should have been open long ago, and decorated with all the heraldry of heaven.
>
> **Peter:** Pretty lordly. But first tell me who you are.
>
> **Julius:** As if you couldn't see for yourself.
>
> **Peter:** See? What I see is new to me, like nothing I ever saw before, and I might say monstrous.
>
> **Julius:** But if you're not stone-blind, you're bound to recognize this key, even if you aren't familiar with the golden oak tree. You can certainly see my triple crown, as well as my cloak all gleaming with gold and gems.
>
> **Peter:** That silver key of yours I do recognize, though there's only one of them, and it's very different from those that were given to me long ago by the one true

shepherd of the church, that is, Christ. But that glorious crown of yours, how could I possibly recognize it? No tyrant ruling over barbarian peoples ever ventured to wear one like it, much less anyone who came here asking for admission. Your cloak doesn't impress me either; for I always used to consider gold and jewels as trash to be despised. But what does this amount to really? In all this stuff—the key, the crown, the cloak—I recognize marks of that rascally cheat and impostor who shared a name with me but not a faith, that scoundrel Simon whom I once flung down with the aid of Christ.

THE LAST PAGE OF ERASMUS' *NOVUM INSTRUMENTUM*, SHOWING THE LAST VERSES OF REVELATION

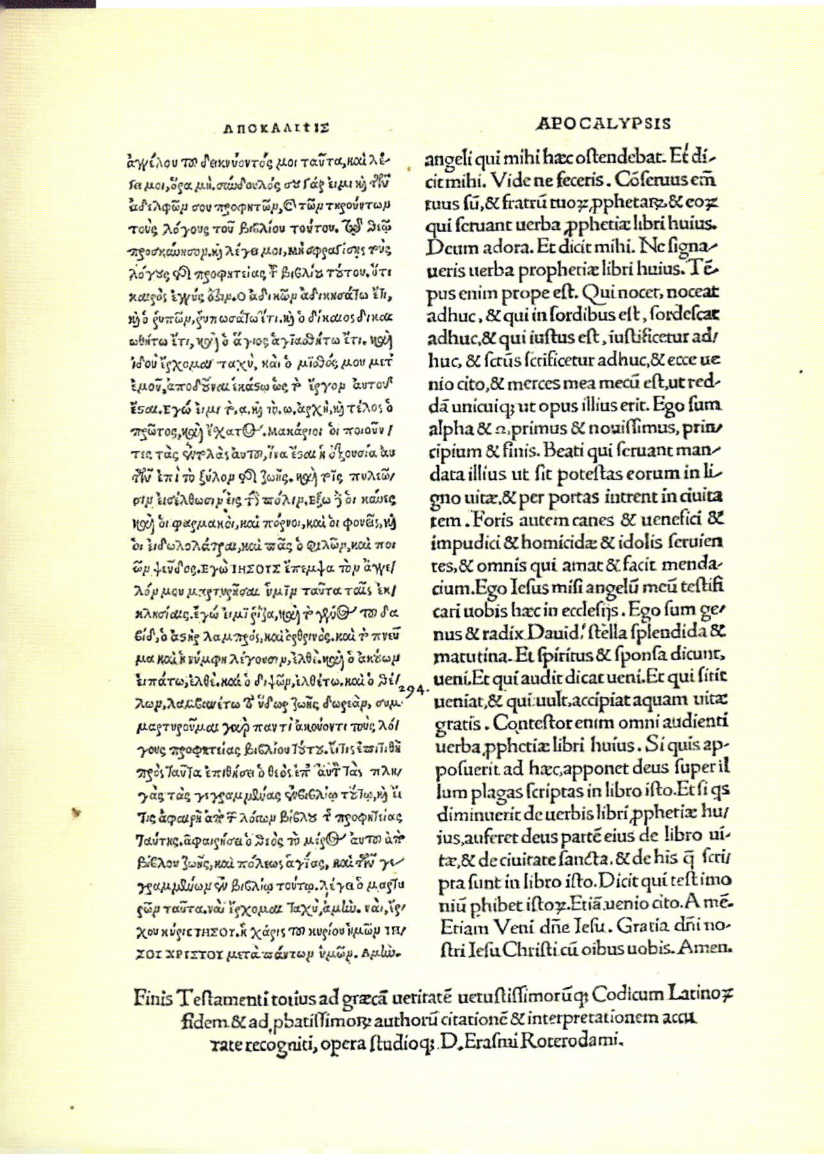
ΑΠΟΚΑΛΥΨΙΣ

APOCALYPSIS

angeli qui mihi hæc oſtendebat. Et dicit mihi. Vide ne feceris. Cõſeruus eñ tuus ſũ, & fratrũ tuoꝝ ꝓphetarꝝ & eoꝝ qui ſeruant uerba ꝓphetiæ libri huius. Deum adora. Et dicit mihi. Ne ſignaueris uerba prophetiæ libri huius. Tẽpus enim prope eſt. Qui nocet, noceat adhuc, & qui in ſordibus eſt, ſordeſcat adhuc, & qui iuſtus eſt, iuſtificetur adhuc, & ſctũs ſctificetur adhuc, & ecce uenio cito, & merces mea mecũ eſt, ut reddã unicuiq; ut opus illius erit. Ego ſum alpha & ω, primus & nouiſſimus, principium & finis. Beati qui ſeruant mandata illius ut ſit poteſtas eorum in ligno uitæ, & per portas intrent in ciuitatem. Foris autem canes & uenefici & impudici & homicidæ & idolis ſeruientes, & omnis qui amat & facit mendacium. Ego Ieſus miſi angelũ meũ teſtificari uobis hæc in eccleſijs. Ego ſum genus & radix Dauid, ſtella ſplendida & matutina. Et ſpiritus & ſponſa dicunt, ueni. Et qui audit dicat ueni. Et qui ſitit ueniat, & qui uult, accipiat aquam uitæ gratis. Conteſtor enim omni audienti uerba ꝓphetiæ libri huius. Si quis appoſuerit ad hæc, apponet deus ſuper illum plagas ſcriptas in libro iſto. Et ſi qs diminuerit de uerbis libri ꝓphetiæ huius, auferet deus partẽ eius de libro uitæ, & de ciuitate ſancta. & de his q̃ ſcripta ſunt in libro iſto. Dicit qui teſtimoniũ phibet iſtoꝝ. Etiã uenio cito. A mẽ. Etiam Veni dñe Ieſu. Gratia dñi noſtri Ieſu Chriſti cũ oibus uobis. Amen.

294.

Finis Teſtamenti totius ad græcã ueritatẽ uetuſtiſſimorũq; Codicum Latinoꝝ fidem & ad ꝓbatiſſimoꝝ authorũ citationẽ & interpretationem accurate recogniti, opera ſtudioq; D. Eraſmi Roterodami.

Julius: Why don't you stop all this nonsense and open the doors? Perhaps you'd rather I broke them down. Why do we need all this palaver [idle chatter]? You see the sort of troops I have at my command.

Peter: I do indeed see some highly practiced thieves. But you must be aware that these doors can only be opened in other ways.

Julius: Enough words, I say. If you don't hurry up and open the gates, I'll unleash my thunderbolt of excommunication with which I used to terrify great kings on earth and their kingdoms too. You see, I've already got a bull prepared for the occasion.

Peter: Just tell me, please, what you mean by all this bombast about bulls, bolts of thunder, and maledictions. I never heard from Christ a single one of these words.

Julius: You'll feel their full force, if you don't watch out.

Peter: Perhaps you used to terrify people with that bluster, but it counts for nothing here. Here we deal only in the truth. This is a fortress to be captured with good deeds, not ugly words.[1]

This satirical dialogue from Erasmus was controversial, but many Christians in Europe could heartily agree with Erasmus' critique of worldly popes like Julius II.

However, Erasmus' most important contribution to the Reformation was not satirical works or his own writings on Christian doctrine. Rather, it was his publication of the Greek New Testament published as the ***Novum Instrumentum*** in 1516. Erasmus' publication included the text of the Greek New Testament in parallel with a fresh Latin translation produced by Erasmus himself. This publication was one of the earliest attempts to provide the entire Greek New Testament in one volume, based on the collection of various manuscripts available at that time. This Greek New Testament and its successive editions (some revised by Erasmus himself) would serve as the foundation for the later texts of the Greek New Testament used by Bible translators all over Europe.

The increased access to the Greek New Testament was essential for the work of Reformation. Luther and other Reformers could now access the text of the New Testament in the original language (Greek). By reading the New Testament in its original language, the Reformers were able to demonstrate how various teachings and traditions of the church were not in accord with the Bible.

In the Western church, the Latin translation known as the **Latin Vulgate** was the Bible used in the church and university. The Latin Vulgate was not necessarily a poor translation. But like any translation, it had imperfections. And because the Hebrew and Greek originals were not very accessible to scholars and clergy during the Middle Ages, some errors of translation and interpretation persisted. But with the publication of Erasmus' Greek New Testament, men like Luther and Tyndale could translate the New Testament into the common languages of Europe such as German and English. Additionally, the Reformers were also able to identify errors in the Vulgate. Some of these errors had led to or provided support for doctrinal errors in the church. For instance, the Vulgate had mistranslated the Greek word *metanoia*, which means "repent," as "do penance."

Dissatisfaction with the corrupt state of the church, the invention of the movable-type printing press, and the recovery of ancient texts (especially the Scriptures) were each important factors in paving the road toward reformation. In the early years of the 16th century, the Lord would mercifully bring light and life to His church. The Reformation was dawning.

The light of the Scriptures shone once again with great clarity throughout Europe. Because of the Reformation, the truth of God's Word would continue to be promulgated throughout the world. The Reformation Wall in Geneva contains the Latin phrase *Post Tenebras Lux* engraved upon the monument. The phrase translated into English means "After Darkness, Light." This phrase is an appropriate description of the events of the Reformation: the light of God's Word shone with great glory amidst the darkness of Satan and the world. The "god of this world" sought to veil the gospel and keep the light of the gospel from shining. But our Lord is greater than the evil one, despite all his fury. "The light shines in the darkness, and the darkness has not overcome it" (John 1:5 ESV). ■

REFORMATION WALL IN GENEVA

WITTENBERG, GERMANY

The Reformation In Germany

For I am not ashamed of the gospel of Christ, for it is the power of God to salvation for everyone who believes, for the Jew first and also for the Greek. For in it the righteousness of God is revealed from faith to faith; as it is written, "The just shall live by faith." (Rom. 1:16-17)

On a stormy afternoon in 1505, Martin Luther made his way from Erfurt to Mansfeld. Luther was a student at the University of Erfurt. But on that day, he was returning home to see his father and mother. Luther's goal was to become a lawyer, fulfilling the wish of his father.

As the severity of the thunderstorm increased, Luther feared death and the judgment of God. Not far from Luther, lightning struck, and Luther fell to the ground appealing to St. Anna for help. It is reported that as Luther prayed to St. Anna, he promised to become a monk if he would be delivered from the terrible weather.

MARTIN LUTHER (1483-1546)

St. Anna was the saint of miners, and Luther's father was a miner. This may explain why Luther appealed to St. Anna. From this, we have a window into the spirituality of Luther's time. He feared God and judgment, and Luther knew that the Lord had control over the weather. And we see that Luther's appeal was not to His Heavenly Father to deliverance, but rather to a saint. This tells us much about how Luther experienced the faith in his time.

Little did Luther know at the time that he would be used by God to ignite a worldwide movement known as the Protestant Reformation. Luther's promise on that stormy summer day would be used in the providence of God to prepare him for the reforming work he would pursue years later.

Martin Luther's parents were disappointed to hear that their son was now intending to pursue a monastic life. His father Hans exclaimed, "You've heard nothing less than the voice of the devil!" But in time, Martin's parents accepted his decision.[1]

On July 16, 1505, Martin Luther entered the Augustinian monastery in Erfurt. Luther, with a troubled conscience and a lack of assurance, sought fellowship with God. This Luther would pursue by carefully obeying the monastic rule of his brethren in Erfurt.

Luther's Struggles in Monastic Life

Then you will call upon Me and go and pray to Me, and I will listen to you. And you will seek Me and find Me, when you search for Me with all your heart. (Jer. 29:12-13)

Luther dedicated himself zealously to the monastic life. Luther's life consisted of prayer, meditation, study, labor, and regular confession. Nevertheless, Luther's dedication to pursuing a life of godliness did not solve his struggles of conscience. Riddled with guilt over his many sins and fearing the just judgment of God, Luther could not be sure he had ever done enough to please God.

Rather than loving Jesus Christ as His Savior, the Lamb of God who took away his sins, Luther confessed to fearing the judgment of Jesus Christ. He wrote, "Constantly I see him before me, enthroned on a rainbow as a strict, terrible Judge who will punish me for my sins. I cannot believe in him. The moment the day begins, I go to confession. Confess some more, and then again."

It was believed by many in Luther's day that only sins that were confessed would be forgiven by God. As a result, those who confessed sought to mine their souls deeply lest they forget some sin in the process of confession. Luther confessed again and again and tried harder and harder. He described his life as a monk in this way:

> If there was ever a monk who reached his goal, then that should have been me. All my brothers in the monastery who knew me can testify to that. If it had lasted longer, I would have tortured myself to death with vigils, prayers, reading, and other works.

Luther became well known among his brothers in the monastery for his frequent and long confessions. On one occasion, Luther recounted that he confessed his sins for over six hours! It is no surprise that Luther's scrupulous detail in confession eventually wore out the brother he was confessing to.

Though the gospel of grace had been greatly obscured in Luther's day, nevertheless there were godly men and women who had some understanding of God's grace. Luther's mentor in the monastery, **Johann von Staupitz** (c. 1460-1524), often reminded Luther that God was merciful. Yet, since Luther had not come to a right understanding of the gospel, his intense spiritual struggles continued.

During his time as a monk, Luther regularly studied his Bible but struggled to resolve his matters of conscience.

Luther's Visit to Rome

A noteworthy event occurred in Luther's spiritual journey when he visited Rome in 1510. It was customary for monks to go on pilgrimage, and Rome was one of the most important sites. There, the pope resided. There it was believed the Apostle Peter had served the church as the first bishop of Rome. As the epicenter of the Western church's activity, Rome was the site of constant pilgrimage from Christians all over Europe.

Luther set out on foot with another brother from the monastery in November 1510. After forty-eight days, Luther reached Rome on Christmas Eve, 1510. He made an arduous journey

DEPICTION OF ERFURT, GERMANY FROM THE NUREMBERG CHRONICLE, 1493

to see the holy city, but Luther was shocked to find debauchery and superstition everywhere he looked. Luther encountered priests rattling off masses at high speed to take in as much money from pilgrims as possible. Greed drove the religious activities in Rome. Not only was covetousness evident, but inappropriate sexual behavior was also evident among many of the priests in Rome.

One of the common activities of pilgrims in Rome was to fast an entire day from food and water. On that day, pilgrims would visit the seven main churches in Rome and then conclude the day by ascending the Scala Sancta, a long stairway in Rome. It was claimed that the stairway was built with steps taken from the palace of Pontius Pilate, where the Lord had been condemned to be crucified. This was one of the many relics found in Rome. Pilgrims were to ascend the stairs on their knees, reciting the Lord's Prayer as they went up. All this was done because pilgrims were told that by performing this ritual, a soul would be delivered from purgatory.

THE SCALA SANCTA IN ROME

Luther faithfully went through the day-long ritual and finished by ascending the Scala Sancta. As Luther completed the ritual, he had doubts. Was this really true? Where did this teaching come from? How did anyone know that such a ritual really accomplished anything? Luther later recounted:

> In Rome I wanted to rescue my grandfather from purgatory. Therefore, I climbed the stairs of Pilate and prayed the Lord's Prayer on every tread. There was a conviction that whoever prayed in this way could save a soul. But when I arrived at the top, I thought, who knows whether this is really true?

Luther returned to Erfurt, disillusioned by his visit to Rome. His spiritual questions remained unanswered.

Martin Becomes Dr. Luther and Teaches the Bible

For all have sinned and fall short of the glory of God, being justified freely by His grace through the redemption that is in Christ Jesus, whom God set forth as a propitiation by His blood, through faith, to demonstrate His righteousness, because in His forbearance God had passed over the sins that were previously committed, to demonstrate at the present time His righteousness, that He might be just and the justifier of the one who has faith in Jesus. (Rom. 3:23-26)

Luther would not find resolution to his spiritual struggles in his own works or in his pilgrimage to Rome. Instead, answers to Luther's burning questions of conscience would be found in God's Word, the Holy Bible.

Johann von Staupitz urged Luther to gain his doctoral degree in theology. Luther submitted to the counsel of his father in the faith and studied at the University of Wittenberg. Luther graduated with his doctorate in 1512 and thereafter became lecturer in Bible at the university.

As Luther wrestled with the biblical text, he began to understand the gospel of grace that had become so obscured by centuries of encrusted tradition. Luther was also aided by reading the New Testament in the original Greek rather than in Latin translation. It was in 1516, four years after Luther became Dr. Luther, that Desiderius Erasmus (1466-1536) published his edition of the Greek New Testament.

Erasmus' publication was a landmark work. It enabled those who were able to read Greek to see what the authors of the New Testament originally wrote. Erasmus' publication would eventually enable Luther to translate the New Testament into German. Others, such as **William Tyndale** (1494-1536), would do the same for the English language.

In 1519, Luther made a critical discovery as he diligently studied Paul's letter to the Romans. Previous to this time, Luther thought the phrase "the righteousness of God" in Romans 1 referred to God's righteous judgment upon sinners. Luther wrote, "I hated that word, namely, 'God's righteousness'; . . . indeed, I did not love God, but I hated this righteous God who punishes sinners." How could the gospel be good news if it revealed God's righteousness which then condemned people? This bothered Luther greatly. He said, "I raged with an angry and thoroughly confused conscience, and unrestrained I went to Paul concerning this text, because I had a burning desire to know what the holy Paul would say about this."

Finally, Luther understood what Paul was saying. God's righteousness is revealed in the gospel as the righteousness that God Himself provides for sinners, through His Son Jesus Christ. It was in these words that Luther understood what Paul was teaching about justification by faith. Luther recounted this dramatic moment in his spiritual journey:

> The gospel reveals the righteousness of God, namely, the passive, through which God the Merciful justifies us through faith, as is written: "The righteous will live by faith." I felt completely newborn, and it was as if I had gone through the open gates into paradise itself.

Year by year, as Luther taught the Bible to the students in Wittenberg, he increasingly grew in his understanding of the gospel of Jesus Christ. Here we see the illuminating clarity of God's Word. It is a lamp to our feet and a light to our path (Ps. 119:105).

The Indulgences Controversy and the 95 Theses

"Now, therefore," says the Lord,
"Turn to Me with all your heart,
With fasting, with weeping, and with mourning."
So rend your heart, and not your garments;
Return to the Lord your God,
For He is gracious and merciful,
Slow to anger, and of great kindness;
And He relents from doing harm. (Joel 2:12-13)

The beginning of the Protestant Reformation is usually tied to the date October 31, 1517. To understand what happened on that day, we need to learn about the practice of indulgences.

The church of the 16th century was facing spiritual bankruptcy. False doctrine, corruption in leadership, and moral degradation were widespread. Not only was the church in spiritual crisis, but the church faced financial straits as well. The massive church system of Rome had been living beyond its means for years, and the resources needed to cover expenses continued to grow. As we often see in history, where there is a love of money and other earthly possessions, corruption often follows. The love of money is the root of all kinds of evils (1 Tim. 6:10).

The church was spending far beyond its means. This left the papacy with a budget problem that needed solving. There was significant debt. How could the church make the money it needed to pay for its vast expenses? How could it cover the luxurious and indulgent lifestyle of the popes and other leaders in the church? One helpful source of income turned out to be **indulgences**.

An important character in the story is **Albert of Mainz** (1490-1545). This man was the archbishop and elector of the region of Mainz. The electors were seven German princes (including three bishops) who elected the Holy Roman emperor. Nearby but not within Albert's territory was the small town of Wittenberg. There, Martin Luther was teaching the Bible at the university.

Church offices were sometimes sold to the highest bidder. This practice became known as **simony**. This is what Albert had done. He had bought multiple bishoprics with money. Because of this, Albert had significant debts he needed to pay. Therefore, he came up with a plan. He could pay off his debts by selling indulgences that would first go to help build St. Peter's Basilica in Rome and secondly, would help him to pay his various debts. This became a major driver for the sale of indulgences in this part of Germany.

An indulgence was a pardon or a remission of the temporal consequences of sin. It was believed that when you died without being completely free from sin, you would go to purgatory for a period of time to be "purged" by fire from sin. Eventually, after suffering some of the consequences of your sins, you would then leave purgatory and enter into God's presence in heaven. An indulgence, it was promised, would free you or a loved one from that extended time of purgation in purgatory.

Albert and the pope were selling indulgences for personal gain. But this was a secret to the common people, who only heard the positive side of it. The people in Luther's region only heard of the spiritual benefits that would come from purchasing an indulgence.

To sell these indulgences, a Dominican preacher named **Johann Tetzel** (c. 1465-1519) was assigned to journey throughout Albert's territory and sell as many indulgences as possible.

For centuries, theologians had debated the matter of indulgences. Initially, the intent of an indulgence was not to make forgiveness "cheap" and enable people to buy God's forgiveness. But in practice, that is exactly what many believed. Some purchased indulgences to cover future sins they would later commit. In the worst examples, some people purchased indulgences and then used it as a license to sin. Others, driven by anxiety about their loved ones in purgatory, flocked to spend their hard-earned money to free their grandmother, uncle, or deceased wife from the fiery pains of purgatory.

Tetzel was gifted in marketing these indulgences. He would chant a "jingle" to show the value of indulgences. The little jingle that Tetzel used was "The moment the money tinkles in the collecting box, a soul flies out of purgatory." A rhymed English version goes like this, "As soon as the coin in the coffer rings, the soul from purgatory springs."

Tetzel's tour was not without controversy. Some electors of the Holy Roman Empire forbade Tetzel to preach in their realms. But in Albert's lands it was allowed, since it benefited Rome and Albert at the same time.

Luther had for some years found problems with this doctrine and practice of indulgences. When residents of Wittenberg visited a nearby town and listened to Tetzel's preaching and purchased

JOHANN TETZEL (C. 1465-1519)

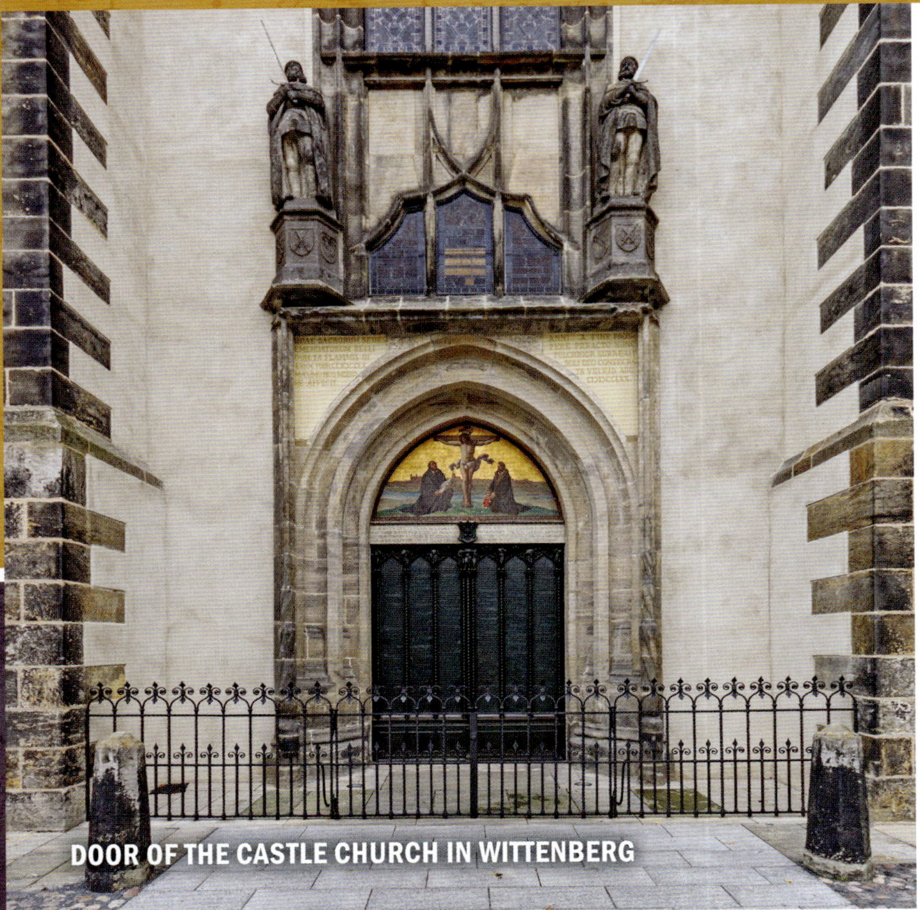

DOOR OF THE CASTLE CHURCH IN WITTENBERG

indulgences, Luther became gravely concerned.

As a student of Scripture and a priest of the church, Luther decided to debate the matter. He wrote 95 points of debate called theses. Luther then posted these **95 Theses** on the door of the Castle Church in Wittenberg on October 31, 1517. Luther's purpose with this document was not to start a movement but simply to debate this important matter with other teachers of the church. Luther wrote in Latin and invited others to debate the matter with him.

It is important to note that Luther did not reject the papacy or indulgences when he posted the 95 Theses. Further reflection on the teaching of Scripture would eventually lead him to reject these things as unbiblical. But the 95 Theses show the early fruit of Luther's reflection upon the Bible. He posted these in 1517, some two years before his discovery concerning "the righteousness of God" in Romans 1.

Here are a few examples of Luther's 95 Theses:

Preface: Out of love for the truth and from desire to elucidate it [make it clear], the Reverend Father Martin Luther, Master of Arts and Sacred Theology, and ordinary lecturer therein at Wittenberg, intends to defend the following statements and to dispute on them in that place. Therefore he asks that those who cannot be present and dispute with him orally shall do so in their absence by letter. In the name of our Lord Jesus Christ, Amen.

1. When our Lord and Master Jesus Christ said, "Repent" (Mt 4:17), he willed the entire life of believers to be one of repentance.

36. Any truly repentant Christian has a right to full remission of penalty and guilt, even without indulgence letters.

43. Christians are to be taught that he who gives to the poor or lends to the needy does a better deed than he who buys indulgences.

45. Christians are to be taught that he who sees a needy man and passes him by, yet gives his money for indulgences, does not buy papal indulgences but God's wrath.

62. The true treasure of the church is the most holy gospel of the glory and grace of God.

The 95 Theses were written in Latin, and Luther did not intend them to be distributed. But someone took them and quickly translated the theses into German. Then, without Luther's permission, the 95 Theses were printed in the common language and began to spread all over Germany. They were then translated into other languages and spread throughout Europe.

The distribution of this document created a firestorm, raising serious concerns about Luther's fidelity to the teaching of the Church. The 95 Theses would only be the first point of controversy. Luther's teaching was challenged by many others. And some accused Luther of heresy.

DISPUTATION BETWEEN LUTHER AND ECK

In 1518 and 1519, Luther participated in two disputations defending his teaching. A learned theologian named Johann Eck debated Martin Luther at the Leipzig Disputation in 1519. Eck backed Luther into a corner, and Luther admitted that he agreed with the Reformer of Prague, John Huss. Huss was condemned as a heretic at the Council of Constance and burned at the stake in 1415. A hundred years later, Luther was aligning himself with the "notorious heretic" of Prague.

Luther was warned to reject his controversial stances. But he refused and kept on writing. Then, on January 3, 1521, the pope excommunicated Martin Luther from the church. This involved more than being barred from the local church. Excommunication in Martin Luther's day usually meant exile from the empire.

Luther was promised safe passage to the assembly, though Luther and others doubted whether this would be honored by the authorities. Nevertheless, Luther agreed and made the journey to Worms.

When Luther arrived and stood before the assembly, he hoped for an opportunity to debate the important theological issues he wrote about. But Luther was disappointed when Johann Eck, in front of the emperor, and other rulers, simply asked Luther: "do you recant of what you have written?" On a nearby table, all of Luther's writings were collected.

Luther was unsure how to answer Eck's question, and he petitioned the emperor for an extension of one day to consider his response. That

The Diet of Worms, 1521

God has not given us a spirit of fear, but of power and of love and of a sound mind. (2 Tim. 1:7)

In March of 1521, Luther was invited by Emperor Charles V (r. 1519-1556) to answer for himself at an Imperial Diet in the city of Worms (pronounced "vurms"). A "diet" as the word was used in Luther's time referred to an assembly of rulers.

LUTHER AT THE DIET OF WORMS

WARTBURG CASTLE

night, Luther wrestled with what to do, and he felt that the devil was attacking him with fear and doubts. But he awoke the next morning resolved to make a defense.

The next morning, Luther stood before Emperor Charles V and others of the assembly and responded to Eck's question. These are some of Luther's most famous words:

> Unless I am convinced by Scripture and plain reason—I do not accept the authority of the popes and councils, for they have contradicted each other—my conscience is captive to the Word of God. I cannot and I will not recant anything, for to go against conscience is neither right nor safe. God help me. Amen.

Luther's courageous stand put him in great danger. Luther and his companions wondered whether he would be captured and killed when he departed for Wittenberg. However, the Lord protected Luther.

On his way back from Worms to Wittenberg, Luther was kidnapped by soldiers. They were soldiers of **Frederick the Wise** (r. 1486-1525), the elector of Saxony. Frederick supported Luther and his work at the university. Frederick's soldiers had kidnapped Luther to protect him. Luther was taken to a secret location called the **Wartburg Castle**. There, Luther disguised himself as a knight, growing out his hair and beard to conceal his identity as the famous monk.

LUTHER'S ROOM IN THE WARTBURG

While living at the Wartburg, Luther translated the New Testament into German from the Greek. Eventually Luther would complete the entire Bible, and his translation would make a significant impact on the standardization of the German language. In fact, Luther's translation (with its various revisions) is still read by German speakers today.

Luther's Later Years as Pastor and Professor

In 1522, Luther returned to Wittenberg despite

the danger this posed to his life. Frederick the Wise continued to protect Luther from harm, and this enabled Luther to continue the work of reforming the church in Wittenberg and throughout the region.

Luther exerted a great influence through his many books, his hymns, and his sermons. Luther also demonstrated his commitment to break with Roman practices by marrying a former nun, **Katherine von Bora** (1499-1552). Luther married Katherine von Bora in 1525 and enjoyed many years of faithful marriage. Together, they had six children. Frederick the Wise generously gave Luther the former monastery in Wittenberg known as the **Black Cloister**. This became Luther's home, a perfect place to raise a large family. Additionally, the Luther family used the former monastery to host frequent guests passing through Wittenberg.

Luther knew that the work of reformation would need to be established through consistent preaching and teaching. To this end, Luther preached frequently in Wittenberg and elsewhere. Additionally, Luther produced various writings to assist in the instruction of God's people. One of Luther's most well-known and beloved writings is his ***Small Catechism***. In this brief instructional manual, Luther sought to provide an introduction to the Christian faith suitable for new disciples and children.

The catechism included teaching on the Ten Commandments, the Apostles Creed, the Lord's Prayer, and the means of grace. A few quotations from *Luther's Small Catechism* show the clarity and simplicity of this little manual.

> **The First Commandment**
> *Thou Shalt Have No Other Gods.*
> What does this mean?
> Answer: We should fear, love, and trust in God above all things.
>
> **The Lord's Prayer**
> *Our Father who art in heaven.*
> What does this mean?
> Answer: God would thereby [with this little introduction] tenderly urge us to believe that He is our true Father, and that we are His true children, so that we may ask Him confidently with all assurance, as dear children ask their dear father.

Luther was also a gifted musician who wrote the words and tunes of about forty hymns and psalm paraphrases, many of which are still sung in churches today. One of the great changes brought by the Reformation was the restoration of congregational singing. During the Middle Ages, singing had come to be restricted to church choirs that sang in Latin, which the people could not understand. The Reformation restored singing to the congregation and produced thousands of vernacular hymns and metrical psalms.

Luther's most well-known hymn is titled ***A Mighty Fortress is Our God***. Luther experienced the attacks of the "ancient foe" Satan who sought to undo him and the work of reformation. But the Lord Jesus Christ strengthened Luther and other godly men and women to stand fast for the truth of Scripture.

Here are the words Luther wrote in English translation:

> A mighty fortress is our God,
> A bulwark never failing;

LUTHER'S LIVING ROOM IN THE BLACK CLOISTER

MARTIN LUTHER PLAYING MUSIC WITH HIS FAMILY

Our helper he, amid the flood
Of mortal ills prevailing.
For still our ancient foe
Doth seek to work us woe;
His craft and power are great,
And armed with cruel hate,
On earth is not his equal.

Did we in our own strength confide,
Our striving would be losing;
Were not the right man on our side,
The man of God's own choosing.
Dost ask who that may be?
Christ Jesus, it is he,
Lord Sabaoth his name,
From age to age the same,
And he must win the battle.

And though this world, with devils filled,
Should threaten to undo us,
We will not fear, for God hath willed
His truth to triumph through us.
The prince of darkness grim,
We tremble not for him;
His rage we can endure,
For lo, his doom is sure;
One little word shall fell him.

That Word above all earthly pow'rs,
No thanks to them, abideth;
The Spirit and the gifts are ours
Through him who with us sideth.
Let goods and kindred go,
This mortal life also;
The body they may kill:
God's truth abideth still;
His kingdom is forever.

Luther's Legacy and Those Who Followed

Luther experienced poor health throughout his life. He suffered from frequent headaches, stomach ailments, kidney stones, tinnitus, vertigo, and other afflictions. The last few years of Luther's life were still quite busy, but his declining health prevented him from traveling and teaching as much. In 1546, Luther became severely ill and then died on February 18, 1546. He was sixty-two years old at the time of his death. A paper was found near Luther at the time of his death with his last words: "We are beggars. This is true." Luther's last written words reflect the truth of the gospel: our hope is not found in ourselves but in Jesus Christ alone.

What should we think of Luther's legacy? Some of the strengths of Martin Luther include his commitment to the Bible as the Word of God, his love for Jesus Christ, and his courageous commitment to the doctrine of justification by faith alone. Luther faced serious dangers, but as a servant of Christ, he did not back down. Luther sacrificed much for the truth of the gospel, and God used him in mighty ways for the recovery of biblical truth.

Yet Luther, to the day of his death, like all of us, was a sinner. Can we make any evaluation of Luther's failings? We should be humble, recognizing that we cannot know a man's heart and we are removed by many centuries from his time. Nevertheless, we can learn from Luther's weaknesses as well as his strengths.

While Luther was bold, he sometimes was not wise in his use of words. Sometimes, Luther was driven by anger in his responses, and sometimes his language was not appropriately gracious. At other times, he may have been overly committed to his own perspective and therefore unwilling to humbly consider the views of others. For instance, Luther spoke harshly of Ulrich Zwingli and other Swiss Reformers with whom he disagreed about the Lord's Supper.

Additionally, Luther's writings against the Jews in his book *On the Jews and Their Lies* contained many false charges against Jews in Europe. Luther had written an earlier book, *That Jesus Was Born a Jew*, that was kinder to the Jews and more hopeful of their conversion to Christ. But Luther's later advocacy of violence against the Jewish people was not justifiable and was not in accord with the teaching of Christ. Luther lacked wisdom in this matter, and his writings on this topic were harmful. But his hostility to the Jews was religious, not racial. Luther longed for the Jews to embrace Jesus Christ as Lord and Savior and become Christians. His frustration was very different than the racial hatred of the Nazis in the 20th century, who targeted all people of Jewish ancestry, whether Christian or not. Yet, sadly, Nazi rallies and propaganda in the 20th century made use of Luther's book.

After the death of Luther, the Lutheran movement faced internal divisions between those who followed the original vision of Luther and those who followed some of the distinct teachings of his successor **Philip Melanchthon** (1497-1560). These internal debates and schisms were settled through a number of important documents collectively known today as ***The Book of Concord***. This collection of documents comprises the Lutheran confessions and catechisms.

Luther's sermons, lectures, and books continue to be read by Christians today. The Lutheran churches maintain much of Luther's teaching in the present day as well. Additionally, Luther can be seen in many ways as one of the most foundational figures of Protestant Christianity.

Of course, as students of church history, it is important to remember that Martin Luther is just one more servant of Jesus Christ in a vast cloud of witnesses who have gone before us. The Lord Jesus, as He built His church, used many different men and women to advance the cause of His kingdom and glory in the world. Let us give all praise to Him for the power of His gospel! ■

TOWN IN BAVARIA, GERMANY

TOGGENBURG, SWITZERLAND

The Swiss Reformation in Zurich

18

So Ezra the priest brought the Law before the assembly of men and women and all who could hear with understanding on the first day of the seventh month. Then he read from it in the open square that was in front of the Water Gate from morning until midday, before the men and women and those who could understand; and the ears of all the people were attentive to the Book of the Law. (Neh. 8:2-3)

A few months after Martin Luther was born in Germany, another boy was born in the Swiss Alps. On January 1, 1484, **Ulrich Zwingli** was born in Wildhaus in the region of Toggenburg. The birth of these two boys, separated only by a few months, are significant because together they left a lasting impact upon world history. It is also an interesting fact of providence that both Luther and Zwingli began the work of reforming the church around the same time.

Many date the beginning of the Protestant Reformation to 1517, All Hallows Eve (October 31). This date is often chosen because on that day Luther nailed the 95 Theses to the Castle Church door in Wittenberg. In the case of Zwingli, 1519 is the pivotal date. It was in 1519 that Zwingli began to preach reform in the **Grossmünster** church in Zurich.

Though there were many similarities between Luther and Zwingli's ideas, the Reformation movements in both regions split ways. Understanding why and how that happened is important for Christians today. The Reformation in Zurich made an enduring impact on the direction of church history to the present day. Let's learn together about the fascinating life of Ulrich Zwingli and the foundational work he did in **Zurich**.

How the Reformation Began in the Swiss Lands

I charge you therefore before God and the Lord Jesus Christ, who will judge the living and the dead at His appearing and His kingdom: Preach the word! Be ready in season and out of season. Convince, rebuke, exhort, with all longsuffering and teaching. (2 Tim. 4:1-2)

As a boy growing up in the Swiss Confederation, Zwingli had a unique heritage. The Swiss lands were the freest in Europe at the time of the Reformation. Each member (canton) of the Swiss Confederation was a self-governing state. At the time of the Reformation, there were thirteen cantons in the Swiss confederacy. They were allied for common defense, but each canton was in charge of its own affairs. This allowed many of the cantons to accept the Protestant Reformation while

ULRICH ZWINGLI (1484-1531)

GROSSMÜNSTER CHURCH IN ZURICH

became a devoted student of the classics. As we learned in an earlier chapter, through Erasmus and other humanists, ancient literature was being recovered and studied anew. Some of these classics were pagan in origin in the case of ancient Greek and Roman literature. But more importantly, the original Hebrew and Greek texts of the Bible were being studied once again.

Inspired by Erasmus' example, Zwingli was an ardent student of the classics. Before Zwingli knew anything of Luther, he was already reconsidering long-held traditions due to his study of the original text of Scripture.

It was in the year 1514 or 1515 that Zwingli read a poem by Erasmus that drove him to reconsider his faith. This is what Zwingli says:

> In 1514 or 1515, I read a poem about the Lord Jesus, written by the profoundly learned Erasmus of Rotterdam, in which with many very beautiful words Jesus complains that people do not seek blessing in Him, so that He might be to them a fountain of every blessing, a Savior, a comfort, a treasure of the soul. So I thought, "Well if this is true, why then should we seek help from any created being?"[1]

During these early years serving as a priest in Glarus and Einsiedeln, Zwingli grew in his understanding of Christ's gospel set forth in the pages of Scripture. But like many other priests of his generation, he was not a man of blameless character (see 1 Tim. 3:2). Zwingli gave in to sexual temptation and committed sexual sin on multiple occasions. These acts of disobedience to God would affect Zwingli's reputation for the rest of his life. However, by God's grace, Ulrich did repent of these sins. At this time in church history, celibacy for all priests was an absolute requirement in the Western church. This man-made rule was disastrous in its effect. Many priests broke

others rejected it. The Swiss Reformation began in Zurich.

Before Zwingli arrived in Zurich, he served as a priest in the towns of Glarus and Einsiedeln. During his early years of ministry, Zwingli

THIRTEEN CANTONS OF THE OLD SWISS CONFEDERACY

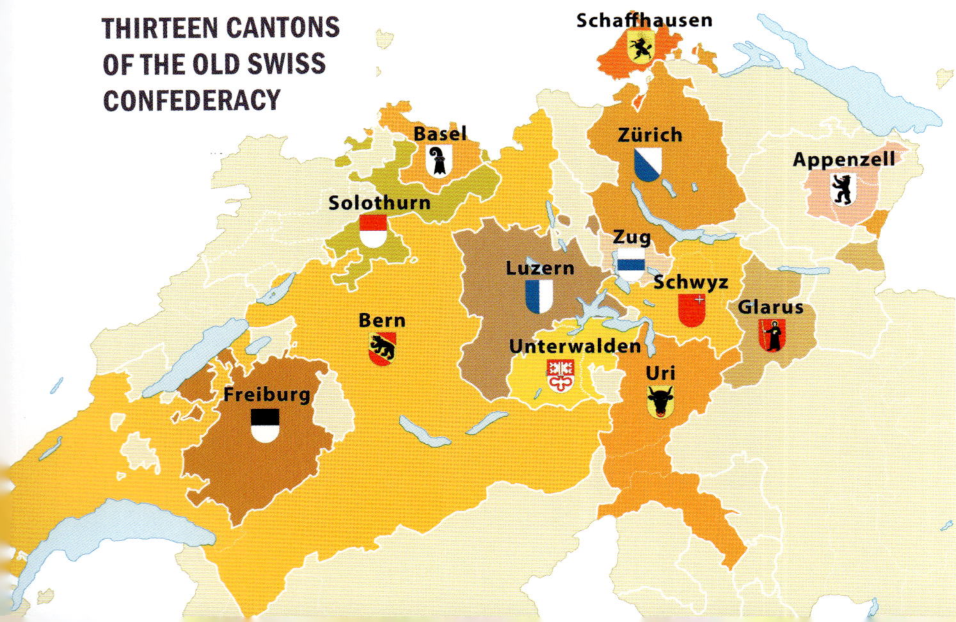

THE HOME WHERE ZWINGLI WAS BORN

God's seventh commandment and fathered children outside of marriage. It would have been much better if many of these men had married instead.

In late 1518, the priestly post at the largest church in Zurich, the Grossmünster, became vacant. Zwingli was elected to the position. In 1518, Zurich was a mid-sized city in the Swiss Confederation consisting of some 6,000 people. Situated on numerous trade routes, many people passed through Zurich, thus giving the city some influence in the region. On January 1, 1519, Zwingli preached his first sermon at the great church. Zwingli's inaugural sermon was unique. Instead of following the assigned readings of the lectionary, Zwingli decided to start preaching from the New Testament right at the beginning: Matthew chapter 1. He began preaching straight through Matthew. Zwingli set out to preach the text of God's Word to God's people. Working directly from Erasmus' edition of the Greek New Testament, Zwingli exposited and applied the Scriptures to the people of Zurich. Although Zwingli had a respect for some of the pagan classics as well as the writings of the church fathers, his primary interest was the Bible.

In 1522, he reflected upon this commitment, writing:

> When I was younger, I gave myself overmuch to human teaching, like others of my day, and when about seven or eight years ago I undertook to devote myself entirely to the Scriptures I was always prevented by philosophy and theology. But eventually I came to the point where led by the Word and Spirit of God I saw the need to set aside all these things and to learn the doctrine of God direct from his own Word.[2]

As was the case with Luther, the authority of Scripture was paramount for Zwingli.

Like Luther, Zwingli attacked the selling of indulgences. A Franciscan preacher named Bernhardin Sanson came to Zurich in January 1519. Zwingli advised the city council not to let Sanson enter the city. The council submitted to this advice, and Sanson was barred entry. This was an early example of the influence Zwingli would have with city officials in Zurich.

The Plague Strikes Zurich

Through the LORD's mercies we are not consumed, because His compassions fail not. They are new every morning; Great is Your faithfulness. "The LORD is my portion," says my soul, "Therefore I hope in Him!" (Lam. 3:22-24)

During Zwingli's first year of ministry in Zurich, calamity visited the city. A terrible plague swept over the German lands and the Swiss Confederation. In Zurich, it was estimated that one third of the population perished. In September 1519, Zwingli became ill and was near to death. Zwingli believed that he was facing his last days. Sometime during or after his illness, Zwingli wrote a poem reflecting upon this difficult season. Here is

MODERN-DAY ZURICH

what Zwingli wrote:

Help, Lord God, help
In this trouble.
I think Death is at the door.
Stand before me, Christ;
For You have overcome him.
To You I Cry....
Console me, Lord God, console me.

Pain and fear seize
My soul and body.
Come to me then,
With Your grace, O my only
Consolation.
It will surely save
Everyone, who
His heart's desire
And hope sets
On You....

Yes, if it please You,
That no spark of sin
Rule me longer on earth.
Then my lips must
Your praise and teaching
Proclaim more
Than ever before,
However it may go,
In simplicity and with no danger.[3]

The plague was severe, and many perished. But the Lord preserved Zwingli's life and by mid-1520, Zwingli had largely recovered. Such plagues, which often struck portions of Europe, were a frequent reminder of the brevity of life. In such times of calamity, God's people were taught to number their days and to gain a heart of wisdom (Ps. 90:12).

A Rebellious Sausage Feast

Therefore do not let your good be spoken of as evil; for the kingdom of God is not eating and drinking, but righteousness and peace and joy in the Holy Spirit. (Rom. 14:16-17)

In the spring of 1522, a private meal was held in the home of Christopher Froschauer (1490-1564). He was the local printer responsible for the production of books in Zurich. On March 9 of that year, Froschauer hosted a sausage feast in his home. You might be wondering, why is someone's sausage meal in a private home of any significance in a chapter on the Reformation?

The reason this sausage meal was so important is because it violated a long-established church tradition. The meal occurred during the forty-day observance of Lent, which commemorated Jesus' forty-day temptation in the wilderness. Roman church authorities required people to abstain from eating meat during Lent even though the Bible did not require such fasting. Froschauer's wife Elsie Flamer prepared the sausages and served the unlawful meats to those in attendance. At some point in the meal, Zwingli joined in. As the minister of the largest church in Zurich, Zwingli's presence provided some endorsement of the sausage feast. Though Zwingli did not partake of the sausage himself, he nevertheless was in support of the meal.

Weeks later, Zwingli preached a message on the freedom of Christians to eat what they want. Defending those who had broken the fast, he explained that eating meat was a matter of Christian liberty. The March 9 sausage feast was another sign that Reformation ideals were beginning to reshape life in Zurich.

Zwingli's Break with the Roman Church

To the law and to the testimony! If they do not speak according to this word, it is because there is no light in them. (Isa. 8:20)

As we learned earlier, the requirement for priests to remain celibate had many damaging effects upon society. It was a man-made tradition that contradicted God's Word. And whenever men come up with rules that contradict God's Word, things don't go well. When Zwingli became minister in Zurich, celibacy was still required of all priests. But Zwingli made a move to defy this requirement in 1522. He secretly married a widow named **Anna Reinhart**. Two years later (in 1524), there would finally be a public celebration of the marriage. Zwingli was the first of the reformers to marry. His marriage was publicly recognized a year before Martin Luther married Katherine von Bora. Eventually, Zwingli and other reform-minded priests would convince the council in Zurich to abolish the celibacy requirement.

It was in 1522 that Zwingli began to publish his perspectives, making his break with the Roman Church even more evident. He wrote a work in 1522 entitled *Concerning the Clarity and Certainty of the Word of God*. In the book, Zwingli rejected the infallibility of the pope, church councils, and church tradition, instead proclaiming the Scriptures to be the final and supreme authority.

Then, in 1523, Zwingli released the 67 Articles that set forth his Protestant views in detail. These articles were to be used in a debate before the city council of Zurich. These 67 Articles teach that justification is by faith alone, purgatory does not exist, the Lord's Supper is not a sacrifice, Christ is the Head of the church, and many other Protestant teachings.

A few articles may be highlighted to show Zwingli's concerns:

1. All who say that the gospel lacks validity unless confirmed by the Church are in error and slander God.
15. Our salvation lies in faith, and our damnation lies in unbelief. For all truth is clear in Christ.
22. Christ is our justification. From this it follows that our works are good, if they flow from Christ; but if they flow from ourselves, they are neither right nor good.
57. The true Holy Scriptures know nothing about any purgatory after this life.

The town council voted in favor of Zwingli's views and thus became a Protestant city. Fees for baptism and burials were eliminated. Monks and nuns were allowed to marry. Images were removed from the churches. In the year 1525, the Roman Catholic mass was abolished, and Protestant worship was established as the only form of worship in the city.

Reforming Worship in Zurich

You shall not make for yourself a carved image—any likeness of anything that is in heaven above, or that is in the earth beneath, or that is in the water under the earth; you shall not bow down to them nor serve them. For I, the Lord your God, am a jealous God, visiting the iniquity of the fathers upon the children to the third and fourth generations of those who hate Me, but showing mercy to thousands, to those who love Me and keep My commandments. (Ex. 20:4-6)

Zwingli's preaching against Roman Catholic traditions, including the idolatrous veneration of Mary and the saints, began to influence the thinking of the Zurich population. The parish churches in Zurich were filled with stained glass, images, and statues of various kinds. Zealous Christians took it into their own hands to destroy various images to cleanse the church. The city council was torn on how to proceed with these acts of iconoclasm. Initially, by law, they had to fine or imprison those who had destroyed church property. But the council ordered a debate to take place in 1523 to discuss images and how they should be handled.

INTERIOR OF THE GROSSMÜNSTER

In the summer of 1524, the city council concluded that images were to be removed from the churches. The council passed this edict and made the decision to:

> Do away with the images of idols in all places where they are worshipped, so that many turn themselves from the idols entirely to the living true God, and each seeks all help and trust in the one God through our Lord Jesus Christ, to call upon and recognize in worship him alone. And the goods and costs that have been laid upon these images should be turned to the poor needy human beings, who are a true image of God.[4]

Churches throughout Zurich were cleansed of all images. All items of value were sold for relief for the poor. The walls of the churches were whitewashed. Stained glass windows were left as is, due to the significant cost of replacing with plain windows. Additionally, all organs within the church were silenced for worship. In addition to the removal of images and relics from churches, the Dominican monastery was turned into a hospital. As news spread to the other cantons of these acts, many were shocked and alarmed. It was clear that Zurich was heading in a new direction.

In 1525, a fellowship of ministers and scholars began meeting in Zurich. Known as the *prophezie*, Zwingli and other learned men would gather to read, translate, and interpret the Scriptures. The format followed in these meetings involved rigorous and detailed study of the Scriptures. Scholars took turns reading the Scriptures in Hebrew, Greek, Latin, and German, followed by commentary. From these meetings, the scholars would take their observations into the pulpit. These meetings were productive in increasing knowledge of God's Word in Zurich. By 1531, a translation of the entire Bible into the Swiss German dialect was published. This was the first complete translation of the Bible in German. Though Luther had already translated the New Testament, it was in a Saxon German dialect, difficult for those in Zurich to understand. Zwingli played an important role in the production of the *Zurich Bible*.

The Anabaptist Movement Begins

That same summer, a group of people within Zurich rejected the practice of infant baptism. Many families refused to bring their children for baptism. Key leaders of this new perspective were **Konrad Grebel** (1498-1526) and **Felix Manz** (1498-1527). This new group became known by their opponents as the **Anabaptists**. The word means "to baptize again" since in the view of those who opposed them, the Anabaptists were performing a second baptism (in addition to their prior infant baptism). But in the view of the Anabaptists, they were simply performing a valid baptism for the first time. Anabaptists would only baptize those who made profession of their faith in Jesus Christ.

To modern readers familiar with a Baptist perspective, a rejection of the practice of infant baptism may not be surprising. But in Zwingli's day, this rejection of infant baptism, which had been practiced consistently for over a thousand years, was a radical perspective.

Through baptism, a newborn not only became a member of the church, but they were also counted as subjects of the city. For this reason, city officials in Zurich considered this a serious matter. A biographer of Zwingli, Bruce Gordon, says the following:

> By refusing to administer the sacrament to their infants, men and women were setting their faith in conflict with their civic duties, raising the question of their allegiance.[5]

This is surprising to modern readers who may be used to seeing a Baptist church, a Presbyterian church, and a Roman Catholic church just a few blocks away from each other. But in Zwingli's day, the Anabaptist perspective was completely novel.

In January 1525, the magistrates called for a public debate over the matter. In this disputation, Zwingli opposed the Anabaptists and argued for the biblical validity of infant baptism. As a result, the city officials made infant baptism mandatory, giving citizens eight days to baptize their children. But the Anabaptists were unfazed.

That same month, the first adult baptisms were performed in Zurich. In Felix Manz's home, Konrad Grebel baptized George Blaurock. Others present were then baptized. At this time, such an act was very dangerous. The city council ultimately ruled that re-baptism was punishable by drowning. On January 5, 1527, Felix Manz was convicted of this crime and was drowned. Sadly, Zwingli was in support of the council's decision in Manz's execution and the drowning of some other Anabaptists in Zurich.

The Anabaptist movement would grow in subsequent decades. It would form another permanent stream out of the Reformation that continues to exist today. In a future chapter, we will learn more about this movement.

Zwingli's Debate with Luther over the Lord's Supper

The cup of blessing which we bless, is it not the communion of the blood of Christ? The bread which we break, is it not the communion of the body of Christ? For we, though many, are one bread and one body; for we all partake of that one bread. (1 Cor. 10:16-17)

The Reformation produced unity around the central truths of God's Word. But those who sought reform were not unified on every matter. Baptism was a subject of debate between the Anabaptists and Zwingli in Zurich. The Lord's Supper was also a matter of division between Martin Luther and Zwingli. Their disagreement over the Lord's Supper kept these two branches of the Reformation from allying in a common cause.

Both Luther and Zwingli rejected the Roman doctrine of **transubstantiation**. This doctrine, codified at the Fourth Lateran Council of 1215, stated the following: When the priest consecrated the elements of bread and wine, they physically turned into the actual body and blood of Christ. The Roman Church maintained that this physical transformation took place even though the elements still tasted and smelled like ordinary bread and wine. Luther and Zwingli rejected this.

However, they disagreed sharply with one another over the question of Christ's physical presence at the Lord's Supper. Luther argued that somehow, mysteriously, the Lord Jesus Christ was physically present to the partakers of the sacrament even though the elements did not change into Christ's physical body and blood. Zwingli, on the other hand, argued that Christ could not be physically present. This was so, in Zwingli's view, because Jesus in His human nature was at the right hand of God and could not be physically present in different places. Instead, Zwingli viewed the Lord's Supper primarily in terms of remembrance. Zwingli connected the Lord's Supper to the Passover celebration, which was a ceremony of remembrance of God's past redemption.

With the goal of unity in mind, a meeting was convened in the town of Marburg. This is known as the **Marburg Colloquy**. (A colloquy is a gathering for discussion on a topic. In contrast with a "disputation," a colloquy was intended more as a meeting in pursuit of unity rather than a debate between two opposing views.) This meeting was held in October 1529. Though unity was the aim of the conference, it was not achieved. Instead, Zwingli and Luther adamantly maintained their divergent perspectives. Zwingli argued that the phrase of our Lord, "This is My body" should be interpreted symbolically. This meant that Zwingli understood Jesus to be saying "This bread represents my body."

Luther was not convinced. He believed that when Jesus said "This is My body" he meant it literally. At one point in the discussion, to make his point, Luther wrote upon the table the words "This is My body" pointing to what he viewed as the plain meaning of Christ's words. Zwingli was willing to grant some kind of spiritual presence of Christ at the Supper. But he could not agree with Luther that our Lord was physically present at the Supper.

MARBURG COLLOQUY

The colloquy ended with no resolution of the matter. Zwingli and Luther were divided on this matter. However, there were some matters agreed upon at Marburg, and fifteen articles were drawn up to describe the results of the meeting.

The fifteenth article summarized the disagreement over the Lord's Supper in this way:

THE DEATH OF ZWINGLI

> And although at this time, we have not reached an agreement as to whether the true body and blood of Christ are bodily present in the bread and wine, nevertheless, each side should show Christian love to the other side insofar as conscience will permit and both sides should diligently pray to Almighty God that through his Spirit he might confirm us in the right understanding. Amen.[6]

The heart behind this article is right: to affirm in Christian love those who disagree and to pray for the Spirit's illumination. However, to this day, Zwingli and Luther's views have not been reconciled. Both views exist within different branches of the Protestant churches (Lutheran, Baptist, and Reformed). There are surely lessons here for us. If we would pursue unity with those who disagree with us, we must do so with love and humility, in submission to God's Word. Only then do we have a chance of finding a Spirit-produced unity.

Conflict in the Swiss Confederation

I came to send fire on the earth, and how I wish it were already kindled! But I have a baptism to be baptized with, and how distressed I am till it is accomplished! Do you suppose that I came to give peace on earth? I tell you, not at all, but rather division. (Luke 12:49-51)

As the Reformation progressed in Zurich and in other cities such as Bern, member cities of the Swiss Confederation divided between Roman Catholic and Protestant. Some of the cantons accepted reform. Others rejected it. Eventually, war broke out between the cantons in 1531. Five of the Catholic cantons declared war on Zurich.

Zurich mobilized an army of some 3,500 soldiers for its defense. Zwingli went out with other men of Zurich to defend the city and to serve as a chaplain in battle. Near Kappel, the Zurich army encountered a much larger force from the five cantons and was quickly defeated. Some 500 of the Zurich force were killed, and Zwingli was among them. At age forty-seven, Zwingli's life work was cut short, but it was in God's providence. Zwingli's wife Anna and their children were left without a husband and father. Zurich lost their primary leader in the Reformation.

But the work of Reformation did not end in Zurich. Zwingli was succeeded by his friend and disciple **Heinrich Bullinger** (1504-1575). For over forty years, Bullinger labored in Zurich to see the church purified and God's people strengthened. The work of Zwingli and the Reformers who followed dramatically altered the church in Europe. Zwingli died at a relatively young age. But his ideas would live on and be further refined by other Reformation leaders such as William Farel, John Calvin, Pierre Viret, and others. ■

VINEYARDS IN SCHAFFHAUSEN, SWITZERLAND

The Anabaptist Movement

In the previous chapter, we learned how the Anabaptist movement had its beginnings in Zurich. Ulrich Zwingli was the primary leader of reformation in Zurich. But others in Zurich grew dissatisfied with Zwingli's leadership. In their view, Zwingli and the city council were not going far enough in purifying the church. They also were not going fast enough. As a result, division occurred in Zurich. This division gave birth to a movement that would continue separately from the Lutheran and Reformed churches.

The Protestant Reformation resulted in different streams of thought and branches of the church. As a generalization, we may divide the streams of the Protestant Reformation into the following.

First, there is the **Lutheran** stream. This stream was especially influenced by Martin Luther and became predominant in Germany and Scandinavia. Luther was adamantly against his name being used to identify the church. He was rightly concerned about the church being identified with one man. Nevertheless, the term Lutheran became commonly used, and it is still used today to identify those churches that hold to the Lutheran confessions and catechisms found in ***The Book of Concord***.

Second, there is the **Reformed** stream which had its beginnings in Zurich. The Reformed churches also made steady advances in Geneva under the leadership of John Calvin and others. The Reformed stream made a significant impact upon other countries as well. Countries that particularly followed in the Reformed stream include portions of Germany, Switzerland, the Netherlands, England, Scotland, and Hungary.

Third, there is the **Anabaptist** stream. Sometimes this is called the **Radical Reformation**. It is called radical because the Anabaptists made claims more radical and revolutionary than the Lutheran and Reformed.

In a later chapter, we will study the Catholic **Counter-Reformation**, which had as its purpose not only opposing the Protestant Reformation but also encouraging reformation within the Roman Catholic Church. However, reformation for the Roman Catholics did not involve an embrace of the biblical teachings of the Protestant Reformers. Some corrupt practices were reformed, but false doctrine was not corrected. On the contrary, the Protestant Reformers and their teachings were thoroughly rejected and condemned.

In this chapter, our purpose is to understand the Anabaptist stream more fully. How did it arise? What were the primary teachings of those who led this movement?

The Anabaptist Movement Begins in Zurich

But the wisdom that is from above is first pure, then peaceable, gentle, willing to yield, full of mercy and good fruits, without partiality and without hypocrisy. Now the fruit of righteousness is sown in peace by those who make peace. (Jas. 3:17-18)

The roots of division between the Anabaptists and the Reformed in Zurich can be traced back to 1523. As Zwingli preached through the Scriptures, he noted many ways in which the Roman Catholic Church had departed from the teaching of Scripture. One important matter that Zwingli preached about was the use of statues and images in churches. Zurich's parish churches were filled with various statues and other artwork. Zwingli argued that the Second Commandment required that pure worship would be absent of any such images. Yet Zwingli did not pursue his reformation efforts apart from the approval of the city council. He did not advocate the removal or destruction of images apart from the magistrates' permission. Zwingli believed that the city magistrates held the responsibility for making such decisions. Zwingli was content to keep on preaching and wait for the magistrates to take action.

Zwingli's patient approach frustrated some in Zurich who wanted the churches to be purged of images immediately. Those impatient with Zwingli's gradual approach denounced him. Konrad Grebel spared no words when he said, "whoever thinks, believes or declares that Zwingli acts according to the duty of a shepherd thinks, believes and declares wickedly."[1] These words drew a line in the sand between those who would follow the more radical Zurich brethren and those who followed Zwingli's approach.

Many decided they could wait no longer and began to vandalize churches in an effort to purge them of idolatry. Some who participated in these acts of iconoclasm were punished by the city magistrates. But in 1524, the city council would authorize the removal of images and statues. Many who engaged in these image-destroying acts also became proponents of the new movement then forming.

In 1525, a number of people within Zurich rejected the practice of infant baptism. Many families refused to bring their children for baptism. Key leaders of this new perspective were **Konrad Grebel** (1498-1526) and **Felix Manz** (1498-1527). This new group became known by their opponents as the **Anabaptists**. The word means "to baptize again." In the view of those who opposed them, the Anabaptists were performing a second baptism (in addition to their prior infant baptism). But in the view of the Anabaptists, they were simply performing a valid baptism for the first time. Anabaptists would only baptize those who made profession of their faith in Jesus Christ. However, it is important to note that the early Anabaptists administered baptism by pouring (also known as "effusion"). Water was poured over the head. The later Baptist movement which developed among English separatists would argue that immersion was the only valid mode of baptism.

As we learned in the previous chapter, in January 1525, the magistrates called for a public debate over the matter. In this disputation, Zwingli opposed the Anabaptists and argued for

ZURICH, SWITZERLAND

the biblical validity of infant baptism. As a result, the city officials made infant baptism mandatory, giving citizens eight days to baptize their children. But the Anabaptists were unfazed. They persisted in maintaining their rejection of infant baptism.

THE DROWNING OF FELIX MANZ

That same month, the first adult baptisms were performed in Zurich. In Felix Manz's home, Konrad Grebel baptized George Blaurock. Others present were then baptized. At this time, such an act was very dangerous. The city council ultimately ruled that re-baptism was punishable by drowning. On January 5, 1527, Felix Manz was convicted of this crime and was drowned. Manz was the first Anabaptist executed. But he would not be the last.

Zwingli also set out to refute the claims of the Anabaptists. In 1525, he wrote ***Baptism, Rebaptism, and Infant Baptism***. In this work, Zwingli coined the term "Anabaptist" to describe those who were committed to the baptism of those who made professions of faith. Zwingli argued for the validity of infant baptism as a covenant sign given to the children of believing parents. Another Anabaptist advocate living outside Zurich named **Balthasar Hubmaier** (1485-1528) wrote a response to Zwingli's book titled ***The Christian Baptism of Believers***. The lines of division between the Reformed and the Anabaptists were becoming clearer.

The Anabaptist movement began to grow rapidly. It was no longer limited to Zurich. Following the execution of Felix Manz, a group of Anabaptists met in February 1527. They met in the town of Schleitheim (within one of the Swiss cantons) and created a confession of faith that summarized their beliefs. The document is known as the **Schleitheim Confession**. It provides a helpful and clear summary of what the earliest Anabaptists believed and what set them apart from Lutheran and Reformed Christians.

Excerpts from the *Schleitheim Confession* (1527)

The *Confession* details some of the unique beliefs of the Anabaptists in comparison with the other Reformers.

> Baptism shall be given to all those who have learned repentance and amendment of

LOCATION OF SCHLEITHEIM, SWITZERLAND

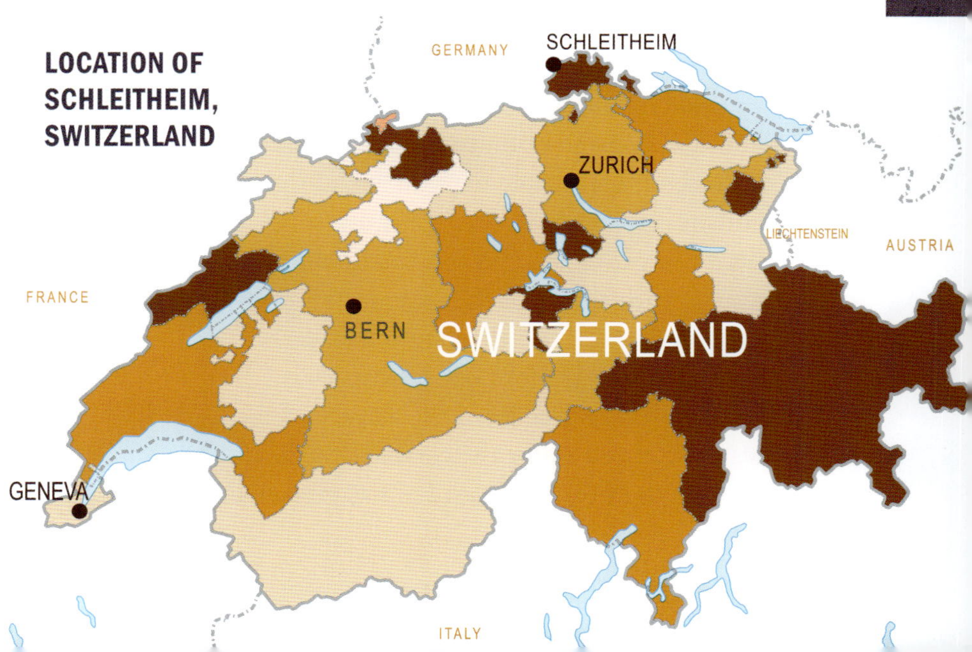

> life, and who believe truly that their sins are taken away by Christ, and to all those who walk in the resurrection of Jesus Christ, and wish to be buried with Him in death, so that they may be resurrected with Him and to all those who with this significance request it (baptism) of us and demand it for themselves. This excludes all infant baptism, the highest and chief abomination of the Pope. (Article 1)

In Article 1, the Anabaptists explain that baptism is only to be administered to those who repent and commit to a new life. Baptism was only to be administered to those who professed faith in Christ. This excluded infants and young children who were not yet able to make such a profession of faith. The Anabaptists also exclaim that infant baptism was an abomination propagated by the papacy. However, Reformers such as Martin Luther and John Calvin would argue that infant baptism was a biblical practice.

Article 4 explains some of the unique commitments Anabaptists made concerning oaths and civil service.

> From this we should learn that everything which is not united with our God and Christ cannot be other than an abomination which we should shun and flee from. By this is meant all Catholic and Protestant works and church services, meetings and church attendance, drinking houses, civic affairs, the oaths sworn in unbelief and other things of that kind, which are highly regarded by the world and yet are carried on in flat contradiction to the command of God, in accordance with all the unrighteousness which is in the world. From all these things we shall be separated and have no part with them for they are nothing but an abomination, and they are the cause of our being hated before our Christ Jesus, Who has set us free from the slavery of the flesh and fitted us for the service of God through the Spirit Whom He has given us. (Article 4)

Anabaptists believed that Christians ought not to participate in the civil government at all. Additionally, Anabaptists were **pacificists** and would under no circumstances participate in violent action. This included a total rejection of participation in any kind of war or any kind of civil punishments involving physical violence. This is found in Article 6:

> Lastly, one can see in the following points that it does not befit a Christian to be a magistrate: the rule of the government is according to the flesh, that of the Christians according to the Spirit. Their houses and dwelling remain in this world, that of the Christians is in heaven. Their citizenship is in this world, that of the Christians is in heaven. (Article 6)

Melchior Hoffman

But the prophet who presumes to speak a word in My name, which I have not commanded him to speak, or who speaks in the name of other gods, that prophet shall die. And if you say in your heart, "How shall we know the word which the Lord has not spoken?"— when a prophet speaks in the name of the Lord, if the thing does not happen or come to pass, that is the thing which the Lord has not spoken; the prophet has spoken it presumptuously; you shall not be afraid of him. (Deut. 18:20-22)

Many Anabaptists upheld classic Christian orthodoxy on most doctrines. But others moved far from biblical doctrine in radical and dangerous directions. One such Anabaptist leader was **Melchior Hoffman** (1495-1543). In 1523, influenced by Martin Luther, Hoffman adopted Reformation views. But very quickly, Hoffman abandoned Luther's teachings and claimed that he was a prophet. Hoffman claimed special spiritual insight into the Scriptures that others did not have. He also prophesied that Jesus would return in 1533.

Hoffman held many radical and unbiblical views. But Hoffman did not restrict himself to

MELCHIOR HOFFMAN (1495-1543)

teaching only. He took action and led riots in various towns to smash church images. Due to his violence and radical teaching, Hoffman became an outcast. However, from 1530-1533, Hoffman gained many disciples as he preached throughout Europe. In 1533, another radical "prophet" prophesied that Hoffman must return to Strasbourg, Germany and be imprisoned. After Hoffman's imprisonment, Christ would return in 1533, as Hoffman had originally prophesied. Hoffman then went back to Strasbourg as the prophecy commanded. But the prophecy didn't come to pass. Hoffman stayed in prison for ten years and then died. Hoffman and many of his followers were false prophets.

The Disaster in Münster

Where do wars and fights come from among you? Do they not come from your desires for pleasure that war in your members? You lust and do not have. You murder and covet and cannot obtain. You fight and war. (Jas. 4:1-2)

Hoffman's teaching had disastrous consequences. One of his disciples was named **Jan Beukels** (John of Leiden) (1509-1536). Beukels led a revolt and made himself "king" of the "New Jerusalem" in Münster, Germany. In 1534, Beukels and other Anabaptist leaders took over Münster and declared it to be "New Jerusalem." Beukels crowned himself king and persecuted those who opposed him. The death penalty was instituted for all sorts of crimes. In 1535, the practice of polygamy was introduced.

Roman Catholics and Lutherans joined forces to besiege Münster and put an end to the revolt there. In June 1535, the city was taken and most of the inhabitants were slain by the invading army. The radical leaders of Münster who had created such a disaster made it more difficult for other Anabaptists (most of them peaceful) to avoid persecution at the hands of authorities throughout Europe. The stain of the Münster rebellion tarnished the reputation of the Anabaptist movement as a whole.

JAN BEUKELS (JOHN OF LEIDEN, 1509-1536)

Menno Simons and the Mennonites

Melchior Hoffman is an example of a dangerous radical who went beyond Scripture, elevating his own opinions (claimed as prophecy). However, there were other Anabaptist leaders that were more conservative and sought to align their views more to Scripture. One of the most influential early Anabaptist leaders was a man named **Menno Simons** (1496-1561). He was the founder of the **Mennonite** group of Anabaptists which still

MÜNSTER, GERMANY

exist today.

Menno was ordained as a Roman Catholic priest in 1524. But as he heard about the Reformation, he began to have doubts about traditional Roman doctrines including transubstantiation. However, Menno quietly kept his views to himself and continued serving as a priest.

But in March 1535, Menno's brother Peter Simons joined the Anabaptists and participated in a violent seizure of a monastery near Bolsward. Government forces besieged the monastery and killed some 300 Anabaptists. Menno deeply grieved the loss of his brother, but he did not condone the violent actions of Anabaptists like his brother. But he did admire his brother's convictions and decided he could no longer continue as a priest with his Anabaptist views in secret.

Menno began traveling and preaching as an evangelist for the Anabaptist cause. He later settled in Groningen in 1537 and became an Anabaptist pastor there. Persecution against the Anabaptists continued to increase. As a result, Menno did much of his ministry in secret. Menno's leadership of some of the Anabaptists kept the movement from descending into radical chaos. Menno strongly denounced the radicalism of those who followed Melchior Hoffman in using violence to establish God's kingdom on earth. He guided the Anabaptist movement to an embrace of pacifism. Anabaptist pacifists argued that Christians should not be civil magistrates or be involved in the state. They also believed it was sinful to wage war or practice self-defense. They also refused to take oaths or vows.

MENNO SIMONS (1496-1561)

In 1539, Menno Simons summarized his view of what it meant to be a Christian. These words are found in his work *Why I Do Not Cease Teaching and Writing*.

> For true evangelical faith is of such a nature that it cannot lie dormant; but manifests itself in all righteousness and works of love; it dies unto flesh and blood; destroys all forbidden lusts and desires; cordially seeks, serves and fears God; clothes the naked; feeds the hungry;

> consoles the afflicted; shelters the miserable; aids and consoles all the oppressed; returns good for evil; serves those that injure it; prays for those that persecute it; teaches, admonishes and reproves with the Word of the Lord; seeks that which is lost; binds up that which is wounded; heals that which is diseased and saves that which is sound. The persecution, suffering and anxiety which befalls it for the sake of the truth of the Lord, is to it a glorious joy and consolation.[2]

Another influential work that produced further unity around pacifism was a book titled ***The Martyr's Mirror***. This was a book containing testimonies of martyrdom written by Dutch Anabaptists. The stories contained in this volume showed Anabaptists calmly and peacefully facing martyrdom. This encouraged many Anabaptists to embrace pacifism.

In 1540, Menno Simons wrote an influential work of theology titled ***The Foundation of Christian Doctrine***. This became a standard work for Mennonites. Much of Menno's book is consistent with orthodox Christian teachings on the Trinity and other doctrines. However, there were ways in which Menno differed from the Protestant Reformers. For example, Menno received the apocryphal books as divinely inspired by God and part of the Old Testament. But on the other hand, Menno rejected Rome's views of authority. He believed that Scripture was the supreme and final authority. Also, Menno primarily emphasized use of the New Testament. He downplayed the role of the Old Testament. He also downplayed the importance of the early church creeds and councils. This had a significant effect on how the Anabaptists understood biblical teaching. Menno's leadership of the Anabaptists left an enduring legacy. The Amish and Mennonites carried on Menno's teachings and still exist in various parts of the world today. ■

HINDELOOPEN, REGION OF FRIESLAND, NETHERLANDS. MENNO SIMONS GREW UP IN FRIESLAND.

ST. PIERRE'S CATHEDRAL, GENEVA, SWITZERLAND

The Reformation in Geneva

Therefore I testify to you this day that I am innocent of the blood of all men. For I have not shunned to declare to you the whole counsel of God. Therefore take heed to yourselves and to all the flock, among which the Holy Spirit has made you overseers, to shepherd the church of God which He purchased with His own blood. (Acts 20:26-28)

In modern-day Geneva, there stands an important monument to the Reformation. The monument is known as the Reformation Wall. Portrayed on this wall are four leading Reformers: **Theodore Beza**, **William Farel**, **John Calvin**, and **John Knox**. Each of these men were highly influential in the Reformation in Geneva and elsewhere. Perhaps the Reformer who has made the most significant influence upon the church is John Calvin (1509-1564). In this chapter, we will learn more about Calvin's reforming efforts in Geneva and the legacy he left for future generations.

The Reformation continued to progress in Zurich under Zwingli's successor **Heinrich Bullinger** (1504-1575). But due to Zwingli's early death, Zurich lost its strongest and most vocal leader. It was in Geneva that the Reformation advanced further under the leadership of John Calvin and some of the other men associated with him. Geneva became a sort of "capital" for the Reformed churches. Men from all over Europe came to Geneva to be trained for ministry. Then they returned to their home countries, taking with them the ideals of the Reformation.

Calvin's Background and Early Life

Your eyes saw my substance, being yet unformed.
And in Your book they all were written,
The days fashioned for me,
When as yet there were none of them. (Ps. 139:16)

Before we give our attention to the Reformation in Geneva, it is important to learn something about John Calvin's background and how he came to arrive in Geneva.

John Calvin was born in the small town of Noyon, France in 1509. At the time, Martin Luther was twenty-six years old. He was a monk and a professor at the University of Wittenberg. Within ten years of Calvin's birth, Luther would begin to pursue reformation in Wittenberg.

Calvin's father Gerard directed his son to enter

HEINRICH BULLINGER (1504-1575)

JOHN CALVIN (1509-1564)

the University of Paris when John was fourteen. Calvin's aim was to study theology and enter the priesthood upon completing his studies. Upon graduation, however, Calvin decided to study law instead and entered the University of Orleans. In 1531, Calvin's father died, and Calvin then moved back to Paris. He received a law degree in 1532 and published his first book, which was a study of the Roman author Seneca's *De Clementia* (*On Mercy*). Like others dedicated to the study of the humanities, Calvin was well versed in the classic literature of the Greeks and Romans. However, it was in 1532 that Calvin's attention would be redirected from the secular classics to the teaching of Holy Scripture. At the University of Bourges in 1532, Calvin encountered Reformation thought. As he considered the claims of the gospel as revealed in Holy Scripture, Calvin was brought to conviction. He recounted his conversion in this way:

> God by a sudden conversion subdued and brought my mind to a teachable frame, which was more hardened in such matters than might have been expected from one at my early period of life. Having thus received some taste and knowledge of true godliness, I was immediately inflamed with so intense a desire to make progress therein, that although I did not altogether leave off other studies, yet I pursued them with less ardour.[1]

In 1533, Calvin demonstrated his Protestant convictions by supporting a friend at the University of Paris. **Nicolas Cop**, friend of Calvin, was given an opportunity to make a speech before the university. Calvin assisted Cop in writing the speech. It was a call to return to the teaching of the New Testament and a right understanding of the gospel. Such ideas were not welcome at the University. As a result, Calvin fled Paris for safety.

TITLE PAGE OF THE 1536 *INSTITUTES*

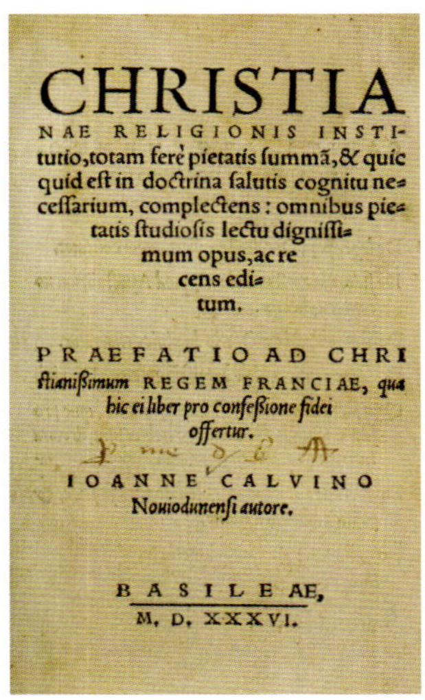

CHRISTIA
NAE RELIGIONIS INSTI-
tutio, totam ferè pietatis summã, & quic
quid est in doctrina salutis cognitu ne-
cessarium, complectens: omnibus pie-
tatis studiosis lectu dignissi-
mum opus, ac re
cens edi-
tum.

PRAEFATIO AD CHRI
stianißimum REGEM FRANCIAE, qua
hic ei liber pro confeßione fidei
offertur.

IOANNE CALVINO
Noviodunensi autore.

BASILEAE,
M. D. XXXVI.

After fleeing Paris, Calvin met a Reformation-minded man named **Louis du Tillet**. Calvin spent five months in du Tillet's home, where he studied the Bible and the writings of the church fathers. His time in du Tillet's home was instrumental in moving Calvin to completely embrace the Reformation cause and to renounce the Roman Church.

Calvin then journeyed to Basel where he began writing the first edition of his most important work, ***Institutes***

UNIVERSITY OF PARIS

of the Christian Religion. What started as a small handbook of Christian doctrine eventually grew into an extensive work of theology. Calvin continued to revise and expand the *Institutes* until he released a final Latin edition in 1559. The *Institutes* laid foundations for Western theology. It remains one of the most important works of Christian literature ever produced. However, the 1536 edition was quite short. It briefly covered the Ten Commandments, the Apostles Creed, the Lord's Prayer, and the sacraments. The purpose of Calvin's short book was to give Christian disciples a foundation of instruction in the Christian Faith.

Calvin also intended to defend the faith against charges of heresy. In the *Institutes*, Calvin addressed the work to the French king, **King Francis I** (r. 1515-1547). Calvin's desire was to demonstrate to King Francis that the Protestant cause was not heretical. His hope was that the French rulers would no longer persecute the Protestants. With this goal in mind, Calvin wrote an opening address to King Francis. Here is a portion of what Calvin wrote to the king:

> Sire . . . My intention was only to furnish a kind of rudiments, by which those who feel some interest in religion might be trained to true godliness. And I toiled at the task chiefly for the sake of my countrymen the French, multitudes of whom I perceived to be hungering and thirsting after Christ, while very few seemed to have been duly imbued with even a slender knowledge of him. That this was the object which I had in view is apparent from the work itself, which is written in a simple and elementary form adapted for instruction.
>
> But when I perceived that the fury of certain bad men had risen to such a height in your realm, that there was no place in it for sound doctrine, I thought it might be of service if I were in the same work both to give instruction to my countrymen, and also lay before your Majesty a Confession, from which you may learn what the doctrine is that so inflames the rage of those madmen who are this day, with fire and sword, troubling your kingdom. [2]

While Calvin's book did not change King Francis' mind concerning Protestants, it did serve as a valuable tool for instructing Christians in the faith. After Calvin published his first edition of the *Institutes*, he intended to move to Strasbourg to study and write for the Protestant cause.

Calvin Is Called to Geneva

A man's heart plans his way,
But the LORD directs his steps. (Prov. 16:9)

If Calvin had his way, he never would have lived in Geneva or served the church there. While we all make plans for the future, it is ultimately the Lord that directs our steps. So it was for Calvin. In July of 1536, Calvin happened to be passing through Geneva on his way to Strasbourg. There

KING FRANCIS I (1515-1547)

he was confronted by the Reformer **William Farel** (1489-1565). Farel was desirous to see the Reformation established in Geneva. He had already been sent to Geneva from the city of Bern to guide Geneva toward embracing the Reformation. Now, if this work were to continue in Geneva, Farel needed help. He saw Calvin as the perfect fit for the job.

Farel was known for his fiery, zealous personality. And true to his personality, he exhorted Calvin with the strongest possible words to move to Geneva and assist with reforming the church. But Calvin did not wish to settle in Geneva. Instead, he wanted to study and write in seclusion. But Farel would not let Calvin go. Farel warned Calvin of God's judgment if he should not obey the call to join the Reformation work in Geneva. Calvin tells the story in his own words:

> Farel, who burned with an extraordinary zeal to advance the Gospel, immediately strained every nerve to detain me. And after having learned that my heart was set on devoting myself to private studies, for which I wished to keep myself free from other pursuits, and finding that he gained nothing by entreaties, he proceeded to utter a threat that God would curse my retirement, and the tranquility of the studies which I sought, if I should withdraw and refuse to give assistance, when the necessity was so urgent. I was so struck with fear by this threat that I desisted from the journey which I had undertaken, but mindful of my natural bashfulness and timidity, I would not bring myself under any obligation to discharge any particular office.[3]

MARTIN BUCER (1491-1551)

Calvin and Farel joined forces and offered their services to the city authorities in Geneva. From 1536 to 1538, Calvin and Farel sought to reform the church in Geneva. However, the first few years did not go well. Calvin and Farel both firmly believed that the church's officers, not the city council, should exercise church discipline. But the city council was not willing to give up this authority. When Calvin and Farel sought to impose a new confession of faith upon all Genevans, they were also resisted.

In 1538, the city council adopted the liturgy used in the city of Bern. Calvin and Farel both disagreed with the council's decision. They argued that it was the duty of church shepherds (pastors and elders) to make such decisions. This disagreement resulted in the council banishing Calvin and Farel from Geneva.

Calvin then spent three years in Strasbourg working closely with and being mentored by the German Reformer **Martin Bucer** (1491-1551). During Calvin's time in Strasbourg, he participated in several conferences with Martin Bucer. Together, they defended Protestant teachings against the Roman Church. Also, while living in Strasbourg, Calvin married a widow named Idelette in August 1540. Idelette had two children from her first marriage. Calvin was now a husband and father.

Calvin was impressed with the hearty psalm singing of Bucer's congregation and decided to produce a French metrical psalter. The resulting *Genevan Psalter* quickly spread throughout Europe and was translated into German, Dutch,

Czech, Polish, Hungarian, and even Turkish, forming a common bond among Continental Reformed churches. Metrical psalm singing spread to England and Scotland as well.

In 1540, the citizens of Geneva wrote to Calvin, asking him to return. Calvin was extremely reluctant to return to Geneva after the hardships he encountered there in previous years. Calvin wrote, "There is no place under heaven I am more afraid of. I would rather submit to a hundred other deaths, than to that cross on which I would have to perish a thousand times every day!"[4] Nevertheless, Calvin agreed to the request and prepared to return to Geneva. "I offer my heart a slain victim in sacrifice to the Lord."[5] When he returned to the pulpit in Geneva, Calvin picked up preaching right where he had left off three years before, at the very next verse.

IDELETTE CALVIN

Though Calvin's presence was requested, not everyone in Geneva liked him. He faced opposition throughout his ministry from 1541 until his death in 1564. Calvin was eager to see the church strengthened in Geneva. But he often found himself in conflict with the city council. For example, Calvin desired to celebrate the Lord's Supper each week on the Lord's Day. But the city council would not allow it. Calvin settled for celebration of the Lord's Supper four times a year. Yet in other cases Calvin was successful in seeing advances in reform.

Calvin and his fellow pastors believed church discipline should be by the officers of the church, not the magistrates of the city. The Genevan Reformers came into conflict with the Genevan magistrates on this point and had many enemies in the city. Calvin's lawless opponents were called Libertines. At one point, some excommunicated, impenitent Libertines approached the table to partake of communion. But Calvin interposed himself to block the way. Lifting up his hands, he exclaimed: "I will lay down my life ere these hands shall reach forth the holy things of God to those who have been branded as despisers."[6]

INTERIOR OF ST. PIERRE'S CATHEDRAL

Calvin's courage won the day on that occasion, but the long, hard struggle continued.

Calvin desired the church to be purified in its doctrine, government, and life. Influenced by Bucer, Calvin developed a doctrine of the Lord's Supper that was between Luther's view and Zwingli's view. He argued for the real spiritual presence of Christ in the sacrament and for the real spiritual partaking of Christ by believers through the power of the Holy Spirit and faith. Calvin worked hard for church unity. Through the efforts of Calvin, Heinrich Bullinger, and others, the Reformed churches came to an agreement on the Lord's Supper called the *Consensus Tigurinus* in 1549. But despite Calvin's efforts and his friendship with Philip Melanchthon, the Lutherans never reached an agreement with the Reformed.

Calvin strove for the reformation and purity of worship. The Lutherans had taught a **Normative Principle of Worship**. This said that what was not forbidden in Scripture might be done in worship. In contrast to this, Calvin and the Reformed taught the **Regulative Principle of Worship**. This said that every element of worship must have some basis in Scripture. This led to some differences in worship between the two groups of Protestants. The Reformed rejected images of Christ and images in worship, while the Lutherans retained them. Lutherans wrote and sang many hymns while the Reformed largely sang psalms.

Calvin also worked for the reformation of church government. He along with other Reformers worked for the restoration of church government by representative assemblies consisting of a plurality of godly elders. This form of church government is known as Presbyterianism today. They also sought to restore the diaconate to its Biblical function of caring for material needs. Reformed representative church government would also have an influence on the development of representative political government.

Calvin was also committed to the purification of society. He strove to see the city council enact various ordinances to enforce laws against various sins including adultery, drunkenness, gambling, swearing, disobedience of children, among others. New ordinances against these kinds of sins provoked violent opposition from some within the city. Some who held heretical views and lived immoral lives opposed Calvin at every step. The city council not only enacted punishments against societal ills. But they also were constructive in seeking to improve life in Geneva. Church historian Nick Needham explains some of the ways Geneva sought to improve social conditions:

> The authorities created an outstanding system of free public education; they stimulated business by helping to establish a highly successful cloth and silk industry, which provided much-needed employment; they made the sale of food subject to strict health and hygiene laws; they supplied latrines free of charge for all houses that lacked them; they built a high-quality hospital, and a place of residence for the homeless; they set up an agency to find work for the unemployed; and they organized a noble system of social care for the poor and aged.[7]

As the Reformation in Geneva progressed, refugees from other lands came to Geneva for both refuge and training. **John Knox** (1514-1572), a leader of the Reformation in Scotland, fled to Geneva for refuge. He was discipled there by Calvin. Many Protestants persecuted in France also fled to Geneva for refuge. Calvin founded an academy for the training of ministers in 1559. This institution later became known as the University of Geneva, which still exists today.

During his years of ministry in Geneva, Calvin exercised a great deal of influence. However, the only office he ever held was pastor of **St. Pierre's Cathedral** in Geneva. Calvin never held any office as a civil magistrate. He brought change to Geneva through the spoken word. He was first and foremost a preacher of Scripture. Calvin was also a faithful pastor and cared deeply for those under his pastoral care in Geneva. His collection of letters shows his wisdom and the love he showed to others. One example is found in a letter he wrote in April 1549 where Calvin described how pastors are to care deeply about Christ's flock. He wrote, "We ought to weep with those who weep. That is to say, if we are Christians, we ought to have such compassion and sorrow for our neighbors that we should willingly take part in their tears, and thus comfort them."[8]

The Controversy over Michael Servetus

One of the most well-known events in Calvin's life was the execution of a man named **Michael Servetus** (1511-1553). Michael Servetus was a medical doctor from Spain who also had an interest in theology. He wrote several works denying Christian doctrine, including the deity of Christ, the Trinity, and original sin. In 1531, Servetus wrote a book detailing how the Trinity was a false doctrine. In 16th century Europe, to deny the Trinity was to brand yourself as a heretic. It was still the common practice to execute heretics, both in Roman Catholic and Protestant lands.

MICHAEL SERVETUS (1511-1553)

In 1545, Calvin and Servetus began to write letters back and forth debating different topics.. Calvin sought to persuade Servetus to repent of his heretical beliefs. But he would not. Eventually, Roman Catholic authorities in France arrested Servetus and convicted him of heresy. The sentence was death. But Servetus escaped execution in France by fleeing.

In 1553, Servetus decided to go to Geneva and attend worship at St. Pierre's Cathedral. Servetus knew the risks of making himself known in Geneva, but he went there anyway. Upon his arrival, French refugees identified Servetus, and he was arrested. Servetus was put on trial by the city council. It is important to note that Calvin did not hold any civil office. He was not even a citizen of Geneva until 1559. However, because he was a theologian familiar with Servetus' views, Calvin did testify regarding Servetus' false teaching. The council concluded that Servetus was a heretic and condemned him to death. Farel and Calvin sought to persuade Servetus to recant of his false teaching. But he would not.

The city council of Geneva condemned Servetus to death by burning at the stake. Calvin pled with the city council to behead Servetus instead as a quicker form of execution. But the council refused and Servetus was burned. Calvin's role in the execution of Servetus has been controversial among Christians. Yet it is important to note that the execution of heretics was almost universally practiced throughout Europe during this time. What happened in Geneva was not unique.

Calvin's Preaching Ministry in Geneva

Therefore, brethren, seek out from among you seven men of good reputation, full of the Holy Spirit and wisdom, whom we may appoint over this business; but we will give ourselves continually to prayer and to the ministry of the word. (Acts 6:3-4)

Calvin was especially gifted as a preacher and teacher. He preached through many books of the Bible and wrote many commentaries on Scripture. His sermons and commentaries are still read by many today. Calvin kept himself busy in constant study and preaching. Calvin preached from the New Testament on Sunday mornings, from the New Testament or the Psalms on Sunday afternoons, and from the Old Testament every morning of the week. Calvin preached an average of 170 sermons per year.

His method of preaching was simple. He worked verse by verse through entire books of the Bible. His method was to carefully expound the text and then apply its meaning to his hearers. Here is a sample of Calvin's preaching on Micah.

> Let us learn, therefore, not to become drunk on our foolish hopes. Rather, let us hope in God and in God's promises, and we will never be deceived. But if we base our hopes on our own presumptuousness, God will strip everything away. This is one of our most essential doctrines, since human nature is so driven by presumptuousness. For we are so influenced by insupportable pride that God is forced to punish us harshly. We think we are so much higher than God that we ought to be more powerful than God. Consequently, seeing how inclined we are toward this vice, all the more ought we to pay heed to what Micah says here: that we must not rest content with the thought that whatever happens will happen. Rather, we must realize that so long as God's hand is upon us, we are condemned to be miserable. For there is no other cure shy of our returning to God and founding our hopes on his promises. Therein lies our surest remedy, equal to any and all disasters that might befall us.[9]

Calvin's commitment to preaching through the Bible verse-by-verse set an important pattern that would be followed by churches of the Reformation. Thanks to the work of a scribe named Dennis Raguenier, who wrote down many of Calvin's sermons as they were delivered, we can still read many of Calvin's sermons today.

Genevan Missionary Efforts

How beautiful upon the mountains
Are the feet of him who brings good news,
Who proclaims peace,
Who brings glad tidings of good things,
Who proclaims salvation,
Who says to Zion,
"Your God reigns!" (Isa. 52:7)

In the first decades of the Protestant Reformation, missionary efforts were limited. The Protestant Reformers directed their attention to the reform of the church in their own region. However, the Reformation did inspire a missionary enterprise. Zealous Christians spread Reformation ideals all over Europe. Geneva was among the most influential cities because people from all over Europe found refuge in Geneva. Persecution against Protestants was on the rise throughout Europe. To find safety, many fled to Geneva. One refugee, an Englishman named John Bale, described what he saw in Geneva.

> Geneva seems to me to be the wonderful miracle of the whole world. For so many from all countries come here, as it were, to a sanctuary. Is it not wonderful that Spaniards, Italians, Scots, Englishmen, Frenchmen, Germans disagreeing in manners, speech, and apparel, should live so lovingly and friendly, and dwell together like a spiritual and Christian congregation?[10]

Monarchs who opposed the Reformation were not happy with Geneva's growing popularity. Philip II of Spain, committed to the Roman Church, wrote to the King of France with these words:

> Geneva is the source of all misfortune to France, the refuge of all heretics, the most terrible enemy of Rome. I am ready at any time, with all the power of my kingdom, to aid in its destruction.[11]

Protestants from France were the largest group of refugees. Many of the French who found refuge in Geneva were trained and then sent back to France. The Reformed church grew rapidly due to Geneva's missionary-sending efforts.

Europe was the primary focus of mission efforts by the early Reformers. However, there were a few exceptions to this. In 1557, a group of missionaries were sent to Brazil. The French Protestants who made the journey sought both refuge as well as missionary advance in the New World. On March 10, 1557, two missionaries named Pierre Richier and William Chartier landed in the region of modern-day Rio de Janeiro, Brazil. The missionaries faced severe trials from the local natives and did not see much success. Nevertheless, this early missionary effort shows how the Protestant Reformers were committed to evangelism and missions.

Legacy of the Genevan Reformation

The labors of Calvin and his successors in Geneva influenced the Western world in many ways. Calvin's teachings on theology, the church, politics, ethics, and economics influenced the church in Europe, North America, and throughout the world for centuries. Calvin's view of politics would also affect the political landscape of the Western world. Countries most impacted by Calvin's thought include Switzerland, Hungary, the Netherlands, England, Scotland, and the United States. ■

LAKE GENEVA, SWITZERLAND

KING'S COLLEGE CHAPEL, CAMBRIDGE, ENGLAND

21 William Tyndale and the English Bible

I have rejoiced in the way of Your testimonies,
As much as in all riches.
I will meditate on Your precepts,
And contemplate Your ways.
I will delight myself in Your statutes;
I will not forget Your word. (Ps. 119:14-16)

The Bible, the written Word of God, is a precious gift to God's people. The words of Holy Scripture have always been the daily bread of Christ's people. Through the preaching of God's Word, the church advances. Through believing God's Word, sinners are saved. Through meditation and practice of God's Word, Christians mature. Without the Word of God, the church languishes. Without access to Scripture, God's people are cut off from a knowledge of the gospel and the precepts of God.

WILLIAM TYNDALE (C. 1494-1536)

The recovery of access to the Bible through translation, preaching, and distribution was one of the most important developments of the Protestant Reformation. In this chapter, we will learn about the life and work of **William Tyndale** (c. 1494-1536), who gave up his life to make the Word of God accessible to the English people.

Before Tyndale was executed for his work of Bible translation, he faithfully produced two editions of the New Testament in English. He also translated a large portion of the Old Testament, but he was prevented from finishing. Tyndale's influence upon English translations of the Bible is enormous. It is estimated that around 85% to 90% of the words in the New Testament of the **Authorised Version (King James Version)** are drawn directly from Tyndale's New Testament translation. From the Authorised Version, later English translations also appeared that still retain much of Tyndale's original work.

Tyndale believed the Bible to be so important that he was willing to die as he sought to translate the Bible faithfully into English. His love for God's Word is an example we too should follow.

William Tyndale's Early Years

William Tyndale was born around 1494 near Gloucestershire, England. There is much we do not know about William's early years. However, we do know that his family was prosperous enough to send him to study at Oxford when he was a young man. Tyndale graduated from Oxford in 1512 with a bachelor's degree from Magdalen College and entered the priesthood around the same time.

Tyndale later observed how students in the universities were shielded from the Holy Scriptures and forced to study the Greek philosophers rather than the most valuable book in the world: the Bible. Tyndale wrote:

> In the universities, they have ordained that no man shall look on the Scripture until he be nursed in heathen learning eight or nine years, and armed with false principles with which he is clean shut out of the understanding of the Scripture . . . The Scripture is locked up with . . . false expositions, and with false principles of natural philosophy.[1]

In 1515, Tyndale distinguished himself as a master of languages when he graduated from Oxford again, now with a master's degree. In 1519, Tyndale went to study at Cambridge, the great intellectual rival of Oxford. In these early years of the Reformation, Cambridge was becoming a hotbed of Protestant ideas as the writings of Martin Luther became available to Cambridge students and professors.

TYNDALE'S CONFRONTATION WITH THE ROMAN CATHOLIC CLERGYMAN

At a local pub called the **White Horse Inn**, scholars gathered to discuss Reformation ideas. This group became known as the "little Germany." Participants in these discussions included such luminaries as Robert Barnes, Nicholas Ridley, Hugh Latimer, Miles Coverdale, Thomas Cranmer, and Thomas Bilney. It is possible that William Tyndale participated in these conversations at the White Horse Inn.

In 1521, as Tyndale reflected on the teachings of the Reformation, he decided to step away from his academic post in order to continue in private study. He took a job as a private tutor for the Walsh family. Tyndale tutored John Walsh's children while he studied the Greek New Testament and Reformation writings. As Tyndale reflected on the poor spiritual condition of England, he realized that the truth of Scripture was the only thing that could establish the English people in the faith. Though churches existed in every village and town, many were ignorant of the gospel of Jesus Christ. Tyndale wrote, "It was impossible to establish the lay people in any truth, except the Scripture were laid before their eyes in their mother tongue."[2]

In time, Tyndale's controversial views became known, and he sometimes had to answer for them to the authorities of the church. One well-known occasion was recorded in ***Foxe's Book of Martyrs***, originally titled ***Acts and Monuments of These Latter and Perilous Days*** by the Protestant leader **John Foxe** (c. 1517-1587). This may be the most well-known quote of William Tyndale. This interchange recorded by Foxe illustrates how committed some were to the authority of the pope and the Roman Church. At dinner one night at the Walsh manor, Tyndale debated with a Roman Catholic clergyman. The priest stated one of the most appalling and shocking statements one could imagine: "We are better without God's laws than the pope's."

How did Tyndale respond? In his typically bold manner: "I defy the pope and all his laws. If God spare my life ere many years, I will cause a boy that drives the plough to know more of the Scripture than thou dost."[3]

Tyndale's challenge to the Catholic priest was no empty threat. In fact, Tyndale ultimately accomplished this. Though his life was cut short before finishing the translation of the entire Bible, Tyndale was instrumental in giving the Scriptures to every ploughboy in England. After this event, the translation of the Scriptures into English became the dominating goal of Tyndale's life. He was committed to it heart and soul.

In 1523, Tyndale went to London seeking permission to create an English translation of the New Testament. He asked permission from the Bishop of London **Cuthbert Tunstall** (1474-1559). Tunstall had worked with Desiderius Erasmus (1466-1536) on Erasmus' edition of the Greek New Testament. Because of this connection, Tyndale thought that Bishop Tunstall would gladly receive his proposal.

However, it didn't work out that way. Tunstall was suspicious of Tyndale's theology and did not trust Tyndale to do the translation work. Tunstall also was concerned that an English New Testament would create mayhem in England. He, along with other church authorities, believed giving the common people access to the Bible would create anarchy and division. Tyndale was disappointed but undeterred from fulfilling his mission.

Tyndale Translates and Prints the English New Testament

"Is not My word like a fire?" says the LORD, "And like a hammer that breaks the rock in pieces?" (Jer. 23:29)

Realizing that neither the church nor the English crown would authorize his translation work, at age thirty, Tyndale left England in 1524. He moved to the European continent and began his translation work illegally. He would translate the Bible there and then send the books into England against the law.

Why did Tyndale break the law? He was a man of conviction. He believed it to be his duty before God to give access to the Word of God to the English people, no matter what the cost. He loved God's Word, and he wouldn't submit to the authorities of a rebellious church that had sought to keep God's oracles from Christ's sheep. The English authorities were disobeying God when they forbade the Bible to be translated. Tyndale would obey God rather than men (Acts 5:29).

Tyndale first went to Germany in 1524 to meet Luther in Wittenberg. Then in 1525, he traveled to Cologne and worked on his translation of the New Testament from Greek into English. However, while in Cologne, a bitter opponent of the Reformation, John Cochlaeus, heard about Tyndale's plans and raided the print shop. Thankfully, Tyndale knew about Cochlaeus' plan beforehand and grabbed his

cxix.
The Gospell off
Sancte Jhon.
The fyrst Chapter.
In the begynnynge was that worde/ ād that worde was with god: and god was thatt worde. The same was in the begynnynge wyth god. All thyngf were made by it/ and with out it/ was made noo thige/ that made was. In it was lyfe/ And lyfe was the light of mē/ And the light shyneth i darcknes/ ād darcknes cōprehēded it not.
There was a mā sent from god/ whose name was Jhon. The same cā as a witnes/ to beare witnes of the light/ that all men through hī myght beleve. He was nott that light: but to beare witnes of the light. That was a true light/ which lighteneth all men that come ito the worlde. He was in the worlde/ ād the worlde by hī was made: and the worlde knewe hym not. ... ed hī not. vns ... receaved hī/ gave he power to be the sōnes of god: i that they beleved ō his name: which were borne not of bloude nor of the will of the flesshe/ nor yet of the will of men: but of god. And that worde was made flesshe/ and dwelt amonge vs/ and we sawe the glory off yt/ as the

THE GOSPEL OF JOHN IN TYNDALE'S 1526 NEW TESTAMENT

copies of the manuscript and fled the city.

Tyndale fled to Worms, Germany. While in Worms, he successfully printed his first edition of the English New Testament in 1526. Copies were then smuggled into England hidden in bales of cotton. They were collected by a secret Protestant society and widely distributed throughout England to many who were eager to read God's Word in their own language. The first printing consisted of some 3,000 copies.

Soon church authorities caught word of the illegal Tyndale New Testament being distributed throughout the country. Bishop Tunstall preached a scathing sermon against Tyndale in London and publicly burned confiscated copies of Tyndale's New Testament.

In 1527, Tyndale's opponents formed a plan to stop the spread of these illegal New Testaments. **William Warham** (c. 1450-1532), the archbishop of Canterbury, sought to purchase all the copies of Tyndale's New Testament that could be found to have them burned. Warham's plan seemed to be an excellent way to stop Tyndale's translation work. But the plan backfired.

The money used to purchase all the remaining copies made it back to Tyndale. In seeking to destroy this first edition from Tyndale, his own opponents provided the needed funds to produce a second, revised edition of the New Testament. Thus, Tyndale's enemies enabled him to produce a better edition and print even more copies this time. The Lord providentially provided Tyndale exactly what he needed to continue his mission.

In 1528, Tyndale gained sufficient knowledge of Hebrew to begin translating the Old Testament as well. He worked for years on this translation while he was on the run from English authorities who were searching the continent for him. In Antwerp, Tyndale completed his translation of the Five Books of Moses (the Pentateuch). Once Tyndale's location became known to local authorities, Tyndale fled Antwerp and set out for Hamburg. Tragically, while aboard a ship, he was caught in a storm and lost all his books, including his translation manuscript of the Five Books of Moses. Tyndale had to begin his translation of the Old Testament anew at Genesis 1:1.

Having lost so much work was surely discour-

ANTWERP, BELGIUM

aging. But this did not stop Tyndale. He was driven by conviction, and his love for God's Word drove him to begin the Old Testament translation once again.

While in Hamburg, Tyndale reunited with a Cambridge classmate, **Miles Coverdale** (1488-1569). Coverdale helped Tyndale retranslate the Pentateuch, speeding up the work's progress. Coverdale himself would be responsible for ongoing translation work as well, culminating in the **Coverdale Bible**, first published in 1535.

In 1534, Tyndale returned to Antwerp and completed his second edition of the Greek New Testament. This is considered by most to be Tyndale's crowning achievement, his very best work. Six thousand copies were printed, and they sold out within a month. A third edition would follow later that year with few corrections.

Tyndale's New Testament was a remarkable production of enduring excellence. Here are a few selections from Tyndale's 1534 edition. Many of these sections of Scripture will be familiar to English readers who have heard echoes of this translation in the Authorised Version (KJV) or other English translations. (Tyndale's New Testament did not have verse numbers, but it did use chapter divisions.)

MILES COVERDALE (1488-1569)

Ye are the salt of the earth: but and if the salt have lost her saltness, what can be salted therewith? It is thenceforth good for nothing, but to be cast out, and to be trodden under foot of men. Ye are the light of the world. A city that is set on an hill, cannot be hid, neither do men light a candle and put it under a bushel, but on a candlestick, and it lighteth all that are in the house. (Matthew 5)

For God so loveth the world, that he hath given his only son, that none that believe in him should perish: but should have everlasting life. (John 3)

But the law in the meantime entered in, that sin should increase. Neverthelater where abundance of sin was, there was more plenteousness of grace. That as sin had reigned unto death, even so might grace reign through righteousness unto eternal life, by the help of Jesus Christ. (Romans 5)

Seeing then that we have a great high priest which is entered into heaven (I mean Jesus the Son of God) let us hold fast our profession. For we have not an high priest, which cannot have compassion on our infirmities; but was in all points tempted, like as we are: but yet without sin (Hebrews 4)

Tyndale's translation is accurate, clear, and beautiful. By re-examining the New Testament in the original Greek, Tyndale also rendered certain words with English words that better represented the original meaning. Instead of "church" he used "congregation." Instead of "priest" he used "elder." "Charity" was translated as "love" by Tyndale in 1 Corinthians 13. Rather than the term "do penance," Tyndale translated the word in the New Testament more accurately as "repent." These translation choices influenced later English translations. However, when the Authorised Version was translated during the reign of King James I in 1611, some of Tyndale's translation choices were rejected in favor of more common terminology (for example, "church" in the KJV instead of Tyndale's "congregation").

Tyndale Betrayed and Executed

I will speak of Your testimonies also before kings,
And will not be ashamed.
And I will delight myself in Your commandments,
Which I love. (Ps. 119:46-47)

Over in England, church authorities still wanted to get their hands on William Tyndale. English authorities sent numerous men from England to the continent to find and apprehend him.

It was a man named **Henry Phillips** who became the successful betrayer of Tyndale. Phillips found himself in debt after gambling a large portion of money away that had been given to him by his father to pay off a debt. Church officials became aware of Henry Phillips' predicament. They offered him money if he would locate Tyndale and befriend Tyndale in order to betray him. He was the Judas of the story who would betray Tyndale after acting as a friend towards him.

Phillips went to Antwerp in 1535 and quietly asked around until he was able to locate Tyndale. For some time, he established a sham friendship with Tyndale. Phillips eventually was able to lead Tyndale into a back-alley where English authorities lay in wait for him. Tyndale was arrested and taken to a castle six miles north of Brussels. He was imprisoned for more than a year awaiting his trial in the damp and cold dungeon of the castle.

THE EXECUTION OF WILLIAM TYNDALE

Even here, Tyndale did not give up on his translation work. We have one of Tyndale's letters from prison, requesting certain books so that he could continue his Old Testament translation. Here is a portion of that letter:

> I beg your lordship . . . that if I am to remain here through the winter, you will request the commissary to have the kindness to send me, from the goods of mine which he has . . . a warmer coat also, for this which I have is very thin; a piece of cloth too to patch my leggings. . . . But most of all I beg and beseech your clemency to be urgent with the commissary, that he will kindly permit me to have the Hebrew Bible, Hebrew grammar, and Hebrew dictionary, that I may pass the time in that study.[4]

All Tyndale wanted was a warm coat, some cloth to patch his ragged leggings, but most of all, this man wanted his Hebrew Bible, his Hebrew grammar, and Hebrew dictionary so he could continue his life work: the translation of God's Holy Word.

In August 1536, Tyndale was brought to trial and accused of a number of crimes. His criminal beliefs included:

- Justification by faith alone
- Human traditions cannot bind the conscience
- The human will is bound by sin
- There is no purgatory
- Mary nor the saints offer prayers for us
- We are not to pray to Mary or the saints

Tyndale was condemned as a heretic for these convictions. The tradition at this time, if a priest was accused of heresy, was to bring them out in their priestly robes and excommunicate them. The accused priest was forced to kneel as his hands were scraped with a knife, symbolizing the loss of all the privileges of the priesthood. The bread and wine of the mass would be placed in his hands and then removed. He was stripped of his priestly vestments. He would then be delivered over to the authorities for the sentence of death.

In October 1536, Tyndale was led out to be executed. Near Brussels he was led out of the castle into the town. An execution stake was placed in the town square. Hanging from the top of the beam was a strong iron chain. Straw and logs were piled at the base. Tyndale's feet were bound and a chain was fastened around his neck. Wood was arranged around Tyndale so that he would burn amidst the fire. Gunpowder was also sprinkled on the wood and brush.

John Foxe recorded that Tyndale simply prayed at this moment and looked up to heaven, praying, "Lord, open the king of England's eyes."[5]

The executioner was then given the signal. The iron noose was tightened around Tyndale's neck, suffocating him. After Tyndale died from suffocation, the wood was lit and caught fire. Soon the fire hit the gunpowder, causing an explosion. William Tyndale's earthly sojourn had ended.

In a short period of time, Tyndale's final prayer was answered. Just two years after Tyndale's death, **Thomas Cranmer**, the archbishop of Canterbury, convinced King Henry VIII to approve the publication of an English Bible. In 1538, the king issued a decree that a copy of the Bible should be placed in every church in England. In the decades that followed, every ploughboy and every housewife began to encounter the living Word of God translated into English by the faithful labors of Tyndale and the men who followed Him. Tyndale died for his conviction that the Word of God is the most precious possession in the world. The Word of God is worth dying for.

If you possess a written copy of the Bible, now is a good time to give thanks to God for faithful Christians like William Tyndale who gave up everything so that Christ's people can hear their Shepherd's voice. ■

BRUSSELS, BELGIUM

WESTMINSTER ABBEY, LONDON, ENGLAND

The Reformation in England

For by grace you have been saved through faith, and that not of yourselves; it is the gift of God, not of works, lest anyone should boast. (Eph. 2:8-9)

William Tyndale's death was not in vain. His life work of translating and distributing God's Word in England continued after his martyrdom. A few years after Tyndale's death in 1536, reading the Bible in English would be authorized by **King Henry VIII** (r. 1509-1547). It was during Henry's reign that the Reformation began in England. But the circumstances in England were quite different than Germany or the Swiss lands.

The English church would separate from the Roman Church not for doctrinal reasons, but as a matter of personal expediency for King Henry VIII. The king was anxious to have a male heir to the throne. Henry's first wife, **Catherine of Aragon** (1485-1536), had given birth to a daughter, **Mary Tudor** (1516-1558). The other children Catherine gave birth to were either stillborn or lived just a month or two. Henry became concerned about the future of his throne. At this time, a male heir to the throne of England was considered essential. However, in later years, with Mary I and Elizabeth I, the monarch of England would be a woman.

Previous to her marriage to King Henry VIII, Catherine had been married for a brief period to Henry's older brother Arthur. But within months of their marriage, Arthur died, leaving Catherine a widow. Subsequently, Henry married Catherine. This fact became important to Henry when Catherine continued to lose children in birth, leaving Henry without a male heir. At the same time, Henry was interested in a young lady named **Anne Boleyn** (c. 1501-1536), whom he wished to marry. But Henry could not marry Anne without ending his marriage with Catherine.

To find a justification for ending his marriage with Catherine, Henry observed what Leviticus 20 said about marrying one's brother's wife.

If a man takes his brother's wife, it is an unclean thing. He has uncovered his brother's nakedness. They shall be childless. (Lev. 20:21)

Henry thought that Catherine's childlessness (in producing a surviving male heir) perhaps was a fulfillment of the curse this verse describes. However, Henry misinterpreted the passage which forbids such a relationship when one's brother is

KING HENRY VIII (1509-1547)

alive. It did not address the matter of marrying a widow such as Catherine.

The Roman Church did not recognize any grounds for divorce, and to the present day still does not believe divorce is a valid practice. But the Roman Church in Henry's time and today can grant an **annulment**. This is a declaration by the church that the marriage was not valid to begin with, and therefore the relationship can be dissolved. Henry sought an annulment from the pope of Rome so he would be free to marry Anne Boleyn. He petitioned Cardinal Wolsey to seek an annulment from the pope, but his petition was denied. Not giving up, Henry persuaded many in the English clergy to make an argument on his behalf in favor of annulment. This too failed. Henry then decided he would break with Rome and declare himself to be the head of the English Church. From 1532 to 1534, a series of acts in the English Parliament made the English Church separate from the authority of the Roman Church.

The Reformation Progresses in England

We have also a more sure word of prophecy; whereunto ye do well that ye take heed, as unto a light that shineth in a dark place, until the day dawn, and the day star arise in your hearts: Knowing this first, that no prophecy of the scripture is of any private interpretation. For the prophecy came not in old time by the will of man: but holy men of God spake as they were moved by the Holy Ghost. (2 Pet. 1:19-21 KJV)

One of Henry's supporters was a priest named **Thomas Cranmer** (1489-1556). Cranmer argued in favor of Henry's view that his marriage with Catherine should be annulled. This made Cranmer a favorable choice to lead the English Church following its separation from Rome. Henry appointed Thomas Cranmer as archbishop of Canterbury in 1533. He would serve in this position for over twenty years.

Thomas Cromwell (c. 1485-1540) served as Henry's chief minister. Along with Thomas Cranmer, Cromwell assisted Henry in the pursuit

ANNE BOLEYN (C. 1501-1536)

THOMAS CRANMER (1489-1556)

of reformation in England. As part of the Reformation effort, Cromwell was tasked with the dissolution of the monasteries in England. Monasteries and their lands were taken over by the English monarchy.

Cromwell and Cranmer both urged Henry to make the Bible available in English. Two different translations of the English Bible were eventually authorized and distributed, including the **Coverdale Bible** and the **Matthew's Bible**. These two versions then culminated in the issuance of the 1539 **Great Bible** which contained the work of Tyndale, Coverdale, and John Rogers (responsible for the *Matthew's Bible*). Cromwell directed the clergy to make the volume accessible to members of the church who could come and read from it. God's people began to read the Bible for themselves. Now, laypeople in the church could knowledgeably discuss the teaching of Scripture with the clergy. Tyndale's vision of the ploughboy knowing more Scripture than the priest was coming to pass.

Despite Henry's support of these efforts in England, it appears that Henry never truly embraced Protestant views. Before England's separation from the Roman Church, Henry wrote a book in defense of the Roman view of the sacraments, opposing Martin Luther. The pope was so pleased with Henry's book that he gave him the title, "Defender of the Faith," which the British monarchs still use today. Roman Catholics and Protestants were burned side by side at the stake during Henry's reign. Henry died with most of his Roman Catholic beliefs still intact.

The story need not be told in detail here. But it is important for the reader to know that Anne Boleyn was not the last wife of Henry VIII. In fact, Henry had six wives in total. The names of Henry's six wives with the dates when they were queen are Catherine of Aragon (1509-1533), Anne Boleyn (1533-1536), Jane Seymour (1536-1537), Anne of Cleves (1540), Catherine Howard (1540-1542), and Catherine Parr (1543-1547). The story of how Henry went through six wives is a sordid tale, and Henry broke many of God's commandments in the process. But God used this wicked king in His providence to further the Reformation in England.

The Brief Reign of Edward VI

Josiah was eight years old when he became king, and he reigned thirty-one years in Jerusalem. His mother's name was Jedidah the daughter of Adaiah

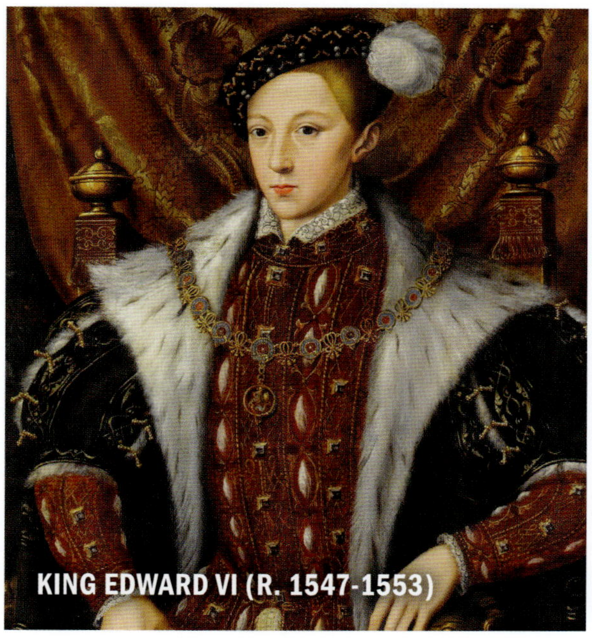

KING EDWARD VI (R. 1547-1553)

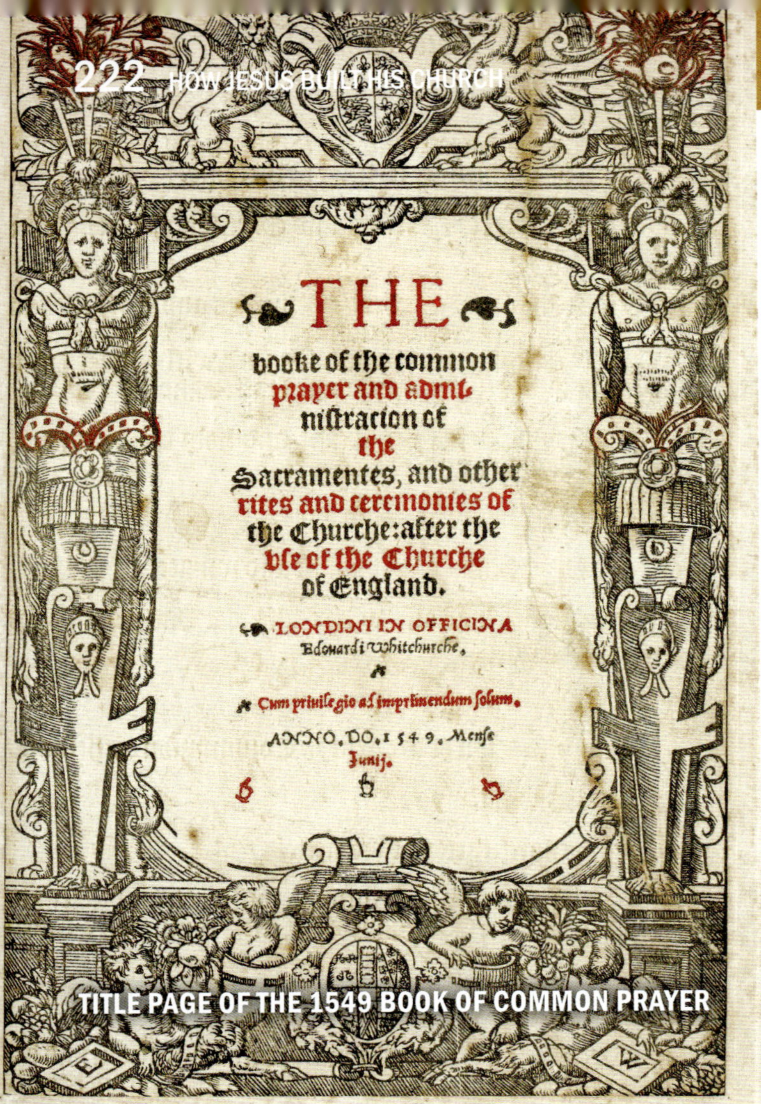
THE
booke of the common
prayer and admi-
nistracion of
the
Sacramentes, and other
rites and ceremonies of
the Churche: after the
use of the Churche
of England.
LONDINI IN OFFICINA
Edouardi Whitchurche.
Cum privilegio ad imprimendum solum.
ANNO. DO. 1549. Mense
Junij.

TITLE PAGE OF THE 1549 BOOK OF COMMON PRAYER

of Bozkath. And he did what was right in the sight of the Lord, and walked in all the ways of his father David; he did not turn aside to the right hand or to the left. (2 Kings 22:1-2)

Jane Seymour, Henry's third wife, did give birth to Henry's long-desired male heir. Their son Edward became **King Edward VI** (r. 1547-1553) at age nine. Protestant leaders such as Cranmer, **Nicholas Ridley** (1500-1555), and **Hugh Latimer** (1487-1555) saw this as an important opportunity to further the reformation of the English church. During Edward's brief reign, the English Church became increasingly Protestant.

One of Cranmer's most important productions was a new prayer book that reshaped the worship of the English (Anglican) Church. Two editions of the book were issued in 1549 and 1552, primarily written by Archbishop Thomas Cranmer. This book, and its later editions, became known as the ***Book of Common Prayer***. As was the case with Zwingli and Luther, the Lord's Supper was a significant matter of controversy in England. Cranmer changed his views on the Lord's Supper over time, moving away from the Roman view to Reformed views.

This shift in perspective is seen in the 1549 and 1552 prayer books Cranmer authored. In the 1552 language, the emphasis was upon remembrance of Christ's death rather than identifying the elements of bread and wine with Christ's body and blood. (See comparison below.)

Cranmer's work on the *Book of Common Prayer* would shape English language and worship for centuries. The literary beauty and power of Cranmer's prayer book can be seen, for example, in this prayer of general confession recommended in the 1552 prayer book:

> Almighty and most merciful Father, we have erred and strayed from thy ways, like lost sheep. We have followed too much the devices and desires of our own hearts. We have offended against thy holy laws. We have left undone those things which we ought to have done, and we have done those things which we ought not to have

1549 Words of Administration	1552 Words of Administration
• The body of our Lord Jesus Christ, which was given for thee, preserve thy body and soul unto everlasting life. • The blood of our Lord Jesus Christ, which was shed for thee, preserve thy body and soul unto everlasting life.	• Take and eat this in remembrance that Christ died for thee, and feed on him in thy heart by faith, with thanksgiving. • Drink this in remembrance that Christ's blood was shed for thee, and be thankful.

> done, and there is no health in us: but thou, O Lord, have mercy upon us miserable offenders. Spare thou them, O God, which confess their faults. Restore thou them that be penitent, according to thy promises declared unto mankind, in Christ Jesus our Lord. And grant, O most Merciful Father, for his sake, that we may hereafter live a godly, righteous, and sober life, to the glory of thy holy name. Amen.[1]

In 1553, the Reformation in England was cut short by the death of Edward VI. On July 6, 1553, Edward died of tuberculosis. He was fifteen years old. Though Edward was young, he died a committed Protestant. Some of his dying prayer is recorded for us.

> Lord God, deliver me out of this miserable and wretched life. . . . Lord, I commit my spirit to You. O Lord, you know how happy it were for me to be with You. . . . O my Lord God! Bless Your people, and save Your inheritance! O Lord God, save Your chosen people of England! O my Lord God, defend this realm from papistry, and maintain Your true religion; that I and Your people may praise Your holy name, for Your Son, Jesus Christ's sake![2]

At this time in England, the future of the Protestant church hung in the balance. Would the Church of England be aligned with Rome and its pope? Or would the Church of England join the Protestant Reformation? Would the Word of God be of supreme authority in England, or would the Roman Church act as the ultimate authority?

A crisis of succession occurred following Edward's death. An attempt was made to place the young Protestant Lady Jane Grey on the throne. But this ended in her execution. Mary Tudor, the daughter of Henry VIII and Catherine of Aragon, inherited the throne. Mary was firmly committed to Roman Catholicism and wanted to see the English church return to the Catholic fold. As Mary consolidated power, she began to purge Protestant leaders from positions of influence. She put many English Protestants to death, both leaders and common people. Many fled to the European Continent to escape her persecution and were discipled there in places like Geneva. Queen Mary soon earned the name **Bloody Mary** because of the executions she ordered. From 1555 to 1558, some 300 to 400 Protestants were killed during her bloody reign. Much of Mary's persecution against faithful men and women is recorded in **John Foxe's *Book of Martyrs***.

QUEEN MARY I, "BLOODY MARY" (1553-1558)

In October 1555, Nicholas Ridley and Hugh Latimer were burned at the stake together. Queen Mary had sentenced them to death for heresy. Latimer's last words were recorded by John Foxe as follows:

> Be of good comfort, and play the man, Master Ridley; we shall this day light such a candle, by God's grace, in England, as I trust shall never be put out.[3]

Latimer was right. The bloody persecutions of

RIDLEY AND LATIMER BURNED AT THE STAKE

Queen Mary did light a candle in England. They led many English people to reject Roman Catholicism and become Protestants. The works of darkness were exposed. The truth of God's Word would shine more brightly in the years that followed.

The Martyrdom of Thomas Cranmer

Shortly after taking the throne, Mary I imprisoned Thomas Cranmer. He was to be tried for treason (because he supported Lady Jane Grey on the throne) and for heresy (because he supported the Reformation). It did not help that many years previously, Cranmer had supported Henry in considering his marriage to Catherine of Aragon as illegitimate. This also meant that Mary was viewed as a daughter of an illegitimate marriage.

As Latimer and Ridley were executed by fire, Cranmer watched from a prison cell and became fearful for his life. He was pressured to recant of his Protestant views, and out of fear he did recant, signing a number of documents. (To recant is to say that one no longer holds an opinion or belief.) News of Cranmer's recantation of Protestant views was spread far and wide through England. At first, Cranmer was promised a safe release if he recanted of his Protestant views. But Mary decided to have Cranmer executed anyway.

On the day of his execution, March 21, 1556, Cranmer preached a final sermon at the University Church in Oxford. But instead of recanting his Protestant views publicly, Cranmer instead recanted his recantation! Cranmer saw his turning back to Rome as a cowardly betrayal of God's truth. Cranmer was dragged out of the pulpit during his final sermon and quickly taken to the place of execution. John Foxe recorded some of the words from Cranmer's final sermon and his execution:

> And then rising, he said, "Every man desireth, good people, at the time of their deaths, to give some good exhortation, that others may remember after their deaths, and be the better thereby. So I beseech God grant me grace, that I may speak something, at this my departing, whereby God may be glorified, and you edified.... And now I come to the great thing that troubleth my conscience more than any other thing that ever I said or did in my life: and that is, the setting abroad of writings contrary to the truth. Which here now I renounce and refuse, as things written with my hand, contrary to the truth which I thought in my heart, and written for fear of death, and to save my life, if it might be: and that is, all such bills, which I have written or signed with mine own hand since my degradation: wherein I have written many things untrue. And forasmuch as my hand offended in writing contrary to my heart, therefore my hand shall first be punished: for if I may come to the fire, it shall be first burned. And as for the pope, I refuse him, as Christ's enemy and

> antichrist, with all his false doctrine."… Fire being now put to him, he stretched out his right hand, and thrust it into the flame, and held it there a good space, before the fire came to any other part of his body; where his hand was seen of every man sensibly burning, crying with a loud voice, "This hand hath offended." As soon as the fire got up, he was very soon dead, never stirring or crying all the while.[4]

Thus ended the life of Archbishop Cranmer, who in his last hours repented of denying Christ's truth. The news of Cranmer's courageous stand spread all over England and encouraged Protestants in their cause. Two years later, in 1558, Queen Mary died. She was forty-two years old. Having died without any children, Mary's sister Elizabeth took the throne.

Elizabeth was the daughter of Henry VIII and Anne Boleyn. She reigned from 1558 to 1603. Elizabeth reversed the earlier course taken by Mary I and restored Protestantism. Many Protestant exiles returned to England. Elizabeth restored the Church of England to where it had been at the end of Edward VI's reign. But she did not allow further reformation. This is sometimes called the **Elizabethan Settlement**. Elizabeth's long forty-five-year reign brought stability to the church.

QUEEN ELIZABETH I (1558-1603)

As a result of the Elizabethan Settlement, the English or Anglican Church was different from the other Reformed churches. Like them, it was Reformed in doctrine. But in its worship and church government it retained many Roman Catholic elements and was closer to Lutheranism. Many Protestants in England wanted to further reform and purify the Church of England to make it more Biblical and more like the other Reformed churches. They became known as **Puritans**. In a later chapter, we will give our attention to these English Puritans. ■

THE TRIAL OF THOMAS CRANMER

In him was life, and the life was the light of men. The light shines in the darkness, and the darkness has not overcome it. (John 1:4-5 ESV)

ST. GILES CATHEDRAL, EDINBURGH, SCOTLAND

The Reformation in Scotland

23

**The wicked flee when no one pursues,
But the righteous are bold as a lion. (Prov. 28:1)**

The man most responsible for bringing the Reformation to Scotland was **John Knox** (1514-1572). He was a man of great courage, a servant of Christ who did not fear man. At Knox's funeral, one of his friends summarized John Knox this way: "Here lies he that neither feared nor flattered any flesh."[1] Reforming the church in Scotland was not a safe mission. It took courageous men and women to stand for the truth, sometimes at the cost of their lives. But where does such courage come from? The answer, of course, is that it is the work of God. John Knox wrote in the ***History of the Reformation in Scotland*** why there was such a bold movement for the truth. He wrote: "God gave his Holy Spirit to simple men in great abundance."[2]

Knox saw himself this way: a simple man filled with the Holy Spirit. He was not naturally strong or bold. But he was made mighty by God!

JOHN KNOX (1514-1572)

One of Knox's contemporaries, Thomas Smeaton described Knox in this way: "I know not if God ever placed a more godly and great spirit in a body so little and frail."[3] This reminds us that God uses weak vessels to accomplish His great purposes in the world.

John Knox is considered by most to be "the Reformer" of Scotland. He was instrumental in the early work of reformation. Knox also wrote the first history of the Reformation in Scotland, titled *The History of the Reformation of Religion in the Realm of Scotland*.[4] The Reformation in Scotland began around the same time as the English Reformation. Martin Luther's influential writings were smuggled into the British Isles. Men and women in England and Scotland eagerly devoured these works. Additionally, many Scots who studied in Germany returned to Scotland with Luther's ideas. The Scottish church leaders sought to stop these ideas from proliferating, but they were not successful.

The Influence of George Wishart

For he hath said, I will never leave thee, nor forsake thee. So that we may boldly say, The Lord is my helper, and I will not fear what man shall do unto me. (Heb. 13:5-6 KJV)

In 1528, a Protestant preacher named Patrick Hamilton was executed as a martyr. As he was dying, he cried out:

> How long, O Lord, shall darkness cover this realm? How long wilt thou suffer this tyranny of men? Lord Jesus, receive my spirit.[5]

Despite the danger, another preacher named George Wishart kept on preaching the Word. Wishart inspired John Knox to eventually take up the cause of the Reformation as well.

We know little about Knox's birth and upbringing. But we do know that at age twenty-five, Knox was ordained to the priesthood, despite never finishing a formal education. Thus, Knox was born and raised in the corrupt church of his day, where idolatry and ignorance largely prevailed. But somehow, by God's grace, Knox heard faithful gospel preaching and was converted to a true understanding of the faith. Later in life, when he was dying, Knox asked his wife to read "where I first cast my anchor," and she read from John 17:3:

GEORGE WISHART (C. 1513-1546)

And this is life eternal, that they might know thee the only true God, and Jesus Christ, whom thou hast sent. (John 17:3 KJV)

This text, then, must have had a significant influence upon Knox and was used by God in Knox's conversion to the true gospel.

Around the year 1546, John Knox became a bodyguard for George Wishart as he preached throughout Scotland. Knox, with broadsword in hand, traveled alongside Wishart, protecting the life of his friend and mentor.

One of the most corrupt clerics in Scotland was **Cardinal David Beaton** (c. 1494-1546). Beaton was well-known as a tyrant among the people, and deeply corrupt. Beaton lived in sumptuous luxury, enjoying the profits collected by the church while most in Scotland lived in extreme poverty. Beaton had seven illegitimate children with his various mistresses despite the fact that he was supposed to live a life of chastity and celibacy. Beaton, through his influence, saw a law passed in Scottish parliament that would punish "damnable opinions contrary to faith and the laws of the Holy Kirk [church]." By this act, parliament outlawed Protestant ideas that were then spreading throughout the land.

One example of how this law was enforced is found in 1544. Cardinal Beaton had four men hanged because they did not observe Lent and refused to pray to the saints. Beaton then arrested

CARDINAL DAVID BEATON (C. 1494-1546)

one of the men's wives. She was accused of the "crime" of praying in Christ's name while in labor instead of praying in Mary's name. The woman was condemned to public drowning, and her child was taken from her. Such was the horrific tyranny and monstrous evil of Cardinal Beaton and the corrupt Scottish Church before it was reformed.

On the night of January 16, 1546, George Wishart was arrested at midnight by Cardinal Beaton's henchmen. Wishart was then tried, convicted, and sentenced to be burned. Wishart languished in the dungeon at St. Andrews for months, but was then brought to his execution. At the Castle of St. Andrews, Wishart was to be burned. Cardinal Beaton had the cannons pointed at the crowds in order to keep back any from stopping the execution. Minutes before his execution, Wishart testified before the cardinal and the crowds, saying:

> For this cause I was sent, that I should suffer this fire for Christ's sake. I fear not this fire. And I pray that you may not fear them that slay the body, but have no power to slay the soul.[6]

Then, turning to the executioner, he kissed him, and said:

> Lo, here is a token that I forgive thee. Do thine office.[7]

Wishart was then burned before the people. A public outcry because of this injustice arose among the people. A conspiracy was hatched to assassinate Cardinal Beaton. Several men snuck into the castle at night and raided Cardinal Beaton's room. They slew Cardinal Beaton with a sword.

Though Knox did not take part in this plan, he was glad to hear that the tyrant was no more. The assassins then secured the castle and sought to negotiate with the Queen Regent Mary of Guise. James Melville, one of the men, invited Knox to occupy the castle with them. The men occupied the castle for some months. Cardinal Beaton had reinforced the castle with almost impregnable walls and lots of food and supplies to endure a long siege.

Knox's Ordination to the Ministry

And the things that you have heard from me among many witnesses, commit these to faithful men who will be able to teach others also. You therefore must

RUINS OF ST. ANDREW'S CASTLE

endure hardship as a good soldier of Jesus Christ. No one engaged in warfare entangles himself with the affairs of this life, that he may please him who enlisted him as a soldier. (2 Tim. 2:2-4)

It was during this time that some of the brothers called Knox to labor in the ministry. Knox tutored some young men holed up within the castle. Knox's private tutoring eventually became preaching to the entire castle garrison. It was evident to all that Knox had a gift for proclaiming God's Word. The men were convinced that Knox was called to this work. Though Knox was ordained as a priest already, the brothers wanted to commission John Knox as a preacher of the gospel. Initially, Knox refused their call to the ministry because he did not want to labor where God had not called him. One of the men said to Knox in the presence of all:

> In the name of God, and of His Son Jesus Christ, and in the name of these that presently call you by my mouth, I charge you that you refuse not this holy vocation, but that you have regard to the glory of God, the increase of Christ's kingdom, and the edification of your brethren . . . that you take upon you the public office and charge of preaching, even as you look to avoid God's heavy displeasure, and desire that he should multiply his graces with you.[8]

In response to this exhortation, Knox burst into tears and went to his bedchamber. Knox was reluctant to take on such a momentous duty. But eventually, Knox accepted the call and preached before the castle garrison. Knox preached his first sermon from Daniel 7:24-25 and from this text compared the true and false church. The men who heard him were astounded by his plainness of speech and boldness. Some commented, "Mr. George Wishart never spoke so plainly; and yet he was burnt. Even so will John Knox be."[9]

Slave to the French

"Because he has set his love upon Me, therefore I will deliver him; I will set him on high, because he has known My name." (Ps. 91:14)

The Queen Regent over Scotland was a French noblewoman named **Mary of Guise**. She was **Regent**, reigning in place of the rightful heir to the throne: her daughter Queen Mary of Scots. Queen Mary would eventually take the throne once her mother, the regent, died.

Mary of Guise called for reinforcements from France to attack the Castle of St. Andrews and capture the rebels. France sent twenty-one heavily armed galleys. The ships bombarded the castle as the queen regent landed French forces. The Scots were hemmed in on all sides.

On July 31, 1547, the garrison surrendered to the French. The men were now prisoners of the French. Knox himself became a slave rowing on a French galley. For a year and a half, Knox toiled under the oppressive bondage of his French masters. Those nineteen months serving as a slave rower took a toll on Knox's health. He would endure various physical maladies for the rest of his life.

During his time as a slave, Knox endured frequent efforts to convert him to Roman Catholicism and to deny his biblical convictions. On one occasion, the French forced a painted wooden image of Mary on Knox. Knox replied, "Trouble me not, such an idol is accursed, and therefore, I will not touch it." His captors then forced the image into his face and his hands. Knox then took the image and cast it into the river and said, "Let our Lady now save herself. She is light enough. Let her learn to swim."[10]

Meanwhile, changes were happening in England. In late 1547, King Henry VIII died. His son Edward VI succeeded him on the throne of England. Edward was just a young man, but he received much instruction from godly Reformers such as Hugh Latimer. Edward managed to secure the release of Knox and the other Scots captured by the French at St. Andrews.

After Knox was released, he was asked by Hugh Latimer to assist in the work of Reformation taking place in England. Knox spent the next few years laboring as a minister in England. But Knox often found himself uncomfortable there due to his convictions. The Reformation in England had proceeded slowly, and there were many remnants of Roman Catholic practice still practiced in the church. Knox found himself in disagreement with Thomas Cranmer over the **Book of Common Prayer**. The *Book of Common Prayer* still required kneeling at the Lord's Supper. Knox believed that this practice was idolatrous since in Roman Catholic worship the elements were worshiped as the actual body and blood of Christ.

Due to his uncompromising stance and bold preaching, Knox was given the charge of a small congregation in Northern England, in Berwick-on-Tweed, near the border of Scotland. Today, this town is still the northernmost town in all of England. In God's providence, Knox met the woman who would become his first wife, Marjory Bowes. Though Knox did not marry Marjory for some years, they became betrothed and eventually united in marriage.

Exile in Geneva

The English government's support for the Reformation in England was suspended for a time when Edward VI died in 1553. Edward VI was succeeded by Queen Mary Tudor, a staunch Roman Catholic who became known as Bloody Mary. Under the reign of Mary, England's Protestants would face severe persecution. Some 300 to 400 were executed by Queen Mary, including Thomas Cranmer, Hugh Latimer, and Nicholas Ridley.

Knox, as usual, minced no words when it came to describing the reign of Bloody Mary. He wrote:

> After the death of this most virtuous Prince [Edward VI], of whom the godless people of England for the most part were not worthy, Satan intended nothing less than that the light of Jesus Christ utterly to have been extinguished within the whole Isle of Britain; for after him was raised up, in God's hot displeasure, that idolatress Jezebel, mischievous Mary, of the Spaniard's blood; cruel persecutrix of God's people.[11]

Knox debated whether he should flee to the continent. He struggled as to whether leaving England was an act of cowardice. Eventually, with some hesitation, he determined to depart for Geneva for refuge. To preserve his life now would give him

BERWICK-ON-TWEED, ENGLAND

the opportunity to fight another day. Knox then journeyed to Geneva to study with John Calvin and other prominent Reformers. Knox spent about five years in continental Europe, laboring in the ministry in Germany and in Geneva. While he was there, he played an influential role in the production of the ***Geneva Bible***, an influential English translation of the Bible. According to Knox, Geneva was:

> The most perfect school of Christ that ever was in the earth since the days of the apostles. In other places I confess Christ to be truly preached; but manners and religion so sincerely reformed, I have not yet seen in any other place.[12]

For Knox, Geneva was an essential training ground for the Reformation work in Scotland. Ministry and training in Geneva strengthened John Knox for his eventual return to his homeland.

Reformation Work in Scotland

And Micaiah said, "As the LORD lives, whatever the LORD says to me, that I will speak." (1 Kin. 22:14)

Knox returned to Scotland in 1559 to continue his ministry among the people of his own land. Many of the Scots were frustrated with the French influence over Scotland, and numerous Scottish nobles sought help from Queen Elizabeth, the newly-crowned queen of England.

Elizabeth understood that French troops in Scotland would be a threat to the security of England. In 1560, she sent money to the Scots along with a fleet to fight the French. The **Treaty of Edinburgh** was signed that same year. This treaty allowed only 120 French troops to remain in Scotland, forbade Frenchmen from holding public office in Scotland, and stipulated that Francis II, the husband of Mary Queen of Scots, was not to engage in war against England. This treaty ended French control of Scotland and enabled the work of Reformation to continue.

The Scottish Parliament met in 1560 and proceeded to reform the church with the help of John Knox and others. The rule of the pope over the Church of Scotland was ended. The mass was declared illegal. The ***Scottish Confession of Faith*** was established as the doctrinal standard of the church (also known as the Scots Confession). The next year (1561), a *Book of Discipline* and a *Book of Common Order* were written and adopted. The church was reorganized into a Presbyterian form of government in which pastors and elders led the church.

This was a tremendous victory for God's truth

EDINBURGH CASTLE IN EDINBURGH, SCOTLAND

in Scotland. But of course, this was not the end of the battle. It is one thing to legislate Roman Catholicism out of the country and to write a confession of faith. It is another thing to win the hearts of the people to the truth. That work requires the Holy Spirit to open eyes. By God's grace, there was much opening of eyes to the truth in the decades that followed. There was a reformation of true worship, and Christian doctrine and practice throughout Scotland.

Extracts from the *Scottish Confession* of 1560

Below are a few selected quotations from the *Scottish Confession* of 1560. Here we see some of the most important matters of the Scottish Reformation summarized.

> Long have we thirsted, dear brethren, to have notified unto the world the sum of that doctrine which we profess, and for the which we have sustained infamy and danger. But such has been the rage of Satan against us, and against Christ Jesus' eternal verity lately born amongst us, that to this day no time has been granted unto us to clear our consciences, as most gladly we would have done. For how we have been tossed a whole year past, the most part of Europe (as we suppose) does understand. But seeing that of the infinite goodness of our God (who never suffers his afflicted utterly to be confounded), above expectation, we have obtained some rest and liberty, we could not but set forth this brief and plain confession of such doctrine as is proponed unto us, and as we believe and profess; partly for satisfaction of our brethren, whose hearts, we doubt not, have been and yet are wounded by the despiteful railing of such as yet have not learned to speak well; and partly for stopping of the mouths of impudent blasphemers, who boldly damn that which they have neither heard, nor yet understand. (A portion of the Preface)

> As we believe and confess the scriptures of God sufficient to instruct and make the man of God perfect, so do we affirm and avow the authority of the same to be of God, and neither to depend on men nor angels. We affirm, therefore, that such as allege the scripture to have no authority, but that which is received from the kirk [church], to be blasphemous against God, and injurious to the true kirk [church], which always hears and obeys the voice of her own Spouse and Pastor, but takes not upon her to be mistress over the same. (Chapter 19 – The Authority of the Scriptures)

> We confess and acknowledge empires, kingdoms, dominions, and cities to be distinguished and ordained by God: the powers and authorities in the same (be it of emperors in their empires, of kings in their realms, dukes and princes in their dominions, or of other magistrates in free cities)

JOHN KNOX AND MARY, QUEEN OF SCOTS

> to be God's holy ordinance, ordained for manifestation of his own glory, and for the singular profit and commodity of mankind. (Chapter 24 – Of the Civil Magistrate)

Confronting Mary, Queen of Scots

After the death of the queen regent, **Mary Queen of Scots**, the daughter of the regent, took the throne in Scotland. Having grown up in France much of her life, Mary was zealously committed to Roman Catholicism. In 1561, Mary Queen of Scots returned to Scotland to reign. She was a zealous Roman Catholic who tried to undo the work of Reformation. Mary was able to charm many Scots. But John Knox courageously opposed her efforts and confronted her with the truth. Knox reminded Mary that monarchs are not rulers with unlimited authority but are under God's law.

Knox was summoned by the queen on numerous occasions. In these dialogues, many of which are recorded in Knox's ***History of the Reformation in Scotland***, we find a remarkable example of speaking the truth in love.

Knox's First Interview with Queen Mary

When Queen Mary arrived in Scotland in 1561, she practiced a private Roman Catholic Mass in the palace. Knox addressed the church on this occasion, saying:

> One Mass is more fearful to me than ten thousand armed enemies landing in any part of the Realm to suppress the whole Religion. In our God there is strength to resist and confound multitudes if we honestly depend upon Him, and this we have already experienced. But when we join hands with idolatry, both God's peaceful presence and comfortable defense leaves us, and what will then become of us? I fear that experience will teach us leading to the grief of many.[13]

As you can imagine, the queen did not take kindly to Knox's words, and she summoned him to answer for "stirring up" her subjects against her lawful rule. Here is a portion of Queen Mary's conversation with John Knox:

> **Queen Mary:** But yet you have taught the people to receive another religion than their Princes can allow. How can that doctrine be of God since God commands subjects to obey their Princes?
>
> **John Knox:** Madam, since right religion takes neither its original strength nor authority from worldly princes, but from the Eternal God alone, so the subjects are not bound to frame their religion according to the appetites of their princes. Princes are often the most ignorant of all others in God's true religion, as we may read in the Histories, both before the death of Christ Jesus and after. If all the seed of Abraham was of the religion of Pharaoh, to whom they were long subjects, I ask you, Madam, what religion should there have been in the world? Or, if all men in the days of the Apostles were of the religion of the Roman Emperors, what religion should there have been upon the face of the earth? Daniel and his fellows were subjects to Nebuchadnezzar and to Darius, and yet, Madam, they would not be of their religion; for the three children said: "We make it known unto you, O King, that we will not worship your Gods." Daniel also did pray publicly to his God against the expressed commandment of the King. And so Madam, you may perceive that subjects are not bound to the religion of their princes, although they are commanded to give them obedience.[14]

Mary went on:

> **Queen Mary:** Yes, but you are not the Kirk that I will nourish. I will defend the Kirk of Rome, for it is, I think, the true Kirk of God.

John Knox: Your will, Madam, is no reason for this belief; neither does your thought make that Roman harlot to be the true and immaculate spouse of Jesus Christ. Do not be amazed, Madam, that I call Rome a harlot; for that Church is altogether polluted with all kind of spiritual fornication, both in doctrine and in practice. Yes, Madam, I offer myself to prove, that the Church of the Jews which crucified Christ Jesus, was not as degenerate from the ordinances which God gave by Moses and Aaron to his people, when they manifestly denied the Son of God, as the Church of Rome has declined, and more than five hundred years has declined, from the purity of that religion which the Apostles taught and established.

Queen Mary: My conscience does not say so.

John Knox: Conscience, Madam, requires knowledge, and I fear that you do not have the right knowledge.[15]

In God's mercy, Queen Mary's efforts to re-catholicize Scotland failed. In 1567, Mary arranged to have her husband Lord Darnley murdered. She then married his murderer, the Earl of Bothwell. The Scottish lesser magistrates rose up and deposed Mary, who fled to England. She was succeeded by her infant son James VI, and Scotland was ruled by regents for many years. Reformed Presbyterian Protestantism became firmly established there.

Through bold confrontation such as we see in this interview between John Knox and Queen Mary, the truth of the gospel and the pure worship of God was preserved in Scotland for many centuries. Though the legacy of the Reformation has faded much in modern-day Scotland, God's truth endures. The church in Scotland, reformed according to God's Word, would influence the church of Jesus Christ all over the world and send out many missionaries to other lands in the centuries that followed. ■

So shall my word be that goeth forth out of my mouth:
It shall not return unto me void,
But it shall accomplish that which I please;
And it shall prosper in the thing whereto I sent it.
(Isa. 55:11 KJV)

KILCHURN CASTLE RUINS, LOCH AWE, SCOTLAND

TRENTO (TRENT), ITALY

The Catholic Counter-Reformation

24

The Protestant Reformation was a direct assault on the authority, doctrine, and practice of the Roman Church. The Reformers were unsparing in their condemnation of the papacy as the antichrist. Luther and Calvin argued that the truth of the gospel had been veiled in the darkness of heresy and superstition. The Word of God, the source of light and truth, had also been largely kept from the people of God for centuries. The kingdoms of Europe divided between allegiance to the Roman Catholic Church and the new Protestant movements. It was now time for Rome to respond to the tidal wave challenge of the Reformation.

In the decades that followed the birth of the Reformation, several significant efforts were made by leaders of the Roman Church to respond to the Reformation. The efforts of Rome to defend itself and to attack the Protestant cause is known as the **Counter-Reformation**. Other historians call this period the **Catholic Reformation** because the Roman Church did seek to reform some of its institutions, purifying them from moral corruption. We can recognize both elements by calling it the "Catholic Counter-Reformation."

Efforts to Seek Unity with Protestants

Therefore if there is any consolation in Christ, if any comfort of love, if any fellowship of the Spirit, if any affection and mercy, fulfill my joy by being like-minded, having the same love, being of one accord, of one mind. (Phil. 2:1-2)

Not all Roman Church leaders were hostile to the cause of the Reformers. Some leaders within the Roman Church were quite sympathetic to the ideas set forth by the Reformers. An early example of this is Luther's spiritual mentor **Johann von Staupitz** (1460-1524). We learned in an earlier chapter how Staupitz was a faithful brother to Luther who often gave him good counsel. Though Staupitz remained an Augustinian monk, he agreed with much that Luther wrote. But eventually they parted ways. When Luther broke off allegiance with the pope, Staupitz did not follow Luther. Saddened that Staupitz did not embrace the Reformation, Luther wrote to his former mentor with these words:

> I am afraid that you hesitate between Christ and the pope, though they are utterly opposed. You seem to me to be a very different Staupitz from the one who used to preach grace and the cross.[1]

Others in the Roman Church like Staupitz interacted with the Reformers' writings, often finding much to agree with. But they were not willing to go as far as separating from the Roman Church. To pursue unity, some Catholic leaders dialogued with the Reformers through letters and books.

In 1541, a meeting was held in Regensburg, Germany. This is known as the **Colloquy of Regensburg**. The meeting involved a gathering of key Roman Catholic leaders including Gasparo Contarini (1483-1542), Johann Gropper (1503-1559), and Albert Pighius (1490-1542). Reformers Martin Bucer (1491-1551), Philip Melanchthon (1497-1560), and John Calvin (1509-1564) represented the Protestant cause. The Catholic and Protestant leaders engaged various issues including the Bible's authority, free will, justification by faith, the sacraments, and other matters. The two sides were able to reach some agreement on justification. But when it came to the Lord's Supper, there was no unity. The meeting showed that there were Roman Catholics who were sympathetic to Protestantism. However, at the end of

REGENSBURG, GERMANY, THE SITE OF THE COLLOQUY OF REGENSBURG

the meeting, it was clear that unity was not possible.

PHILIP MELANCHTHON (1497-1560)

IGNATIUS OF LOYOLA (1491-1556)

Ignatius of Loyola and the Jesuits

We learned in a previous chapter how the Dominican order arose in response to heresies in the late Middle Ages. A similar event occurred during the Reformation. The Catholic order of the **Jesuits** (or the **Society of Jesus**) was founded by **Ignatius of Loyola** in 1540. Loyola was a Spaniard with a military background and desired to serve as a knight to the Spanish kings. But in 1521, Loyola experienced a difficult trial. That year, Loyola shattered one of his legs in battle and became a cripple. Loyola was confined to his home.

During this time, Loyola turned his attention to spiritual matters. He began reading religious books. One of these was by a Carthusian monk named Ludolph of Saxony. The book's title was *The Life of our Lord Jesus Christ*. The book was an exposition and application of the life of Christ as contained in the Gospels. Ludolph's book inspired Loyola to give up his military career and devote his life to the service of the church.

Loyola joined a Dominican monastery and from 1522 to 1523 dedicated all his time to seeking God through monastic disciplines. During this time, Loyola claimed to receive a series of spiritual visions. Loyola collected his experiences into a manual called *Spiritual Exercises*. This became a foundational work that defined the Jesuit order. The book contained various prayers and spiritual meditations intended to bring about a real spiritual experience of the things of God. Loyola urged the reader to imagine the reality of heaven, hell, Christ's death and resurrection, and other foundational doctrines and events.

Loyola also made clear in his book that he was steadfastly devoted to the authority and teaching of the Roman Church. For Loyola, the authority of Rome was never to be questioned. Obedience to the church, no matter what the church said, was Loyola's commitment. In his *Spiritual Exercises*, he wrote:

> We should leave to one side all personal opinions of our own, and keep our minds prepared and zealous to obey in all things our holy mother, the Catholic Church, the true Bride of Christ our Lord . . . To ensure that we enjoy perfect certainty, we should maintain the following attitude: I will believe that something that seems white is actually black, if the Catholic Church proclaims it to be black. For I believe that there is one and the same Spirit who unites Christ our Lord the Husband with the Church His Bride. This Spirit rules and guides our souls for our good; the same Spirit and the same Lord who gave the Ten Commandments guides and rules our holy mother the Church.[2]

After his time in the Dominican monastery, Loyola went on to study in Spain and then in Paris. While in Paris, he formed a group of disciples who joined Loyola. In 1534, Loyola with some other disciples made an oath to journey to the Holy Land. One of those disciples of Loyola was **Francis Xavier** (1506-1552). Xavier would become one of the most traveled Roman Catholic missionaries of all time. He would eventually travel to India, Malaysia, and Japan. Xavier would see tens of thousands converted through his missionary journeys.

Due to conflicts occurring in the region, Loyola, Xavier, and the other Jesuits did not make this missionary journey to the Holy Land. But there would be many missionary endeavors in later years. In 1540, Pope Paul III officially recognized the Jesuits as a new order in the Catholic church. The Jesuit order grew rapidly and established schools all over Europe. The Jesuits were committed to a rigorous course of study. The process to become a member of the order was quite extensive. A novice who wished to become a Jesuit had to wait a trial period of two years. After two years, the novice would then take the vows of poverty, chastity, and obedience. After this, the new

FRANCIS XAVIER (1506-1552)

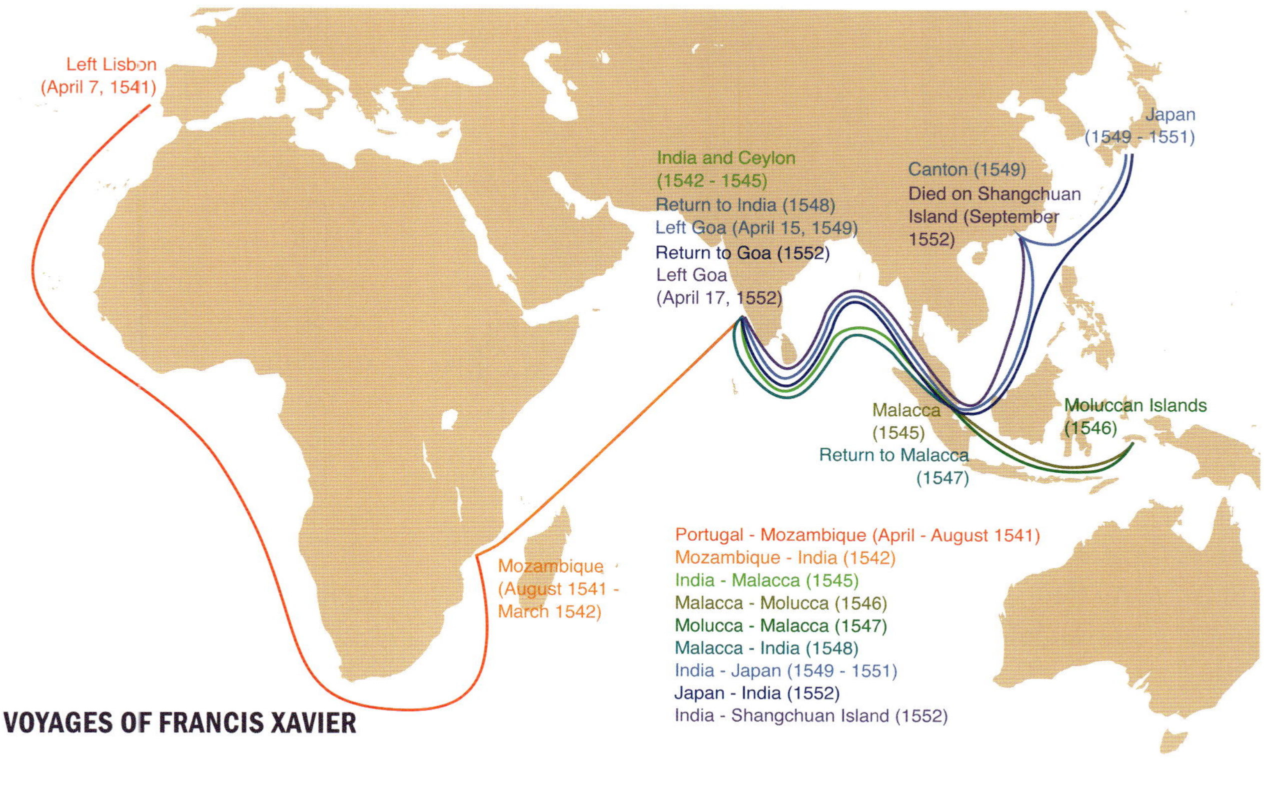

VOYAGES OF FRANCIS XAVIER

member would spend ten years in rigorous study of philosophy and theology.

The Jesuits were committed to the teaching of Aristotle and Thomas Aquinas. They also committed themselves to attacking the heresy of the Reformation. To this end, the Jesuits read the writings of the Protestants and then responded to them with their own writings. Because of their missionary zeal, Jesuits went into many regions dominated by Protestant churches and sought to win back the populace to the Roman Church. In some cases, they were quite successful. They established schools to disciple children into Romanism. Much like the Dominicans of the Middle Ages, the Jesuits of the Reformation period did much to defend the Roman Church.

Index of Prohibited Books

Another way in which the Roman Church tried to counter the Reformation was through banning books. Book banning has a poor history of success in suppressing ideas. In many cases, banning a book makes people even more curious about it. Sometimes banning a book makes it more popular. Nevertheless, the Roman Church decided to counter the Reformation by banning various books they deemed dangerous to the Catholic faithful.

Pope Paul IV issued a list of prohibited books in 1559. The document issued was known as the **Index Librorum Prohibitorum** (*Index of Prohibited Books*). The index continued to be updated by the Roman Catholic Church until 1966. Writers who were banned included Erasmus, John Calvin, Martin Luther, and Philip Melanchthon. In addition to human authors, the *Index* also banned numerous Bible translations that were seen as subversive of Rome's authority.

INDEX LIBRORVM PROHIBITORVM,

CVM REGVLIS CONFECTIS per Patres a Tridentina Synodo delectos, auctoritate Sanctiss. D.N. Pij IIII, Pont. Max. comprobatus.

VENETIIS, M. D. LXIIII.

TITLE PAGE OF THE INDEX OF PROHIBITED BOOKS: NOTE THE REFERENCE TO THE COUNCIL OF TRENT (TRIDENTINE SYNOD)

The Council of Trent

I marvel that you are turning away so soon from Him who called you in the grace of Christ, to a different gospel, which is not another; but there are some who trouble you and want to pervert the gospel of Christ. But even if we, or an angel from heaven, preach any other gospel to you than what we have preached to you, let him be accursed. (Gal. 1:6-8)

One of the most significant efforts of the Catholic Counter-Reformation was the **Council of Trent**. The council met in various sessions from 1545 to 1563. Unlike the Colloquy of Regensburg, the council did not seek to gain unity with Protestants. Instead, the Council of Trent condemned Protestant beliefs. The council further cemented the division between the Roman Church and the Protestant Reformation.

For almost twenty years, and under three popes, the council met in Trent, Italy. Many important decisions were made at Trent. Statements from this pivotal church council continue to define what Roman Catholics believe to the present day. It is important for us to learn about some of the statements this council made.

First, we can look at what the council had to say about the relationship between the Bible and the traditions of the church. For Protestants, the Bible was and is the supreme authority. All decisions about our beliefs and practices are to be judged according to the standard of the Bible. But for the Roman Catholic church, the Bible is on the same level of authority as the tradition of the church. The Council of Trent said this about the Bible and tradition:

> Following the example of the orthodox fathers, the Council accepts and venerates with the same sense of devotion and reverence all the books of the Old and New Testaments (for God alone is the source of both), together with all traditions regarding faith and morality, as proceeding from the mouth of Christ, or inspired by the Holy Spirit, and preserved in unbroken succession in the Catholic Church.[3]

THE COUNCIL OF TRENT

This is why Roman Catholics do not have to use Scripture to establish all of their beliefs. They can also look to the traditions of the church and believe it on the basis of the church's authority. The council also made the Latin Vulgate version of the Bible the authoritative version of Scripture.

Second, the council also responded to the Reformers' teaching on justification. How a man is justified in the sight of God was among the most important doctrines the Reformers sought to recover and preach. The Council of Trent firmly rejected what the Reformers taught about justification. By doing so, the Council of Trent also rejected what the Bible teaches about justification. The council declared:

> If anyone says that a sinful man is justified by faith alone . . . let him be anathema.[4]

The word anathema means "to be accursed" or "damned." The council further added:

> If anyone says that men are justified either through the imputation of Christ's justice [righteousness] alone, or through the remissions of sins alone . . . let him be anathema.[5]

By such declarations, the Roman Church condemned belief in the gospel of God's grace. The Roman Church denied exactly what the Bible plainly taught in passages like these:

But to him who does not work but believes on Him who justifies the ungodly, his faith is accounted for righteousness, just as David also describes the blessedness of the man to whom God imputes righteousness apart from works: "Blessed are those whose lawless deeds are forgiven, and whose sins are covered; blessed is the man to whom the Lord shall not impute sin." (Rom. 4:5-8)

For He made Him who knew no sin to be sin for us, that we might become the righteousness of God in Him. (2 Cor. 5:21)

Third, the Council of Trent condemned the Protestant's views on the sacraments. The Lord's Supper was a major point of controversy even among Protestants. Yet Protestants were united in rejecting Rome's views of the sacraments. The council once again condemned the Protestants to eternal judgment for their beliefs. The Council said the following:

> If anyone says that . . . there are more or less than seven sacraments let them be anathema.[6]

The council did not only respond to the Protestant Reformation. It also attempted reform within the Catholic Church itself. In particular, the council condemned various ills including simony and sexual immorality among the clergy. The council concluded its work on December 4, 1563. The decisions of the council were then submitted to the pope for approval. By doing this, the council acknowledged the pope's authority over its decisions.

The Council of Trent was unsparing in its condemnation of the Protestant Reformation. There was no unity possible. Rome had cursed the Protestants, consigning them to God's judgment. However, despite Trent's efforts, the Protestant Reformation would continue. The Protestant movement would grow in almost every country in Europe and eventually spread all over the world. But some countries stayed firmly in Rome's grip. These included Spain, Portugal, and Italy.

The Reformation spread in France but was fiercely opposed. The French Protestants, called Huguenots, took up arms to defend themselves from persecution. In 1572, French Romanists slaughtered tens of thousands of Huguenots in the **St. Bartholomew's Day Massacre**. This treacherous massacre took place during a truce for a wedding which was supposed to bring peace between the two sides. Instead, the fighting continued for many years. The Huguenot leader Henry IV (r. 1589-1610) eventually became king of France. Although he converted to Romanism to gain the throne, he did grant freedom of worship and protections to the Huguenots. But after Henry's death, these protections were gradually removed. King Louis XIV (r. 1643-1715) persecuted and drove most of the Huguenots out of France. Roman Catholicism triumphed in France. But the prosperous, hard-working Huguenots enriched the Protestant countries they fled to.

The Story of the Reina-Valera Bible

How sweet are Your words to my taste,
Sweeter than honey to my mouth! (Ps. 119:103)

The Reformation significantly impacted some places such as Germany, Switzerland, and the British Isles. But in other regions like Spain, the Reformation made little to no progress. Even though the Reformation was heavily persecuted in Spain, there were still faithful disciples there who embraced the Reformation. One of the most noteworthy of these was a man named **Cassiodoro de Reina** (1520-1594). Reina was a Spanish monk who learned about the Reformation and embraced it. He devoted himself to Bible study and set out to create a translation of the Bible into Spanish. The Inquisition was strong in Spain, so Reina fled to Geneva for refuge. Reina stayed in Geneva for a time but eventually set-

PALAZZO PRETORIO IN TRENTO (TRENT), ITALY

tled in London in 1559. Reina became a preacher for other Spaniards living in England. It was in London that Reina began his translation of the Bible into the mother tongue of his people.

Even though Reina found refuge in England, the Spanish authorities did not stop pursuing him. They brought false charges against Reina to English authorities. Reina fled back to the continent and stayed in various cities, on the run from Spanish authorities. Despite the pressures of persecution, Reina finished his translation of the Bible into Spanish in 1569. Copies were smuggled into Spain, but the Inquisition attempted to rid the country of every copy. Despite the Inquisition's assaults upon Reina's translation, it survived. In 1602, **Cipriano de Valera** (1531-1602) revised Reina's translation, creating what became the most-used Bible in Spanish. The translation is known as the ***Reina-Valera Bible***. Various revisions of the Reina-Valera are still read by Spanish-speaking Christians today. Heroic, courageous men like Tyndale and Reina enabled God's people to read the Bible in their own language. Thanks be to God for access to His eternal and inspired Word!

Cyril Lucaris and the Failed Eastern Orthodox Reformation

There were also attempts to reform the Eastern Orthodox Church. **Cyril Lucaris** (1572-1638) was born on the Greek island of Crete. He traveled to Western Europe and studied there, where he came in contact with Protestant ideas. Cyril seems to have adopted Protestant theology and sought to bring reformation to Eastern Orthodoxy.

In 1620, Cyril became the patriarch of Constantinople, the highest position in the Eastern Orthodox Church. Cyril corresponded with leading Reformed theologians in Switzerland, the Netherlands, and England, including the archbishop of Canterbury. Cyril sent Eastern Orthodox theological students to those countries to study, where they learned Reformed theology. He also spearheaded the translation of the New Testament into modern Greek. In 1629, Cyril wrote a confession of faith that taught Protestant doctrine. Cyril's confession affirmed the supreme authority of Scripture and said that the church could err. It also affirmed justification by faith and God's sovereign grace in salvation.

CYRIL LUCARIS (1572-1638)

Cyril Lucaris' reforming efforts met with much opposition. The Jesuits were very active at this time in Eastern Europe. They were seeking to subject the Eastern Orthodox Church to the pope and they hated Cyril. The Jesuits trained many Eastern Orthodox church leaders in their schools. In 1638, Cyril's enemies falsely accused him of inciting rebellion against the Turkish sultan. The sultan had Cyril strangled and his body thrown into the sea. After his death, Cyril's followers continued to try to reform the church. But at the Synod of Jerusalem in 1672, Protestant teachings were condemned. The synod condemned Cyril's Confession but said he hadn't written it. The Eastern Orthodox Reformation had failed.

Thankfully, even though man may curse, God can still bless. So it was with the Protestant Reformation. Despite the failure of the Reformation in Southern and Eastern Europe, Protestantism continued transforming church and society in Northern and Western Europe. And from there it would spread across the world in the coming centuries. ■

AD 1492
Columbus Discovers America

AD 1571
39 Articles Written

AD 1603-1625
Reign of King James I

AD 1611
Authorised (King James) Version Printed

AD 1618-1648
Thirty Years War

AD 1618
Synod of Dort

AD 1620
Plymouth Plantation Established

AD 1741
Jonathan Edwards Preaches *Sinners in the Hands of an Angry God*

AD 1774
Theophilus Lindsey forms the first Unitarian denomination

AD 1776
George Mason writes *The Virginia Declaration of Rights*

AD 1859
Charles Darwin Publishes *The Origin of Species*

AD 1887-1888
Downgrade Controversy

AD 1924
Auburn Affirmation

Unit 5

The Post-Reformation Period (AD 1600-1750)

AD 1620
Mayflower Compact

AD 1625-1649
Reign of King Charles I

AD 1630
Founding of the Massachusetts Bay Colony

AD 1642-1648
English Civil War

AD 1643-1648
Westminster Assembly

AD 1648
Peace of Westphalia

AD 1662
The Great Ejection

AD 1666
Great Fire of London

AD 1666
Great Fire of London

AD 1685-1688
Reign of King James II

AD 1707
Philadelphia Baptist Association Founded

AD 1707
Latitudinarians takes over Harvard College

AD 1730-1740
The Great Awakening

CANTERBURY CATHEDRAL, CANTERBURY, ENGLAND

Puritans, Separatists, and Covenanters

25

Husbands, love your wives, just as Christ also loved the church and gave Himself for her, that He might sanctify and cleanse her with the washing of water by the word, that He might present her to Himself a glorious church, not having spot or wrinkle or any such thing, but that she should be holy and without blemish. (Eph. 5:25-27)

Despite the persecutions under Queen Mary I, the English Reformation endured. As we learned in a previous chapter, Queen Elizabeth I's long reign (r. 1558-1603) brought stability to the English Church. The Church of England was Protestant. During Elizabeth's reign, the core statement of faith was finalized in 1571. The ***Thirty-Nine Articles*** of the Church of England summarize what the Church taught.

In the *Thirty-Nine Articles*, we find sound expressions of biblical truth. Here are a few examples of the brief articles of faith from the *Thirty-Nine Articles*.

> **Of the Justification of Man**
> We are accounted righteous before God, only for the merit of our Lord and Saviour Jesus Christ by Faith, and not for our own works or deservings. Wherefore, that we are justified by Faith only, is a most wholesome Doctrine, and very full of comfort . . . (Article 11)
>
> **Of Good Works**
> Albeit that Good Works, which are the fruits of Faith, and follow after Justification, cannot put away our sins, and endure the severity of God's judgment; yet are they pleasing and acceptable to God in Christ, and do spring out necessarily of a true and lively Faith insomuch that by them a lively Faith may be as evidently known as a tree discerned by the fruit. (Article 12)

The *Thirty-Nine Articles* repudiated many teachings of the Roman Church. The Articles rejected the doctrine of purgatory, and the Roman view of the sacraments.

> **Of Purgatory**
> The Romish Doctrine concerning Purgatory, Pardons, Worshipping and Adoration, as well of Images as of Relics, and also Invocation of Saints, is a fond thing, vainly invented, and grounded upon no warranty of Scripture, but rather repugnant to the Word of God. (Article 22)

The Roman requirement for priests to remain unmarried was also rejected.

> **Of the Marriage of Priests**
> Bishops, Priests, and Deacons, are not commanded by God's Law, either to vow the estate of single life, or to abstain from marriage: therefore it is lawful for them, as for all other Christian men, to marry at their own discretion, as they shall judge the same to serve better to godliness (Article 32)

The Lord was gracious to the people of England to provide a period of peace for the church during Elizabeth's reign. However, this did not mean the church had been perfected in its teachings or that God's people in England were without need of change and growth. The Church of England still needed to mature in faithfulness and holiness.

The Puritan Desire for a Pure Church

Therefore, having these promises, beloved, let us cleanse ourselves from all filthiness of the flesh

and spirit, perfecting holiness in the fear of God. (2 Cor. 7:1)

It was this desire for the purification of the church that drove those godly ministers of the **Puritan** movement. The word "puritan" was not a title adopted by those within the movement. Instead, it was a negative term used by opponents of the Puritans who thought they were overly zealous in their attempts to purify the church. Much like the word "legalist" or "Pharisee" is a negative word, the word "puritan" was used negatively of these pastors who labored for the purity of the English church.

Those men known as Puritans were grateful to God for restoring so much faithful teaching to the Church of England. But they were concerned about some elements of worship and practice that appeared to be remnants of Roman Catholicism. Such elements included kneeling while partaking of communion, the wearing of vestments, making the sign of the cross when performing baptism, and the number of holy days observed on the church calendar. Puritans were also concerned about nominalism and a lack of church discipline in the Church of England.

Some of the Puritans also desired to see the form of church government in England changed. The Church of England, after its separation from Rome, continued with an Episcopal form of church government. This form of government involves the rule of bishops over a city or region. Under the bishops are priests or pastors serving in local churches. Under the priests, there are also deacons in the church. Some of the Puritans held Presbyterian or Congregational convictions. This meant that they did not believe that bishops should hold rule over a city or region above the office of the pastors or elders. These different forms of church government are summarized in the table below.

The Puritans who longed for the purification of the church were also committed to staying in the church and continuing to seek its ongoing purity. Among the Puritan-minded men in the church, some eventually determined that they would instead have to worship separately from the Church of England. Because of issues of conscience, some of these pastors could not continue in the Church of England. Those who separated and worshiped independently from the Church of England became known as **Separatists**.

Both the Puritans and Separatists encountered resistance from those within the Church of England. But it was the Separatists who received the most persecution. By separating from the national church, they made themselves a target. Separation from the national church was seen as a subversive act. Elizabeth, though committed to some tenets of Protestant belief, still oversaw some of these persecutions.

However, the ill-begotten **Star Chamber** was used to condemn many an innocent man to imprisonment and death during Elizabeth's reign. **Archbishop John Whitgift** (1530-

Three Forms of Church Government

Episcopal Bishops, Priests, and Deacons	Presbyterian Pastors/ Elders and Deacons	Congregational Pastors/ Elders and Deacons
• Bishop has rule over a city or region. Bishops are responsible for ordaining priests.	• Pastors/Elders rule the local church but are connected together in an assembly called a Presbytery (a council of elders). Elders in the Presbytery examine and ordain other elders.	• Pastors/Elders lead the local church. Each local church is independent. In matters of church discipline, authority resides with the majority vote of the congregation itself.

ARCHBISHOP JOHN WHITGIFT

1604) oversaw this tribunal. It functioned much like the tyrannical Inquisition in Spain. This court was vested with the power to apprehend a person without a charge and without an accuser. If the individual would not answer the questions directed to him, he would be remanded to jail until he was willing to do so.

Between 1583 and 1593, twenty-five Separatist pastors were confined to jails in London, many of whom were cruelly beaten. At least three died while in prison. On May 29, 1593, three Christian men were executed at St. Thomas-a-Watering in Central London, just south of the river Thames. John Penry, Henry Barrow, and John Greenwood were sentenced to death by hanging for authoring books on the subject of church discipline. The Puritans and Separatists became increasingly controversial groups within England.

The Growth of the Puritan Movement

Pursue peace with all people, and holiness, without which no one will see the Lord. (Heb. 12:14)

What were the core ideals of the Puritans? Joel Beeke and Randall Pederson, two scholars of Puritan thought, summarize Puritanism with these five distinguishing characteristics:

1. The Puritans sought to search the Scriptures, bring together their findings, and apply them to all areas of life.
2. The Puritans were passionately committed to focusing on the Trinitarian character of theology. They never tired of proclaiming the electing grace of God, the dying love of Jesus Christ, and the work of the Holy Spirit in the lives of sinners.
3. The Puritans believed in the significance of the church in the purposes of Christ. Puritanism was a movement that focused on plain and earnest preaching, liturgical reform, and spiritual brotherhood.
4. The Puritans looked to Scripture for light on the duties, powers, and rights of king, Parliament, and citizen-subjects.
5. The Puritans focused on personal, comprehensive conversion. They excelled at preaching the gospel, probing the conscience, awakening the sinner, calling him

WILLIAM PERKINS (1558-1602)

to repentance and faith, leading him to Christ, and teaching him the way of Jesus' commands.[1]

These core values drove the Puritans in their quest for a purer church.

There were certain regions of England where Puritanism especially flourished. Cambridge University was a major center for Puritanism in Elizabethan England. **William Perkins** (1558-1602) is sometimes considered the father of Puritanism, passing on his theology to men such as **William Ames** (1576-1633), **Richard Sibbes** (1577-1635), and **John Cotton** (1585-1652). Ten years after Perkins died, Thomas Goodwin reported that Cambridge was "filled with the discourse of the power of Mr. William Perkins' ministry."[2] Beeke and Pederson write of Perkins' influence:

> Nearly one hundred Cambridge men who grew up in Perkins' shadow went to New England, including William Brewster of Plymouth, Thomas Hooker of Connecticut, John Winthrop of Massachusetts Bay, and Roger Williams of Rhode Island. Richard Mather (father of Increase Mather, and grandfather of Cotton Mather) was converted while reading Perkins. Jonathan Edwards was also fond of reading Perkins more than a century later. Samuel Morison remarked that "your typical Plymouth Colony library comprised a large and a small bible, Ainsworth's translation of the Psalms, and the works of William Perkins, a favorite theologian."[3]

KING JAMES I (1603-1625)

Elizabeth I died in 1603 without any descendants of her own. The House of the Stuarts from Scotland took the English throne in 1603, beginning with **King James I** (r. 1603-1625). James grew up in Scotland, where Reformed and Presbyterian thought had become a dominant perspective. James' arrival as the monarch now over both Scotland and England excited the Puritans. They assumed James would be sympathetic to their aims for the English church. But they were to be sadly disappointed. James did not receive the Presbyterian views imparted by his teachers in Scotland. He hated the Scottish Presbyterians who had resisted his attempts to rule over the church.

James preferred the Episcopal government of the English church. He could appoint the bishops, and they tended to defer to him. James sought to rule as an absolute monarch, and he hated the Puritans and Separatists. He said of them: "I will make them conform themselves, or else I will harry them out of the land, or else do worse."[4] When James said they must "conform," he meant that the Puritans and Separatists must agree with the established practice of the Church of England.

Persecution and resistance to these movements continued during King James' reign. It was again the Separatists who received the most mistreatment. The persecutions caused many Separatists to flee to the Netherlands, where they enjoyed religious toleration. In 1620, a group of these separatists known as the Pilgrims made their way to Plymouth, Massachusetts. They established **Plymouth Plantation**. Nine years later, a ship filled with Puritans led by John Winthrop landed in Boston, Massachusetts where these reforming Christians set out to build a "city on a hill." The Puritans and Separatists had a significant influence in shaping the North American colonies, which later became the United States of America.

GREAT HALL OF THE HAMPTON COURT PALACE

The Hampton Court Conference and the Authorised Version

The law of the Lord is perfect, converting the soul;
The testimony of the Lord is sure, making wise the simple;
The statutes of the Lord are right, rejoicing the heart;
The commandment of the Lord is pure, enlightening the eyes. (Ps. 19:7-8)

Shortly after the beginning of James' reign in England, an important conference was held in January 1604. The **Hampton Court Conference** was a meeting of various English Church leaders with King James. The Puritans petitioned King James for further reforms in the Church of England. While King James chose not to give the Puritans most of their requests, he did grant one: the petition for a new English translation of the Bible.

Since Tyndale's first English translation of the New Testament from the original Greek, various English translations had been made. These included the *Great Bible* of 1539, the Geneva Bible of 1560, and the *Bishop's Bible* of 1568. The Puritans often favored the Geneva Bible. But the *Bishop's Bible* was the primary translation used in the Church of England at that time. Some desired that a primary translation that would unite English-speaking Christians be produced. We do not know all the reasons why King James agreed to the production of a new translation. But it is possible that one reason was his dislike of the *Geneva Bible*. The *Geneva Bible* contained commentary notes that justified resistance to monarchs under certain circumstances. James required that the new translation contain no notes of commentary. The translators were allowed to put notes in the margin where an alternate translation was justified. But no interpretation or explanation was allowed. When the Puritan John Reynolds, at the conference, petitioned the king for a new translation, King James replied:

> I could never yet see a Bible well-translated into English but I think that of all, that of

> Geneva is the worst. I wish some special pains were taken for an uniform translation; which should be done by the best learned in both universities, then reviewed by the bishops, presented to the privy council, lastly ratified by royal authority, to be read in the whole church, and no other.[5]

James supported the translation effort and appointed forty-seven scholars to work on the translation. The translators came from a variety of backgrounds within the Church of England. Some were Puritans. Others were not. From 1607 to 1610, various committees worked on the translation. Once the work was completed, the translation was printed in 1611. It became known as the **Authorised Version**, also called the **King James Version**. Original editions of the translation, like the *Bishops' Bible* before it, contained the books known as the Apocrypha.

The *Authorised Version* was a revision bringing together the best of all previous translations including Tyndale, Coverdale, the *Great Bible*, and the *Bishops' Bible*. Though the translation was published in 1611, it took many decades before it became more widely used than existing translations. But by the 1700s, the *Authorised Version* was firmly established as the dominant English translation of the Bible.

The original edition of the *Authorised Verison* contained a letter dedicated to King James I. In this brief introductory letter, the translators show their godly zeal and love for God's Word. Here is a portion of their introductory letter to King James:

> But among all our joys, there was no one that more filled our hearts, than the blessed continuance of the preaching of God's sacred Word among us; which is that inestimable treasure, which excelleth all the riches of the earth; because the fruit thereof extendeth itself, not only to the time spent in this transitory world, but directeth and disposeth men unto that eternal happiness which is above in heaven.

No translation of the Bible is perfect since the Bible was originally inspired in Hebrew and Greek. Nevertheless, faithful translations provide God's people access to His Word so they can read it with understanding and edification. The *King James Version* was used by God to provide a unified translation for English speaking Christians all over the world. The *King James Version* continues to be read with profit by Christians today. It also continues to influence more recent translations of the Bible.

TITLE PAGE OF THE *AUTHORISED VERSION*

The Puritans and Covenanters after King James I

James died in 1625. His son, Charles I (1625-1649), ascended to the throne. Like his father, **Charles I** sought to rule as an absolute monarch. But he was less cautious than his father. He ruled without a parliament for eleven years, raised illegal taxes, and trampled on English liberties. The Star Chamber and Court of the High Commission censored books and punished his enemies without fair trial. These courts whipped, fined, pilloried, imprisoned, and cut off the ears of those who dared criticize the king's tyranny. Charles also appointed **William Laud** (1573-1645) as archbishop of Canterbury. Laud was zealous to move the Church of England closer to Rome. He hated and persecuted the Puritans. Charles' tyrannical reign and Laud's leadership of the church provoked much controversy in the realm. During this time of persecution, many Puritans left old England to found New England.

The Stuart kings had been trying to control the Scottish church for years. But in 1637, Charles I and Archbishop Laud made a fatal mistake. They tried to impose a high church Anglican liturgy on the Church of Scotland. But the Scots would have none of it. The story goes that as the dean of Edinburgh was beginning the new service, a Scottish woman named Jenny Geddes threw her stool at him, shouting, "Villain, dare you say Mass in my lug [ear]?"[6] The Scots rose up against the Anglican liturgy and Episcopacy in the Scottish Second Reformation. They signed the National Covenant in 1638. This covenant pledged the nation to resist all Roman Catholic and Episcopalian innovations and restore Presbyterianism in the Kirk (church). Some Scots even signed the covenant with their own blood.

Charles was furious and invaded Scotland. But his army was disastrously defeated by the Scots. The king had no standing army and could not raise money for one without the English Parliament. So Charles was forced to summon Parliament in 1640. The new Parliament had many Puritans who demanded redress of grievances. They abolished the Star Chamber and the Court of High Commission and imprisoned Archbishop Laud. But King Charles continued in his tyrannical ways. Tensions between the king and Parliament eventually led to the outbreak of the **English Civil War** (1642-1648). The English Parliamentarians and most of the Scots allied with each other, signing the Solemn League and Covenant in 1643. This covenant promised the preservation of the Reformed religion in Scotland and the reformation of religion in England and Ireland "according to the Word of God and the example of the best reformed churches." Those Scots who signed the National and Solemn

KING CHARLES I (R. 1625-1649)

ARCHBISHOP WILLIAM LAUD (1573-1645)

JENNY GEDDES THROWING HER STOOL

League and Covenants became known as **Covenanters**.

During the war, the English Parliament called the **Westminster Assembly** (1643-1653) to reform the Church of England. The Westminster Assembly consisted of about 150 members, most of whom were English ministers and theologians. They are sometimes called "divines" because they were doctors of divinity. The Church of Scotland also sent several commissioners who had great influence at the Assembly, such as Samuel Rutherford (1600-1661) and George Gillespie (1613-1648). The Assembly produced the ***Westminster Confession of Faith***, the ***Westminster Larger Catechism***, and the ***Westminster Shorter Catechism***, which are known as the *Westminster Standards*. Although these documents were never adopted by the Church of England, they were adopted by the Church of Scotland. To this day, Presbyterian churches in Scotland, America, and throughout the world hold to the *Westminster Standards*.

THE WESTMINSTER ASSEMBLY

Eventually, Parliament won the English Civil War. William Laud was executed. In 1649, Charles I himself was beheaded for treason. England, Scotland, and Ireland became a commonwealth ruled by Lord Protector **Oliver Cromwell** (1599-1658). For a time, England, Scotland, and Ireland were without a King. Oliver Cromwell's son Richard Cromwell (1626-1712), served as lord protector for a short time. But in 1660, **Charles II** (r. 1660-1685), son of Charles I, was restored to the throne. The monarchy was back.

The **Restoration** brought back persecution for the Puritans. In 1662, thousands of Puritan pastors were expelled from their churches in what is known as the **Great Ejection**. At this time, most Puritans left the Church of England to form dissenting churches. The English government also prohibited nonconformist church services and forbade Puritan pastors from coming within five miles of their former churches. The Puritans and Separatists suffered terribly under Charles II. Many were imprisoned, including **John Bunyan** (1628-1688), who wrote ***Pilgrim's Progress*** while in Bedford Jail.

In Scotland, the persecution was even worse. Charles II and the Scottish Parliament repudiated the National and Solemn League and Covenants, imposed Episcopacy on the Scottish Kirk, and outlawed Presbyterianism. Over 250 ministers were ejected from their churches because they refused to accept this tyranny. An act known as the "Bishop's Dragnet" crippled people with ruinous fines if they did not attend the service of their local parish.

The Scottish Covenanters, who continued to hold fast to the Covenants, disobeyed this act and met for worship in open air meetings known as "conventicles." Parliament outlawed conventicles, defining them as any meeting for worship outside the established kirk at which more than five people were present. Royal dragoons tried to hunt down and break up these conventicles and arrest whomever they caught. Some of the Covenanters took up arms to defend themselves but were mostly unsuccessful. Thousands of Covenanter

THE GREAT FIRE OF LONDON

men, women, and children were killed in these dark days known as the "**Killing Times**." They were martyred because they believed that Christ, not the king, was the head of the church.

Charles II and his court were ungodly and immoral, and they badly misgoverned the land. But God is not mocked. In 1665-1666, London was struck by the **Great Plague**, which killed

SCOTTISH COVENANTERS WORSHIPING OUTDOORS

about 100,000 people. In September 1666, the **Great Fire of London** swept through the city, burning down large portions of London. The next year the English suffered a humiliating defeat in their war with the Dutch. A Dutch fleet sailed up the Thames River almost to London, destroying English ships and burning some English buildings on shore. After these calamities, Puritan pastor Thomas Vincent wrote a book called *God's Terrible Voice in the City*. Vincent warned the nation to heed these warnings and repent, lest the Lord send worse judgments on an unfaithful people.

But the immorality and the persecution continued. In 1685, two Scottish women, eighteen-year-old **Margaret Wilson** and sixty-three-year-old **Margaret McLachlan**, were arrested and sentenced to death for attending Covenanter conventicles. The two women were tied to stakes on the seashore at Wigtown to be drowned by the incoming tide. Margaret McLachlan's stake was tied further out, and Margaret Wilson had to watch the older woman drown. This was to weaken the younger Margaret's resolve. But when she was asked what she thought of her older friend, she replied:

> What do I see, but Christ in one of his members wrestling there? Think you that we are the sufferers? No; it is Christ in us, for he sends none a warfare upon their own charges.[7]

Both women died as martyrs for Christ's Crown and Covenant.

In 1685, **James II** (r. 1685-1688) became king. He was an open Roman Catholic who attempted to make England and Scotland Roman Catholic countries. He also sought to control the American colonies and overthrow their colonial charters. James was a close ally of King Louis XIV of France (r. 1643-1715), who was cruelly persecuting his own French Protestant subjects, known as Huguenots.

James II was so tyrannical that he alienated most Anglicans, and they joined with the Puritans in opposing him. Fearing the triumph of popery and tyranny, English Protestants called on **William** and **Mary** for help. William of Orange married the daughter of James II. William was a Protestant from the Netherlands. In 1688, William landed in England and King James II fled. Parliament deposed James II and made William and Mary king and queen. This is known as the **Glorious Revolution**. A bill of rights was enacted and Protestant dissenters were finally given freedom of worship. Presbyterianism was restored in Scotland. Persecution in England and Scotland came to an end.

The legacy of the Puritans and Covenanters today is found in the many writings they have left behind. The Puritans wrote on numerous subjects. But they are particularly well known for their lengthy sermons expositing Scripture and their writings on Christian piety and practice. Their writings are still read with much profit today. The maturity and holiness of the Puritans should be imitated by Christians today. Insofar as they imitated Christ, may we also imitate them. ■

Imitate me, just as I also imitate Christ. (1 Cor. 11:1)

COUNTRYSIDE IN SAXONY-ANHALT, GERMANY

26 Pietists, Arminians, and Baptists

And let us consider one another in order to stir up love and good works, not forsaking the assembling of ourselves together, as is the manner of some, but exhorting one another, and so much the more as you see the Day approaching. (Heb. 10:24-25)

In the 1500s, the Lutheran form of Protestantism became predominant in Germany. Germany at this time was not one country. It was made up of many small territories. The 1555 **Peace of Augsburg** allowed each ruler to choose whether his territory would be Lutheran or Roman Catholic. But during the Thirty Years War (1618-1648), Roman Catholics tried to stamp out Protestantism in Germany. They almost succeeded. But the Swedes came to the aid of the German Protestants, led by **King Gustavus Adolphus** (r. 1611-1632). Protestantism in Germany was saved, but Central Europe had been devastated. For thirty years, the armies of both sides had lived off the land and wasted it. About one out of four people in Germany had died.

The 1648 **Peace of Westphalia** that ended the war reaffirmed the principle that each ruler could choose whether his territory was Protestant or Roman Catholic. Lutheranism remained predominant in Germany. The Lutheran confessions and catechisms collected in the ***Book of Concord*** shaped what the Lutheran church believed and practiced. However, just because Protestantism had become firmly rooted in Germany did not automatically mean that a living faith was rooted in the heart of every person in Protestant Germany. Many who attended worship did so out of tradition or under compulsion.

It was the desire of some godly, zealous Christians that churchgoers in Germany would become zealous and committed disciples of the Lord Jesus Christ. These Christians desired that the faith would be living and active in the hearts of every German churchgoer. They sought a living faith instead of a dead orthodoxy. Eventually a movement developed in Germany that became known as the **Pietist** movement. The word **piety** is another way of describing godliness. To be godly is to love the Lord and to be spurred on by that love to worship the Lord in daily life and to devote oneself to a life of holiness and Christian service. This kind of active and engaged spiritual life is described by the Apostle Paul in Romans 12:

Do not be slothful in zeal, be fervent in spirit, serve the Lord. (Rom. 12:11 ESV)

GUSTAVUS ADOLPHUS (R. 1611-1632)

The Founders of Pietism: Spener and Francke

Philip Jakob Spener (1635-1705) is considered by many the founder of Pietism. Often in church history, a "movement" develops around certain emphases that have been lost or neglected by previous generations. So it was with the Pietists. They wanted to recover the living, active faith of previous generations that seemed to have declined. The Pietists accepted the doctrines of the Lutheran church. They had no desire to change the orthodox teaching of the church. Instead, their desire was to cultivate a life of sincere godliness and holiness. However, some Pietists did downplay the importance of doctrine, and some failed to apply Scripture beyond one's personal life.

Spener's classic work, ***Pia Desideria***, published in 1675, summarized the emphases of the Pietists in six points:

1. To better acquaint believers with Scripture by adding private readings and study groups to preaching.
2. To emphasize the gifts of the body and to encourage involvement of all the members in spiritual ministry to one another.
3. To emphasize that believers be "doers of the Word" and not hearers only, to apply their faith and knowledge of God.
4. To restore humility and love in the church, avoiding unnecessary controversy.
5. To ensure that pastors live pious lives while also assuring that they are well taught in the Word.
6. To focus preaching on developing faith in ordinary believers.

AUGUST HERMANN FRANCKE (1663-1727)

One of the unique emphases of the Pietists was the development of group gatherings of believers in homes to study the Bible and to pray together. Before the rise of the Pietist movement, gatherings for group Bible studies outside of the worship services of the church were uncommon. Pietist teachers thought it beneficial for believers to gather together more frequently to read and pray together and to spur one another on to love and good works. These gatherings were known as **conventicles**. In our day, "small group" gatherings are quite common in Evangelical churches. This pattern of Christian community owes much to the Pietist movement.

In 1705, a school was established in **Halle**, Germany in line with these Pietist principles. A man named **August Hermann Francke** (1663-1727) founded the school first in his home. He wanted to disciple other young men

HALLE, GERMANY

for a life of active Christian service. An important aspect of Pietist theology was the emphasis upon conversion. Early Pietist leaders like Spener and Francke would recount their experiences of conversion. Francke said this of his conversion to the Lord:

> Suddenly, God heard me. As easily as one turns a hand, my doubts vanished. In my heart, I was certain of the grace of God in Jesus Christ. Since then I was able to call God, not only "God," but also "Father." Sadness and anxiety immediately left my heart. And I was suddenly overcome by a wave of joy, such that I praised and magnified God aloud, who had granted me such grace.[1]

One of Francke's desires in establishing a school was to train men for Christian missions. Francke's efforts in Halle make him an important figure in the rise of the modern missionary movement. He also inspired many other Christians to engage in care for orphans. He began his work with orphans in 1698, working with one hundred young children. He was the inspiration for **George Müller** (1805-1898), the great evangelist and orphanage director of the 19th century. One of Francke's most influential disciples at Halle was a young man named **Count Nicolaus von Zinzendorf** (1700-1760). For eight years, Francke taught Zinzendorf the life of piety.

At age twenty-one, Zinzendorf came into possession of a large estate. With a portion of his vast estate, Zinzendorf purchased land from his grandmother which included the town of Berthelsdorf. Then, in May 1722, he met a man from Moravia. His name was **Christian David**. This man had fled Moravia in search of a place where he and his fellow Moravians could worship the Lord freely. Zinzendorf offered his estate as a potential location where the Moravians might temporarily lodge.

Christian David sent word to his fellow Moravians back home. Soon a number of families were on their way to Berthelsdorf. With Zinzendorf's permission, the Moravian refugees began building structures on the land for housing and worship. The Moravians soon named the new spot Herrnhut. Translated, this means, "on the watch for the Lord."

COUNT NICOLAUS VON ZINZENDORF (1700-1760)

At first, Zinzendorf knew little about these Moravian Christians. But he was glad to provide a safe place for them. As he spent more time with them, he learned that these Moravians had a rich history. They maintained the Protestant legacy that dated back to John Huss. Huss was the great church reformer of the 14th century who was martyred for his faith. As with the man whose name they bore, these Hussites had encountered great persecution. The freedom that many Hussites had enjoyed in Bohemia came to an end with the Thirty Years War. Led by the Jesuits, Roman Catholics began severely persecuting them. The Moravians buried Bibles in their gardens and held their church meetings in barns at midnight. They preserved sacred records in birdhouses as well as in their cottage roofs. Finally, however, persecution at the hands of Roman Catholic civil leaders had reached such an intolerable level that they were forced to flee. The Moravians found a place of refuge on Zinzendorf's estate.

Over the next ten years, Herrnhut grew to house hundreds of Christians with similar ideals. Most of the community came from Moravia. But other Christians from a Lutheran and Reformed background heard about the community. They also wanted to join. Herrnhut was a unique community of spiritual devotion. Zinzendorf and his wife the countess were excited to be part of a community dedicated to spiritual pursuits.

Herrnhut was unique in several ways. For one, the community gathered for worship every single day. Each day ended with a ser-

ST. THOMAS

vice of hymn singing. Thousands of hymns were produced by the Christians at Herrnhut. It was also a community dedicated to continual prayer. Starting on August 27, 1727, the Christians at Herrnhut began a pattern that would continue for one hundred years. For each hour of the day, someone was assigned to engage in intercessory prayer. The prayer warriors would gather weekly to meet and share letters and other news. These weekly meetings prepared the intercessors with content to bring to the Lord in prayer.

Herrnhut was not a community of perfect people. But it was a community centered on the unifying truth of Jesus Christ and His death and resurrection for sinners. The Moravians' zeal for the Lord would bear much fruit in the generations that followed.

The Beginning of Moravian Missions

Surely you shall call a nation you do not know,
And nations who do not know you shall run to you,
Because of the Lord your God,
And the Holy One of Israel;
For He has glorified you. (Isa. 55:5)

Count Zinzendorf had long been committed to spreading the gospel. Now, the community of Herrnhut provided a path to do just that. The Moravians were ready to take the message of Jesus to other parts of the world. The first missionaries set out in 1732. Two men left for the small island of **St. Thomas** in the Caribbean. **Leonard Dober** and **David Nitschmann** said their goodbyes to the community on August 18, 1732. That night, before the missionaries departed, the community sang one hundred hymns together.

As this new missionary effort began, Zinzendorf and the Moravians committed themselves to certain principles. These included:

1. Instead of aiming at converting the whole nation (and transforming the culture) at least initially, they would look for individuals who were seeking the truth. In the past, kings and princes had taken an interest in the Christian message. This wasn't the case as much anymore. Now, a new strategy came into play. They would work to find individuals who were interested in the gospel. They would labor to convert these people before attempting a top-down discipleship of the nations.
2. They would speak directly of the life and death of Jesus Christ. Before speaking of the necessity of faith and repentance, it becomes necessary to teach first the work of God in salvation. This is the thing that men and women must believe to be saved.
3. They would not consider themselves above the native people as if they were superior to them. Instead, they would

humble themselves and mix in with the people. They would pray with and work alongside those they ministered to.

JOHN WESLEY (1703-1791)

Moravians continued to make their way across the Atlantic. Missions were established in Jamaica, Antigua, Barbados, St. Kitts, and Tobago. Another Moravian mission was launched far to the north in **Greenland** in 1733. The Moravian work in Greenland became so well established that it survived until 1900. In that year, the church joined with the existing Danish Lutheran church. The geographical spread of Moravian missions continued into Suriname (on the northern coast of South America), South Africa, Canada, and the American Colonies.

The dedication of the Moravians to the cause of missions was outstanding in the history of the Christian church. Their dedication to the cause of Christ's kingdom would inspire future missionaries for generations to come. The Moravians' earnest love for Christ, fanned by the flames of spiritual devotion at Herrnhut, resulted in a significant kingdom work that changed the world. Praise be to God for Moravian missions and the fruit they produced!

The Moravians also influenced both **John Wesley** (1703-1791) and **George Whitefield** (1714-1770), evangelists that God used mightily during the first Great Awakening of the 1740s. On a voyage to Savannah, Georgia where he was sent to minister, John Wesley first encountered the Moravian Brethren and he was impressed by their faith. During a frightening storm at sea, the Brethren sang hymns and prayed while others panicked. After two years of ministering to the colonials and Native Americans, Wesley returned to England and allied himself with the Moravians, even paying a visit to their Herrnhut community in Saxony. Writing of the Moravians, Wesley observed that, "They walked worthy of the vocation wherewith they were called, and adorned the Gospel of our Lord in all things."[2]

The convictions of the Pietists and the Moravians would contribute to the revivals of religion that took place in the 1700s and 1800s in Great Britain and America.

The Arminian Controversy

Blessed be the God and Father of our Lord Jesus Christ, who has blessed us with every spiritual blessing in the heavenly places in Christ, just as He chose us in Him before the foundation of the world, that we should be holy and without blame before Him in love, having predestined us to adoption as sons by Jesus Christ to Himself, according to the good pleasure of His will. (Eph. 1:3-5)

In the early 1600s, a theological controversy broke out in the Dutch Reformed Church. A man named **Jacob Arminius** (1560-1609) began to depart from the teaching of the Reformed Church. His teaching reduced God's sovereignty in salvation, emphasized man's free will, and taught that God's saving grace could be resisted by men. Arminius' theology, which came to be known as **Arminianism**, made salvation ultimately depend on man's choice rather than God's. Arminianism caused great controversy in the Dutch Reformed Church because the Arminians opposed the Augustinian and Reformed view of grace, which is sometimes called **Calvinism**.

After Arminius' death, his followers set forth

their views in **Five Articles of Remonstrance**. A remonstrance is an act of protest. In this case, the Arminians were protesting the doctrine of the Reformed churches. The Five Points of Arminianism include the following:

1. Conditional Election: God looks into the future, sees those who will believe on Him, and chooses those people for salvation.
2. Unlimited Atonement: Christ died for all men without exception. The atonement is unlimited in its extent but is limited in its efficacy (what it accomplishes). The atonement does not actually secure salvation for anyone. It makes salvation possible for those who choose to believe.
3. Total Depravity: The Arminians affirmed that man is affected in the whole nature by sin. As a result, without God introducing "cooperative grace," a sinner cannot turn to Christ.
4. Prevenient Grace: God's saving grace can be resisted and rejected by men.
5. Conditional Preservation of the Saints: Arminians were divided on this point. Some said that since man chooses Christ, he can unchoose Him and lose his salvation. Others say that man cannot lose his salvation no matter how he lives, which can lead to carnal security.

LOCATION OF DORDRECHT, WHERE THE SYNOD OF DORT WAS HELD

The Dutch Arminians repeatedly used civil power to block the attempts of Dutch Reformed pastors and elders to meet in a synod (church council) to deal with the important theological issues involved in the controversy. At last in 1618-1619, the **Synod of Dort** convened. In this council, representatives were also present from the Reformed churches of Switzerland, Germany, England, and Scotland.

The synod discussed the points of controversy and the arguments of both sides at length. In the end, it affirmed the Augustinian and Calvinistic position in five points, formulated in response to the five points of Arminianism. The **Five Points of Calvinism**, as they have come to be known, can be summarized with the acronym **TULIP**:

1. **T – Total Depravity:** Man is depraved in every aspect of his being. Man is dead in trespasses and sins. In this state, he hates God. Man cannot prepare himself for salvation and cooperate with God in salvation unless God first grants the sinner new life (the new birth).
2. **U – Unconditional Election:** God chooses men for salvation solely because He loved them and chose to have mercy on them. He did not choose them because He foresaw they would believe, because all hated Him, and none would choose Him if He had not first chosen them.
3. **L – Limited Atonement** (Particular Redemption): Christ died for all His people, all those whom the Father had given Him. Christ died for all men without distinction, that is, all kinds of men, those from every tribe, people, language, and nation. The atonement is limited in its extent but

is unlimited in its efficacy. The atonement actually secures salvation for all those for whom Christ died.

4. **I – Irresistible Grace:** Men can resist God's outward call. But God's inward call of saving grace cannot be resisted by the sinner but will surely result in his regeneration, faith, and repentance.
5. **P – Perseverance of the Saints:** All those whom the Father predestined, the Son died for, and the Spirit regenerates will be preserved by God's power and can never totally or finally fall from grace and lose their salvation.

The decrees of the council, known as the ***Canons of Dort***, were adopted as the doctrinal standards of the Dutch Reformed Church along with the ***Belgic Confession*** and the ***Heidelberg Catechism***. These three documents are known as the ***Three Forms of Unity***. They remain the doctrinal standards of Dutch Reformed churches to this day.

The decisions of Dort were affirmed by all the Reformed churches. Arminianism was rejected. However, the doctrinal perspective of the Arminians would continue to reappear at various times in church history.

The Baptists

Or do you not know that as many of us as were baptized into Christ Jesus were baptized into His death? Therefore we were buried with Him through baptism into death, that just as Christ was raised from the dead by the glory of the Father, even so we also should walk in newness of life. (Rom. 6:3-4)

In previous chapters on the Reformation in Switzerland, we learned about the rise of the Anabaptist movement and how it continued in various groups that still exist today such as the Mennonites. However, in the early 1600s, a separate movement arose in England. The English Baptists shared one common trait with the Anabaptists: they would only baptize professing believers. But on many other points of theology, the English Baptists were more in line with other Protestant churches in Great Britain and the continent of Europe.

It is estimated that over 60% of modern-day Protestant Christians in the world are made up of descendants of the English Baptists and Independents. This family of churches was founded by **Thomas Helwysse** (1575-1616) and **John Spilsbury** (1593-1668). Because Baptists make up such a large portion of Protestant Christianity, it is important that we understand their roots.

Among the English Baptists, there may have been ideological roots in the Anabaptists of the earlier Reformation. However, it is the modern Mennonites, the Amish, and the Brethren groups

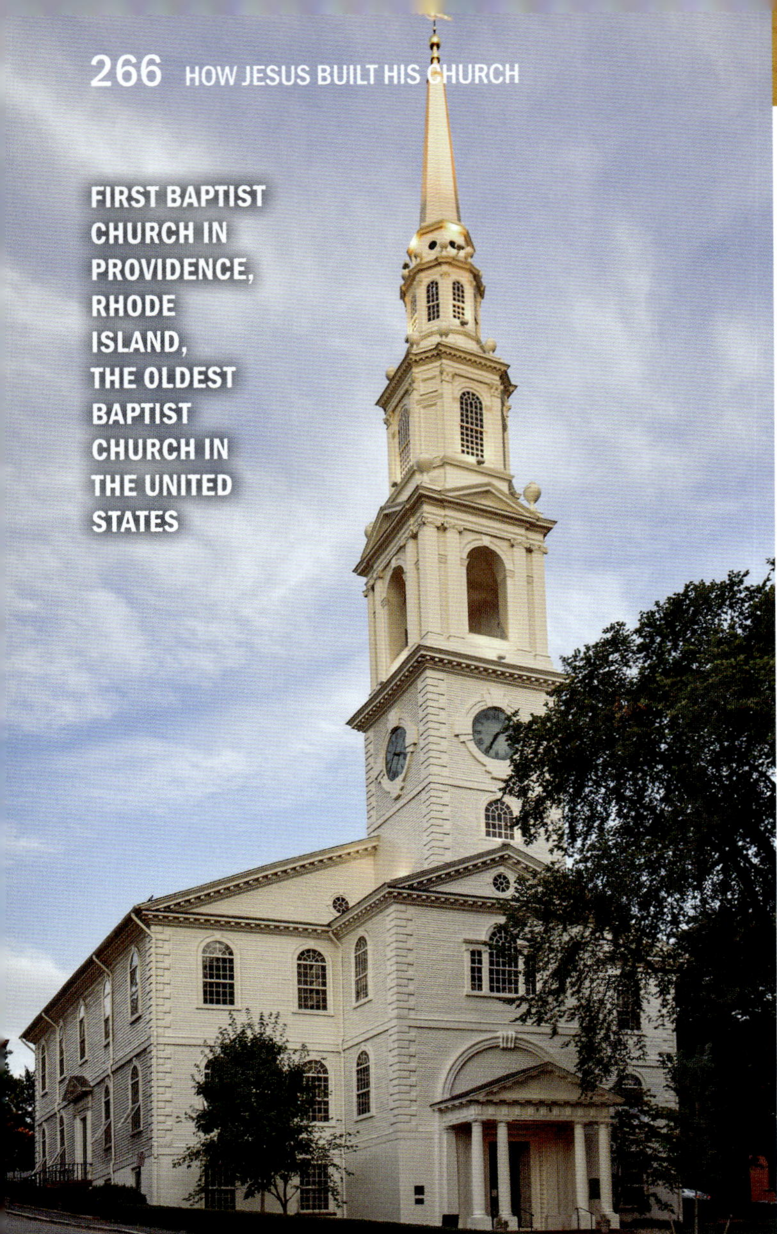

FIRST BAPTIST CHURCH IN PROVIDENCE, RHODE ISLAND, THE OLDEST BAPTIST CHURCH IN THE UNITED STATES

that flow directly from the original Anabaptist movement. The English Baptists have their roots in English Separatists who left the Church of England. Many of them fled to the Netherlands for religious freedom. The primary distinctive of the English Baptists was their rejection of infant or household baptisms in favor of baptisms after profession of faith. The English Baptists also practiced an independent form of church government whereby each church was governed by local pastors/elders and independent of all other churches.

Thomas Helwysse moved from Holland back to England and planted a church at Spitalfields in London in 1612. These first English Baptist churches became known as **General Baptists** for their Arminian view of Christ's atonement. The General Baptists believed that Christ had died for the sins of all mankind rather than intending to die for the sins of the elect only. Several church splits in the 1630s resulted in the formation of the **Particular Baptists**, John Spilsbury being one of the first Baptist pastors taking the Calvinist view of Christ's atonement (holding to the doctrine of "particular atonement").

The Baptists found more fertile soil in America where individualism was more cherished and radical conversion experiences were more encouraged (in the early Puritan years). The first London Baptist Confession of 1644 upheld particular atonement. Article 21 states:

> Jesus Christ by His death did purchase salvation for the elect that God gave unto Him: These only have interest in Him, and fellowship with Him, for whom He makes intercession to His Father in their behalf, and to them alone doth God by His Spirit apply this redemption; as also the free gift of eternal life is given to them, and none else.

***Westminster Confession of Faith* (1647) on Baptism**	***Second London Baptist Confession of Faith* (1689) on Baptism**
• Not only those that do actually profess faith in and obedience unto Christ, but also the infants of one, or both, believing parents, are to be baptized. • Dipping of the person into the water is not necessary; but baptism is rightly administered by pouring, or sprinkling water upon the person.	• Those who do actually profess repentance towards God, faith in, and obedience to, our Lord Jesus Christ, are the only proper subjects of this ordinance. • Immersion, or dipping of the person in water, is necessary to the due administration of this ordinance.

A later confession was adopted and became used by many English and American Baptists. This confession is called the **Second London Baptist Confession** of 1689. It was modeled after the content of the **Westminster Confession of Faith** of 1647. The distinctive Baptist views of the *London Baptist Confession* can be seen by comparing the two confessions side by side (see table on previous page).

Benjamin Keach (1640-1704) was a prolific Baptist writer and a signer of the 1689 confession. A few years before the signing of the confession, Keach's son immigrated to America (in 1686). He organized a church in Pennepek, Pennsylvania and preached throughout Pennsylvania and New Jersey. The **Philadelphia Baptist Association** was formed in 1707. The Association adopted the *Second London Baptist Confession* in 1742 with several modifications. Meanwhile, the General Baptists formed in New England under the leadership of **Roger Williams** (1603-1683). Williams was responsible for founding the colony of Rhode Island. By 1780, there were 457 Baptist churches in America (up from 33 in 1700).[3] By 1850, the Baptists had become the largest Christian denomination in the country.

The Baptists may have been strengthened in part due to the persecution they received in New England in the 17th century and in the southern states through the American War for Independence. The **Virginia Declaration of Rights** was written by George Mason and adopted on June 12, 1776. This document guaranteed liberty to the Baptists (and Presbyterians) in Virginia. Article 16 of the declaration contains the critical clause: "All men are equally entitled to the free exercise of religion, according to the dictates of conscience." This view of religious liberty would become a distinguishing marker of American life. In previous centuries of church history, the freedom to join any Christian denomination you wanted without fear of persecution was not commonplace. But in the United States, this kind of religious liberty became normal.

However, the 19th century marked a period in which revivalism downplayed the importance of doctrine, creeds, and confessions. The majority of American Baptists became Arminians. Some American Baptists were more given to **Hyper-Calvinism** in the form of the Primitive Baptists under the leadership of **Daniel Parker** (1781-1844). Hyper-Calvinism rejects human responsibility in evangelizing, resting on the notion that God is going to save whomever He wants to save with or without human means. This doctrine is contrary to God's Word which commands us to preach the gospel to every creature (Mark 16:15) and to disciple the nations in the commands of Christ (Matt. 28:19-20).

In the late 19th century and early 20th centuries, the Baptists faced the attacks of Modernism and Theological Liberalism. In liberal theology, the infallibility and authority of Scripture is rejected in favor of man-made ideas. Baptist preacher **Charles**

METROPOLITAN TABERNACLE IN LONDON

CHARLES SPURGEON (1834-1892)

Spurgeon (1834-1892) in London engaged in the **Downgrade Controversy** in 1887-1888. Liberalism was creeping into the Baptist Union. Spurgeon stated his concerns in this way: "Our warfare is with men who are giving up the atoning sacrifice, denying the inspiration of Holy Scripture, and casting slurs upon justification by faith."[4] In the end, Spurgeon and his congregation, the **Metropolitan Tabernacle**, left the Baptist Union because the Union had compromised the truth. This spiritual battle took a heavy toll on Spurgeon's health. His wife, Susannah believed that "his fight for the faith cost him his life."[5]

Yet Charles Spurgeon's worldwide ministry of books and sermons published in newspapers had a tremendous effect upon Baptists and evangelicals even to the present day. His writings would continue to serve as an inspiration for other pastors and Christian leaders like **A.W. Pink** (1886-1952), **Lorraine Boettner** (1901-1990), **John Piper** (1946-), **R.C. Sproul** (1939-2017), and **John MacArthur** (1939-). These men helped preserve and spread Calvinistic theology.

Northern Baptists largely succumbed to Liberalism in the early to mid 1900s. Liberals also infiltrated the Southern Baptist Convention (SBC). But in the 1970s-1990s, Southern Baptists affirmed the inerrancy of Scripture, disciplined the Liberals, and saved their denomination for evangelical orthodoxy in what became known as the Conservative Resurgence.

There was also a revival of Calvinism among Baptists. Reformed Baptist churches formed in the 1960s and 1970s under the leadership of men like **Albert N. Martin** and **Walter Chantry**. By 2013, about 30% of Southern Baptist churches (the largest Protestant denomination in America) claimed to be Calvinist. Sometimes called the "Founders Movement," these Calvinistic Baptists spread quickly. Most notable in this resurgence of Reformed thinking is the influence of **R. Albert Mohler** (1959-), president of Southern Baptist Theological Seminary in Louisville, Kentucky, which may be the largest Christian seminary in the world. Baptists continue to play an important role in Christ's church as one of the largest Protestant groups in the world. ■

SOUTH FERRY CHURCH IN NARRAGANSETT, RHODE ISLAND, BUILT IN THE 1850S AS NARRAGANSETT BAPTIST CHURCH

COAST OF MAINE, USA

Christianity in Colonial America

No king is saved by the multitude of an army;
A mighty man is not delivered by great strength.
A horse is a vain hope for safety;
Neither shall it deliver any by its great strength.
Behold, the eye of the LORD is on those who fear Him,
On those who hope in His mercy. (Ps. 33:16-18)

The 1400s marked a new period of world exploration. From the 1400s to 1600s, ships from Europe crossed all over the globe. Historians call this the **Age of Discovery**. At first, Spain and Portugal led the way by traveling new sea routes. Discovery and trade expanded into the Americas and into Asia. In 1492, Italian explorer **Christopher Columbus** (1451-1506) discovered the Americas. He was not the first European to reach the Americas. **Leif Erickson** (c. 970-1025), the Norseman, landed in Greenland and Canada around AD 1000. But it was not until after Columbus that Europeans began to colonize the "New World." The first colonial efforts in the Americas were made by Spain and Portugal. These nations brought Roman Catholicism to Central and South America.

In the early 1600s, England began to expand its colonization efforts as well. Through the 1600s and into the 1700s, numerous colonies were founded by the English in North America. In total, thirteen colonies were established. Each of the colonies had a somewhat different background and purpose. But eventually, these colonies would join in an American War of Independence and then become the United States of America.

In God's providence, the United States of America has played an important role in church history. Learning about how these colonies formed will help us understand how the United States became what it is. In this chapter, we will learn about the early foundations of the American colonies. We will also look at the Christian background of each colony.

Virginia, the Carolinas, and Georgia

Blessed is the nation whose God is the LORD,
The people He has chosen as His own inheritance.
(Ps. 33:12)

In the early 1600s, travel across the Atlantic was long and dangerous. An ocean journey from Great Britain to North America took around two months. If you had made such a journey, you would not have arrived in North America to find a bustling port city filled with inns, businesses, and restaurants. The earliest colonists left Great Britain and traveled across the ocean for two months only to enter largely uncultivated wilder-

CHRISTOPHER COLUMBUS (1451-1506)

JAMESTOWN SETTLEMENT

ness lands. For the earliest colonists, embarking on such a journey was costly and dangerous. It came with many risks. But the journey also opened many opportunities. There were opportunities for business. There was the opportunity to gain greater religious liberty. And for Christians, there was a missionary opportunity. Christ's crown rights as King of kings would be advanced into new parts of the world.

The story of the United States begins in the state of **Virginia**, very close to the modern-day capital of Washington DC. The first lasting colony established by the English was the colony of Virginia. While there were a few failed colonial efforts in the region (such as the failed Roanoke Colony), the first permanent settlement was **Jamestown**, established in 1607.

A minister of the Church of England arrived with the first settlers of Jamestown. One of the earliest structures in Jamestown is the church building. Some of the foundation stones from that building still exist in Jamestown to this day. One purpose for the Jamestown settlement was to put a stop to Spanish expansion into the north from Florida. Another goal for the colony was to make money. Establishing a colony came with great sacrifice and many risks. Stockholders and the colonists both intended to make a profit. Many early colonists were attracted by the economic opportunities of the New World. North America was a land abundant in untapped natural resources. Colonists wanted to use the resources the land provided and generate income through their labors.

The colony of **Carolina** was founded in 1663, just south of Virginia. To encourage immigration to these new colonies, Carolina was founded with a decree of religious freedom. This attracted many **dissenters** from Virginia who differed in their convictions from the Church of England. Dissenters were those who objected to worship in the Church of England. They were not willing to participate in the established state church. But

JAMES OGLETHORPE (1696-1785)

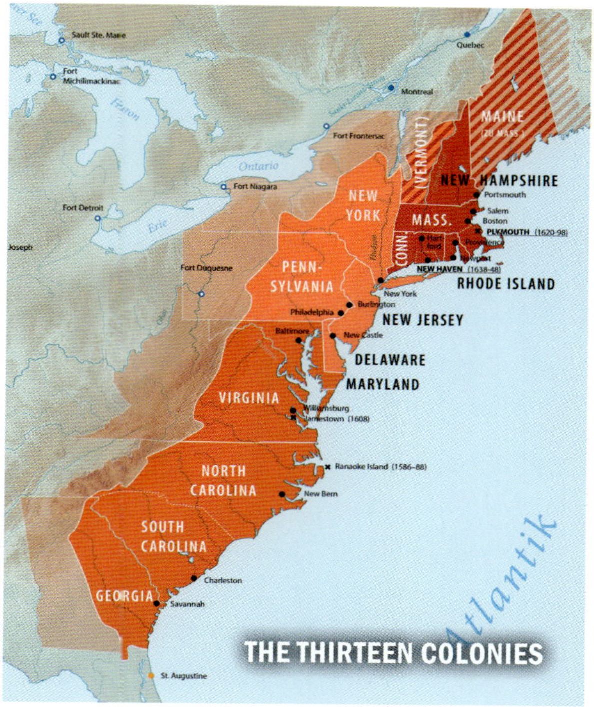

in Virginia, religious freedom was limited. Worship in any other church besides the established Church of England was for a time forbidden. In Carolina, the higher classes were often part of the Church of England. The lower classes were often attracted to the dissident groups such as the Presbyterians, the Baptists, and the Quakers. Until 1712, Carolina was one colony. But in that year, it was split into two colonies (North Carolina and South Carolina).

The colony of **Georgia** was established in 1733. **James Oglethorpe** (1696-1785) was the founder and first governor of the colony. Most of Georgia's colonists were members of the Church of England. The English identity of the colony was evident in the colony's name. Georgia was named after **King George II** (r. 1727-1760). Though most colonists considered themselves members of the Church of England, Georgia became a place of religious refuge for Christians of other backgrounds as well. Georgia's charter, issued in 1732, included this decree securing religious liberty:

> That forever hereafter, there shall be a liberty of conscience allowed in the worship of God, to all persons inhabiting, or which shall inhabit or be resident within our said province, and that all such persons, except papists, shall have a free exercise of their religion, so they be contented with the quiet and peaceable enjoyment of the same, not giving offence or scandal to the government.[1]

Christians of different backgrounds were granted religious liberty. But the charter indicated that Roman Catholics (called "papists") were not granted the same liberty.

Georgia was founded with two basic purposes. The first purpose was to halt the Spanish expansion from Florida. Georgia was in a strategic location between Florida and the other English colonies. This made the land a good spot to establish a colony. The second purpose for Georgia's founding was to serve as an alternative place for those sentenced to debtor's prison. By the beginning of the 18th century, there were many in England who wanted to reform the prison system. Debtor's prison did little to help those in debt get out of debt. Prisoners often suffered from poor conditions. Nor were prisoners acting as productive contributors to society since they were imprisoned rather than working to pay off their debts. Georgia became a place where the indebted could go and work with their hands.

The New England Colonies

You are the light of the world. A city that is set on a hill cannot be hidden. Nor do they light a lamp and put it under a basket, but on a lampstand, and it gives light to all who are in the house. Let your light so shine before men, that they may see your good works and glorify your Father in heaven. (Matt. 5:14-16)

It was in the Northern colonies of **New England** that Puritanism had its greatest influence, particularly in Massachusetts. The region of New England comprises the states of **New Hampshire**, **Massachusetts**, **Vermont**, **Rhode**

THE MAYFLOWER PILGRIMS

Island, **Connecticut**, and **Maine**. From the beginning, the historic center of this region has been the colony (and later the state) of Massachusetts.

Several colonies were planted in the New England region for specifically religious reasons. The first of these colonies was **Plymouth Plantation** south of modern-day Boston, Massachusetts. The courageous men and women who founded Plymouth are sometimes called the Pilgrims. The Pilgrims were a group of Separatists originally from England. Separatists were those who worshiped in congregations separate from the established Church of England. For a time, the Separatists lived and worked in the Netherlands. There, they could practice their faith without fear of persecution by English authorities.

The Pilgrims did appreciate the freedom they experienced among the Dutch. But they were concerned that the culture of the Netherlands was not a good influence on their children. Some of their children were being corrupted by the Dutch youth, who cared little for the things of God. Also, economic conditions in the Netherlands were difficult. Many of the English Separatists found it difficult to make a living.

The Pilgrims then determined to establish a colony in North America. Not only did the pilgrims desire freedom and new opportunities. They also wanted to see the gospel of Jesus Christ advance into new lands. **William Bradford** (1590-1657), who wrote the first account of the Plymouth Colony, described the purpose of their journey to the New World in the following way:

> Lastly, (and which was not least,) a great hope and inward zeal they had of laying some good foundation, or at least to make some way thereunto, for the propagating and advancing the gospel of the kingdom of Christ in those remote parts of the world; yea, though they should be but even as stepping-stones unto others for the performing of so great a work.[2]

With this purpose in mind, 102 Separatist settlers set out for the New World in 1620 on board the ***Mayflower***. Their planned destination was a region in Virginia. But the Lord had other plans for them. The Separatists ended up arriving about 400 miles north of their intended destination. This was far beyond the limits of the Virginia Colony. They found themselves in what is now called Cape Cod Bay in Massachusetts. As it was now the beginning of winter, they could not safely sail south to Virginia. They decided to disembark and to establish a new colony near Cape Cod.

Before they landed, the Pilgrims organized themselves into a political body. They recognized that if they were to be alone in this new land, they would need a proper government over the colony. Together, they signed the *Mayflower Compact*, setting forth the covenant by which they would live together. Below is the text of the *Mayflower Compact*:

> In the name of God, Amen.
>
> We, whose names are underwritten, the Loyal Subjects of our dread Sovereign Lord King James, by the Grace of God, of Great Britain, France, and Ireland, King,

Defender of the Faith, etc.

Having undertaken for the Glory of God, and Advancement of the Christian Faith, and the Honour of our King and Country, a Voyage to plant the first Colony in the northern Parts of Virginia; Do by these Presents, solemnly and mutually, in the Presence of God and one another, covenant and combine ourselves together into a civil Body Politick, for our better Ordering and Preservation, and Furtherance of the Ends aforesaid: And by Virtue hereof do enact, constitute, and frame, such just and equal Laws, Ordinances, Acts, Constitutions, and Officers, from time to time, as shall be thought most meet and convenient for the general Good of the Colony; unto which we promise all due Submission and Obedience.

IN WITNESS whereof we have hereunto subscribed our names at Cape-Cod the eleventh of November, in the Reign of our Sovereign Lord King James, of England, France, and Ireland, the eighteenth, and of Scotland the fifty-fourth, Anno Domini; 1620.

JOHN WINTHROP (1587-1649)

The first months of Plymouth colony's existence were exceedingly difficult. The Pilgrims suffered from a variety of illnesses including scurvy, pneumonia, and tuberculosis in the cold weather. About half of them died the first winter. However, once spring came, the local native tribes assisted the Pilgrims. They gave the Pilgrims advice on how to best cultivate the land. The Pilgrims worked hard to learn their new environment and secure food stores for the next winter. They were able, by God's provision, to survive and to grow. The colony lasted many more decades until 1691, when it was absorbed into neighboring Massachusetts.

Ten years after Plymouth's founding, a group of English Puritans organized the **Massachusetts Bay Company**. It was founded in 1630.

MODERN RECREATION OF PLYMOUTH PLANTATION

The seal of the Massachusetts Bay Colony included an Indian exclaiming: "Come Over and Help Us." These words were derived from the "Macedonian Call" contained in Acts (Acts 16:9). The words of the seal indicate something of the missionary aim of the colony, which was to see the Christian faith received by the natives of the Massachusetts region.

The first colonists to arrive came under the leadership of a man named **John Winthrop** (1587-1649). The New England Puritans sought to build a godly society on the Bible. Their law codes cited Deuteronomy and incorporated biblical laws from the Old Testament. The Puritans also sought to ground their education in the Word of God. ***The New England Primer***, a book written to teach children the alphabet, began, "In Adam's fall, we sinned all." Like other Reformed Christians, the Puritans sang metrical psalms. In fact, the first book published in North America was the 1640 ***Bay Psalm Book***. The other New England colonies of **Connecticut** and **New Hampshire** were also founded by the Puritans.

One of the first missionaries to the native American tribes was a man named John Eliot (1604-1690). Eliot developed an alphabet for the **Algonquin** language so that the Algonquin Native Americans could begin to read and write their own language. Then Eliot translated the Bible into Algonquin, providing a foundational tool for the conversion and discipleship of this tribe. Many Indians came to faith in Christ through Eliot's preaching. Eliot organized the converted natives into Christian communities called Praying Towns.

Let the peoples praise You, O God;
Let all the peoples praise You.
Then the earth shall yield her increase;
God, our own God, shall bless us.
God shall bless us,
And all the ends of the earth shall fear Him.
(Ps. 67:5-7)

ROGER WILLIAM'S BANISHMENT

Rhode Island and the Baptists

The founding of the colony of **Rhode Island** began with a dispute between the minister **Roger Williams** (1603-1683) and the authorities in Boston. Williams arrived in Massachusetts in 1631 to serve in the Christian ministry. Williams rejected the idea that the civil magistrate should enforce the first four of the Ten Commandments, a radical position at that time. He believed in absolute religious toleration for all religions. He thought that order in society could be preserved using human reason and natural law, which he believed would prevent crimes like murder and theft.

The Puritans asked Williams what would happen if a group of unbelievers, whose minds were not shaped by the moral laws of the Bible, held control of the government? The Puritans were concerned that without the standard of God's Word, society would not have a basis to define right and wrong. Williams responded by arguing that through natural law, revealed in

ROGER WILLIAMS STATUE IN PROVIDENCE, RHODE ISLAND

nature and in the human conscience, there would be order in society on that basis.

There were other disagreements between the Puritans and Roger Williams. Williams was highly critical of the Puritans for taking land which he believed belonged to the Native Americans. Because of these disagreements with the authorities in Massachusetts, Williams was eventually expelled from the colony.

Williams left Massachusetts and founded the colony of Rhode Island. Williams wished to establish a colony where a greater degree of toleration of other religious views would be allowed. The colony was founded as Rhode Island and Providence Plantations. Williams named it Providence Plantations because the colony was "in a sense of God's merciful providence unto me in my distress."

Williams established the colony with broader religious liberties than were found in the Massachusetts Bay Colony. Various groups like the Quakers moved to Rhode Island to practice their convictions freely. However, even though Rhode Island tolerated more views than other colonies, its 1663 charter still expressed a Christian aim for the colony. Here is a portion of that charter:

> With peaceable and loyal minds, their sober, serious and religious intentions, of godly edifying themselves, and one another, in the holy Christian faith and worship as they were persuaded; together with the gaining over and conversion of the poor ignorant Indian natives, in those parts of America, to the sincere profession and obedience of the same faith and worship... to defend themselves, in their just rights and liberties against all the enemies of the Christian faith.[3]

Williams assisted in establishing a church in **Providence**, Rhode Island in 1639. It was one of the first Baptist congregations in the English colonies. Yet Williams did not stay long in this church. His views became increasingly radical and unorthodox. Williams concluded that all churches were false and that Scripture was to be understood in merely spiritual terms. This brought further attacks against Williams from the New England Puritans. Even the Baptists in Providence disagreed with Williams. Yet Roger Williams' view of religious liberty would become influential in America in the centuries that followed.

The God of Israel said,
The Rock of Israel spoke to me:
"He who rules over men must be just,
Ruling in the fear of God." (2 Sam. 23:3)

The Middle Colonies

Most of the American colonies were colonized by Protestants. These groups included Anglicans, Puritans and Separatists, Presbyterians, and Baptists. England had become an "officially Protestant" nation by its separation from the Roman Catholic Church. For this reason, most colonists from England were Protestant in their convictions.

Nevertheless, Roman Catholicism soon came to the shores of America, through the founding of the colony of **Maryland**. In 1632, **King Charles I** (r. 1625-1649) granted **Lord Baltimore** (1605-1675) rights of property and colonization over a portion of the territories that had been claimed for Virginia. Lord Baltimore was himself a Roman Catholic. Many Catholics in England wished to have a place where they could avoid persecution in England by coming to America. Maryland became a haven for English Roman Catholics to practice their religion. Lord Baltimore could not forbid Protestants from entering the colony. But early on, Roman Catholicism had a strong presence in Maryland. Maryland was another example of the unique experiment in religious liberty practiced in many of the American colonies.

WILLIAM PENN (1644-1718)

The colonies founded between New England and Maryland were **New York**, **New Jersey**, and **Delaware**. These colonies were not, in the beginning founded by a singular Protestant group. But as with the other colonies, Protestantism had a significant influence upon the lives of the colonists in these middle colonies.

The colony of **Pennsylvania**, which played such an important role in the birth of the nation, was founded as a haven for the Quakers. **William Penn** (1644-1718), a Quaker, founded Pennsylvania as a safe place for Quakers to practice their faith. Quakers were often persecuted in England due to their nonconformity to the Church of England. Because Pennsylvania, New Jersey, and Delaware did not have established state churches, the middle colonies became a melting pot of many different Christian denominations. Even colonies that did not have established state churches still had religious tests that required officeholders to believe in the Trinity and the inspiration of the Bible.

In the late 1700s, the thirteen English colonies would join together to fight the **American War for Independence** (1775-1783) to form a new nation independent from the British Empire. Many colonial pastors played an important role in the war, supporting the American cause. They are often called the black-robed regiment because of the black preaching robes they wore. One of these pastors was **John Witherspoon** (1723-1794). Witherspoon was a Scottish pastor and leader of the evangelicals in the Church of Scotland. He spent years fighting the apostasy and doctrinal decline in Scotland. In 1768, he moved to America to serve as president of the **College of New Jersey** (now Princeton University). Witherspoon would teach at Princeton for the next 26 years, training many men who would become America's Founding Fathers, many of whom were Christians. Witherspoon also helped organize the American Presbyterian church, and he was the only minister to sign the Declaration of Independence.

The founding of the United States would open a new chapter in the history of Christ's church. Christians from various denominations would be sent out from this young nation to all different parts of the world. Eventually, for a time, the United States became the nation that sent out the most missionaries of any nation in the world. Part of the reason for America's widespread influence in Christianity was due to the spiritual awakenings that occurred in the mid-1700s and during the 1800s. In the next chapter, we will learn how the Lord blessed the churches of America with times of spiritual refreshing. ■

JOHN WITHERSPOON (1723-1794)

THE BATTLE OF LONG ISLAND, 1776

LAKE BALA, WALES

The Great Awakening

28

Restore us, O God of our salvation,
And cause Your anger toward us to cease.
Will You be angry with us forever?
Will You prolong Your anger to all generations?
Will You not revive us again,
That Your people may rejoice in You?
Show us Your mercy, Lord,
And grant us Your salvation. (Ps. 85:4-7)

The 20th century Christian leader J.I. Packer (1926-2020) defined revival as "the visitation of God which brings to life Christians who have been sleeping and restores a deep sense of God's near presence and holiness. Thence springs a vivid sense of sin and a profound exercise of heart in repentance, praise, and love, with an evangelistic outflow."[1] Throughout church history, God has been gracious to send His Holy Spirit to the church to bring times of revival and refreshing. Packer's definition of revival rightly notes that revival is a visitation of God. It is not something that man produces. It is a work of God.

By the early 1700s, churches in Britain and America were in desperate need of God's visitation. Genuine piety and holiness were at a low ebb. If anybody would reveal an earnestness in prayer or preaching, it would be perceived as a threat to the peace of the realm. Christianity in Britain had largely descended into an empty and external form of religion. The populace was taken by drunkenness, and immorality was widespread. Prisons were filling with criminals and debtors. Even though the church had a large presence in life, the condition of religion in Great Britain looked much like the description Christ provided the church at Laodicea in Revelation 3:

So then, because you are lukewarm, and neither cold nor hot, I will vomit you out of My mouth. Because you say, "I am rich, have become wealthy, and have need of nothing"—and do not know that you are wretched, miserable, poor, blind, and naked—I counsel you to buy from Me gold refined in the fire, that you may be rich; and white garments, that you may be clothed, that the shame of your nakedness may not be revealed; and anoint your eyes with eye salve, that you may see. (Rev. 3:16-18)

If revivals should bring about discernible improvements of life and culture in localities and nations, then it would be hard to find many

GEORGE WHITEFIELD
(1714-1770)

JONATHAN EDWARDS
(1703-1758)

national revivals since the period of the Reformation. But the **Great Awakening** of the 1730s and 1740s was one such revival. And it was not only a national revival but an international revival because it affected both sides of the Atlantic. The regions of England, Scotland, Wales, and North America were greatly impacted by this work of God through men like **George Whitefield** (1714-1770), **John Wesley** (1703-1791), and **Jonathan Edwards** (1703-1758). In America, this revival became known as the Great Awakening, but in Britain it is called the Evangelical Revival.

The Preaching Ministry of George Whitefield

But you be watchful in all things, endure afflictions, do the work of an evangelist, fulfill your ministry. (2 Tim. 4:5)

George Whitefield is generally considered the greatest evangelist of the modern age. Whitefield was greatly influenced by **Thomas à Kempis** (c. 1380-1471) and Puritans **Henry Scougal** (1650-1678), **Joseph Alleine** (1634-1668), and **Richard Baxter** (1615-1691). He was also a friend of John and Charles Wesley. In his *Journals*, Whitefield describes his conversion or "new birth" in his nineteenth year. He confessed that he was delivered from "sect religion" or denominationalism and repented of frequenting stage plays. He testified how God worked in his soul the grace of the new birth. One day, Whitefield cried out on his bed "I thirst! I thirst!" He then wrote: "Soon after this, I found and felt in myself that I was delivered from the Burden that had so heavily oppressed me! The Spirit of Mourning was taken away from me, and I knew what it was truly to rejoice in God my Savior."[2]

Whitefield began his teaching ministry by visiting prisoners, which he found of the greatest use to prepare himself for a more public ministry. Ordained to the ministry at twenty-one years of age, the evangelist began working in a small country parish called Dummer. There he maintained a rigorous daily schedule of eight hours in study and prayer, eight hours in visitation, and eight hours in sleep. Upon the encouragement of John Wesley, he began making plans to organize an evangelistic outreach to Georgia in America. As he made preparations to leave England in 1737, Whitefield began a traveling preaching ministry in various churches and meetinghouses. Instantly, a fire was lit that would continue for the rest of his life. Whitefield writes:

> Neither church nor house could contain the people that came. I found uncommon manifestations granted me from above. Early in the morning, at noonday, evening, and midnight, nay, all the day long, did the blessed Jesus visit and refresh my heart.[3]

Weeks later, Whitefield writes again in his journals:

> The congregations contin-

BRISTOL, ENGLAND

> ually increased, and generally, on a Lord's Day, I used to preach four times to very large and very affected auditories... Henceforward, for near three months successively, there was no end of the people flocking to hear the Word of God... I now preached generally nine times a week... On Sunday mornings, long before day, you might see streets filled with people going to church with their lanterns in their hands, and hear them conversing about the things of God.[4]

In February 1739 on a cold day outside Bristol, England, George Whitefield preached in the open air for the first time. It was in a small region called **Kingswood**. The district was inhabited by many low-wage coal miners. Evangelist George Whitefield went from house to house, inviting the residents to gather and hear the preaching of the Word. On the first day he preached, Whitefield proclaimed the gospel to some two hundred people.

The next Wednesday, Whitefield preached again in Kingswood. This time, there were about 2,000 people present. Two days later, about 4,000 gathered. Then, on Sunday, Whitefield estimated he preached to over 10,000 people. He recounted, "The trees and hedges were full. All was hush when I began. The sun shone bright. God enabled me to preach for an hour with great power, and so loudly that all, I was told, could hear."[5] Open air preaching allowed Whitefield and other evangelists to reach people who were not regular churchgoers. They preached the gospel to all classes of society, from the highest to the lowest.

BENJAMIN FRANKLIN (1706-1790)

Whitefield's crowds grew to 20,000 at a time in some cases. His preaching caused controversy, especially with the clergy. The doctrine of the new birth greatly bothered them because his preaching called into question the faith of nominal church members. Whitefield did not push for "decisions" or public professions at his services. Nonetheless, thousands were impacted by his messages. Charles Wesley reported that "The whole nation is in an uproar,"[6] and James Hervey wrote that "All London and the whole nation ring of the great things of God done by his ministry."[7]

Though many embraced the Word of God as Whitefield preached, there were also many opponents. Some clergy barred him from their pulpits. Many mocked Whitefield's ministry. Due to issues with his eye, some people joked about Whitefield, calling him "Dr. Squintum." Sometimes he would experience hecklers in the crowds who would pelt him with stones or rotten eggs.

George Whitefield's work in America was even more extensive than his preaching in Great Britain. Biographer Arnold Dallimore claims there is "little doubt that far more than half of the total population of the Colonies had heard him preach."[8] Whitefield's work extended beyond preaching in America. He raised funds to build orphanages in Georgia. He argued for American liberties to the point of attending a parliamentary meeting with **Benjamin Franklin** (1706-1790).

In the early 1740s, Whitefield's preaching enjoyed great success in Scotland as well. Tens of thousands gathered to hear him preach. In a letter to his wife Elizabeth, Whitefield wrote of the unusual response:

> I preached at two to a vast body of people,

> and at six in the evening and again at nine at night. Such a commotion surely never was heard of, especially at eleven at night. It far outdid all that I ever saw in America. For about an hour and a half there was such weeping, so many falling into deep distress and expressing it in various ways, as is inexpressible . . . Their cries and agonies are exceedingly affecting . . . All night in the fields could be heard the voice of prayer.[9]

For weeks he preached in Scotland, once to a crowd of 40,000 as they stood in the rain to hear this man of God.

Whitefield died on September 30, 1770 in Newburyport, Massachusetts while on a preaching tour in America. No doubt, millions of lives and every Protestant denomination in Britain and America were impacted by his ministry. Many American preachers and evangelists from different denominations were active throughout the colonies during the Awakening, and Whitefield worked with many of them.

Jonathan Edwards (1703-1758) was a Congregationalist pastor in Northampton, Massachusetts. His congregation and others were blessed by the Great Awakening. The Lord especially used the preaching of Edwards' sermon ***Sinners in the Hands of an Angry God*** in Enfield, Connecticut in 1741. Edwards would become a great theologian who wrote many books. He also served as a missionary to American Indians on the Massachusetts frontier.

Elsewhere in the colonies, Dutch Reformed pastor **Theodore Frelinghuysen** (1691-1747) and Presbyterians **William Tennent** (1674-1746) and **Gilbert Tennent** (1703-1764) preached in New Jersey and Pennsylvania. Presbyterian **Samuel Davies** (1723-1761) preached in Virginia. Patrick Henry heard Samuel Davies' sermons as a boy.

The Great Awakening had a great impact on America. Many of America's founding fathers commended George Whitefield, including Benjamin Franklin, George Washington, John Adams, and Patrick Henry. Later evangelists like **Dwight L. Moody** (1837-1899) and **Billy Graham** (1918-2018) would build upon Whitefield's evangelistic fervor.

JOHN WESLEY (1703-1791)

John and Charles Wesley

Ho! Everyone who thirsts,
Come to the waters;
And you who have no money,
Come, buy and eat.
Yes, come, buy wine and milk
Without money and without price.
Why do you spend money for what is not bread,
And your wages for what does not satisfy?
Listen carefully to Me, and eat what is good,
And let your soul delight itself in abundance.
(Isa. 55:1-2)

Whitefield's preaching ministry dramatically impacted the lives of people in Great Britain and North America. But Whitefield was not the only evangelist who traveled far and wide. John and Charles Wesley were also instrumental during the period of the Great Awakening. Around the time Whitefield began preaching, John Wesley traveled to America. He set out to engage in evangelism in the new colony of Georgia. On the long ocean voyage, John met a group of **Moravian** Christians. John was impressed by the Moravians' faith and love. He watched as these people gladly took on any difficult or menial task that needed to be done aboard the ship.

Sometime during the Atlantic crossing, a tempestuous storm struck the ship. John Wesley and others on board panicked. Screams of fear arose from the ship. Wesley confessed that he was afraid to die. But there was one group that did not seem afraid. As the storm raged and the waves pummeled the ship, the Moravians didn't cry out in fear. Instead, they sang hymns of trust and praise to God. Amazed at their lack of fear, John desired to have that same faith in God.

In 1738, after returning to England, John did put all his trust in Jesus Christ. While visiting a church gathering at **Aldersgate Street**, London, he experienced a sense of confidence and assurance of salvation through Christ. A man was reading a portion of Martin Luther's commentary on Romans. It was the powerful, gospel words of Romans that gave assurance to John. He later wrote: "I felt my heart strangely warmed. I felt I did trust in Christ, Christ alone for salvation. And an assurance was given me that he had taken away my sins, even mine, and saved me from the law of sin and death."[10]

Around the same time, John's brother Charles came to a similar confidence. On May 21, 1738, he gave up trying to save his own soul. He trusted in Christ alone to save him. To remember how Jesus had saved him, Charles wrote one of his greatest hymns, ***And Can It Be***. Here are some words of that hymn:

And can it be that I should gain
An int'rest in the Savior's blood?
Died He for me, who caused His pain?
For me, who Him to death pursued?
Amazing love! how can it be
That Thou, my God, shouldst die for me?

Amazing love! how can it be
That Thou, my God, shouldst die for me!

No condemnation now I dread;
Jesus, and all in Him is mine!
Alive in Him, my living Head,
And clothed in righteousness divine,
Bold I approach th'eternal throne,
And claim the crown, through Christ my own.

Amazing love! how can it be
That Thou, my God, shouldst die for me!

Charles' gifts for poetry were evident. Eventually, he would write some 6,500 hymns. Charles' excellent hymns continue to be sung by Christians today. For example, one of the most famous Christmas carols of all time, ***Hark! The Herald Angels Sing***, was written by Charles Wesley.

Hark! the herald angels sing,
"Glory to the newborn King:
Peace on earth, and mercy mild,
God and sinners reconciled!"
Joyful, all ye nations, rise,
Join the triumph of the skies;
With th'angelic host proclaim,
"Christ is born in Bethlehem!"

CHARLES WESLEY (1707-1788)

Hark! the herald angels sing,
"Glory to the newborn King."
Christ, by highest heav'n adored,
Christ, the everlasting Lord!
Late in time behold him come,
Offspring of the Virgin's womb.
Veiled in flesh the Godhead see;
Hail th'incarnate Deity,
Pleased as man with men to dwell,
Jesus, our Emmanuel.

Hail, the heav'n-born Prince of Peace!
Hail, the Sun of Righteousness!
Light and life to all he brings,
Ris'n with healing in his wings.
Mild he lays his glory by,
Born that man no more may die,
Born to raise the sons of earth,
Born to give them second birth.

It was these times of spiritual refreshing that brought about such significant contributions to preaching, evangelism, Christian literature, and hymnody.

Whitefield and the Wesleys became known as "Methodists" because of their steadfast commitment to methods or spiritual disciplines. The Methodist movement grew rapidly under the leadership of Whitefield and the Wesleys. It is estimated that from 1771 to 1791, under the leadership of Wesley and others, the Methodist movement increased from 26,000 to around 57,000 in England and Wales.

Initially, the Methodists were a movement within the Church of England. For this reason, John and Charles Wesley established "societies" rather than separate churches. John gave this definition to a "society" in contrast with a church:

> A company of men having the form and seeking the power of godliness, united in order to pray together, to receive the word of exhortation, and to watch over one another in love, that they may help each other work out their salvation.[11]

The Methodists were unusual in employing many in lay leadership. Men without theological training were sent forth to preach the gospel. Wesley exhorted these lay preachers to focus upon the salvation of souls. He said:

> It is not your business to preach so many times and to take care of this or that society; but to save as many souls as you can; to bring as many sinners as you possibly can to repentance, and with all your power to build them up in that holiness without which they cannot see the Lord.[12]

It is important to remember that we cannot save anybody. But God does use His people to spread the gospel. We can be an instrument in the Redeemer's hands to deliver the truth of the gospel to sinners.

George Whitefield and John Wesley disagreed with each other on some issues. Whitefield was a Calvinist who believed in predestination while Wesley was an Arminian who rejected it. Wesley also believed in sinless perfection, the view that one can become completely sanctified and free from sin in this life. Whitefield disagreed with this. In the

THE FIRST METHODIST CHAPEL

end, the two men went their separate ways, and their differences led to a split in the Methodist movement. Eventually, many separated from the Church of England to form new Methodist denominations. In England and America, these Methodists followed Wesley and became Arminian. But in Wales, the Methodists followed Whitefield and were Calvinistic. Calvinist evangelicals in England mostly remained within the Church of England and revitalized it.

WESLEY'S CHAPEL IN LONDON

Results of the Great Awakening and Evangelical Revival

A young ten-year-old boy named **William Wilberforce** (1759-1833) was deeply impacted by Whitefield's preaching in England. The words preached, further impressed on his heart years later by the writings of **Philip Doddridge** (1702-1751), led to his conversion. Wilberforce became a major evangelical leader in Britain. Serving forty-five years in parliament, Wilberforce dedicated his life to the abolition of the slave trade and the reformation of morals.

WILLIAM WILBERFORCE (1759-1833)

Wilberforce was part of a group of devout evangelical members of the Church of England who sought to reform corrupt British society. They became known as the **Clapham Sect** or **Clapham Circle**. Many of them looked to **John Newton** (1725-1807) as a spiritual father. Newton was an English slave ship captain who was converted to Christ. He became an Anglican pastor who wrote many letters of wise spiritual counsel. He was also a hymnwriter who coauthored the *Olney Hymns* with his friend, the poet **William Cowper** (1731-1800). Newton's most famous hymn is ***Amazing Grace***. Newton encouraged Wilberforce and other members of the Clapham Circle in their labors.

The Clapham Circle's goals included abolishing the slave trade, promoting world missions, reforming the prison system and penal code, helping the lower classes, and improving morals. British evangelicals were largely successful in

JOHN WESLEY PREACHING IN CORNWALL

transforming British society. This transformation would have global effects as the British Empire spread around the world in the 19th century. One historian summarized the effects of the Evangelical Revival in Britain this way:

> A religious revival burst forth at the close of Walpole's administration, which changed after a time the whole tone of English society. The Church was restored to life and activity. Religion carried to the hearts of the people a fresh spirit of moral zeal, while it purified our literature and our manners. A new philanthropy reformed our prisons, infused clemency and wisdom into our penal laws, abolished the slave trade, and gave the first impulse to popular education.[13]

Some revivals occurred in Great Britain and Ireland after the Evangelical Revival but on a smaller scale. Decline of commitment to the Christian faith in the British Isles resumed in the 20th century. Church attendance in England would fall to about 5% by the 21st century when the apostasy had fully matured. Church attendance in North America remains higher. Nevertheless, the 20th and 21st century have been times of significant spiritual decline. May the Lord send more revivals to His church!

Countless additional stories could be told from this exceptional period of history. The testimonies we read above give us a window into what Christ was doing in His church at this time. Not everything that happened during the Great Awakening was perfect. Some preachers that participated in the revivals were not faithful to the Bible. Sometimes, people acted in a divisive way and claimed to be superior to other Christians because of what they learned or how they lived. Some were quick to judge others as unconverted, thinking they could read their hearts. And some who claimed to be converted later did not continue in the faith. When the Holy Spirit moves in mighty ways, the forces of the evil one also come to distract, deceive, and divide.

Nevertheless, we must praise God for His power and mercy in saving sinners. No human being can know how many were redeemed during the Great Awakening. Yet we must acknowledge the evident work of God in bringing about this time of spiritual awakening and renewal. ■

I will hear what God the LORD will speak,
For He will speak peace
To His people and to His saints;
But let them not turn back to folly.
Surely His salvation is near to those who fear Him,
That glory may dwell in our land. (Ps. 85:8-9)

OLNEY, ENGLAND, WHERE JOHN NEWTON SERVED AS PASTOR

GLASGOW UNIVERSITY, GLASGOW, SCOTLAND

Apostasy and Doctrinal Decline in the Church

Now the Spirit expressly says that in latter times some will depart from the faith, giving heed to deceiving spirits and doctrines of demons, speaking lies in hypocrisy, having their own conscience seared with a hot iron. (1 Tim. 4:1-2)

One of the mottos used to describe the Reformation is the Latin phrase ***Post Tenebras Lux***. Translated into English, this means "after darkness, light." By the grace of God, the light of the gospel shone once again with great clarity. The church in Europe was immensely blessed by faithful preaching and teaching from God's Word. The Reformation influence continues today in the worldwide Protestant movement.

Yet, wherever the gospel goes forth with power, the forces of darkness are present to oppose it. It was no different in the Reformation and in the centuries that followed. A new intellectual movement would arise in the 17th and 18th centuries. This movement is called by many the **Enlightenment**. The word suggests a period where the light of truth dawned upon many. But as we will see, the Enlightenment was a movement that was hostile to Christianity. Leaders in this movement rejected the authority of God's revelation in the Bible. In place of the Bible, human reason was exalted as the standard for truth.

Even before the 17th and 18th centuries, there were signs of radical departures from Christian truth. Apostasy and doctrinal heresy are to be found in every period of Christ's church. Here are a few examples of heresy in and after the Reformation period. Certain Anabaptist groups, such as that led by Jan van Batenberg, practiced polygamy. The Anabaptist community at Munster was one of the earliest experiments with a form of communism. As we learned in a previous chapter, that experiment ended in disaster.

One essential doctrine that came under attack during the Reformation was the doctrine of the Trinity. **Fausto Sozzini** (1539-1604) was among the earliest Anti-Trinitarians. Sozzini used his own human reasoning to determine that the Trinity did not make sense. As a result, he rejected it. Sozzini claimed that Jesus was not the eternal Son of God. He also rejected the foreknowledge of God. These ideas quickly became popular with humanist rationalist thinkers. If an idea does not make sense to the human mind, it is rejected by rationalists. These were the roots of further apostasy that came in the 18th century in Europe and America. Sozzini's false teaching would continue to reappear through other teachers.

FAUSTO SOZZINI (1539-1604)

It is important to remember that ideas have consequences. Denying key doctrines of the Christian faith is a serious matter. When core doctrines concerning God's nature are denied, the individual who embraces false teaching ends up worshiping a false god. We dare not create a god of our own imagination. We must worship the one true God who reveals Himself in the Bible as one God in three persons: God the Father, God the Son, and God the Holy Spirit.

Do you see a man wise in his own eyes? There is more hope for a fool than for him. (Prov. 26:12)

Bad Teachers and Doctrinal Departures

Whoever transgresses and does not abide in the doctrine of Christ does not have God. He who abides in the doctrine of Christ has both the Father and the Son. (2 John 9)

In the late 1600s and early 1700s, two kinds of false teaching gained ground in Great Britain. The two groups are known as the **Latitudinarians** and the **Unitarians**. The term Latitudinarian refers to someone who allows for a diversity of views on theology and practice. Latitudinarians generally saw certain fundamental Christian beliefs as optional (such as the Trinity or the deity of Jesus Christ). The term Unitarian refers to someone who denies the doctrine of the Trinity and believes that God is only one person. The biblical doctrine of the Trinity teaches that there is only one God but that there are three persons in the Godhead.

John Locke (1632-1704) is a noteworthy example of a Latitudinarian. Latitudinarians wanted to allow for a wide variety of beliefs including Deism, Unitarianism, and the Quakers. Locke was born of Puritan parents and raised in the Wrington parish in Somerset under the Puritan Dr. Samuel Crook. But he quickly shifted to one of London's more liberal churches in 1668, under the leadership of **Benjamin Whichcote** (1609-1683). Whichcote rejected the doctrines of total depravity, hell, God's omnipotence, God's eternality, and God's omnipresence. Whichcote called human reason "the divine governor of man's life" and the very "voice of God."[1] By saying this, Whichcote elevated human reason above the authority of the Bible.

Deism also gained popularity in Great Britain. Deism is the belief that there is a God who exists, but this God has no interaction with human creatures. He is like a watchmaker. He created the world like a man makes a watch, then wound it up and left it to run its own course according to natural laws. Deists denied miracles, the supernatural, and God's providential hand in history. The Deists affirmed the existence of some god. But they rejected the Bible as God's revelation of Himself.

The first Unitarian denomination formed in

JOHN LOCKE (1632-1704)

BENJAMIN WHICHCOTE (1609-1683)

CHARLES CHAUNCY (1705-1787)

England in 1774 under the leadership of **Theophilus Lindsey** (1723-1808). **Jonathan Mayhew** (1720-1766) became one of the first Unitarian pastors in America. He took the pulpit of the Old West Church in Boston in 1747. Another Unitarian, **Charles Chauncy** (1705-1787) pastored the First Church in Boston from 1727-1787. The rise of Unitarianism was a troubling development in Christ's church. This false teaching unsettled the faith of many.

The Influence of the Universities

Now concerning things offered to idols: We know that we all have knowledge. Knowledge puffs up, but love edifies. And if anyone thinks that he knows anything, he knows nothing yet as he ought to know. (1 Cor. 8:1-2)

Before he died, the Scottish Reformer John Knox (1514-1572) warned the church with these words: "Above all, preserve the kirk [church] from the bondage of the universities."[2] Knox's warning contained much wisdom. Many of the Reformers did not realize the damage to the faith that would come through the universities. Universities like Edinburgh, Oxford, Harvard, and Yale would become sources of false teaching.

Harvard College in America was given over to the Latitudinarians by 1707. This was the year **John Leverett** (1662-1724) became president. **Increase Mather** (1639-1723) is considered one of the last faithful teachers at Harvard. He kept the Reformation light alive in Harvard until the Latitudinarians took control. In 1805, Reverend **Henry Ware** (1764-1845), a self-professed Unitarian, was appointed the professor of divinity at the college. Then **Yale College** and **Princeton University** abandoned their Christian heritage in the 19th century. The battle for orthodoxy against apostasy was fought vigorously in the universities. But in most cases, faithful Christians lost ground in these institutions.

These attacks upon Christian truth impacted Christ's church in the West. Nevertheless, Jesus Christ was still on His throne. He continued accomplishing His purposes and building His church throughout the world (Eph. 1:22-23). Even though apostasy was on the rise in the West, the church was spreading throughout the world. The rise of the modern missionary movement exported

MEMORIAL HALL AT HARVARD IN CAMBRIDGE, MASSACHUSETTS

the faith into far-off lands all over the world.

Attacks on the Bible

Every word of God is pure;
He is a shield to those who put their trust in Him.
Do not add to His words,
Lest He rebuke you, and you be found a liar.
(Prov. 30:5-6)

LUDWIG ANDREAS VON FEUERBACH (1804-1872)

During the 18th and 19th century, many poisonous teachings flowed out of European universities. Some modern developments in science and technology were a blessing to the world. But theology (as it was taught in the universities) by and large departed from the faithful teaching of the Word of God. Universities in Germany were among the most influential sources of false teaching in the West. The development of **Liberal Theology** made rapid advances in Germany.

Most of the attacks upon Christianity in German universities came through biblical studies. The development of methods known as Higher Criticism put the Bible under the microscope of human reason and wisdom. The Higher Critical method set out with a few goals, including:

1. To determine who originally authored the biblical books
2. To study the books of Scripture in their ancient historical context
3. To examine how the books of the Bible were formed
4. To trace the transmission of the biblical text

Critics in biblical studies claimed to use a scientific approach that would deliver sure results. But in most cases, their methods were based on human reason and guesswork. In the end, the Higher Critical movement was just another expression of human autonomy. Man wants to pick and choose what he will take from God's revelation. The Higher Critics set out to do this under the pretense of being "scientific."

Johann Gottfried Eichorn (1752-1827) is generally recognized as the father of the Higher Critical movement. He denied the supernatural events recorded in the Old Testament. He rejected most of the Old Testament books as accurate historical records. Eichorn also rejected the Pauline authorship of the pastoral epistles (Timothy, Titus). He also argued that 1 Peter, 2 Peter, and Jude were not written by Peter or Jude.

Another liberal theologian, **Ludwig Andreas von Feuerbach** (1804-1872) had a profound influence upon some of the most influential humanists of the 19th century. These include the communists **Karl Marx** (1818-1883) and **Friedrich**

KARL MARX (1818-1883)

Engels (1820-1895). Feuerbach began his studies as a student of theology. But he became skeptical of Christian belief. He eventually published a book titled ***The Essence of Christianity***. In this book, Feuerbach argued that Christianity was a man-made idea. Ultimately, for Feuerbach, God was just a projection that human beings made up. Perhaps it was from Feuerbach that Marx got the idea that religion was just a "crutch" for weak people.

Another German biblical scholar, **Julius Wellhausen** (1844-1918), developed the **Documentary Hypothesis** in the 1870s. In this hypothesis, Wellhausen claimed that Moses was not the author of the first five books of the Bible. Instead, Wellhausen identified four different unnamed authors. These four authors combined and then added material. The eventual result was the first five books of the Bible (the **Pentateuch**). This hypothesis was a rejection of the words of the Lord Jesus Christ who said that Moses wrote about Him.

Do not think that I shall accuse you to the Father; there is one who accuses you—Moses, in whom you trust. For if you believed Moses, you would believe Me; for he wrote about Me. But if you do not believe his writings, how will you believe My words? (John 5:45-47)

The speculative man-made ideas of Eichorn, Feuerbach, Wellhausen, and others would do much to shipwreck the faith of many.

Science and Evolution

For in six days the Lord made the heavens and the earth, the sea, and all that is in them, and rested the seventh day. Therefore the Lord blessed the Sabbath day and hallowed it. (Ex. 20:11)

CHARLES DARWIN (1809-1882)

In November 1859, an English scientist named Charles Darwin published an important book. It was titled ***On the Origin of Species by Means of Natural Selection, or the Preservation of Favoured Races in the Struggle for Life***. The book's publication was a development of seismic importance. In this work, Darwin proposed a theory of natural evolution for all species on earth. Darwin was not the first to propose the theory of evolution. But he was the most influ-

PRINCETON THEOLOGICAL SEMINARY

CHARLES HODGE (1797-1878)

ential popularizer of this doctrine.

Darwin argued that all species evolved through a process of natural selection without the direct involvement of a Creator. He also proposed that mankind was not created by God. Rather, he postulated that mankind had evolved over many millennia out of the animal kingdom. This novel belief was immediately welcomed by the academic world, a world that was looking for a reason to escape moral responsibility to a Creator.

Between 1860 and 1920, Darwin's book influenced almost every institution and profession in America, including seminary professors, law schools, judges, and American presidents. As modern nations were running away from God, they were looking for an intellectual basis for their apostasy. Darwin gave them one. Darwin's doctrine of evolution quickly became a formidable challenge to the Christian faith in America.

About fifteen years after Darwin's book was published, a Christian theologian responded to Darwin's doctrines. He was a professor of theology at Princeton Seminary. **Charles Hodge** (1797-1878) wrote a book called ***What is Darwinism?*** Hodge rightly understood how dangerous Darwin's views were, and how those views contradicted the Christian faith. Hodge wrote:

> What is Darwinism? It is Atheism. This does not mean, as before said, that Mr. Darwin himself and all who adopt his views are atheists; but it means that his theory is atheistic; that the exclusion of design from nature is . . . tantamount to atheism.[3]

Hodge understood that in Darwinism there was no place allowed for God as Creator or Providential Sustainer. He wisely foresaw the devastating consequences Darwin's doctrine of evolution would have upon the Christian faith and the gospel itself. If mankind did not descend from the first Adam, then how could Christ, the second Adam, overcome the curse of sin and death for mankind through His act of obedience? The Bible plainly teaches that the first human being is Adam, who introduced sin into the world.

Therefore, just as through one man sin entered the world, and death through sin, and thus death spread to all men, because all sinned—(For until the law sin was in the world, but sin is not imputed when there is no law. Nevertheless death reigned from Adam to Moses, even over those who had not sinned according to the likeness of the transgression of Adam, who is a type of Him who was to come.) (Rom. 5:12-14)

Charles Hodge wisely rejected Darwinism. Nevertheless, he was still influenced by some of the scientific theories of his day. He accepted the belief that the universe and the earth were much older than 6,000 years. Although he recognized the "days" of Genesis 1 as ordinary twenty-four-hour days, he felt obligated to harmonize the account with the common geological perspectives of his day—that the earth had "existed for countless ages."[4]

The Advance of Liberal Theology in the United States

Higher Critical Liberal Theology began in Germany. But in the 1800s and 1900s, it swept into Britain and North America. Charles Hodge served as a professor at Princeton Seminary. This institution served the Presbyterian Church in the United States. Led by men such as Charles and **A.A. Hodge** (1823-1886), **B.B. Warfield** (1851-1921) and **J. Gresham Machen** (1881-1937), Princeton Seminary stood as a bulwark of orthodoxy against Theological Liberalism for generations. Many important battles over truth would occur in Protestant denominations in the 1800s and 1900s. The year 1924 was pivotal for the Northern Presbyterian Church. Five doctrines were at stake. These were doctrines over which the conservatives fought hard for thirty years. The doctrines were:

1. The inerrancy of the Bible
2. The virgin birth and the deity of Christ
3. The doctrine of substitutionary atonement
4. The bodily resurrection of Jesus Christ
5. The authenticity of Christ's miracles

At least two of these doctrines had appeared in the Apostles' Creed. All five doctrines had been defended by the Reformation. The various Lutheran and Reformed Confessions all contained affirmations of these five essential truths. A petition was circulated just prior to the General Assembly of the Presbyterian Church USA in 1924 that garnered the support of 1,274 liberal ministers. The petition was called the **Auburn Affirmation**. The Auburn Affirmation rejected the inerrancy of Scripture and recommended against using the five "essential" doctrines as a test for who could be ordained into the ministry. This controversy also raged at the same time in the Northern Baptist Convention. It was lost in both denominations. One by one, most of the Mainline Protestant denominations fell to Theological Liberalism. Bible-believing Protestants left these denominations to form new evangelical ones.

This pattern of new denominations splitting off from a larger, original denomination has continued throughout the 20th and 21st centuries. As apostasy has increased, faithful remnants of Baptists, Lutherans, Presbyterians, Methodists, and others have come out from larger denominations. For example, in 2009 a conservative group of Anglicans broke away from the liberal American Episcopal Church and Canadian Anglican Church, calling themselves the Anglican Church in North America. They maintained full communion with the African Anglican Church (in Nigeria, South Sudan, Sudan, and Uganda). While the Western world apostatized, the faithful defenders of orthodoxy shifted to Africa, Asia, and South America. Small but vibrant communions continued in the West as a remnant. ■

But what does the divine response say to him? "I have reserved for Myself seven thousand men who have not bowed the knee to Baal." Even so then, at this present time there is a remnant according to the election of grace. (Rom. 11:4-5)

B.B. WARFIELD (1851-1921)

AD 1793
William Carey Arrives in Calcutta

AD 1795
Yale College Revival

AD 1798
Revival Through the Ministry of James McGready

AD 1807
British Parliament Abolishes the Slave Trade

AD 1813
Adoniram Judson Arrives in Burma

AD 1827
Joseph Smith Writes the *Book of Mormon*

AD 1829
Sati Banned in India

AD 2018
Native Missionaries in Asia and Africa Exceeds the American Mission Force

AD 1991
Collapse of the Soviet Union

AD 1989
Fall of the Berlin Wall

AD 1980
Communist China Establishes the Three-Self Church

AD 1967
Richard Wurmbrand Founds Voice of the Martyrs

AD 1961
Morris and Whitcomb's *The Genesis Flood* Written

AD 1955
Brother Andrew Founds Open Doors

Unit 6

The Age of Missions and the Modern Period
(1750-Present)

AD 1844
The "Great Disappointment"

AD 1858
John Paton Starts His Ministry in the New Hebrides

AD 1859
Welsh Revival

AD 1864
Samuel Crowther Ordained as First African Anglican Bishop

AD 1899
Boxer Rebellion

AD 1902
Woodrow Wilson Assumes Presidency of Princeton

AD 1905
Azusa Street Revival

AD 1907
The Korean Pentecost

AD 1917
Bolshevik Revolution

AD 1939
Martin Lloyd-Jones Takes up Pastoral Role at Westminster Chapel

AD 1939-1945
World War II

AD 1945-1946
Nuremberg Trials

AD 1948
Richard Wurmbrand's Imprisonment

AD 1950-1953
The Korean War

BAGAN, MYANMAR

The Modern Missionary Movement

30

In His abundant love and mercy for the world, the Lord saw fit to bring about great expansion of the church in the 19th and 20th centuries. The church expanded into new regions through the efforts of pioneering missionaries. Our Lord's Great Commission was further advanced in this era of modern missions. In this chapter, we will learn about some of the most influential missionaries of the last few hundred years. We will see how they labored through many trials. Through their suffering, the Lord brought about a harvest for His glory. Our Lord Jesus promises that those who give up their lives for the sake of the gospel will not only gain the great treasure of eternal life, but their lives will also be used for the cause of kingdom growth. Jesus said in John 12:

Most assuredly, I say to you, unless a grain of wheat falls into the ground and dies, it remains alone; but if it dies, it produces much grain. He who loves his life will lose it, and he who hates his life in this world will keep it for eternal life. If anyone serves Me, let him follow Me; and where I am, there My servant will be also. If anyone serves Me, him My Father will honor. (John 12:24-26)

Missions to India: William Carey

All the ends of the world
Shall remember and turn to the Lord,
And all the families of the nations
Shall worship before You.
For the kingdom is the Lord's,
And He rules over the nations. (Ps. 22:27-28)

The 19th century is often called the "greatest century of missions." The expansion of the church was unprecedented. The church had never expanded so far and wide with such speed. This massive missionary movement was the fruit of both the Protestant Reformation and the Great Awakening and Evangelical Revival of the faith in America and the British Isles in the 18th century. After William Carey, the English-speaking nations provided the majority of the world's missionaries during the 19th and 20th centuries.

On May 31, 1792, an English cobbler (a shoemaker) named **William Carey** (1761-1834) preached a sermon that laid out a missionary vision. The result of Carey's sermon would be the beginning of a new era in missions' history. Carey's sermon is sometimes called the "Deathless Sermon" because of its continuing impact. The sermon was based on the text of Isaiah 54:2-3:

WILLIAM CAREY (1761-1834)

Enlarge the place of thy tent,
And let them stretch forth the curtains of thine habitations:
Spare not, lengthen thy cords, and strengthen thy stakes;
For thou shalt break forth on the right hand and on the left;
And thy seed shall inherit the Gentiles,
And make the desolate cities to be inhabited.
(Isa. 54:2-3 KJV)

Carey presented two points in the sermon: (1) Expect great things from God; (2) Attempt great things for God. Carey also wrote a pamphlet called ***An Enquiry into the Obligations of Christians to use Means for the Conversion of the Heathens***. His little booklet was a clarion call to the church to evangelize people in lands all over the world who had not yet heard the gospel.

Carey's call to missions was initially rejected by the assembly of Particular Baptists. But a small group of twelve Baptist ministers formed **The Particular Baptist Society for Propagating the Gospel among the Heathens** several months later. The society then sent Carey as a missionary to India.

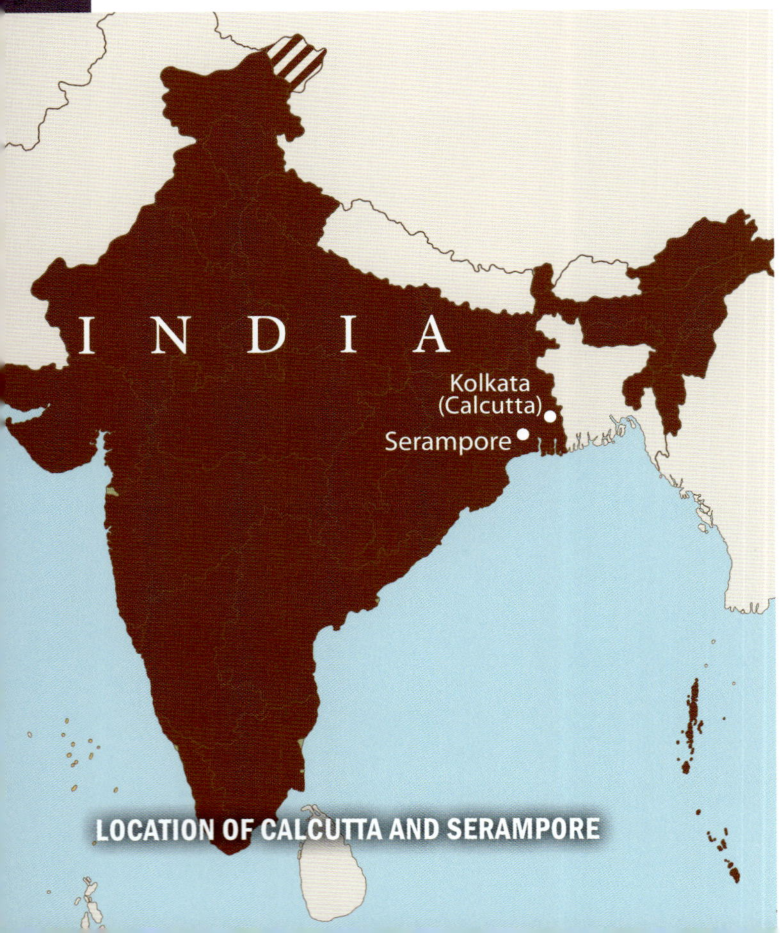

LOCATION OF CALCUTTA AND SERAMPORE

Carey arrived in **Calcutta**, India in November 1793. He faced enormous obstacles. This pioneer missionary did his work alone, and his wife offered little support (she suffered from mental problems). He faced opposition from the British East India Company authorities, hostility from the native people, and internal treachery within the mission. The climate was unhealthy for Europeans. Carey ended up burying two wives on the mission field. The language was difficult, and a fire destroyed much of his initial translation work.

For the first six years, Carey saw no conversions. Despite all these difficulties, Carey was not discouraged. He wrote:

> When I left England, my hope of India's conversion was very strong; but amongst so many obstacles, it would die, unless upheld by God. Well, I have God, and His Word is true. Though the superstitions of the heathen were a thousand times stronger than they are, the example of the Europeans a thousand times worse; though I were deserted by all and persecuted by all, yet my faith, fixed on that sure Word, would rise above all obstacles and overcome every trial. God's cause will triumph. [1]

Carey's commitment to the mission, his patience, incomparable diligence, and the strength that can only come from Christ produced a successful mission. The historian of Christian missions, Stephen Neill, calls Carey's work "a heroic epoch in missions, the consideration of which arouses in the mind of the student an equal measure of awe and inspiration."[2]

William Carey settled in **Serampore**, a Danish colony not far from Calcutta (West Bengal State). Thankfully, the Danes were more supportive of Christian missions than were the British authorities at this time. His faithful mis-

SERAMPORE COLLEGE

sionary team included William Ward and Joshua Marshman.

This small team produced six translations of the Bible and twenty-three translations of the New Testament into various Indian languages and dialects. The mission also established a college at Serampore and founded India's Agri-Horticultural Society. William Carey wrote essays on forestry and cultivated public gardens such as the Serampore Gardens and Calcutta's Botanical Gardens. He also introduced the printing press to India.

Taking seriously the Great Commission's call to teach every commandment of Christ, Carey fought for righteous and just laws in India. On multiple occasions, he petitioned for a government ban on infanticide (the killing of infants), which he successfully obtained in 1802. He fought polygamy and the Indian practice of ***Sati*** (the burning of widows on the funeral pyre of their husbands). He gained a monumental victory in this cultural battle when the Edict of 1829 banned Sati in India. When the Hindu priests protested the law as a violation of their cultural practice, British Commander in Chief Sir Charles Napier responded:

> Be it so. This burning of widows is your custom; prepare the funeral pile. But my nation has also a custom. When men burn women alive we hang them, and confiscate all their property. My carpenters shall therefore erect gibbets on which to hang all concerned when the widow is consumed. Let us all act according to national customs.[3]

Carey's prime motivation came through a strong sense of the historical progressive reign of the Lord Jesus Christ. He wrote from the mission field, "We only want men and money to fill this country with the knowledge of Christ. We are neither working at uncertainty nor afraid for the result . . . He must reign, till Satan has not an inch of territory."[4] William Carey was sure of the inevitable success of the Great Commission in history. He played an important role in the fulfillment of that commission.

Missions to India and Persia: Henry Martyn

**He shall have dominion also from sea to sea,
And from the River to the ends of the earth. (Ps. 72:8)**

By God's grace, Carey and his team were not to be the last missionaries sent to India. The Church of England sent **Henry Martyn** (1781-1812) to Calcutta to minister to the British colonials there. Martyn, a deeply pious man, was encouraged to go to the mission field by the evangelical pastors **Charles Simeon** (1759-1836) and

HENRY MARTYN (1781-1812)

TABRIZ, PERSIA

John Newton (1725-1807) (the converted slave trader). Martyn sailed for India in 1805, leaving behind the woman he loved and whom he wished to marry, Lydia Grenfell. It would be the greatest sacrifice of his life.

His new home in Aldeen was an old temple that used to serve a heathen god. Within a few weeks of settling down, he heard a commotion at the local temple and ran out to see what was happening. He found a blazing fire, people gathered around, and a widow already thrown into it—he was too late to save her. He writes, "I felt my spirit more inflamed with zeal than I ever conceived it would be; and I thought that if I had words, I would preach to the multitudes all the day, if I lost my life for it."[5]

Martyn was soon off to **Patna**, some 350 miles northeast of Calcutta up the Ganges River. He was alone among pagan Europeans and pagan Indians in Patna, but he was persistent in sharing the gospel with everyone he met. He was rejected almost everywhere he went, but he found some success in starting schools for Indian children. He witnessed to the English, Muslims, and Hindus.

Then he moved to **Cawnpore** (Kanpur), another 300 miles up the Ganges River towards New Delhi. There he opened up his house on Sunday afternoons, offering food to the poor. Hundreds showed up, and he began to preach the gospel to them. They were mostly beggars, some clothed in "abominable rags, some nearly without clothes, some plastered with mud and cow-dung."[6] These first meetings produced a single convert from the Muslim faith, a man named **Abdul Masih**. Another early convert named Sabat had been a fanatical Muslim as well. This Arab had killed a Christian but was haunted by the victim's peaceful demeanor as he died. The gospel came upon Sabat as a "flood of light."

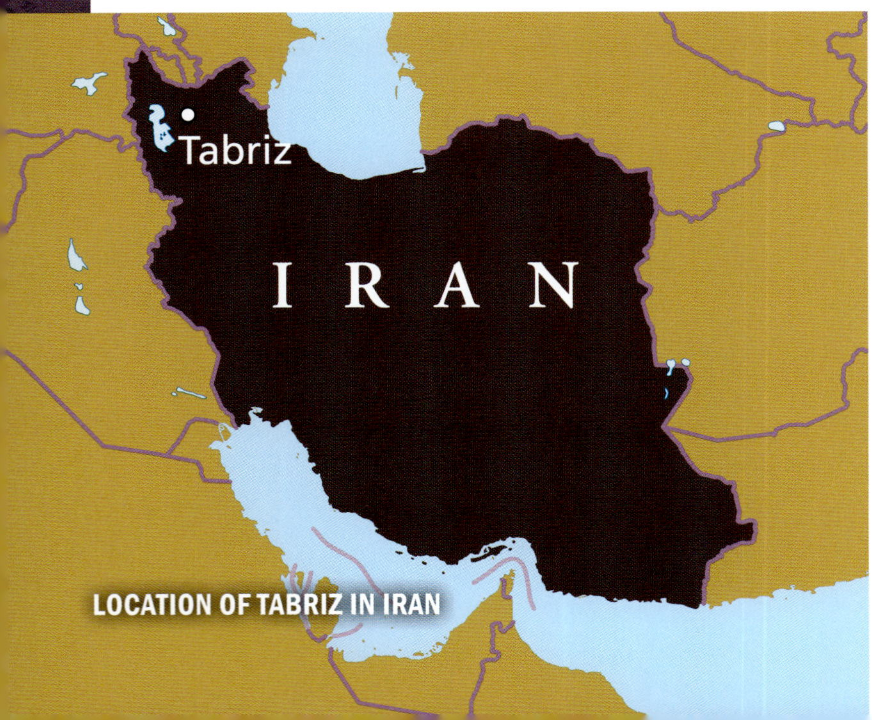

LOCATION OF TABRIZ IN IRAN

Sensing his health was rapidly deteriorating and he would not live much longer, Henry Martyn left India in 1811. On the return trip, he stopped in **Persia** (Iran) and became one of the most important pioneering missionaries to Muslims in the Persian Gulf. Suffering from high fevers and laboring through 126-degree weather, he somehow made his way to Shiraz. Here he found Muslim scholars who helped him translate the New Testament into Persian in just eight and a half months. Martyn's rapidly-produced translation was a tremendous feat.

Martyn spent many hours defending the faith, reading the Bible, and building friendships with some of the brightest Muslim scholars of the day. After finishing his translation of the New Testament into Persian, he made the 700-mile journey across mountains and deserts to reach the Shah of Iran in **Tabriz**. Martyn intended to present the Shah with the treasure of God's Word. When he arrived in Tabriz, Martyn was too ill to seek a personal audience with the Shah. But his New Testament translation was delivered to the Shah by the English ambassador, Sir Gore Ouseley. The response on the part of the Shah was surprisingly positive, exceeding all expectations. He required that the book be read out loud, cover-to-cover, in his presence. This was the first time that the Muslim world had the revelation of the Lord Jesus Christ in the Persian language.

At this point in his life, Henry Martyn decided to return home to England. But before reaching Constantinople, he died and was buried by Armenian Christians in an obscure grave a long way from home. He was only thirty-one years old, but he had fought the good fight, finished the race, and kept the faith (2 Tim. 4:7). The British under-secretary of state, Sir James Stephen, called Henry Martyn, "the one heroic name which adorns the annals of the Church of England from the days of Elizabeth to our own."[7]

The British East India Company, which ruled most of India, had been keeping missionaries like William Carey out because it feared they would interfere with the company's trade. But the company's charter had to be renewed by the British Parliament every twenty years. When the charter came up for renewal in 1813, William Wilberforce and other evangelicals in Parliament compelled the company to allow missionaries into India. And as the British Empire expanded in the 19th century, it would open doors for missionaries to take the gospel to the ends of the earth.

Missions to Burma: Adoniram and Ann Judson

His name shall endure forever;
His name shall continue as long as the sun.
And men shall be blessed in Him;

ADONIRAM JUDSON (1788-1850)

ANN HASSELTINE JUDSON (1789-1826)

All nations shall call Him blessed. (Ps. 72:17)

While William Carey labored in India, another region of Asia was yet unreached for Christ. The land of Burma remained sunk in the darkness of pagan religion. **Adoniram Judson** (1788-1850) was the first missionary to **Burma** (modern-day **Myanmar**) and the first American foreign missionary. Though raised in a Christian home, Judson professed **Deism** as a young man studying at Brown University in Rhode Island. This was not unusual for young academics attending university in the 19th century.

Though Judson committed himself to a life of unbelief, the Lord had other plans for Adoniram. Judson was converted by the power of God in 1808. He then committed himself to a life of missionary service and set his sights on Burma. Before he left for Burma, he married **Ann Hasseltine** (1789-1826) from Bradford, Massachusetts.

While on their way to Burma, the couple stopped in for a visit with William Carey in India. Adoniram and Ann Judson became convinced of the Baptist view of baptism, and they asked William Carey to re-baptize them. Arriving in Rangoon in July 1813, the Judsons set to work against much opposition. Two of their children quickly died on the field. When their second child died, Ann wrote:

> Our hearts were bound up with this child; we felt he was our earthly all, our only source of innocent recreation in this heathen land. But God saw it was necessary to remind us of our error, and to strip us of our only little all. O, may it not be vain that he has done it. May we so improve it that he will stay his hand and say "It is enough."[8]

It took seven years before the gates of brass and bars of iron gave way (Ps. 107:16), and Adoniram had his first convert. During the **Anglo-Burmese War** of 1824-1826, he spent seventeen months in a filthy Burmese prison. At night, the missionary would be forced to sleep hanging upside down with only his shoulders touching the ground. Then in 1826, his beloved wife Ann and their third child died.

After the death of his wife, Judson teamed up with another young missionary, George Boardman and his wife Sarah. Together, they formed a mission work in **Tavoy** on the southeast coast of Burma. It was at this time that Judson ran into a slave of the Karen peoples named Ko Tha Byu. The man had been a bandit and a murderer, having killed at least thirty people in the past. However, Judson bought his freedom and proceeded to disciple him in the gospel of the Lord Jesus Christ. Ko was radically saved, and God used him to reach out to his tribe—the animist, primitive Karen tribe that roamed through the jungles of the Salween River.

George Boardman died of tuberculosis in 1831, and Judson did what a practical missionary would do in the jungles of Burma. He married the widow Sarah Boardman and they proceeded with the mission work. Together they had eight children, and Sarah contributed much to the work. She translated *The Pilgrim's Progress* into Burmese. Her translation is still used among Christians in that country today. She also translated the New Testament into the Peguan language. Judson himself finished a Burmese translation of the Bible in 1834 and an English-Burmese dictionary in 1849.

By the time of his death at sixty-one years of age, Judson could claim sixty-three churches planted throughout Burma with some 100,000 members, mostly of the Karen tribes. Many of the Karens have held on to the faith through thick and thin despite much persecution that continues to this day. It was obvious what motivated Adoniram Judson on the field. He could never have done his work without a firm faith in the sovereign mercy of God. He would write in his diaries:

> O slow of heart to believe and trust in the constant presence and overruling agency of our almighty Saviour![9]

> Had it not been for the consolations of religion, and an assured conviction that every additional trial was ordered by infinite love

JOHN G. PATON (1824-1907)

and mercy, I must have sunk under my accumulated sufferings.[10]

Missions in the South Pacific: John G. Paton

Let the peoples praise You, O God;
Let all the peoples praise You.
Oh, let the nations be glad and sing for joy!
For You shall judge the people righteously,
And govern the nations on earth. (Ps. 67:3-4)

There are few missionary stories as exciting as that of John G. Paton's account of missionary life in the New Hebrides Islands of the South Pacific (modern-day Vanuatu). Throughout the story, we read of missionaries murdered and harrowing escapes on multiple occasions. The tests of faith, the missionary vision, the threats of demonic powers, and the conquering power of the gospel all come to life as we read John Paton's *Autobiography*.

John G. Paton (1824-1907) was born into a godly Christian home in Scotland. He writes of his upbringing:

> Each of us, from very early days, considered it no penalty, but a great joy, to go with our father to the church; the four miles were a treat to our young spirits.... We had, too, special Bible Readings on the Lord's Day evening,—mother and children and visitors reading in turns, with fresh and interesting question, answer, and exposition, all tending to impress us with the infinite grace of a God of love and mercy in the great gift of His dear Son Jesus, our Saviour.[11]

Paton's father was a man of prayer. Paton wrote of him:

> How much my father's prayers at this time impressed me I can never explain, nor could any stranger understand. When, on his knees and all of us kneeling around him in Family Worship, he poured out his whole soul with tears for the conversion of the Heathen world to the service of Jesus, and for every personal and domestic need, we all felt as if in the presence of the living Savior, and learned to know and love

TANNA ISLAND, VANUATU

him as our Divine friend. As we rose from our knees, I used to look at the light on my father's face, and wish I were like him in spirit,—hoping that, in answer to his prayers, I might be privileged and prepared to carry the blessed Gospel to some portion of the heathen world.[12]

When he grew up, the Lord called John Paton to be a missionary to the savage cannibals of the New Hebrides. These cannibals practiced infanticide and widow sacrifice. Like the Indians, they killed the widows of men after they died so that they could serve their husbands in the next world. Their whole religion revolved around propitiating angry evil spirits. As Paton put it: "Their whole worship was one of slavish fear; and, so far as ever I could learn, they had no idea of a God of mercy or grace."[13] Many people tried to dissuade Paton from becoming a missionary to these people. He writes:

> Amongst many who sought to deter me, was one dear old Christian gentleman, whose crowning argument always was, "The cannibals! you will be eaten by cannibals!" At last I replied, "Mr. Dickson, you are advanced in years now, and your own prospect is soon to be laid in the grave, there to be eaten by worms. I confess to you, that if I can but live and die serving and honoring the Lord Jesus, it will make no difference to me whether I am eaten by cannibals or by worms; and in the Great Day my resurrection body will arise as fair as yours in the likeness of our risen Redeemer."[14]

Paton and his wife Mary went to the island of **Tanna** in 1858. Within the first year of their arrival, Paton's wife and newborn child died of disease. While Paton's life was threatened almost daily for several years, he continued to preach the Word of God "in season and out of season" (2 Tim. 4:2). Paton boldly confronted those trying to kill him. He rebuked them for their sin and warned them of God's judgment. He often told them, "If you kill me, my Jehovah God will punish you." God protected him on numerous occasions. Paton wrote of these times:

> Without that abiding consciousness of the presence and power of my dear Lord and Saviour, nothing else in all the world could have preserved me from losing my reason and perishing miserably. His words, "Lo, I am with you alway, even unto the end of the world," became to me so real that it would not have startled me to behold Him, as Stephen did, gazing down upon the scene. I felt His supporting power, as did St. Paul, when he cried, "I can do all things through Christ which strengtheneth me." It is the sober truth, and it comes back to me sweetly after twenty years, that I had my nearest and dearest glimpses of the face and smile of my blessed Lord in those dread moments when musket, club, or spear was being leveled at my life. Oh the bliss of living and enduring, as seeing "Him who is invisible!"[15]

During tribal wars, Paton would attempt peace-making at every opportunity. Sometimes he would hold Sunday worship on the battlefield for anyone who would lay down their weapons and listen to the teaching. On many occasions, Paton intervened for the lives of widows who were going to be killed.

Eventually, the gospel penetrated, and some lives were radically changed. As one converted cannibal chief died on the island, he cried out:

> I am happy, looking unto Jesus! One thing only deeply grieves me now; I fear God is taking us all away from Tanna, and will leave my poor people dark and benighted as before, for they hate Jesus and the Worship of Jehovah. O Missi, pray for them, and pray for me once more before I go.... Farewell, Missi, I am very near death now; we will meet again in Jesus and with Jesus.[16]

Paton was deeply impressed with the powerful work of regeneration in the hearts and lives of the natives. He wrote, "Thus died a man who had been a cannibal chief, but by the grace of God and love of Jesus, changed, transfigured into a character of light and beauty."[17]

On May 20, 1861, several natives, at the urging of the white traders, murdered a missionary couple on Erromanga, Mr. and Mrs. Gordon. The blood of the martyrs serves as the seed of the church in most nations to which the gospel comes.

Eventually, Paton was forced off the island of Tanna. But he left several chiefs there who would live to serve Christ for many years—Nowar, Manuman, and Sirawia. Paton himself moved to the neighboring island of Aniwa. The people of **Aniwa** self-righteously considered themselves morally superior to the Tannese because they were cannibals who didn't eat the bones of their victims. Nevertheless, Paton and his second wife Margaret labored faithfully in Aniwa for forty-one years. At the end of his life, Paton was able to say, "I claimed Aniwa for Jesus, and by the grace of God, Aniwa now worships at the Savior's feet."[18]

Entire islands came under the influence of the gospel shared by Paton, and these natives who once consumed human flesh sat at the Lord's Table and formed the church of Jesus Christ in the New Hebrides, now named Vanuatu. It was Paton's *Autobiography* that inspired multiple generations of missionaries well into the 20th century to take up this worthy calling. Today, some 80% of the population of Vanuatu claim to be Christian.

Missions to Africa: Samuel Crowther

Many missionaries also took the gospel to Africa in the 1800s. **Samuel Ajayi Crowther** (c. 1809-1891) was an African born into a pagan home in modern-day Nigeria. When he was about twelve years old, Ajayi was kidnapped by Muslim slave raiders and sold to Portuguese slave traders, who put him on a slave ship. But British ships boarded the Portuguese ship and rescued

BLUE LAGOON, PORT VILA, VANUATU

Ajayi from slavery. Thanks to the leadership of William Wilberforce, the British had banned the slave trade in 1807. Now they were seeking to put an end to it. The British freed Ajayi and took him to Sierra Leone, where he was cared for by missionaries of the evangelical Anglican Church Missionary Society (CMS). The Church Missionary Society had been founded by evangelical Anglicans of the Clapham Circle. The missionaries taught Ajayi to speak English and read the Bible. He came to believe the gospel and was baptized in 1825. He took the name Samuel Crowther.

SAMUEL AJAYI CROWTHER (C. 1809-1891)

A brilliant student, Crowther was sent to England for further education. He especially loved theology and languages. He served as an interpreter for English missionaries in Nigeria. Then he was ordained as an Anglican minister in 1843. He translated the Bible and the *Book of Common Prayer* into the Yoruba language. In 1864, Crowther was ordained as the first African Anglican bishop. He helped to oversee the church in Nigeria, including the training of African church leaders and Bible translation efforts in other African languages. His ordination was a milestone in Western missionary efforts to plant indigenous churches with native leaders that would be self-supporting, self-governing, and self-propagating. Today, there are many churches in Africa. Christianity continues to grow rapidly there.

Missions to Israel: Robert Murray M'Cheyne and Andrew Bonar

And they also, if they do not continue in unbelief, will be grafted in, for God is able to graft them in again. For if you were cut out of the olive tree which is wild by nature, and were grafted contrary to nature into a cultivated olive tree, how much more will these, who are natural branches, be grafted into their own olive tree? For I do not desire, brethren, that you should be ignorant of this mystery, lest you should be wise in your own opinion, that blindness in part has happened to Israel until the fullness of the Gentiles has come in. And so all Israel will be saved, as it is written: "The Deliverer will come out of Zion, and He will turn away ungodliness from Jacob." (Romans 11:23-26)

Since the Protestant Reformation, the Holy Spirit has laid it on the hearts of Christ's people to reach out to the Jews. Early Reformers like Martin Bucer and Theodore Beza as well as many of the Puritans envisioned the uniting of Jew and Gentile once again in Christ. Puritan William Gouge wrote the book *The Calling of the Jews* in 1621. The *Westminster Directory for Public Worship* specified that prayer should be made every Sunday "for the propagation of the gospel and kingdom of Christ to all nations; for the conversion of the Jews, the fulness of the Gentiles..." Additionally, the Westminster Larger Catechism said this concerning the petition of the Lord's Prayer, "Thy Kingdom Come":

> In the second petition (which is, *Thy kingdom come*), acknowledging ourselves and all mankind to be by nature under the dominion of sin and Satan, we pray, that the kingdom of sin and Satan may be destroyed, the gospel propagated throughout the world, the Jews called, the fullness of the Gentiles brought in...[19]

ROBERT MURRAY M'CHEYNE (1813-1843)

Many Puritans prayed for the Jews and longed to convert them to Christ. **Cotton Mather** (1663-1728) wrote in his diary:

> This Day, from the Dust, where I lay prostrate before the Lord, I lifted up my Cries ... for the conversion of the Jewish Nation, and for my own having the Happiness, at some time or other, to baptise a Jew that should by my own ministry be brought home to the Lord.[20]

ANDREW BONAR (1810-1892)

Missions to the Jews increased in the 19th century. In 1839, the Church of Scotland established a committee for the conversion of the Jews. It sent **Robert Murray M'Cheyne** (1813-1843), **Andrew Bonar** (1810-1892), and two other men on an extensive journey through Europe and the Middle East, to learn about current Christian outreach to the Jews and to look for a good place to aid the work.

While in Alexandria, they attended a Jewish synagogue and examined a copy of the Hebrew Scriptures. Out of these Scriptures, M'Cheyne and Bonar talked about sin and atonement with the men. Bonar and M'Cheyne found many portions of the Old Testament that spoke of the person and work of Christ. They shared these with the Jews.

> We told them that we had come from Scotland out of love to their souls. We spoke of Messiah, how he came the first time to die for sin, and is coming soon the second time to reign in glory.[21]

By camel and by donkey, the team worked their way into Palestine to Jerusalem. They found the Jews there more hardened to the gospel. They were "poor and despised, and sadly divided among themselves,"[22] and generally treated badly by the law. Polygamy and adultery among the Jews were common.

About fifteen people assembled to worship the risen Christ in Jerusalem on a Sunday morning. Together with a missionary named Dr. Nicolayson, Bonar and M'Cheyne visited the home of a converted Jew named Simeon and held a short service there in the afternoon. Simeon's entire family had been baptized (he, along with his wife and two children) in a household baptism the year before. Shortly thereafter, another Jew named Hymen Paul was baptized also. The first native Jew from Jerusalem converted to the Christian faith in the 19th century was Rabbi Joseph. The controversy was so intense in the city that Joseph was sent away to Constantinople for baptism. Three more rabbis followed him into the Christian faith, but this produced great resistance to the missionaries. These were the humble beginnings of modern missions to the Jews.

At the time, Bonar and M'Cheyne estimated 10,000-15,000 Jews were living in the Holy Land in the 1830s. The cultural tensions between different groups did not make winning the Jews to Christ any easier. The men reported: "Greeks, Armenians, and Roman Catholics—are even more bitter enemies to Jews than Mahometans [Muslims]."[23] Only the Protestants had decent relations with the Jews.

The most successful outreach to Jews during these years, however, came from Germany, Hungary, and Russia. Here there was a stronger interest in the Christian faith. On their journey, the team came across a Jew named Mr. Moritz in Hamburg, Germany who had worked with the Jews in Germany and Russia for thirty-two years. His evangelistic tour through Russia, Crimea, Western Ukraine, and Latvia between 1817 and 1825 produced much interest among the Jews. Moritz was even able to preach in some synagogues. Among his first converts were his aunt and her two sons.

Bonar and M'Cheyne related this story of an outreach they witnessed with a few Jews who assembled. Moritz tells the story:

> The Jews present requested an explanation of the parable, which he gave them, by referring to Isaiah 9:6, and the Second Psalm. A deep silence followed. At last some young men asked—"And will the

OLD CITY WALL, JERUSALEM

> bandage always be on our eyes?" He told them to pray that the Spirit of God might take it away. Five of these young men seemed to receive saving impressions that evening![24]

On their journey, Bonar, M'Cheyne, and the other men stopped in Budapest and found fertile soil there. They recommended that the Church of Scotland send missionaries to Budapest. So in 1841, the Scottish church sent a group of missionaries there under the leadership of "Rabbi" **John Duncan** (1796-1870). "Rabbi" Duncan was a Scottish minister known for his love of the Jews, knowledge of Hebrew, and witty aphorisms.

The Scottish missionaries came to evangelize Hungarian Jews, encourage revival and evangelism among Hungary's many Protestants, and provide pastoral care for Scots working in Budapest. Duncan, a brilliant linguist, learned Hungarian in three months. He and his fellow missionaries befriended the Hungarian Jews, inviting them into their homes. They also held public services each Lord's Day. Although conducted in English, they attracted many Jews who wanted to improve their English. A breakthrough came when Israel Saphir, a highly respected member of the Jewish community, believed in Jesus as the Messiah. Another significant convert was **Alfred Edersheim** (1825-1889), whose books on Jewish culture in the time of Christ, such as ***The Life and Times of Jesus the Messiah***, are still widely read today.

JOHN DUNCAN (1796-1870)

Evangelism of the Jews greatly increased in the 20th century. This was especially the case as converted Jews began to enthusiastically reach out to their communities. In 1973, Moishe Rosen formed Jews for Jesus, and today the organization has nine branches and 200 full-time employees/missionaries.

Conclusion

The triumph of Jesus in modern missions shows the truth of God's promises. Eventually, every knee will bow and every tongue will confess that Jesus is Lord (Phil. 2:10-11). No man and no devil on earth or in hell will be able to counter the kingdom of Jesus Christ. We are called, just as the apostles were, to continue the same Great Commission (Matt. 28:19-20). ■

CHURCH IN NEW ENGLAND DURING THE FALL

Revivals and Cults in the 19th Century

31

Repent therefore and be converted, that your sins may be blotted out, so that times of refreshing may come from the presence of the Lord, and that He may send Jesus Christ, who was preached to you before, whom heaven must receive until the times of restoration of all things, which God has spoken by the mouth of all His holy prophets since the world began. (Acts 3:19-21)

The period of church history known as the Great Awakening was a short period of just a few years, in the 1740s. While the Holy Spirit is always at work within the church, there are times of greater Spirit outpouring, leading to times of refreshing in Christ's church. With that spiritual refreshing comes increased love for Christ, abundant joy in the Holy Spirit, and evangelistic zeal for the lost.

The Lord Jesus blessed His church through various times of reviving during the 19th century. In Great Britain and the United States, the church was strengthened. As Acts 9 describes, by the filling of the Holy Spirit, the churches "were edified and walking in the fear of the Lord and in the comfort of the Holy Spirit, they were multiplied" (Acts 9:31). The various revivals of the 19th century are sometimes called the **Second Great Awakening**.

Early 19th Century Revivals in America

A Presbyterian named **James McGready** (1763-1817) is generally considered the first evangelist in the "Second Awakening" in America. McGready was a humble preacher who was trained not at Harvard or Yale but in a log cabin school in Washington County, Pennsylvania. He arrived in Logan County, Kentucky in 1796 to preach the Word. The new settlements were filled with unbelief and general immorality. After McGready dedicated a whole year to prayer and fasting, one young woman was converted in the congregation where McGready served. Then revival broke out in 1798 with what the pastor called a "remarkable spirit of prayer and supplication.... a sensible, heart-felt burden of the dreadful state of sinners."[1] By 1801, tens of thousands were attending revival meetings throughout the state of Kentucky. When George A. Baxter, president of Washington College, visited the state in the same year, he reported that, "I found Kentucky . . . the most moral place I have ever been. A profane expression was hardly ever heard. A religious awe seemed to pervade the country."[2]

By the late 1700s and the early 1800s, most of the American universities were capitulating to unbiblical philosophies and worldly behavior. Yale College, founded to train young men for the ministry, was also affected by such worldly philosophies. **Timothy Dwight** (1752-1817), a grandson of Jonathan Edwards, accepted the position of president of Yale College in 1795. On his first day addressing Yale's senior class, President Dwight posed the question, "Are the Scriptures of the Old and New Testament the word of God?"[3] Not one member of the class had the faith to answer the question in the affirmative. This was a tragic sign of the lapse in faith among students at Yale. Dwight spent the next six months arguing the case for the Bible's inspiration in the college chapel. It took seven years before revival finally broke out on the campus. At that time around a third of Yale's 230 students professed faith in Christ. One student commented on the revival: "The whole college was shaken. It seemed for a time as if the whole mass of the students would press into the kingdom. It was the Lord's doing,

TIMOTHY DWIGHT (1752-1817)

and marvelous in all eyes. Oh, what a blessed change! It was a glorious reformation."[4]

Lapses in Faith

If anyone teaches otherwise and does not consent to wholesome words, even the words of our Lord Jesus Christ, and to the doctrine which accords with godliness, he is proud, knowing nothing, but is obsessed with disputes and arguments over words, from which come envy, strife, reviling, evil suspicions, useless wranglings of men of corrupt minds and destitute of the truth, who suppose that godliness is a means of gain. From such withdraw yourself. (1 Tim. 6:3-5)

Despite various instances of revival, the Christian heritage brought to America continued to degrade. By the early 1800s, **Unitarianism** (the denial of the Trinity) became a widely held belief in the United States. There were other forms of unbiblical teaching that also infected American churches.

Joseph Bellamy (1719-1790) and **Samuel Hopkins** (1721-1803) were students of Jonathan Edwards. Some of the most remarkable revivals occurred during Edwards' ministry. But not all of Edwards' students held fast to his faith convictions. Bellamy and Hopkins began to develop a new theology that rejected the doctrines of original sin (the guilt of Adam's original sin transferred to every child born into the world) and penal substitutionary atonement. **Nathaniel W. Taylor** (1786-1858) went further and emphasized man's absolute free will and ability to choose salvation. Christian pastors began to interpret the Bible by "what seemed right" according to their own thinking. This was an effect of the humanist Enlightenment of the 1700s.

By this time, most Americans were looking for a theology where they could be in control of their own salvation. Instead of trusting the Holy Spirit to change men's hearts, preachers more and more wanted to take over this work for themselves. **Charles Grandison Finney** (1792-1875) became the most famous Christian leader of the 19th century in America. Though educated in the Presbyterian tradition, Finney's theology strayed from these roots. He rejected the idea that Jesus imputes His righteousness to us (in the doctrine of justification). He also advocated a doctrine of perfectionism (that Christians can obtain sinless perfection in this life.)

Earlier revival preachers like George White-

CHARLES GRANDISON FINNEY (1792-1875)

ASAHEL NETTLETON (1783-1844)

field and Jonathan Edwards understood that men and women are born with a depraved sin nature. They are enemies of God and slaves of sin who will not repent and believe unless the Holy Spirit first regenerates them. Therefore, the preacher's job is to preach the Word faithfully and pray for the Lord to open the hearts of those He has ordained to eternal life (Acts 16:14, 13:48). Revival is an extraordinary outpouring of the Spirit in awakening sinners. God is the one who sends revival in His time according to His sovereign plan. We can pray for revival, but we can't schedule it or make it happen. **Asahel Nettleton** (1783-1844) was a widely known preacher during the Second Great Awakening who held to these views.

In contrast, Charles Finney and other evangelists believed that people are not born with a sin nature and are not slaves of sin. Rather, their wills simply need to be persuaded to accept the truth and believe. Revivals can be brought about simply by employing special evangelistic methods. These new methods came to be known as the New Measures. These New Measures included praying for sinners by name in public meetings and using overly familiar language with God in prayer. In worship services, women spoke publicly to groups of both men and women, contrary to Scriptural teaching (1 Cor. 14:34-35, 1 Tim. 2:11-12). Preachers protracted the length of meetings to pressure people into making decisions and scheduled meetings at abnormal times. They called on emotionally affected hearers to come forward to a place at the front of the church, known as the **Anxious Bench** where they would be coached through a conversion prayer. People were encouraged and pressured to "make a decision for Christ." Those who did so were counted. The number of these "converts" was taken as evidence that there had been a revival. Other preachers who did not produce similar results were despised and criticized. The emphasis on a crisis conversion also downplayed the importance of Christian education and discipleship.

Nettleton encountered Finney at a revival in New Lebanon in July 1827. As the Apostle Paul corrected Peter (Gal. 2:11), Nettleton brought Finney a list of concerns he had with Finney's revival methods. But Finney did not listen. His influence grew, and his new methods became common in revival meetings in the 19th and 20th centuries.

The Second Great Awakening produced mixed results. In areas where the New Measures were used, while many were genuinely converted to Christ, many merely made temporary professions and apostatized later. Towards the end of his life, Finney had to admit that "The glory has been departing and revivals have been becoming less and less frequent—less powerful."[5] He also came to realize that many of those he thought were converted became what he called a "disgrace to religion."[6] There were more positive results where man-centered teaching and approaches were avoided, as with Nettleton.

New Movements and New Cults

Beloved, do not believe every spirit, but test the spirits, whether they are of God; because many false prophets have gone out into the world. (1 John 4:1)

In 1801, a Presbyterian named **Barton Stone** (1772-1844) participated in a revival in Cane Ridge, Kentucky (continuing what had begun in Logan County the year before). However, Stone rejected all written creeds and certain Christian doctrines like the depravity of fallen man and predestination, in hopes that he could get back to the more genuine, primitive "apostolic church." Stone eventually joined forces with **Alexander Campbell** (1788-1866), another former Presbyterian who shared his views. Together, they founded what became known as the **Restoration Movement**. Out of this movement came the group of churches that call themselves the **Church of Christ**. By the 21st century, the Churches of Christ claimed about 2,000,000 members worldwide. Generally, these churches hold to baptism as a necessary part of salvation. Many of them believe one cannot be saved without water baptism.

In the early 1800s, Finney and other revival preachers spent much time in the region of Western New York, hosting revival meetings. It happened to be in this same region that several new movements and new cults were born.

WILLIAM MILLER (1782-1849)

CHARLES TAZE RUSSELL (1852-1916)

In 1833, a Baptist lay-preacher named **William Miller** (1782-1849) announced that Christ was coming back on October 22, 1844. It was known as the "Great Disappointment" when the Lord did not comply with Miller's announcements. Nonetheless, a group of "Adventists" met in Albany, New York in April 1845 to readjust the message. Out of this group came the modern **Seventh Day Adventists** formed by **Hiram Edson** (1806-1882) in the Rochester, New York area.

The **Jehovah's Witnesses** cult evolved out of the same movement, formed by **Charles Taze Russell** (1852-1916). The Jehovah's Witnesses cult separated itself from the church and began to advocate numerous heretical doctrines. The Witnesses deny the doctrine of Christ's eternal existence (viewing Him as a creature). They also deny the doctrine of hell. Over the years, the Watchtower Society (the secretive and controlling leadership arm of the Witnesses) has made numerous false prophecies.

The **Spiritualist** movement of the 19th century came out of Hydesville, New York, where the Fox sisters conducted their first séances (in 1848).

The human desire to maintain contact with the spirit world was strong. By turning to the occult, those engaging in such behavior opened themselves up to demonic influence or even demonic possession.

MORMON TEMPLE IN PALMYRA, NEW YORK

Between 1817 and 1825, a young boy named **Joseph Smith** (1805-1844) and his family attended Charles Finney's revivals, passing through Palmyra, New York, where his family lived. In 1820 (at fifteen years of age), Smith says he received a vision that settled his "religious confusion." He was told in the vision that all Christian churches had "turned aside from the Gospel." In 1827, Smith claimed to receive golden plates containing a "message from God" which he began translating into English. This became the ***Book of Mormon***. This was the origin of the cult known as the **Church of Jesus Christ of Latter-Day Saints** (LDS). The Mormons, or Latter-Day Saints grew rapidly. By 2017, they numbered around 16 million members.[7]

Nineteenth century America, especially western New York State, provided the fertile ground out of which many modern sects and cults developed. Most of these sects and cults believed that the church had become corrupt shortly after the apostles or in Constantine's time. They sought to restore the church to the "purity" of New Testament times. They failed to see God's faithfulness to build His church against the gates of hell throughout history.

Then many false prophets will rise up and deceive many. And because lawlessness will abound, the love of many will grow cold. But he who endures to the end shall be saved. And this gospel of the kingdom will be preached in all the world as a witness to all the nations, and then the end will come. (Matt. 24:11-14)

JOSEPH SMITH (1805-1844)

Scotland's 19th Century Revivals

Truth shall spring out of the earth,
And righteousness shall look down from heaven.
Yes, the LORD will give what is good;
And our land will yield its increase. (Ps. 85:11-12)

God was also at work in the British Isles in the 19th century. While the devil came to divide, deceive, and destroy, the Lord Jesus' saving work continued. Scotland's spiritual revivals during the 19th century kindled significant interest in missionary work. As a result, many Christian missionaries came from Scotland during this period.

Scotland's "killing times" during the reigns of

Charles II and James II (r. 1660-1688) produced many faithful martyrs. The early church father Tertullian first made the great statement: "The blood of the martyrs is the seed of the church."[8] Men like **Samuel Rutherford** (1600-1661), James Guthrie, James Renwick, and **George Gillespie** (1613-1648) strengthened the church in Scotland through their testimony and suffering.

Future generations lost sight of this great contribution of the Covenanters. By the late 1700s, Enlightenment philosophies infiltrated much of the Church of Scotland. Iain Murray explains the condition of the church at that time:

> The Moderates preached morality, with almost nothing of the supernaturalism of true Christianity. They ignored the Fall of man, sneered at the idea of a new birth and said nothing of the perfection and power of the work of the Son of God.[9]

Yet God was merciful to Scotland. He blessed the church in Scotland with another awakening. A man named **Thomas Chalmers** (1780-1847) would be used by the Lord to disciple many in faithful gospel ministry. When Chalmers first entered the University of St. Andrews, he adopted many false philosophies of the Enlightenment. But in 1808, Chalmers witnessed the death of his sister and uncle. He too became ill and almost died. The Lord used this trial in Chalmers' life to wake him up to his sinful condition and his need for a Savior. Seeking spiritual guidance, Chalmers turned to the classic writings of Jonathan Edwards, John Calvin, John Newton, John Owen, and others. The message of truth he found in the writings of these men helped him better understand the Scriptures.

THOMAS CHALMERS (1780-1847)

With a burning zeal and passion, Chalmers began passing on the same message to his students at St. Andrews. He reintroduced the Puritans to his classes at the University of St. Andrews when he became a professor in 1827. He taught his ministerial students to preach and to visit their congregants and engage in evangelistic outreaches. Chalmers released into the world students on fire to reach the world for Christ. Murray summarizes Chalmers' work:

> Few professors of divinity have had such students that crowded Chalmers' classroom in the 1830s. Many of them, as their subsequent biographies reveal, were to become men of outstanding usefulness . . . by 1843, Chalmers was able to say that he could travel from one end of Scotland to the other and spend each night in the manse of one of his former pupils.[10]

His students included such luminaries as **Robert Murray M'Cheyne** (1813-1843), **Andrew Bonar** (1810-1892), and **Horatius Bonar** (1808-1889). Between 1839 and 1843, revivals broke out in Kilsyth and Perth under the ministry of Robert M'Cheyne, William Chalmers Burns, and John Milne. The Scottish revival fervor lit a fire that spread around the world. The missionary movement grew rapidly. The preacher **William Chalmers Burns** (1815-1868) felt a call to China and left Scotland to minister in the Far East. His missionary work did not have much immediate effect. However, he did serve as a mentor for another missionary named **Hudson Taylor** (1832-1905) who was struggling in his spiritual life. According to Hudson Taylor's biographer, "William Burns was better to [Taylor] than a college course with all its advantages, because he lived out before him right there in China the reality of all he most needed to be and know."[11]

HUDSON TAYLOR (1832-1905)

The Welsh Revival of 1859

Therefore I make known to you that no one speaking by the Spirit of God calls Jesus accursed, and no one can say that Jesus is Lord except by the Holy Spirit. (1 Cor. 12:3)

The country of Wales lies on the western portion of Great Britain. The religious condition of Wales was much like other portions of Great Britain during the 19th century. Though it had been affected by the Great Awakening, interest in the things of God had declined. But in 1859, in answer to prayer, the churches were strengthened.

The Welsh revival of the 19th century began with a meeting of two preachers. Pastor **Humphrey Jones** (1832-1895) and Pastor **David Morgan** (1814-1883) met together. They decided to bring their two congregations together for prayer in 1859. They had two concerns they wanted to pray for: "The deadness of the church" and the lack of "earnest prayer."[12] This corporate prayer continued daily until "old backsliders began to return. Men came in crowds from the mountains, and all the country round, to our meetings, until we were afraid the chapel would come down—men who were never seen in any place of worship, except in church at a christening or a funeral, and knew nothing of worshipping God!"[13]

The revival began in Pastor David Morgan's town of **Llangeitho**. From there it spread all over Wales. The awakening impacted the Baptists, the Congregationalists, the Wesleyans, and the Calvinist Methodists. According to Thomas Phillips' eyewitness account of the Welsh revival, there were common features of Christian revival identified in the Welsh experience. First, there was unified, fervent prayer of the church body. Secondly, there was a unified zeal to renounce sin and lead godly lives. Families were committed to discipling their children in the gospel of Christ. The third element was aggressive outreach.[14]

The testimony of Scripture and history teach us that there are times where the Holy Spirit's work is greater in measure. Of course, we should never despise or ignore the working of God's Holy Spirit in Christ's church. Whenever we see love for God, devotion to Scripture, the fruit of the Spirit, and the faithful teaching of the gospel, we must praise God as the source of those things. At times, Christ's people have grieved the Holy Spirit through sin and rebellion. But when the Lord's people pray for the Holy Spirit, we can be sure that the Lord will answer this prayer. The timing and size of spiritual revivals is in the hands of God. It is for us to pray for Jesus' church to grow, for us to be filled with the Spirit, and to labor faithfully in what our Lord has commanded us to do. ■

If you then, being evil, know how to give good gifts to your children, how much more will your heavenly Father give the Holy Spirit to those who ask Him!" (Luke 11:13)

LLANGEITHO, WALES

THE WORD OF GOD IS THE CHRISTIAN'S SOURCE OF AUTHORITY AND TRUTH

Fundamentalists and Liberals

32

For I delivered to you first of all that which I also received: that Christ died for our sins according to the Scriptures, and that He was buried, and that He rose again the third day according to the Scriptures, and that He was seen by Cephas, then by the twelve. (1 Cor. 15:3-5)

How important is the historical fact that Jesus was born of a virgin? Or how important is it that Jesus Christ rose from the dead? Is it possible to be a Christian and deny either of those doctrines? Is there such a thing as Christianity without the physical resurrection? Identifying the essential beliefs of the Christian faith is very important. Since we are saved from sin and death through Jesus, who is the way, the truth, and life, it is vital that we know who He is and put our trust in Him.

In a previous chapter, we learned how the ideas of the Enlightenment swept across Europe and then America. Liberal theology, which rejected the inspiration of Scripture and the miraculous, was a destructive force in the Western church. By the 1920s, the forces of modernism and anti-supernaturalism had affected most universities and seminaries. There were not many Christian leaders left who were willing to take a strong stand against the secular academic elite. Most Protestant denominations compromised with the onslaught of Darwin's evolutionary theories and the religion of scientism.

Some of the Christian West apostatized, turning to atheism. But others wanted to hold on to a veneer of Christianity. They wanted to retain the pretense of the Christian faith, while compromising with the world on key doctrines. They argued that one could be a true Christian and yet disbelieve such essential truths as the virgin birth and the resurrection.

In this chapter, we will learn about some of the crucial battles for truth fought in the early 1900s. There were many Christians who courageously stood for God's truth against the forces of modern liberal theology. Many of those Christians we do not know by name. They included fathers, mothers, grandfathers, and grandmothers who faithfully taught God's Word to the rising generation. The faith was often retained through faithful and godly parents passing on the truth of the gospel to their children. Let us always remember that the Lord can use every one of us to stand for truth in a hostile world. Some of the Lord's works in His church are known in the pages of history books. Others will only be told when we enter into glory and spend eternity contemplating how the Lord Jesus built His church. We know that He builds His church with living stones of men, women, and children who love Him and serve Him.

Though we cannot account for all the ways Christ's truth was defended and passed on, we can look at a few of the well-known figures who stood for God's Word in the 20th century. We will look at several important figures in this battle. First, we will learn about a man named **J. Gresham Machen** (1881-1937). Machen was particularly well equipped to stand for the truth of the Bible in the academy. Machen had an extensive academic background. He argued vigorously that Christianity could not exist without the virgin birth, the resurrection, and numerous other central Christian beliefs. If you don't believe in the resurrection of Jesus Christ, Machen argued, you are simply not a Christian. If the resurrection of Jesus Christ is defined as the very heart of the gospel in 1 Corinthians 15, then rejecting this must be a fatal compromise of the faith. By holding to this conviction, Machen contended for the faith "once for all delivered to the saints" (Jude 3). He was waging war for the truth of the faith against compromising church leaders. These accommodating leaders wanted to

J. GRESHAM MACHEN (1881-1937)

make Christianity acceptable to the world. But we must remember this is impossible. Friendship with the world is enmity with God (Jas. 4:4).

Conflicts with Liberal Theology

Now I urge you, brethren, note those who cause divisions and offenses, contrary to the doctrine which you learned, and avoid them. For those who are such do not serve our Lord Jesus Christ, but their own belly, and by smooth words and flattering speech deceive the hearts of the simple. (Rom. 16:17-18)

An important battleground in this narrative is Princeton University. Princeton had been compromising with liberalism and evolution since the days of the presidency of **Woodrow Wilson** (1856-1924). Before Woodrow Wilson became the 28th president of the United States, he also served as president of Princeton.

Woodrow Wilson had descended from rich Christian roots (in the Southern Presbyterian tradition). But when he assumed the presidency of Princeton in 1902, he put a stop to the college's regular Bible instruction classes. In 1907, Woodrow Wilson and his wife Ellen appealed to a Ouija board hoping to conjure up James McCosh (dead for thirteen years) on matters relating to Princeton politics. This descent into witchcraft was a frightening example of apostasy. Unsurprisingly, Wilson had become a liberal progressive in his ideas by 1908. His rationale for his progressivism was contained in a book he wrote called *The Constitutional Government of the United States*. He argued for an evolutionary view of government. This meant the rejection of fixed absolutes and fixed laws. Wilson wrote: "In our own day, whenever we discuss the structure or development of anything, whether in nature or in society, we consciously or unconsciously follow Mr. Darwin . . . Living political constitutions must be Darwinian in structure and practice."[1]

At the same time, higher critical theories from Germany were seeping into America. German theologians like **Albrecht Ritschl** (1822-1889) and **Adolf von Harnack** (1851-1930) rejected certain books of the Bible (like the Gospel of John). For Ritschl and Harnack, the Word of God did not judge them. Instead, they stood in judgment over God's Word. They went so far as to teach that the Apostle Paul invented "Christianity" and this imposition was very different from the "simple, ethical monotheism" taught by Jesus. Such teachings undermined the authority and unity of Scripture

WOODROW WILSON (1856-1924)

ADOLF VON HARNACK (1851-1930)

in the most sinister, demonic way. Many American seminary students studied in Germany, imbibed these unbelieving ideas, and brought them back home with them. These false teachings infected churches and seminaries in America in the early 20th century.

J. Gresham Machen (1881-1937) was a New Testament scholar and professor at Princeton Seminary. Machen had studied in Germany and almost lost his faith there. But he came away with a renewed commitment Christian orthodoxy and an awareness of the danger of liberalism. In 1921, Machen released his first book entitled ***The Origin of Paul's Religion***. He convincingly argued the case that Paul's theology was not fabricated by Paul. Instead, it was a faith that was revealed to him through a revelation of the Lord Jesus Christ (Gal. 1:11-12). Against the skeptics and the higher critics of the day, Machen affirmed the New Testament record. On the Damascus Road, Paul encountered the risen and ascended Christ (Acts 9). There he was truly and dramatically converted to the faith he once tried to destroy (Gal. 1:13-17). This was the first of many books that Gresham would write to defend orthodox historic Christianity against the anti-supernatural, liberal attacks on the faith. Two years later, in 1923, Gresham wrote his most famous book, ***Christianity and Liberalism***. This was the book that would make the greatest impact upon the American church. In this book Gresham explained the real issues at stake.

In Machen's day, liberal theology was spreading throughout Christian denominations. Across the nation, Christians were tempted to compromise on essential Christian doctrines such as the resurrection of Christ, the virgin birth of Christ, the miracles of Jesus, and the inspiration and infallibility of the Scriptures. In many cases, seminary professors and pastors who abandoned biblical teaching were allowed to continue teaching and preaching in the churches and on the mission field. Machen became gravely concerned. He saw these departures from biblical orthodoxy as a serious threat to the church.

Theologian **H. Richard Niebuhr** (1894-1962) once summarized liberal theology with these memorable words: "A God without wrath brought men without sin into a kingdom without judgment through the ministrations of a Christ without a cross."[2] Niebuhr's summary shows how liberal theology attacks the foundations of Christian belief. Obviously, this sort of theology was diametrically opposed to the biblical faith.

The Fundamentalists and Modernists

If anyone teaches otherwise and does not consent to wholesome words, even the words of our Lord Jesus Christ, and to the doctrine which accords with godliness, he is proud, **knowing nothing, but is obsessed with disputes and arguments over words, from which come envy, strife, reviling, evil suspicions, useless wranglings of men of corrupt minds and destitute of the truth, who suppose that godliness is a means of gain. From such withdraw yourself. (1 Tim. 6:3-5, emphasis added)**

The battle between those holding to biblical truth and those departing from it became known as the **Fundamentalist-Modernist Controversy**. The term "fundamentalist" came into use after a

HARRY EMERSON FOSDICK (1878-1969)

FIRST PRESBYTERIAN CHURCH, NEW YORK CITY, NY

1910 book called **The Fundamentals** was published. This was a large work of articles by various pastors and professors defending the fundamental doctrines of the Christian faith. On the other side were the Modernists. The Modernists were those attempting to reframe Christian beliefs and bring them into harmony with modern ideas.

This conflict reached a critical point in 1922 when a pastor in New York preached a sermon called "Shall the Fundamentalists Win?" That pastor was the Baptist **Harry Emerson Fosdick** (1878-1969), who filled the pulpit of the First Presbyterian Church in New York City. In his sermon he called for tolerance of those who could not believe that the Bible was inspired, that Christ died a substitutionary death on the cross, that Christ was born of a virgin, and other basic doctrines. Fosdick presented the "Fundamentalists" as intolerant and unkind. However, the Scriptures teach that heretics and schismatics are the ones in error. Fosdick suggested that the church needed to be more tolerant of new ideas. In his sermon, he stated:

> As I plead thus for an intellectually hospitable, tolerant, liberty-loving church, I am, of course, thinking primarily about this new generation. We have boys and girls growing up in our homes and schools, and because we love them we may well wonder about the church which will be waiting to receive them. Now, the worst kind of church that can possibly be offered to the allegiance of the new generation is an intolerant church.[3]

Fosdick was concerned that the next generation would be lost if the church did not become more "liberal" and open to new ideas. Ironically, however, the denominations of America most liberal in their theology are shrinking at a rapid pace today.

Harry Emerson Fosdick and the other liberals were striking at the very heart of the Christian faith. J. Gresham Machen boldly labeled these liberal ideas as a false religion. His book, *Christianity and Liberalism,* answered Fosdick and other liberals. Machen explained the purpose of his powerful little book in an advertising blurb:

> What is the difference between modern "liberal" religion and historic Christianity? An answer to this question is attempted in the present book. The author is convinced that liberalism on the one hand and the religion of the historic church on the other are not two varieties of the same religion, *but two distinct religions proceeding from altogether separate roots.* This conviction is supported by a brief setting forth of the teachings of historic Christianity and of the modern liberalism with regard to God and man, the Bible, Christ, salvation, the Church, and Christian service. If Christianity, in its historic acceptation, is really to be abandoned, it is at least advisable that men should know what they are giving up and what they are putting in its place. (emphasis added)[4]

Some liberals argued that Christianity was nothing but a lifestyle taught by Jesus. What you believed did not matter so much. To this, Machen pointed out that the Christian faith as recorded throughout the entire New Testament was based upon a message to be believed—the message of the gospel. Machen agreed that following Jesus does require a certain way of life. But a Christian, he argued, is also one who believes in the gospel of Jesus Christ. That gospel of Jesus Christ is a message about acts of God performed in space-time human history, centered on the incarnation of the Son of God, His death and resurrection, His ascension, and His eventual second coming.

If professing "Christians" deny that Jesus is the Son of God, that He was born of a virgin, that He died on the cross for the sins of the world, and that He rose again on the third day, then the Bible says their faith is in vain. That is what the Apostle Paul said.

Now if Christ is preached that He has been raised from the dead, how do some among you say that there is no resurrection of the dead? But if there is no resurrection of the dead, then Christ is not risen. And if Christ is not risen, then our preaching is empty and your faith is also empty. Yes, and we are found false witnesses of God, because we have testified of God that He raised up Christ, whom He did not raise up—if in fact the dead do not rise. (1 Cor. 15:12-15)

In other words, if what the liberals of Machen's day were saying is true, then faith in Jesus Christ is pointless. Machen further explained:

> If Jesus was only what the liberal historians suppose that He was, then trust in Him would be out of place; our attitude toward Him could be that of pupils to a Master and nothing more. But if He was what the New Testament represents Him as being, then we can safely commit to Him the eternal destinies of our souls.[5]

The questions which arose during this time of unbelief and skepticism are just as important today: who is Jesus? Is He merely a good teacher? Or is He the Savior of the world? How we answer that question and what we believe about Jesus Christ is a matter of eternal life or eternal death.

He who believes in the Son has everlasting life; and he who does not believe the Son shall not see life, but the wrath of God abides on him. (John 3:36)

Founding of a New Seminary and a New Church

These kinds of destructive teachings were infiltrating the church of which Machen was a member. The Presbyterian Church in the United States became a critical battleground for Christian truth. The conflict over liberal theology also erupted within Princeton. Eventually, J. Gresham Machen resigned from Princeton Seminary. He could not continue to teach in an institution where Christian truth was being compromised. Several other biblically-minded teachers joined with him to form a new seminary in Philadelphia in 1929. The new institution was named Westminster Theological Seminary. It was an institu-

ALEXANDER HALL, PRINCETON SEMINARY

tion dedicated to training students to be faithful teachers of God's inspired Word, the Holy Bible.

After his departure from Princeton, Machen remained within the mainline Northern Presbyterian Church. But another controversy would lead to Machen's departure from the existing church. For a number of years the Board of Foreign Missions of the Presbyterian Church funded numerous missionaries who openly denied foundational Christian doctrines. Instead of proclaiming the truth of the gospel, these missionaries focused on the alleviation of poverty and sickness. Their missions then became primarily humanitarian efforts. A missions report titled *Rethinking Missions* was funded by John D. Rockefeller and published in 1932. It was then promoted by the Presbyterian Church. A review of the report was published by one of the Presbyterian Church's most well-known missionaries, Mrs. **Pearl S. Buck** (1892-1973). In her own words, she called the report "the only book I have ever read which seems literally true in its every observation and right in its every conclusion."[6] She wrote in her review:

> Let the sole question about that missionary be whether or not he is beloved in the community, whether the people see any use in his being among them, whether or not the way he has lived there has conveyed anything to the people about Christ – not mind you, whether or not he has preached, for that is of no value, but whether by the way he has lived he has conveyed anything. . . . *But above all, let the spread of the spirit of Christ be rather by mode of life than preaching.* I am weary unto death with this incessant preaching. It deadens all thought, it confuses all issues. (emphasis added)[7]

Mrs. Buck's contempt for the "foolishness of preaching" was faithless and fatal. She failed to realize it is the preaching of Christ crucified that is the power and wisdom of God unto salvation (1 Cor. 1:18). The Apostle Paul had a much different perspective of preaching:

How then shall they call on Him in whom they have not believed? And how shall they believe in Him of whom they have not heard? And how shall they hear without a preacher? And how shall they preach unless they are sent? As it is written: "How beautiful are the feet of those who preach the gospel of peace, who bring glad tidings of good things!" But they have not all obeyed the gospel. For Isaiah says, "Lord, who has believed our report?" So then faith comes by hearing, and hearing by the word of God. (Rom. 10:14-17)

PEARL S. BUCK (1892-1973)

Once Machen read Buck's review, he wrote a direct response. He insisted that this *Rethinking Missions* was "from beginning to end an attack upon the historic Christian Faith."[8] A significant number of members in the Presbyterian church could no longer in good conscience provide financial support to the Board of Foreign Missions that had taken such a position against the preaching of the Gospel. Several leaders came together to form an Independent Presbyterian Board of Foreign Missions. This new independent board would support missionaries who were committed to the faithful deposit of biblical truth and the proclamation of the gospel.

The formation of this new missions board produced a new controversy. The New Brunswick Presbytery proceeded to remove Gresham's ministerial credentials. They did this without ever holding a trial or giving Machen the opportunity to defend his actions. Along with several other pastors and elders in the Presbyterian church, Machen formed the Presbyterian Church of America (later renamed the Orthodox Presbyterian Church). This new group of churches committed themselves to the Word of God as the only infallible rule of faith and practice. The Orthodox Presbyterian Church still exists today throughout the United States.

As the mainline Protestant denominations fell to liberalism, Bible-believing Protestants left them to form new evangelical denominations. Conservative Southern Presbyterians would form the Presbyterian Church in America (PCA) in 1973. Conservative Episcopalians would form the Anglican Church in North America (ACNA) in 2009. Some denominations, such as the Lutheran Church Missouri Synod (LCMS) and the Southern Baptist Convention (SBC) were able to resist the onslaught of liberalism.

A Faith Worth Fighting For

A year after the Orthodox Presbyterian Church was formed, Machen died after contracting pneumonia. On January 1, 1937, this defender of the faith entered into the presence of His Lord. He was faithful unto death. Though Machen had gone to his eternal rest, the work he began was continued by many faithful Christians who followed in his footsteps.

Every age presents its own battles and tests of faith for men and women of God. During an age of severe breakdown of faith, even leaders begin to flee from the field of battle. God tests the faith of those who remain and stand. When Shammah continued to stand and fight in the field of lentils after the other fighting men had scattered in fear, he proved his faithfulness and courage for future generations to emulate (2 Sam. 23:11-12). This is what we find with J. Gresham Machen. By the grace of God, he continued to stand and fight in the field of lentils when many others had already given up. Eventually, a faithful, evangelical church emerged in the following decades of the 20th century.

We too must earnestly contend for the truth of the gospel. The Lord Jesus Christ is the only way to the Father (John 14:12). The Bible is inspired by God (2 Tim. 3:16-17). There is only one God (Isa. 45:22). Salvation is by faith in Jesus Christ alone (Acts 4:12). These are fundamental truths worth fighting for. ■

O Timothy! Guard what was committed to your trust, avoiding the profane and idle babblings and contradictions of what is falsely called knowledge—by professing it some have strayed concerning the faith. Grace be with you. Amen. (1 Tim. 6:20-21)

A SOUTHERN BAPTIST CHURCH

RED SQUARE, MOSCOW, RUSSIA

Persecutions in Eastern Europe

33

Here is the patience of the saints; here are those who keep the commandments of God and the faith of Jesus. (Rev. 14:12)

The 20th century was one of the bloodiest centuries in human history. Two world wars brought immense suffering and distress to people all over the world. In addition to these two worldwide conflicts, numerous other revolutions and genocides occurred. The dragon, though a mortally wounded foe, sought to inflict harm upon Christ's people with much vehemence. Certain portions of Christ's church experienced severe attacks. In the 20th century, some of the fiercest persecution occurred in the Soviet Union.

For a time, the Soviet Union was the largest country in the world. But in 1991, the Soviet Union was dissolved. The communist project failed. But for more than seventy years, this godless state would inflict immense suffering on hundreds of millions of people.

In 1917, the **Bolshevik Revolution** occurred in Russia. Under the leadership of **Vladimir Lenin** (1870-1924), the communist Bolsheviks overthrew the existing government in Russia and established the Soviet Union. The Soviet communists were committed to atheism, the belief that there is no God. By adopting this belief system, the Soviets adopted the worldview of the fool. And they doomed their project to failure.

The fool has said in his heart, "There is no God."
They are corrupt,
They have done abominable works,
There is none who does good. (Ps. 14:1)

Christ's Church in the Soviet Union under Attack

The largest church in Russia and surrounding Slavic nations was the **Russian Orthodox Church** and its related church bodies. At the time of the Bolshevik Revolution, most Russians were members of this church. It is not a surprise that the Russian Orthodox Church was the first target for the communists. Between 1917 and 1935, 130,000 Russian Orthodox priests were arrested, and some 95,000 were killed by firing squad.[1] The first Soviet concentration camp, the Solovki Camp of Special Purpose, was formed out of an Orthodox monastery. More purges came in 1937 and 1938, when another 100,000 Orthodox priests were executed.[2]

A Russian Pentecostal missionary from America by the name of Ivan Yefimovitch Voronaev helped to found 350 churches in Russia, Ukraine, Bulgaria,

VLADIMIR LENIN (1870-1924)

RUSSIAN ORTHODOX CATHEDRAL IN MOSCOW

and Poland in the 1920s. He was arrested in 1929 and died in a Siberian prison camp with millions of other Pentecostal brethren. The first Russian Baptist churches had formed in the 1880s. Some two million Baptists faced severe persecution under the Soviets. A Russian believer recorded what he remembers of these early persecutions:

> My mother's father was killed as a criminal with words from the Bible on his lips. As he died, he was praying about his executioners. My mother, who is now in her eighties, is still afraid when somebody knocks loudly on the door. It still reminds her of KGB people knocking at their door during the night in order to make a search. She was always afraid that they would find her Bible and confiscate it . . . for many, many years this old Bible was kept in a secret place in our house.[3]

The Lutheran church also suffered under the severe persecutions of the Soviets. The first Lutheran church was established in Russia in 1576. The church was known as St. Michael's in Moscow. But four years later, the czar of Russia ordered the church burnt down. Lutherans remained a small minority in Russia, mostly composed of ethnic Germans living there. The Russian Orthodox Church was the dominant form of religion. But German Lutherans continued to immigrate to Russia for various reasons. They brought their Protestant theology and practice with them. By 1917, at the eve of the Bolshevik Revolution, it is estimated that there were over 3.5 million Lutherans in Russia and around 1,800 Lutheran churches.[4]

After the communists took power, a decree was made, known as the **Decree on Separation of Church from State and School from Church**. The purpose of this decree was to eradicate every trace of Christian influence in society. The communists would make significant progress with this goal. But they would ultimately fail. Now that Lutherans and Russian Orthodox were both persecuted, this removed some of the divisions that had kept them apart. Patriarch Tikhon of the Russian Orthodox Church called the communists "agents of Satan . . . monsters of the human race."[5] By 1921, it is estimated that the number of Lutheran congregations still existing in Russia was down to 160.[6]

After the Revolution, the communists declared that all property belonged to the state. Now, for any church to gather, even on their own church property, required the permission of the communists.

Frequently, such permission was denied. Church property was confiscated to be used for other purposes. The job of pastor was not considered a valid profession by the communists. Pastors all over Russia struggled to feed their families.

The communists forced Christian children into atheist schools and indoctrinated them into atheism. Matthew Heise details one event in the Christmas of 1921 that illustrates this:

> During school celebrations at Christmastime 1921, the new Communist principal of the former Lutheran school remarked how the children were accustomed to getting presents at Christmas. He then told them, "Kneel down and pray to your God for Christmas gifts." When none appeared after their prayers, he said, "Ask this Soviet government for Christmas gifts." After the children had asked the Soviet government, "the curtains were drawn back and there was a beautiful Christmas tree and there were presents for all the children and there were songs."[7]

JOSEPH STALIN (1878-1953)

Here the communist principal was causing children to stumble by attacking their faith. He was teaching them a wrong understanding of prayer and encouraging them to worship the false religion of Communism.

Whoever causes one of these little ones who believe in Me to sin, it would be better for him if a millstone were hung around his neck, and he were drowned in the depth of the sea. (Matt. 18:6)

Despite the severe persecutions the Lutherans faced, they ultimately outlived the communist state. The church's numbers were dramatically reduced. Many pastors were imprisoned and executed. But the Lutheran church continues in Russia and former Soviet nations today.

Fearful of losing World War II, **Joseph Stalin** (1878-1953) gave a little more freedom to the churches. But the communists sought to infiltrate and control the churches so they wouldn't be a threat to them. After World War II, the Soviets conquered Eastern Europe and employed the same strategy there. They had various ways of doing this. Children were forbidden to attend church and indoctrinated in communist government schools. Any pastor who dared to criticize the state would be severely punished. Some Christians courageously resisted while others weakly complied. The result was a division between the official churches who complied with the communists and the underground churches who resisted them. The underground churches were brutally persecuted by communist governments.

The Ministry of Brother Andrew

Christians in these communist countries had few Bibles. In the 1950s, a Dutch Christian named **Brother Andrew** (**Andrew van der Bijl**, 1928-2022) began visiting these countries. He saw the great need these brothers and sisters had

BROTHER ANDREW (1928-2022)

for the Word of God. So Brother Andrew began to smuggle Bibles into communist countries. He had numerous encounters with police and border guards. As he would approach the border, he would pray this prayer:

> Lord, in my luggage I have Scripture that I want to take to Your children across this border. When You were on earth, You made blind eyes see. Now, I pray, make seeing eyes blind. Do not let the guards see those things You do not want them to see.[8]

The Lord answered Brother Andrew's prayer and made seeing eyes blind many times. Brother Andrew made it to Moscow in 1960. Stuffed in his little blue Volkswagen was a stack of Russian Bibles. He connected with a pastor of a little church of 150 members in Siberia with not a single Bible among them.[9] The pastor had been recently imprisoned and tortured. Upon visiting a church in Ukraine, Brother Andrew's team of Bible smugglers saw the pastor borrow a Bible from a member of the congregation so he could preach the sermon.

Only the East German churches of the Soviet Union had Bibles. But Brother Andrew found the churches in East Germany to be some of the weakest in the Eastern Bloc countries. Many of the churches had allowed the state to control church functions and complied with communist counterfeits of church ceremonies.

Deep in the underground church in Bulgaria, Brother Andrew met a certain Pastor Constantine and reports that the pastor "had been in prison for eighteen months for baptizing converts who were under twenty-one years of age. He had just been released. Constantine told me that the night after his release he had taken twenty-seven teenagers out of town and baptized them secretly in a river in the country."[10]

Brother Andrew and his fellow workers smuggled tens of thousands of Bibles and other Christian literature into communist countries, including the Soviet Union and China. They also encouraged and strengthened the believers there. Brother Andrew founded **Open Doors**, a ministry that continues to serve persecuted Christians worldwide today.

The Persecution of Richard Wurmbrand

Let it be known to you, O king, that we do not serve your gods, nor will we worship the gold image which you have set up. (Dan. 3:18)

In Romania, a congress of 4,000 church leaders was held at the capitol building shortly after the Soviets gained control in 1944. A Lutheran minister of Jewish descent by the name of **Richard Wurmbrand** (1909-2001) attended. He witnessed the priests, pastors, and ministers in attendance elect Soviet leader Joseph Stalin (1878-1953) as the honorary president for the meeting. The religious leaders filed up to the front to render their proper prostration and praise for communism. Wurmbrand wrote of the event:

> My wife and I were present at this con-

> gress. My wife sat near me and told me; "Richard, stand up and wash away this shame from the face of Christ! They are spitting in His face." I said to my wife, "If I do so you lose your husband." She said, "I don't wish to have a coward as a husband." Then I arose and spoke to this congress, praising not the murderers of Christians, but Christ and God and said our loyalty is due first to Him. The speeches at this congress were broadcast and the whole country could hear proclaimed from the rostrum of the Communist Parliament the message of Christ! Afterwards I had to pay for this but it had been worthwhile.[11]

During the 1940s, the true church maintained a robust outreach to the Russian troops and the Romanian public by street preaching, tract distribution, and one-on-one witnessing. Wurmbrand records that two Christian brothers pushed their way in to see the Romanian prime minister, Gheorghiu Dej (1901-1965). They were arrested and imprisoned for their work. But Wurmbrand records that on his deathbed, the prime minister "confessed his sins, accepted the Savior and began to serve Him in his sickness. Not long afterward he died, but went to his new-found Savior all because two Christians were willing to pay the price. And they are typical of the courageous Christians in the communist lands."[12]

RICHARD AND SABINA WURMBRAND

Wurmbrand was arrested on February 29, 1948. Through years of torture, he sustained four broken vertebrae, scars in a dozen places, and numerous burns. Thousands of Romanian Christians were arrested, tortured, and many died under the communists. The testimonies of these suffering believers show the supernatural power of God in sustaining His people. A bride was arrested on her wedding day. She looked towards her groom, kissed her chains, and said, "I thank my heavenly Bridegroom for this jewel He has presented to me on my marriage day. I thank Him that I am worthy to suffer for Him."[13]

Richard Wurmbrand described life in prison as the Christians would continue their preaching. They could not be silenced. "It was a deal. We preached, and they beat us." He recalls a brother who preached in his cell to fellow prisoners. He was dragged off for a beating and was tossed back into the cell hours later, bruised, bleeding, and battered. He picked himself off the floor and said, "Now brethren, where did I leave off when I was interrupted?" and continued his gospel message.[14]

What was particularly remarkable about these persecutions, as related to us by this Romanian pastor, was the amazing love the persecuted believers showed to their persecutors. Wurmbrand wrote:

> I have seen Christians in communist prisons with 50 pounds of chains on their feet, tortured with red-hot iron pokers . . . being kept afterward without water, starving, whipped, suffering from cold, and praying with fervor for the communists. This is humanly inexplicable! It is the love of Christ which was shed into our hearts.[15]

He goes on to speak of some of the torturers who were later themselves delivered into the same prisons. Christians would sometimes give away their last slice of bread (from their thin ration of a slice of bread a week) to save the life of one of these persecutors.

After fourteen years of suffering for Christ in communist prisons, Wurmbrand was released. He soon discovered that many pastors and bishops within almost every denomination were informers. "Most ministers gave information to the secret police,"[16] he wrote. The head of every official denomination was an appointee of the communists, according to Wurmbrand. The totalitarian, persecuting, god-like state tested the church for the presence of true faith. Protestant, Catholic, and Orthodox leaders collaborated with the communist takeovers, including Father Balogh in Hungary, Bishop Sergius in Russia, and Father Burducea in Romania. Wurmbrand reported that, "The president of the Romanian Adventists, Tachici told me that he had been an informer of the communist secret police from the very first day of their coming to power."[17]

Meanwhile, real believers avoided the official churches with their "watered-down gospels." The "faithful Underground Church," said Wurmbrand, "has thousands of members in such places. They have secret meetings in basements, attics, apartments, and homes."[18] The communists especially wanted to control the minds of the children and disallowed all Sunday schools, homeschools, and Christian schools.

In 1964, Wurmbrand and his family came to the West. He testified before the US Senate about communist persecution of Christians. He showed the scars from his tortures. Wurmbrand was saddened by the lack of concern on the part of Christians in the West for their brothers and sisters suffering around the world. He mentioned names nobody has ever heard of, such as Brother Grunvald, Ivanenko, Granny Shevchuk, Taisya Tkachenko, Ekaterina Vekazina, Georgi Vekazin, and so on. So as never to abandon the legacy of these saints who suffered for Christ and His church, Richard Wurmbrand formed an organization called Voice of the Martyrs in 1967. The ministry is still in operation to this day. Wurmbrand died at ninety-one years of age in 2001.

The Dissolution of the Soviet Union

For all that is in the world—the lust of the flesh, the lust of the eyes, and the pride of life—is not of the Father but is of the world. And the world is passing away, and the lust of it; but he who does the will of God abides forever. (1 John 2:16-17)

God brought down communism in Europe very quickly. In June 1989, Hungary opened its border with Austria. This event triggered a chain reaction which brought down communist governments all over Eastern Europe. In East Germany (under the control of the Soviet Union), Lutheran pastor Christian Fuhrer had been holding prayer meetings for seven years in his church in Leipzig. The prayer meetings had gradually grown. In October 1989, nearly 70,000 Germans attended the Leipzig prayer meeting and staged a peaceful demonstration afterwards. The demonstrations quickly spread to other East German cities, the **Berlin Wall** (dividing Soviet Controlled Ger-

NICOLAE CEAUSESCU (1918-1989)

many from the West) was torn down, and the Communist regime collapsed.

At this time, Romania was ruled by brutal communist dictator **Nicolae Ceausescu** (1918-1989). In Transylvania, which had been given to Romania after World War I, there was a sizable Hungarian minority. Laszlo Tokes, Hungarian Reformed pastor of the church of Timisoara, courageously spoke out against the oppression of the Ceausescu regime. He refused to be intimidated by threats. In July 1989, he exposed the evils being committed in Romania to the outside world in a television interview.

Ceausescu was furious. Tokes was ordered to leave his church. His life was threatened. Armed men with knives broke into his apartment. But he and his friends fought off the attackers and refused to leave. On December 15, as the police came to evict him, his congregation in Timisoara gathered round him to protect him, singing hymns. Although the police fired on the crowd, it refused to disperse. It grew larger and larger as Christian and non-Christian, Hungarian and Romanian alike began calling for the overthrow of the regime. The demonstrations quickly spread to other Romanian cities. By December 27, communism was overthrown and Ceausescu was dead.

In 1991, the Soviet Union itself collapsed. Statues of Lenin were toppled all over Eastern Europe. In the 1970s, the Soviet Union seemed very strong. To many it may have seemed invincible at the time. But God brought down communism in Europe in the late 1980s and early 1990s. The evil empires of men always come to an end. But the kingdom of our Lord Jesus Christ continues forever. ■

These will make war with the Lamb, and the Lamb will overcome them, for He is Lord of lords and King of kings; and those who are with Him are called, chosen, and faithful." (Rev. 17:14)

THE BERLIN WALL IN 1986

Christians in World War II

34

Then a third angel followed them, saying with a loud voice, "If anyone worships the beast and his image, and receives his mark on his forehead or on his hand, he himself shall also drink of the wine of the wrath of God, which is poured out full strength into the cup of His indignation. He shall be tormented with fire and brimstone in the presence of the holy angels and in the presence of the Lamb. (Rev. 14:9-10)

In Germany, higher critical views of the Bible weakened the faith in the 18th and 19th centuries. Then, in the 20th century, the country was hit hard by a dangerous strain of secular humanism. Germany was defeated in World War I and had to make many difficult concessions to the victorious allied nations. Germany suffered economic woe and wounded pride after its defeat. This opened the door for a charismatic leader to win the hearts of the German people. **Adolf Hitler** (1889-1945) rose to power in the late 1920s and early 1930s. He promised a glorious, restored future for the German people. With other sympathizers, he formed the **National Socialist Germany Workers' Party** (abbreviated as the **Nazi Party**). In 1933, Hitler took power and became a dictator over Germany.

To restore Germany's power, Hitler and the Nazis built up its industry and military. Hitler and the Nazis initiated conflict in Europe by invading Poland on September 1, 1939. The United Kingdom and France declared war on Germany. Hitler's military forces attempted to conquer all of Europe. The Nazis successfully subdued many nations including Poland, France, the Netherlands, Norway, and Belgium. But the United Kingdom stood fast against the onslaught of the German Air Force (the **Luftwaffe**).

Germany was successful in the early years of war. But Hitler made a fatal miscalculation in 1941 when he invaded the Soviet Union. Hitler wanted to conquer Russia to provide more living space for the German people. But the Soviets along with the Allied nations of the USA and the United Kingdom would eventually defeat Germany. By April 1945, Berlin was surrounded by the Soviets and the other allies. Hopeless and knowing that defeat was near, Hitler committed suicide on April 30, 1945. The wicked and barbarous Hitler was no more.

From 1939 to 1945, the Second World War brought devastation and death to the people of Europe. At least 60 million people died in World

ADOLF HITLER AND BENITO MUSSOLINI

RUINS OF THE REICHSTAG IN BERLIN, JUNE 1945

War II. It is among the most devastating wars in world history. Nonetheless, God preserved a remnant during these harsh and evil times. As our Lord Jesus said, "And because lawlessness will abound, the love of many will grow cold" (Matt. 24:12). This cold world yielded the murder of millions of Jews, the purging of the disabled, and the martyrdoms of Christians under Adolf Hitler. Thousands of Catholic priests and lay leaders were arrested and sent to concentration camps. Several hundred or thousands were executed.[1] Faithful village pastors like **Wilhelm Gottwaldt** of Pomerania continued their work through the 1930s and 1940s. While the Nazis forbade children to attend church and Sunday school, Gottwaldt steadfastly opposed them. He would still conduct his "Gospel campaigns," much to the frustration of the Nazi authorities.

DIETRICH BONHOEFFER (1906-1945)

Courageous Christians attempted to intervene. In May 1934, the **Confessing Church**, made up of Lutheran and Reformed churches, broke from the official state church in Germany on several points with a document known as the *Barmen Declaration*. This declaration repudiated anti-Semitism and announced a formal separation of the church from the Nazi state. It stated:

> If you find that we are speaking contrary to the Scripture, then do not listen to us! But if you find that we are taking our stand upon Scripture, then let no fear or temptation keep you from treading with us the path of faith and obedience to the Word of God.[2]

One Christian leader who steadfastly opposed the Nazi regime was a man named **Dietrich Bonhoeffer** (1906-1945). Bonhoeffer, a pastor and theologian, joined the Confessing Church and resisted the Nazi's evil plans. Those plans included commandeering the national church to support Nazi views. Other plans included the exclusion and ultimate eradication of Jews in Europe. Bonhoeffer supported faithful Christians by forming an underground seminary where he discipled men for pastoral ministry. He wrote a valuable work called ***Life Together*** in 1939. Bonhoeffer gave a beautiful description of Christian community during this time of persecution. In Bonhoeffer's book we learn about how important it is for Christians to confess their sins to one another. Christians live under the cross of Christ, which cleanses them from all sin. Here are a few portions of Bonhoeffer's thoughts on Christian community.

> In confession the break-through to community takes place. Sin demands to have a man by himself. It withdraws him from the community. The more isolated a person is, the more destructive will be the power of sin over him, and the more deeply he becomes involved in it, the more disastrous is his isolation. Sin wants to remain unknown. It shuns the light.
>
> In confession the light of the Gospel breaks into the darkness and seclusion of the heart. The sin must be brought into the light. The unexpressed must be openly spoken and acknowledged. Since the confession of sin is made in the presence of a Christian brother, the last stronghold of self-justification is abandoned. The sinner surrenders; he gives up all his evil. He gives his heart to God, and he finds the forgiveness of all his sin in the fellowship of Jesus Christ and his brother.
>
> The expressed, acknowledged sin has lost all its power. It has been revealed and judged as sin. It can no longer tear the fellowship asunder. He is no longer alone with his evil for he has cast off his sin in confession and handed it over to God. Now he stands in the fellowship of sinners who live by the grace of God in the Cross of Jesus Christ."[3]

One of the questions Bonhoeffer faced as a Christian in Hitler's Germany was, "How do you oppose evil?" How could one oppose evil leaders like Hitler but be faithful to God's Word? Romans 13 requires that we honor civil authorities. But what happens when these civil authorities do evil things like murder Jews or Christians? Bonhoeffer believed it was his duty to oppose Hitler's regime. He even went as far as participating in plans to see Hitler assassinated. This was one of the reasons Bonhoeffer was eventually arrested and imprisoned. Toward the end of World War II, Bonhoeffer was sent to a concentration camp in **Flossenburg**. He was then executed by his Nazi captors on April 9, 1945.

An account of Bonhoeffer's last hours was given to Bonhoeffer's friend Eberhard Bethge by an eyewitness. This is what the man said.

> I saw Pastor Bonhoeffer . . . kneeling on the floor praying fervently to God. I was most deeply moved by the way this lovable man prayed, so devout and so certain that God heard his prayer. At the place of execution, he again said a short prayer and then climbed the few steps to the gallows, brave and composed. His death ensued after a

BARRACKS AT FLOSSENBURG CONCENTRATION CAMP

few seconds. In the almost fifty years that I worked as a doctor, I have hardly ever seen a man die so entirely submissive to the will of God.[4]

The Story of Corrie ten Boom

Do not be overcome by evil, but overcome evil with good. (Rom. 12:21)

The Netherlands has long been a country known to offer freedom to the persecuted. This legacy goes back to the 1570s. William the Silent almost single-handedly halted the bloody inquisitions wrought upon thousands of poor citizens there by the Spanish. The Netherlands gave persecuted Pilgrims, Puritans, and Covenanters refuge in the 1600s.

This tradition continued into the 20th century. Dutch Christians like **Corrie ten Boom** (1892-1983), **Diet Eman** (1920-2019), and many others preserved the lives of many Jews during the German occupation in the 1940s. In all Europe, it was Dutch Christians who offered some of the strongest resistance to Nazi brutality. These courageous Christians stood steadfastly against the tyranny of the state, obeying God rather than men (Acts 5:29). In the dark times of World War II, the light of the gospel of Jesus Christ still shone. Jesus Christ was still on the throne, bringing all His enemies under His footstool (Ps. 110:1, 1 Cor. 15:25). The servants of Christ were also busy about the work of their Lord.

CORRIE TEN BOOM (1892-1983)

Corrie ten Boom and her family's love for the Jewish people is one such story. The ten Booms were a family of watchmakers in Holland who showed love and mercy to those in need in the darkest years of the 20th century. The ten Booms expressed their Christian faith by housing Jewish families and individuals who were being hunted by the **Gestapo**. (The Gestapo was the police force of the Nazis.)

Corrie ten Boom and her family courageously hid Jews in their home for years. To engage in this covert activity was very dangerous. There was the constant potential for discovery and the threat of imprisonment or death. Eventually, in the providence of God, the "hiding place" in the ten Boom home was discovered, and the family was imprisoned. Years of hardship followed for the members of the ten Boom family.

Corrie and her sister Betsy spent years in various jails and concentration camps. There they partook of many of the same sufferings that the Jewish people were undergoing in concentration camps throughout Nazi-occupied Europe. Betsy died in prison, but Corrie was eventually released. Corrie became an advocate for forgiveness and peacemaking between the Jews, the Dutch, and the Germans. She eventually chronicled her story in her classic book, ***The Hiding Place***.

The evils of the war, the concentration camps, and all the other atrocities are hard to fathom. How does one forgive such offenses? Would Christians forgive those who had engaged in some of the most heinous evils ever committed?

Of course, we know that there is forgiveness for all sinners who repent and turn to faith in Christ. And Christians are called to forgive as God in Christ forgave us. Of course, for someone who experienced such evils directly, it is not easy to extend forgiveness to evildoers who repent. Nevertheless, by the grace of God, it can be done.

One particularly moving story from this chronicle is Corrie's encounter with a former prison guard from Ravensbruck concentration camp. Corrie was imprisoned for some time at this concentration camp. She knew who this man was when she encountered him years later. Corrie retells the story this way:

> The place where the hunger was greatest was Germany. Germany was a land in ruin, cities of ashes and rubble, but more terrifying still, minds and hearts of ashes. Just to cross the border was to feel the great weight that hung over the land. It was at a church service in Munich that I saw him, the former S.S. man who had stood guard at the shower room door in the processing center at Ravensbruck. He was the first of our actual jailers that I had seen since that time. And suddenly it was all there—the roomful of mocking men, the heaps of clothing, Betsie's pain-blanched face. He came up to me as the church was emptying, beaming and bowing. "How grateful I am for your message, Fraulein," he said. "To think that, as you say, He has washed my sins away!"
>
> His hand was thrust out to shake mine. And I, who had preached so often to the people in Bloemendaal the need to forgive, kept my hand at my side.
>
> Even as the angry, vengeful thoughts boiled through me, I saw the sin of them. Jesus Christ had died for this man; was I going to ask for more? "Lord Jesus," I prayed, "forgive me and help me to forgive him."
>
> I tried to smile, I struggled to raise my hand. I could not. I felt nothing, not the slightest spark of warmth or charity. And so again I breathed a silent prayer. "Jesus, I cannot forgive him. Give your forgiveness."
>
> As I took his hand the most incredible thing happened. From my shoulder along my arm and through my hand, a current seemed to pass from me to him, while into my heart sprang a love for this stranger that almost overwhelmed me.
>
> And so I discovered that it is not on our forgiveness, any more than on our goodness that the world's healing hinges, but on His. When He tells us to love our enemies, He gives, along with the command, the love itself.[5]

Amen! May we learn to forgive as Corrie learned to forgive—to forgive as God in Christ forgave us (Eph. 4:32).

THE "HIDING PLACE" IN THE TEN BOOM HOME

A Gospel Mission at the Nuremberg Trials

And the tax collector, standing afar off, would not so much as raise his eyes to heaven, but beat his breast, saying, "God, be merciful to me a sinner!" I tell you, this man went down to his house justified rather than the other; for everyone who exalts himself will be humbled, and he who humbles himself will be exalted. (Luke 18:13-14)

After the war ended, an international tribunal was established to bring top-level Nazi leaders to justice. A series of trials occurred in the German city of **Nuremberg**. These trials are known in history as the **Nuremberg Trials** (1945-1946). When the trials began, many high-level Nazi leaders had already ended their own lives to avoid human justice. These included Adolf Hitler, Heinrich Himmler (1900-1945), and Joseph Goebbels (1897-1945). Though they evaded the court of human justice, they had come before the judgment seat of God. "It is appointed for men to die once, but after this the judgment" (Heb. 9:27).

Other Nazi leaders survived the war and were brought to trial to answer for what they had done. Each of the defendants had varying levels of responsibility and involvement in the crimes of the Nazis. Each received different sentences. Some were executed shortly after the trials. Others received prison sentences of varying durations. A few were acquitted.

DEFENDANTS AT THE NUREMBERG TRIALS

Christians, in obedience to Christ, are committed to the weightier matters of the law. Our Lord said that these weightier matters include "justice and mercy and faith" (Matt. 23:23). It was just for the Nazi leaders to be tried in a court of human justice for their crimes. Yet, by God's gracious provision, these men were given an opportunity to repent of their sins and turn to Christ in faith and receive the forgiveness of sins. That opportunity came for many of them through a humble servant pastor named **Henry Gerecke** (1893-1961).[6]

Gerecke was an American Lutheran pastor in his fifties at the time of the Nuremberg Trials. His two sons served in the American military during World War II. During the first few years of the war, Gerecke continued his ministry at home in America. But as he heard about the need for more chaplains to minister to American soldiers, he decided to enlist as a chaplain in the US Army. In 1943, Gerecke enlisted and became a pastor to American soldiers serving overseas. He first served in England to wounded soldiers and then in Germany after the war ended. Gerecke was then assigned to serve as a chaplain in the prison at Nuremberg. Gerecke was chosen for this role for a few reasons. First, Gerecke was fluent in German. This enabled him to communicate easily with the Nazi prisoners on trial. Gerecke also had extensive experience in prison ministry in the US, having preached the gospel for years in US prisons.

Gerecke, along with a Roman Catholic priest named **Sixtus O'Connor** (1909-1983), were chosen to minister to the prisoners. O'Connor ministered to the six prisoners who wanted a Roman Catholic chaplain. Gerecke ministered to the fifteen who preferred a Lutheran Protestant one. Since many of the Nazi leaders grew up in the Lutheran church, Gerecke brought them a familiar message. It was a message they had chosen to forget. But it was a message they urgently needed: the gospel of Jesus Christ.

Over a period of months as the trials proceeded, Gerecke visited each of the Nazi prisoners to visit with them, pray with them, give them Christian literature, and invite them to chapel services. Gerecke visited with some of Hitler's top military leaders including **Rudolf Hess** (1894-1987), one of Hitler's closest confidantes, **Herman Goering** (1893-1946), the commander of the German Luftwaffe (air force), **Albert Kesselring** (1885-1960), and the labor minister **Fritz Sauckel** (1894-1946). Sauckel was responsible for employing slave labor and for other evils that occurred in some of Germany's concentration camps.

As Gerecke ministered, he saw much spiritual progress in Fritz Sauckel in particular. Sauckel would often weep during his meetings with Gerecke and pray to God for mercy. He became devoted to Bible study and would carry his catechism to read during the trials. On one occasion, when Gerecke entered Sauckel's cell, Sauckel threw his hands in the air, and cried out loudly "God be merciful to me, a sinner!"[7] Sauckel's cries were so loud that all the prison guards heard him. Gerecke wrote later, "I believe he meant every word of it."[8]

Gerecke led regular chapel services for the accused war criminals. Sometimes a dozen or more Nazi leaders gathered to sing hymns together and to hear Gerecke preach the Word of God. At the back of the chapel thirteen guards were stationed to keep watch over the prisoners.

HERMANN GOERING AT THE NUREMBERG TRIALS

As the trials proceeded, Gerecke was given an opportunity to end his service and return home. Gerecke missed his wife Alma. They had been apart for years while Gerecke served in Europe. But many of the Nazi leaders came to so love their prison pastor that they wrote a letter to Gerecke's wife and signed it together. They requested that Gerecke stay with them and minister to them in their hour of spiritual need. Here is what the letter said:

> Frau Gerecke,
>
> Your husband Pastor Gerecke has been taking religious care of the undersigned defendants during the Nuremberg trial. He has been doing so for more than half a year. We now have heard, dear Mrs. Gerecke, that you wish to see him back home after his absence of several years. Because we also have wives and children we understand this wish of yours very well.
>
> Nevertheless we are asking you to put off your wish to gather your family around you at home for a little time. Please consider that we cannot miss your husband now. During the past months he has shown us uncompromising friendliness of such a kind, that he has become indispensable for us.[9]

Not only did Gerecke share the gospel with the Nazi prisoners, he spoke with their wives and children when they visited the prison. He would talk to the children of the Nazi prisoners about Jesus. He wrote, "God forbid any boasting at this point, but I have the conviction that some of the little girls and boys who came to visit their daddies during those sessions became better acquainted with the Savior."[10]

The Nuremberg trials ended in October 1946. Sentences were passed upon the Nazi leaders. Twelve of the Nazis were sentenced to death. Seven were handed prison sentences of varying amounts. Three of the men were acquitted. After the sentencing, those men who were sentenced to death spent most of their time with Gerecke and the Catholic priest O'Connor. For some, they had only weeks left to live. The critical question was: would they turn from their sins to God and put their faith in Jesus Christ, the Lamb of God? Gerecke observed different spiritual responses in the last few weeks of ministry. **Joachim von Ribbentrop** (1893-1946), Hitler's foreign minister, spent most of his time reading the Bible. Gerecke noted that **Wilhelm Keitel** (1882-1946), commander of the German army, "was especially interested in certain Bible portions and certain hymns which spoke of the love of God in the redeeming blood of Christ."[11]

Some of Hitler's former leaders humbled themselves before God and trusted in Christ. But others were still resistant to the message of the gospel. This did not stop Gerecke from pleading with them to repent of their sins and turn to the Lord. Hermann Goering, who had once been Hitler's second in command, persisted in his unbelief. Gerecke continued to urge Goering to receive the gospel, speaking to him about "eternal values and how a man can be prepared to die, to meet his God."[12] Goering insisted that he was a member of the Christian church but that he did not accept the teachings of the faith. He mocked the Bible and the doctrines of Christ's atonement and resurrection.

WILHELM KEITEL (1882-1946)

Pastor Gerecke reminded Goering that the message was not his message. It was the Word of God. "This is what Jesus said. This isn't what Gerecke is saying, but this is God speaking to you. Won't you accept this? Just say, 'Jesus, save me.'" Goering refused and said, "I can't do that. This Jesus you always speak of—to me he's just another smart Jew." Gerecke continued, "This Jesus is my savior who suffered, bled, and died that I may go to heaven some day. He paid for my sins." Goering continued his refusal, "You don't believe that yourself. When one is dead, that's the end of everything."[13]

Despite Goering's rejection of the Christian gospel, he still asked Gerecke to serve him the Lord's Supper. Goering, out of tradition, may have wanted to partake of communion despite his unbelief. To some of the Nazis on trial who had confessed their sins and professed Christ, Gerecke had already served communion. But he would not give the bread and wine to Hermann Goering. Gerecke explained this to Goering. "Herr Reichsmarshal, this is the way it is: only those who believe that Jesus is really their savior, who believe in him who instituted the supper should be permitted to attend the Lord's Supper. The others are unfit." Goering was offended. He replied, "I have never been refused the Lord's Supper by a German pastor, never."

Pastor Gerecke stood his ground. "I cannot with a clear conscience commune you because you deny the very Christ who instituted the sacrament. You may be on a church roll, but you do not have faith in Christ and have not accepted him as your savior. Therefore, you are not a Christian, and as a Christian pastor I cannot commune you. Herr Goering, your little girl said she wants to meet you in heaven." But Goering persisted in his proud rejection of Christ. He said to Pastor Gerecke, "Yes, she believes in your savior. But I don't. I'll just take my chances, my own way."[14] Tragically, shortly after this last meeting, instead of believing in Christ, Goering took his own life.

Nevertheless, several of the Nazi leaders whom Gerecke ministered to expressed their trust in Christ to save them from their sins. On the day of execution, Gerecke prayed with them. In Pastor Gerecke's last meeting with Joachim von Ribbentrop, he told Pastor Gerecke that he "put all his trust in the Blood of the Lamb that taketh away the sins of the world. He asked that God have mercy on his soul."[15] Wilhelm Keitel made a similar confession. Before his execution, he prayed "Christ's blood and judgment are my adornment and robe of honor; therein I will stand before God when I go to heaven. Amen." Keitel thanked Gerecke for his faithful ministry to him, saying, "I thank you, and those who sent you, with all my heart."[16] After the trials concluded, it was Pastor Gerecke's belief that at least four of the men he ministered to had been redeemed by the Lord. He believed that Frick, Sauckel, Ribbentrop, and Keitel "died as penitent sinners trusting God's mercy for forgiveness. They believed in Jesus who shed his blood for their sins."[17]

Pastor Gerecke's ministry to the Nazi leaders at Nuremberg was not easy. His duty was to share the gospel with men who were responsible for some of the most heinous evils ever committed. In many cases, these were men whose consciences had been long hardened by their sin. Some believed they were innocent. But by God's grace, the hearts of some of the men softened. Pastor Gerecke knew that there was only one hope for these men. They could not atone for their own sins, even by their own death. Their only hope was the Lamb of God who takes away the sins of the world.

The hymn, "Rock of Ages," reminds us that we can bring nothing to God that will save us. We must simply cling to the cross of Christ.

Not the labors of my hands
Can fulfil thy law's demands;
Could my zeal no respite know,
Could my tears for ever flow,
All for sin could not atone;
Thou must save, and thou alone.

NUREMBERG AFTER THE WAR ENDED

Nothing in my hand I bring,
Simply to thy cross I cling;
Naked, come to thee for dress,
Helpless, look to thee for grace;
Foul, I to the Fountain fly;
Wash me, Savior, or I die.

Some who learned about Pastor Gerecke's ministry were critical of him. Some believed that there was to be no mercy whatsoever for such war criminals. Of course, it was important that these men were brought to justice for their crimes. Yet as Christians, we should desire the salvation of all, even those sinners whom the world most despises. We are to "do justice, and to love mercy" (Mic. 6:8). We must also remember that we too are sinners deserving of God's judgment. We too are saved through the redemption that is in Christ Jesus. ■

For all have sinned and fall short of the glory of God, being justified freely by His grace through the redemption that is in Christ Jesus. (Rom. 3:23-24)

THE GREAT WALL OF CHINA

Persecutions in China and Korea

35

And the dragon was enraged with the woman, and he went to make war with the rest of her offspring, who keep the commandments of God and have the testimony of Jesus Christ. (Rev. 12:17)

Ancient records indicate the first appearance of Christianity in China around AD 635. A missionary named **Alopen** took the Christian faith to the Far East. In the 1600s, Roman Catholic missionaries also brought the Roman faith to China. The earliest Protestant missionaries to China include **Robert Morrison** (1782-1834), **William Chalmers Burns** (1815-1868), and **Hudson Taylor** (1832-1905). By the beginning of the 20th century, the missionary movement in China claimed around 80,000 members and half a million adherents. (An adherent is a follower who is not yet a member of the church.) It is also estimated that there were around 1,500 missionaries, husbands and wives included. The gospel was advancing throughout China.

As we have seen throughout our survey of church history, the dragon continues his futile war against Christ and the saints. This means that wherever the gospel is proclaimed, persecution will follow. Persecution against Christ's followers in China heated up in the **Boxer Rebellion**.

The Boxer Rebellion

Attitudes towards foreigners in China turned sour between 1890 and 1900. It was not long before hostility turned into violence. The Boxer Rebellion started with an organization called the "I Ho Ch'uan," or the "Righteous Harmony Fists." This was a secret society that promoted spirit possession (or what we would call "demon possession") as their primary religious practice. The group boasted of supernatural invulnerability to knives, bullets, and cannon shot. On November 1, 1897, representatives of this secret society burst into the home of a German missionary, killing two Christians. Leading the Chinese government at the time was the **Empress Dowager Cixi** (r. 1861-1908). As tensions increased between China and the European nations over these initial acts of violence, the empress was stirred up to support violence against foreigners. On June 24, 1900, Cixi issued an imperial decree ordering the killing of all foreigners. At least 188 missionaries died in the massacre, including fifty-three children.

BOXERS

Especially serious was the massacre conducted by Governor **Yu Hsien** in **Shansi** district, where 44 Christian missionaries lost their lives. The details of the martyrdoms of **Thomas** and **Jessie Pigott** and their twelve-year-old son Wellesley are worth recounting. Here was a family of great faith who gave up everything for Jesus Christ. Thomas Pigott preached his way from his mission at Shou Yang to Tai Yuan, along with his wife and son. At one point, one bystander told him, "You are to be killed for preaching, and yet go on doing so!"[1] Detained in the prison in Tai Yuan, Jessie Pigott continued witnessing to a woman accused of murdering her husband, "telling her about Jesus."[2] In their last moments, as they stood before the Chinese Nero, Yu Hsien, Thomas "preached to the people till the very last, [until he was executed] ... Mrs. Pigott held the hand of her son, even when she [was executed], and he was killed immediately after her."[3] Young Wellesley had written hopefully to relatives in England, "We can't be martyrs in England, but my father and mother and I might be in China."[4] His desire to serve His Savior Jesus was fulfilled.

Foreign powers eventually crushed the ill-conceived revolution and demanded reparations from the Chinese. But Hudson Taylor and the China Inland Mission refused to receive any compensation from the people they served. They did this to demonstrate to the Chinese the meekness and gentleness of Christ. By God's good providence, the cruel plans of the Evil One backfired. In the aftermath of the Boxer Rebellion, the Chinese people became even more receptive to the gospel. By 1920, the number of missionaries to China had increased fourfold.

The Communist Revolution and Chinese House Churches

For we do not wrestle against flesh and blood, but against principalities, against powers, against the rulers of the darkness of this age, against spiritual hosts of wickedness in the heavenly places. Therefore take up the whole armor of God, that you may be able to withstand in the evil day, and having done all, to stand. (Eph. 6:12-13)

The Boxer Rebellion had ended. But the situation was about to get more difficult for Christians in China. The rise of communism in China once again brought significant persecution against the church. The evil philosophy of communism was propagated by a man named **Karl Marx** (1818-1883). Marx was a lapsed Lutheran who claimed the influence of Satan in some of his poems

LOCATION OF SHANSI PROVINCE, CHINA

MAO ZEDONG (1893-1976)

BROTHER YUN (1958-)

and prose. China's first communist leader, **Mao Zedong** (1893-1976), was influenced by Marx's disastrous doctrines. These are the roots of one of the largest persecutions in the history of Christ's church.

Mao Zedong led a civil war against the Chinese nationalists between 1946 and 1949. The communists prevailed. With the communist takeover of China, Mao Zedong holds the worldwide record for the largest mass killing in recorded history. Accurate numbers are hard to come by, but the best available ones, provided by the authoritative *Black Book of Communism*, put the number of dead at 65 million. An estimated 50 million Chinese were sentenced to serve time in forced labor camps from the 1950s through the 1980s. This number includes many Christians. Of the 600,000 Christians that lived in China at the outset of the Communist Revolution, many of them were doubtless killed or suffered in labor camps during this severe persecution.

What followed this nightmarish reign of terror constitutes some of the most amazing work of Almighty God in the history of Christ's kingdom. Who would have ever imagined that the Chinese Christian church would grow so much in the 20th century? Recent estimates put the Chinese Christian population anywhere between 67 million and 100 million. This compares to some 87 million members of the Communist Party. "The kingdoms of this world have become the kingdoms of our Lord and of His Christ!" (Rev. 11:15).

The story of the Chinese church leader **Brother Yun** (Liu Zhenying, 1958-) gives us a snapshot of the church in China. As a teenager, Yun gained access to a Bible from a stranger who delivered a copy to his home after he prayed to receive a copy. He began to memorize entire books of the Bible. Brother Yun began to travel as an evangelist for several years. He reached hundreds of thousands of people with the gospel. These believers formed the heavily persecuted house church movement in China. Entire villages became Christian and were baptized.[5] Yun was arrested for preaching the Gospel first in 1975 at seventeen years of age. He was imprisoned on three separate occasions. He was often beaten and tortured. He finally escaped China and obtained asylum in Germany in 2001.

During these years, the Chinese church was constantly harassed by wolves in sheep's clothing. In 1980, the government attempted to arrest the growth of these churches with their own alternative. The established a state-controlled organization called the **Three-Self Church**. Leaders with a more liberal man-centered theology crowded in to lead the state-endorsed church, according to Yun.[6] During the organization of the Three-Self Church in his province, Yun reminded the gathering, "The Bible says believers and unbelievers should not be yoked together. How can light and darkness dwell together? God's church has no communion with idols. The Lord and his church will judge you!"[7] "The pure bride of Christ can never be controlled by atheistic government or led by men who hate God."[8] The house church movement continues separate from the state-controlled Three-Self Church in China.

Another influential house church leader in China was Pastor **Samuel Lamb** (1924-2013). Pastor Lamb served for twenty years in communist prisons and labor camps between 1955 and 1978. Upon release from prison, he immediately formed a house church which now claims a membership of 5,000. Lamb, Yun, and others resisted official registration with the state-controlled Three-Self Church. Typical restrictions imposed by this state agency included a prohibition on any Christian education for children, including Sunday schools, homeschools, and Christian schools. Also, the state banned any teaching on the second coming of Christ.

SAMUEL LAMB (1924-2013)

Another important battle line for the true Chinese Christian church involved the secular humanist agenda first espoused by America's Margaret Sanger—the secular vision of contraception, abortion, and infanticide. China's one-child policy was put in place in 1979. The communist government restricted parents to one child with only very limited exceptions. This led to even more mass murders, often by the force of the state. Hundreds of millions of babies lost their lives due to this evil policy. While most of the Chinese churches supported abortion over the decades, a small minority of Christians stood against the murder of children. The Chinese Christian pro-life movement has taken the message to their brothers and sisters since 2012. In 2016, the Chinese government changed to a two-child policy. Then, in 2021, China introduced a three-child policy. The communists realized that their policy was threatening China's continued existence as a nation. The population was shrinking and growing more elderly.

There is much to learn from the great work of the Spirit of God upon the church in China. Our brothers from China can testify to us that the suffering is well worth it. Those who compromise with the world's ideas and state

PRAYER MEETING IN PYONGYANG, KOREA IN 1907

control over the church do not enjoy spiritual growth. Those who stand against ungodliness and unbelief suffer persecution. But their suffering serves as the spiritual seeds of a vibrant church.

COMBAT IN THE STREETS OF SEOUL, KOREA DURING THE KOREAN WAR

Christianity's Growth and Persecution in Korea

When the Day of Pentecost had fully come, they were all with one accord in one place. And suddenly there came a sound from heaven, as of a rushing mighty wind, and it filled the whole house where they were sitting. Then there appeared to them divided tongues, as of fire, and one sat upon each of them. And they were all filled with the Holy Spirit and began to speak with other tongues, as the Spirit gave them utterance. (Acts 2:1-4)

Roman Catholic missionaries reached Korea in the 18th century. But the Koreans began to oppose all foreigners in the 1860s. In 1866, the Korean government killed 8,000 Korean converts. The second Protestant missionary to Korea, **Robert Jermain Thomas** (1839-1866), made two journeys to the country. He was killed during his second visit in 1866. He left a Bible to his executioners. Protestant missionary activity in Korea greatly increased in the late 1800s. Encouraged by the ideas of Presbyterian missionary **John Nevius** (1829-1893), the missionaries worked hard to plant self-propagating, self-governing, and self-supporting indigenous churches.

The Korean church greatly expanded in the early 20th century. This growth occurred when the Spirit of God ignited what came to be known as the **Korean Pentecost**. In 1907, a powerful revival broke out in Pyongyang. The event occurred during the ministry of two Presbyterian missionaries: **Jonathan Goforth** (1859-1936) and **William Blair** (1876-1970). The unusual outpouring of the Holy Spirit of God came as a tremendous surprise to these missionaries. On January 7, 1907, 1,500 people gathered in a meeting hall in Pyongyang. That evening, conviction of sin, confession, and weeping swept through the congregation. It continued for days. William Blair wrote of it:

> It seemed as if the roof was lifted from the building and the Spirit of God came down from heaven in a mighty avalanche of power upon us. I fell at Kim's side and wept and prayed as I had never prayed before. My last glimpse of the audience is photographed indelibly on my brain. Some threw themselves full length upon the floor, hundreds stood with arms outstretched to heaven. Every man forgot every other. Each was face to face with God. I can hear yet that fearful sound of hundreds of men pleading with God for life, for mercy. The

> cry went out over the city till the heathen were in consternation.[9]

The outpouring continued the next night as the elders confessed their sins. Blair records:

> Their sins rose up in all their vileness, till shame and grief and self-loathing took complete possession; pride was driven out, the face of men forgotten. Looking up to heaven to Jesus whom they had betrayed, they smote themselves and cried out with bitter wailing: "Lord, Lord cast us not away forever!" Everything else was forgotten. Nothing else mattered. The scorn of men, the penalty of the law, even death itself seemed of small consequence if only God forgave. We may have our theories of the desirability or undesirability of public confession of sin, I have had mine; but I know now that when the Spirit of God falls upon guilty souls, there will be confession, and no power on earth can stop it.[10]

Persecutions often follow periods of revival. That was the case for Korean believers who would face a series of severe persecutions. From 1910-1945, Japan conquered and ruled Korea. The Japanese tried to impose **Shintoism** on the Koreans and force them to worship the Japanese emperor. Many of the Japanese Christians succumbed to emperor worship. Sadly, this often happened because of the encouragement of American evangelical missionaries to bow the knee. But many of the Korean Christians stood fast against idolatry. Thousands of Korean Christians were imprisoned by the Japanese for refusing to submit to the idolatry of the state. Many of them lost their lives due to their commitment to worshiping the one true God alone. During this persecution, Korean Christians cried out to the Lord and developed a vibrant culture of prayer which continues today. The resistance of Korean Christians to the Japanese endeared them to their fellow Koreans and opened doors for the gospel to spread in Korea.

During the **Korean War** (1950-1953), thousands of Christians in North and South Korea, particularly pastors and elders, were killed. Two sons of a pastor were shot to death by a young communist revolutionary. When the young revolutionary was arrested, Pastor Sohn Yangoon offered to adopt the young man into his own family. The magistrate approved the adoption. The boy was enrolled in the Higher Bible Institute in Pusan. Pastor Sohn was later arrested while he was serving in a leper colony. The communists murdered him about three miles north of the town of Yussoo on September 28, 1950.[11] These stories provide more living pictures of Christ on this earth. Through such examples we better understand how the kingdom comes on earth, as it is in heaven (Luke 11:2).

Since the end of the Korean War, Christianity has grown tremendously in South Korea. Today, South Korea has one of the highest populations of Christians in the Far East. Visitors to Seoul at night will see the sky lighted up with thousands of glowing neon crosses. Many Korean churches have early morning prayer meetings seven days a week.

Immediately after the 1907 revival, seven men were ordained for gospel ministry. The missionary spirit took possession of the church and never subsided. The Korean church is now the fifth largest missionary-sending nation in the world, supporting some 1,000 missionaries per every million members. There were over 10,000 Korean Protestant missionaries serving in 156 countries around the world at the turn of the 21st century.[12] ■

FORBIDDEN CITY, BEIJING, CHINA

PRESBYTERIAN CHURCH IN CAERNARFON, GWYNEDD, WALES

36 Christian Leaders and Movements of the 20th Century

And they overcame him by the blood of the Lamb and by the word of their testimony, and they did not love their lives to the death. Therefore rejoice, O heavens, and you who dwell in them! Woe to the inhabitants of the earth and the sea! For the devil has come down to you, having great wrath, because he knows that he has a short time. (Rev. 12:11-12)

The 20th century was a time of great distress and persecution for Christ's church. Two world wars, revolutions, and genocides affected Christ's people in different places. Yet, no matter how severe the trials or persecutions, the Lord's people are "more than conquerors," and none of these distresses can separate them from the love of God in Christ (Rom. 8:37-39). The power and promises of Jesus Christ continued to sustain the church through the 20th century. Though the church suffered much, it also advanced in new regions of the world. The gates of hell cannot prevail against Christ's church.

In this closing chapter of our survey of our Lord's church, we will learn about influential figures and movements of the 20th century.

Christian Leaders in Great Britain

By the 1940s, there was still a remnant of Christian influence in Great Britain. God had mercy on a few intellectuals who had been steeped in secular humanism. For example, an Oxford scholar named **Clive Staples Lewis** (1898-1963) converted to the Christian faith in 1931. Lewis grew up in Northern Ireland in a nominally Christian home. But in his youth, he abandoned the Christian faith and embraced atheism. For some years, in his pride, he rejected Christian truth. But the Lord was merciful to humble Lewis and soften his heart. Lewis was a professor both at Oxford and later Cambridge. During his years of teaching, Lewis became an influential writer who wrote works of non-fiction, fiction, and Christian apologetics (the defense of the faith).

During World War II, Lewis became an influential voice for Christianity in the United Kingdom. Between 1942 and 1944, as the war progressed, C.S. Lewis gave several radio addresses on Christian themes over the British Broadcasting Corporation (BBC). Those talks reached many in Great Britain. Later, the radio addresses were turned into a book called ***Mere Christianity***. In addition to this popular book, Lewis wrote other well-known works such as *Miracles, The Problem of Pain, The Screwtape Letters, The Great Divorce,* and the children's fantasy series *The Chronicles of*

C.S. LEWIS (1898-1963)

D. MARTYN LLOYD-JONES (1899-1981)

TOWER OF WESTMINSTER CHAPEL, LONDON, ENGLAND

Narnia. Lewis' works continue to be read by many Christians today.

And He Himself gave some to be apostles, some prophets, some evangelists, and some pastors and teachers, for the equipping of the saints for the work of ministry, for the edifying of the body of Christ. (Eph. 4:11-12)

Great Britain was also blessed with a faithful, God-centered preacher named **D. Martyn Lloyd-Jones** (1899-1981). Lloyd-Jones was a brilliant young medical doctor who was trained under the finest medical professionals in London. He experienced a conversion to the Lord in 1925. Though Lloyd-Jones had been raised in a Calvinistic Methodist Church, he had never heard "preaching that would convict me of sin."[1] Because of this, he had not experienced his need for Christ and the gospel until his conversion. It wasn't until he was twenty-five years old that this young doctor realized the power of the gospel. Though Lloyd-Jones had many opportunities open to him in the medical field, he sensed a calling to preach the Word of God. He left his medical profession in London and returned to his home country of Wales for his first pastoral charge. In Aberavon, Wales, Pastor Lloyd-Jones ministered to a then-shrinking congregation. The Lord abundantly blessed his ministry and the church grew rapidly.

After a number of years in Wales, the Lord opened a door of ministry in London. In 1939, he took up a pastoral role at **Westminster Chapel**. He joined Pastor **G. Campbell Morgan** (1863-1945) as an assistant pastor in those first years of ministry at Westminster Chapel. It was a tumultuous year to take up a new ministry opportunity. This was especially so because he was ministering in the heart of London, just blocks from Buckingham Palace. World War II erupted in September 1939, when Germany invaded Poland. Subsequently, the London Blitz would occur as the German Luftwaffe (air force) pummeled London and other English cities for almost a year. Lloyd-Jones and the Christians at Westminster

Chapel continued to meet, though occasionally services were interrupted by air raid sirens.

The people of Great Britain rejoiced when the war finally came to an end in 1945. Lloyd-Jones continued a long and fruitful ministry until 1968. Lloyd-Jones became renowned for his gift of **expository preaching**. For years at a time, he would diligently, faithfully, and accurately work his way through books of the Bible. For example, from 1955 to 1968, Lloyd-Jones preached through Romans on Friday evenings. Eventually, his sermons on this book of Scripture were published in fourteen volumes. Lloyd-Jones' love for God's Word, expressed in his preaching, has influenced Christians all over the world.

American Evangelists and Missionaries

And He said to them, "Go into all the world and preach the gospel to every creature." (Mark 16:15)

The United States remained a major center of Christianity in the 20th century. American evangelists and missionaries continued to spread the gospel. One of the most influential evangelists was a man named **Billy Graham** (1918-2018). Graham grew up on a dairy farm near Charlotte, North Carolina. He felt called to preach and, after studying for the ministry, began evangelistic campaigns in the 1940s. From the 1940s to the early 2000s, Graham held evangelistic campaigns all over the world, reaching millions of people. He led more than 400 campaigns in 185 countries and territories on six continents.

As his fame grew, Graham was careful to guard himself from the moral and financial scandals that plagued other Christian leaders. However, his evangelistic campaigns used some of the man-centered techniques popularized by Charles Finney in the previous century such as the invitation system. This system strongly encouraged people to make immediate decisions for Christ. While many people were genuinely converted to Christ under Graham's ministry, there were also many false converts who fell away from the faith.

Beginning in the 1950s, Graham began to include and cooperate with Liberal Protestants and

BILLY GRAHAM (1918-2018)

ELISABETH ELLIOT (1926-2015)

Roman Catholics in his evangelistic campaigns. Liberals and Roman Catholics would sometimes speak alongside Graham at his campaigns. And converts were sometimes encouraged to attend Liberal or Roman Catholic churches where the gospel was not taught. Some evangelical leaders, such as Martyn Lloyd-Jones and Francis Schaeffer, urged Graham to stop such compromising cooperation and drop the invitation system, but he would not do so. Graham thought such methods were needed to reach more people.

The Lord raised up missionaries as well as evangelists. **Elisabeth Elliot** (1926-2015) grew up in a loving Christian family that was heavily involved in Christian ministry. Her parents, the Howards, had been missionaries in Belgium. Elisabeth went to Wheaton College to study Greek and prepare to be a missionary translator. There she met a fellow Greek student named **Jim Elliot** (1927-1956) who was also preparing to be a missionary. Jim and Elisabeth eventually married and became missionaries to unreached tribes in the jungles of Ecuador.

In January 1956, Jim Elliot, Nate Saint, and three other missionaries were martyred while trying to bring the gospel to the Waorani tribe. Elisabeth and the other four wives of the martyred missionaries became widows. But two years later, she went to live among the Waorani with her three-year-old daughter Valerie and Rachel Saint, the sister of Nate Saint. The women were able to share the gospel with the Waorani and see many of them come to faith in Christ.

In 1963, Elisabeth returned to the United States. For the next forty years, she ministered to many people through her writing, speaking, and radio broadcasts for women. She helped many women and stood against **feminism**, the belief that there are no God-created role differences between men and women and that women should be pastors. Feminism was seeping into many evangelical churches, and Elisabeth joined other Christians in arguing against it from the Bible (1 Tim. 2:12, 1 Cor. 14:34-35).

The Azusa Street Revival and the Origins of Pentecostalism

And when they had prayed, the place where they were assembled together was shaken; and they were all filled with the Holy Spirit, and they spoke the word of God with boldness. (Acts 4:31)

Among the most important developments of the 20th century is the birth of the Pentecostal movement. By the end of the 20th century, the Pentecostal and Charismatic movement was one of the largest Protestant groups in the world. The story of Pentecostalism begins in Los Angeles, California. In 1905, a preacher by the name of **William J. Seymour** (1870-1922) came to minister in an old Methodist Church building on **Azusa Street**. Seymour had been discipled in Houston, Texas by **Charles Fox Parham** (1873-1929). Parham believed in divine

AZUSA STREET MISSION

WILLIAM J. SEYMOUR (1870-1922)

healing and advocated ***xenoglossia***, the supernatural gift of speaking in tongues. At the beginning of the early Pentecostal movement, Parham and his followers believed they were speaking in known languages such as Chinese or Hebrew. Parham taught that speaking in tongues was the sign of being baptized by the Holy Spirit as a second work of grace.

Under Seymour's leadership, the **Azusa Street Mission** grew over three years. The meetings were unique for their time. The services were racially integrated. They did not follow any particular liturgy. Many of the participants spoke and sang in tongues. These "tongues" were now taken to be unknown languages (which could not be verified as a language used by a tribe or nation on the earth).

Pentecostalism spread rapidly partly because of its multi-cultural influence. Soon, Pentecostal beliefs and practices spread into foreign nations. Between 1907 and 1910, Pentecostal mission works were established in Argentina, Brazil, South Africa, and Italy. To the present day, that growth has not slowed down. By some estimates, Pentecostalism is still the fastest growing Christian movement in the world in the 2010s. By 1980, Pentecostals and Charismatics made up about 6% of the Christian population worldwide. Thirty years later the number approached 25% of the worldwide Christian population.[2]

In addition to speaking in tongues, Pentecostals believe in the continuing role of prophecy in the church. Theologians Duffield and Van Cleave offer this explanation for the Pentecostal use of prophecy:

> Normally, in the operation of the gift of prophecy, the Spirit heavily anoints the believer to speak forth to the body not premeditated words, but words the Spirit supplies spontaneously in order to uplift and encourage, incite to faithful obedience and service, and to bring comfort and consolation.[3]

Pentecostals and Charismatics also became known for their boldness in evangelism and strength under persecution. In many cases, such as in the Soviet nations and the Islamic states, these denominations along with others have demonstrated steadfast faith under fire. Pentecostal missionaries spread the faith into dangerous territories.

There are aspects of Pentecostal and Charismatic theology that biblical believers should be critical of. However, there are also strengths that can be observed. One strength of the Pentecostal movement is the recognition of the Holy Spirit as active and powerful. Many Christians who are raised in a materialistic, anti-supernaturalist age begin to see God as very distant, less real, and less sovereign over the sparrow that falls and every hair on their heads. By contrast, many Pentecostals and Charismatics see God's intimate involvement in their lives, and by faith they respond in heartfelt gratitude and praise.

On the other hand, there are dangerous aspects to some sectors of the Pentecostal and Charismatic movements. The very-popular **Word of Faith** movement hinges everything on the faith of the one who seeks health and wealth. Word of Faith teachers lost sight of God's ultimate sovereignty and forgot to include Jesus' words: "nevertheless not my will, but Thine be done," in prayer. Also, an emphasis on physical health and wealth appeals more to the carnal desires of those who are not "seeking to lay up for themselves treasures in heaven" and who do not "set their affections on things above" (Matt. 6:19-20, Col. 3:2).

Additionally, the role of prophecy and miracles is another area of concern. The use of prophecy as the means of conveying one's own ideas, the endless seeking after miracles and signs, and the preeminence of personal experiences trump the authority of God's Word among some in Pentecostal and Charismatic churches. The Jews sought continually for signs (1 Cor. 1:22), but they lacked faith. Faith must believe even when it has not witnessed a miraculous healing or a resurrection. "Faith is the substance of things hoped for, the evidence of things not seen" (Heb. 11:1). Additionally, we should be content with God's written Word. It is sufficient for all our needs in faith and life.

The 20th century Pentecostal and Charismatic movements also became known for numerous moral scandals. Of course, false teachers and immoral leaders can appear in any Christian denomination. But the Pentecostal and Charismatic movements were home to many scandals in particular. Christians must be careful not to be overly condemnatory towards brothers and sisters within this movement. Nevertheless, Jesus's warning in Matthew 7 is an important guide for us.

You will know them by their fruits. Do men gather grapes from thornbushes or figs from thistles? Even so, every good tree bears good fruit, but a bad tree bears bad fruit. A good tree cannot bear bad fruit, nor can a bad tree bear good fruit. Every tree that does not bear good fruit is cut down and thrown into the fire. Therefore by their fruits you will know them. (Matt. 7:16-20)

Reformation Movements of the 20th Century

Be watchful, and strengthen the things which remain, that are ready to die, for I have not found your works perfect before God. Remember therefore how you have received and heard; hold fast and repent. (Rev. 3:2-3)

The worldview of secular humanism steadily advanced in the West during the 20th century. Bad ideas, some many centuries old, were bearing bad fruit. The atheist **John Dewey** (1859-1952) had advocated for education absent of the fear of the Lord. **Karl Marx** (1818-1883) had introduced anti-God philosophies of government and economics. Other anti-Christian thinkers such as **Friedrich Nietzsche** (1844-1900) and **Sigmund Freud** (1856-1939) developed secular psychology. These unbiblical and harmful systems began to dominate the educational institutions in the West. Many Christians, lacking discernment, began to think more like the world rather than with the mind of Christ. The church in the West needed a return to a biblical way of thinking. Every thought needed to be taken captive to the obedience of Christ (2 Cor. 10:4-5).

JAY ADAMS (1929-2020)

In 1965, a Presbyterian pastor named **Jay Adams** (1929-2020) reintroduced what he called "nouthetic counseling" or "biblical counseling." Adams was responding to the church's adoption of secular psychology into Christian counseling. He argued for a return to both the theology and method of Scripture in counseling.

THE GENESIS FLOOD

Christian theologians and philosophers like **Francis Schaeffer** (1912-1984), **Gordon Clark** (1902-1985), **Cornelius Van Til** (1895-1987), and **R. J. Rushdoony** (1916-2001) began to identify differences between humanist thinking and Christian thinking. These men helped Christians to renew their minds according to God's Word. These Christian reformers talked about the **Christian worldview** in contrast with unbiblical worldviews. They argued for a distinctively Christian view of knowledge. This reformation of Christian thought also impacted education. New Christian schools formed in the 1960s and 1970s. Between 1980 and 2015, the Christian homeschool movement in the United States grew from almost zero to around 2.5 million children.

In 1961, an important book on Noah's flood was released. ***The Genesis Flood*** was written by two scientists, **Henry Morris** (1918-2006) and **John C. Whitcomb** (1924-2020). At the time of its publication, many Christian pastors had adopted evolutionary or old-earth views of creation. Most of the church fathers and Protestant Reformers believed the universe was created in six days and was quite young. But Christians in the 19th and 20th centuries were influenced by old earth geology and Darwinian evolution. Many believed the universe was billions of years old. Some Christian pastors believed in theistic evolution, that God used the process of evolution to bring about mankind from a lower species.

R.C. SPROUL (1939-2017)

Morris' and Whitcomb's book sparked a movement that became known as **Young Earth Creationism**. Morris and Whitcomb argued that rock layers and fossils should be interpreted in light of what Scripture teaches. The global flood of Noah (occurring about 4,500 years ago) was a cataclysmic event in world history. The historical reality of that flood was to be taken into account when examining geological evidence. Large ministries formed around the doctrine of creation, including the **Institute for Creation Research** and **Answers in Genesis** (founded by Ken Ham, 1951-). Apologetic ministries and worldview training organizations sprouted everywhere. Christian parents and students were equipped to take on an increasingly aggressive anti-Christian world.

God preserved a remnant of Christian faithfulness during the 20th century. Preachers like D. Martyn Lloyd-Jones kept the flame of Protes-

CHRISTIAN CHURCH IN BRAZIL

tant Reformation burning bright. Through such preaching, the Lord's people were discipled in sound doctrine and practice. Various pastors and authors in the 20th century continued to provide faithful teaching for God's people as well. They include **A.W. Pink** (1886-1952), **A.W. Tozer** (1897-1963), **J.I. Packer** (1926-2020), **R.C. Sproul** (1939-2017), and **Jerry Bridges** (1929-2016).

The Future of Christ's Church in the World

There has been a slow but steady departure from the Christian faith in the Western nations of Europe and North America. As a result, these nations have been contributing less and less to the worldwide task of missions. But today, many nations that were formerly the target for Christian missions are now sending out missionaries!

As secular humanism grows in the formerly Christian countries of the West, they are becoming important mission fields. Many people in the West now have no knowledge of Christ and need to be evangelized. Many people from Muslim, Buddhist, and Hindu countries in Africa and Asia are immigrating to Western countries. Many of these immigrants are becoming secular humanists. But there is a great opportunity to reach them for Christ.

There has also been a resurgence of Islam. Islam is rapidly growing in Europe. Christians have suffered terrible persecution from Muslims in Africa and Asia. But the gospel is going forth among Muslims with greater power and effectiveness than ever before. Many Muslims are becoming disillusioned with Islam and converting to Christ.

Remarkable demographic changes have occurred within the Christian church in the last hundred years. In 1900, about 80% of the world's Christians lived in Europe and North America. Only about 20% lived in the Global South (Africa, Asia, and Latin America). But those figures have dramatically changed. According to a 2011 survey, about 65% of the world's Christians live in the Global South while those in Europe and North America only make up about 35%.[4] Present demographic trends suggest that the Christian population will continue to grow in the Global South. It is also likely that the Christian population will continue to decline in Europe and North America. Of course, the Lord can mercifully bring times of reviving in the West. Nevertheless, current trends suggest that the Global South will be where most Christians live in the future.

For much of the 20th century, the United States had one of the largest Christian populations in the world. The US provided much support for worldwide missions. Church attendance in the US also remained high into the 21st century. Until 2014, at least 46% of Americans still believed God created mankind. However, this number dropped to 38% in 2017.[5] By 2016, the world center of missions and faith shifted away from the United States. The Southern Baptists cut 15% of their missions staff.[6] Indigenous missionaries came to replace Western missions in many nations. Native groups in India are now reached by Indian missionaries. America is still the largest missionary-sending country, but nations in the Global South are catching up. In fact, by 2018 there were 285,000 native missionaries serving in Asia and Africa (exceeding the American mission force of 110,000).[7] Thanks be to God for the growth of the church in these lands!

One of the means the Lord is using to spread the gospel throughout the world is technology. Through the internet, people around the world now have access to the Bible in many different languages. They can communicate with Christians and ask them questions through internet chat rooms. The Bible and other Christian resources can now be distributed rapidly and secretly on smartphones and flash drives. The gospel is spreading even in countries where Christianity is outlawed, including North Korea and Afghanistan. Jesus Christ continues to build His church, and the gates of hell will not prevail against it. There is a day coming when every knee will bow and every tongue will confess that Jesus is Lord (Phil. 2:10-11). Let us pray for that day, and let us labor for the Lord with the time He gives us to serve Him. ■

After these things I looked, and behold, a great multitude which no one could number, of all nations, tribes, peoples, and tongues, standing before the throne and before the Lamb, clothed with white robes, with palm branches in their hands, and crying out with a loud voice, saying, "Salvation belongs to our God who sits on the throne, and to the Lamb!" (Rev. 7:9-10)

SUNRISE OVER THE AFRICAN SAVANNA

Endnotes

Chapter 2
1 Tacitus, *Annals*, 15.44.
2 Ibid.
3 Ignatius of Antioch, *Epistle to the Romans*, 5.
4 *Martyrdom of Polycarp*, 14.
5 Eusebius, *Church History*, 5.1.18-19.
6 Ibid., 5.1.56.
7 Peter Leithart, *Defending Constantine: The Twilight of an Empire and the Dawn of Christendom* (Downers Grove, IL: IVP, 2010), 129.

Chapter 3
1 The Apostolic Fathers are available, with explanatory comments, in *Essential Writings on Church History*, edited by Kevin Swanson and Joshua Schwisow, and available from generations.org.
2 All quotations of the Apostolic Fathers are from the translation of Michael W. Holmes, *The Apostolic Fathers in English*, 3rd ed. (Grand Rapids: Baker, 2006).
3 Ignatius, *Letter to the Smyrnaeans*, Chapter 8
4 Ignatius, *Letter to the Trallians*, Chapter 6
5 *The Didache*, Chapter 7
6 *The Letter to Diognetus*, Chapter 9
7 *Didascalia Apostolorum*, Chapter 6
8 *Didascalia Apostolorum*, Chapter 6
9 *Didascalia Apostolorum*, Chapter 13
10 Quotations from Eusebius are taken from Eusebius, *The Church History*, trans. Paul L. Maier (Grand Rapids: Kregel, 2007), This quotation is from Book 2, Chapter 25.
11 Eusebius, *Church History*, Book 3, Chapter 25
12 Eusebius, *Church History*, Book 10, Chapter 1
13 Eusebius, *Church History*, Book 10, Chapter 1

Chapter 4
1 Justin Martyr, *First Apology*, Chapter 67
2 Clement of Alexandria, *Instructor,* 3.4.
3 *Didache,* 2.

Chapter 5
1 Clement, *Exhortation to the Pagans*, Chapter 6
2 Tertullian, *Prescription Against Heretics*, Chapter 7
3 Tertullian, *Prescription Against Heretics*, Chapter 7
4 Tertullian, *Against Marcion*,1.1.

Chapter 6
1 Justo L. Gonzalez, *The Story of Christianity, Volume 1: The Early Church to the Reformation* (New York: Harper Collins, 2010), 233-234.
2 Basil, "Letter to Gregory of Nyssa"
3 Gregory of Nyssa, *Gregorii Nysseni Opera* (GNO), vol. 5, trans. Stuart G. Hall and Rachel Moriarty, *Homilies on Ecclesiastes,* Homily 4, 336.6.
4 Ibid., 336.20.

Chapter 7
1 Philip Schaff, *History of the Christian Church*, Volume 4, Chapter 1.
2 Jerome, *Letter CXXVII (To Principia).*
3 Gregory the Great, *Register of the Epistles*, Book 7, Epistle 33 to Mauricius Augustus.
4 Gregory the Great, *Pastoral Care*, Chapter 8.
5 Ibid.

Chapter 8
1 *Rule of St. Benedict*, Prologue.
2 Ibid., Chap. 2.
3 Ibid., Chap. 7.
4 Ibid., Chap. 48.
5 Ibid., Chap. 20.
6 Ibid., Chap. 55.
7 Ibid., Chap. 39.

Chapter 9
1 Fulcher of Chartres in Bongars, Gesta Dei per Francos, 1, pp. 382 f., trans. in Oliver J. Thatcher, and Edgar Holmes McNeal, eds., *A Source Book for Medieval History* (New York: Scribners, 1905), 513-517. (emphasis added)
2 Quoted in Samuel Zwemer, *Raymond Lull: First Missionary to the Moslems* (New York: Funk & Wagnalls, 1902), 52-53.

Chapter 10
1 Philip Schaff and David S. Schaff, *History of the Christian Church*, vol. 5, The Middle Ages, AD 1049-1294 (New York: Scribner, 1907), 131.
2 Ibid., 128.
3 Gregory the Great, "First Letter to John of Constantinople," quoted in Nick Needham, *2000 Years of Christ's Power, vol. 1, The Age of the Early Church Fathers* (Fearn, Ross-shire, UK: Christian Focus, 2016), 351-352.
4 Gregory the Great, *Register of the Epistles*, Book 7, Epistle 33 to Mauricius Augustus.
5 The popes vying for the title at this time were Pope Benedict IX, Sylvester III, and Gregory VI.
6 These problems persist today in the Roman Catholic Church which still requires celibacy for all priests. The various sexual abuse scandals plaguing the Catholic Church in recent decades demonstrate the damaging effects of this requirement.
7 Quoted in Nick Needham, *2000 Years of Christ's Power, vol. 2, The Middle Ages* (Fearn, Ross-shire, UK: Christian Focus, 2016), 173-174.

Chapter 12
1 These names and the questions they asked are summarized in Phillip Schaff and David S. Schaff, *History of the Christian Church,* vol. 5, The Middle Ages, AD 1049-1294 (New York: Scribner, 1907), 459-460.
2 Anselm, *Proslogion*, Chapter 1.
3 Ibid.
4 Nick Needham, *2000 Years of Christ's Power*, vol. 2, *The Middle Ages* (Fearn, Ross-shire, UK: Christian Focus, 2016), 272.

Chapter 13
1 A "friar" is a term used to describe members of various religious orders including the Dominicans.
2 *Testament of St. Francis.*
3 *Rule of St. Francis*
4 Philip Schaff and David S. Schaff, *History of the Christian Church*, vol. 5, The Middle Ages, AD 1049-1294 (New York: Scribner, 1907), 247.
5 Quoted in Ibid., 250.

Chapter 14
1 Quoted in Nick Needham, *2000 Years of Christ's Power*, vol. 2, *The Middle Ages* (Fearn, Ross-shire, UK: Christian Focus, 2016), 404.
2 quoted in Philip Ziegler, *The Black Death* (New York: Harper, 2009).
3 Philip Schaff and David S. Schaff, *History of the Christian Church*, vol. 6, The Middle Ages, AD 1294-1517 (New York: Scribner, 1910), 91.
4 Quoted in Needham, 404.
5 Council of Constance, Sacrosancta, 1415, quoted in Joseph Alberigo et al., *Conciliorum Oecumenicorum Decreta* (Basel and Rome, 1962), 385.

Chapter 15
1 John Huss, *The Letters of John Hus,* trans. Herbert B. Workman and R. Martin Pope (London: Hodder & Stoughton, 1904), 231.
2 Dialogue taken from *Foxe's Book of Martyrs.*

Chapter 16

1 Quoted in Nick Needham, *2000 Years of Christ's Power*, vol. 3, *Renaissance and Reformation* (Fearn, Ross-shire, UK: Christian Focus, 2016), 62-63.

Chapter 17

1 Quotations from Martin Luther are drawn from the translations provided by biographer Herman Selderhuis in *Martin Luther: A Spiritual Biography* (Wheaton, IL: Crossway, 2017).

Chapter 18

1 Quoted in Nick Needham, *2000 Years of Christ's Power*, vol. 3, *Renaissance and Reformation* (Fearn, Ross-shire, UK: Christian Focus, 2016), 146.

2 Ulrich Zwingli, *Of the Clarity and Certainty of the Word of God,* in Geoffrey Bomiley, ed., *Zwingli and Bullinger* (Philadelphia: The Westminster Press, 1953), 90-91.

3 Ulrich Zwingli, "The Plague Poem," in *The Latin Works and the Correspondence of Huldreich Zwingli,* ed. Samuel Macauley Jackson, trans. Henry Preble, et. al, vol. 1 (New York: G.P. Putnam's Sons, 1912), 56-57.

4 quoted in Bruce Gordon, *Zwingli: God's Armed Prophet* (New Haven: Yale, 2021), 117.

5 Bruce Gordon, *Zwingli: God's Armed Prophet* (New Haven: Yale University Press, 2021), 124.

6 "The Marburg Colloquy and The Marburg Articles, 1529," trans. Martin E. Lehmann in *Luther's Works*, ed. Helmut T. Lehmann and Martin E. Lehmann (Philadelphia: Fortress Press, 1971), 38:88–89.

Chapter 19

1 Quoted in Bruce Gordon, *Zwingli: God's Armed Prophet* (New Haven: Yale University Press, 2021), 106.

2 Menno Simons, "The Reason Menno Simon Does Not Stop Teaching and Writing," in *The Complete Works of Menno Simons* (Elkhart, IN: John F. Funk, 1871), 1:246.

Chapter 20

1 Quoted in John Dillenberger, *John Calvin, Selections from His Writings* (Oxford: Oxford University Press, 1975), 26.

2 John Calvin, "Prefatory Address to King Francis I of France," in *The Institutes of the Christian Religion*, trans. Henry Beveridge (Edinburgh: Calvin Translation Society, 1845).

3 John Calvin, "Author's Preface," *Commentary on the Book of Psalms*, vol. 1, transl. James Anderson (Grand Rapids: Baker, 1993), xlii-xliii.

4 *John Calvin. Tracts and Letters,* 7 vols., ed. Henry Beveridge and Jules Bonnet (Edinburgh: Banner of Truth, 2009), 4:175.

5 Quoted in Nick Needham, *2000 Years of Christ's Power*, vol. 3, *Renaissance and Reformation* (Fearn, Ross-shire, UK: Christian Focus, 2016), 220.

6 Quoted in Phillip Schaff, *History of the Christian Church*, vol. 8, *The Swiss Reformation* (New York: Scribner, 1910), 452.

7 Nick Needham, *2000 Years of Christ's Power*, vol. 3, *Renaissance and Reformation* (Fearn, Ross-Shire, UK: Christian Focus, 2016), 221.

8 John Calvin, "Letter 240 – To Madame de Cany", April 29, 1549, in *Letters of John Calvin*, ed. Jules Bonnet, vol. 2 (Edinburgh: Thomas Constable, 1857), 208-209.

9 Quoted in Steven J. Lawson, *The Expository Genius of John Calvin* (Sanford, FL: Reformation Trust, 2007), 106–107.

10 Quoted in John T. McNeill, *The History and Character of Calvinism* (New York: Oxford University Press, 1967), 178- 179.

11 Quoted in Phillip Schaff, *History of the Christian Church,* vol. 8, *The Swiss Reformation* (New York: Scribner, 1910), 802.

Chapter 21

1 Quoted in Thomas Russell, ed., *The Works of the English Reformers: William Tyndale and John Frith*, 3 vols. (London: Ebenezer Palmer, 1831), 1:437.

2 Ibid., 1:3.

3 John Foxe, *Book of Martyrs*, Chap. 12: "The Life and Story of the True Servant and Martyr of God, William Tyndale."

4 Quoted in David Daniell, *William Tyndale: A Biography* (New Haven: Yale University Press, 1994), 379.

5 *Foxe's Book of Martyrs*, Chap. 12.

Chapter 22

1 *Book of Common Prayer*, "Confession of Sin for Morning and Evening Prayer."

2 Quoted in Chris Skidmore, *Edward VI: The Lost King of England* (New York: St. Martin's Griffin, 2009), 257-258.

3 *Foxe's Book of Martyrs,* Chap. 16: "Persecutions in England During the Reign of Queen Mary."

4 John Foxe, *Foxe's Book of Martyrs*, Chap. 16: "Persecutions in England During the Reign of Queen Mary."

Chapter 23

1 Quoted in Thomas M'Crie, *The Story of the Scottish Church* (London: Blackie & Son, 1875), 61.

2 John Knox, *History of the Reformation in Scotland* (Glasgow: Blackie, Fullerton, & Co., 1831), 34.

3 Quoted in John Howie, *The Scots Worthies*, ed. W.H. Carslaw (Edinburgh: Oliphant, Anderson, & Ferrier, 1885), 63.

4 John Knox's *History of the Reformation in Scotland* is an incredible, action-packed story of God's work in Scotland. Readers can find a modernized and abridged version of Knox's classic in *Great Christian Classics,* vol. 1, published by Generations.

5 M'Crie, *Story,* 11.

6 Knox, *History,* 58.

7 Ibid., 59.

8 Ibid., 64.

9 Ibid., 66.

10 Ibid., 78.

11 Ibid., 83.

12 John Knox, "Letter to Mrs. Lock," in David Laing, ed., *Works of John Knox* (Edinburgh: Bannatyne Club, 1846), 4:240.

13 Knox, *History,* 250.

14 Ibid., 252.

15 Ibid., 253.

Chapter 24

1 Quoted in Nick Needham, *2000 Years of Christ's Power,* vol. 3, *Renaissance and Reformation* (Fearn, Ross-shire, UK: Christian Focus, 2016), 446.

2 Ibid.

3 Ibid.

4 Decrees of the Council of Trent, Session 6, Chap. 9, Canon 9.

5 Ibid., Session 6, Chap. 9, Canon 11.

6 Ibid., Session 7, Canon 1.

Chapter 25

1 Joel R. Beeke and Randall J. Pederson, *Meet the Puritans: With a Guide to Modern Reprints* (Grand Rapids: Reformation Heritage, 2007), xvii.

2 Quoted in ibid.

3 Ibid.

4 Quoted in Thomas Fuller, *Church History of Britain*, vol. 3 (London: Thomas Tegg, 1842), 188.

5 Ibid., 182.

6 Quoted in Thomas M'Crie, *Story of the Scottish Church* (London: Blackie & Son, 1875), 141.
7 Ibid., 355.

Chapter 26

1 Quoted in Justo L. Gonzales, *The Story of Christianity* (Peabody: Prince Press, 2008), 2:207.
2 An excerpt from John Wesley's February 24, 1736 diary entry in *The Works of Rev. John Wesley in Ten Volumes* (New York: J.&J. Harper, 1827), 1:130.
3 Samuel Waldron, *Baptist Roots in America* (Simpson: Boonton, NJ, 1991), 7.
4 C.H. Spurgeon, *The Sword & the Trowel*, April 1887.
5 Susannah Spurgeon, ed., *Spurgeon's Autobiography*, vol. 4: 1878-1892, 277.

Chapter 27

1 "Charter of Georgia: 1732," *The Avalon Project*, Yale Law School, https://avalon.law.yale.edu/18th_century/ga01.asp
2 William Bradford, *Of Plymouth Plantation*, Chap. 4.
3 "Rhode Island Royal Charter granted by King Charles II, 1663," Rhode Island State Archives, https://catalog.sos.ri.gov/repositories/2/digital_objects/628.

Chapter 28

1 J.I. Packer, *Your Father Loves You: Daily Insights for Knowing God* (Shaw Publications, 1986).
2 George Whitefield, *George Whitefield's Journals* (Lafayette, IN: Sovereign Grace Publishers, 2000), 26.
3 Quoted in Luke Tyerman, *The Life of the Rev. George Whitefield*, vol. 1 (New York: Anson D.F. Randolph & Co., 1877), 76.
4 Ibid., 84.
5 Quoted in Robert Philip, *The Life and Times of the Rev. George Whitefield* (London: J.R. & C. Childs, 1837), 103.
6 Luke Jackson, *The Life of the Rev. Charles Wesley* (New York: G. Lane & P.P. Sandford, 1842), 94.
7 Arnold Dallimore, *George Whitefield: The Life and Times of the Great Evangelist of the Eighteenth-Century Revival*, vol. 1 (Edinburgh: Banner of Truth, 1970), 140.
8 Ibid., 587.
9 George Whitefield, *The Works of the Reverend George Whitefield*, vol. 1 (London: Edward & Charles Dilly, 1771), 405.
10 John Wesley, *Journal of John Wesley*, ed. Percy L. Walker (Chicago: Moody Press, 1951), 55.
11 John Wesley and Charles Wesley, *The Nature, Design, and General Rules, of the United Societies* (Bristol: Felix Farley, 1743).
12 John Wesley, *Works of the Rev. John Wesley*, vol. 5 (New York: J. Emory & B. Waugh, 1831), 219.
13 J.R. Green, *A Short History of the English People*, vol. 4 (London: Macmillan & Co., 1903), 1612.

Chapter 29

1 Benjamin Whichcote, *Moral and Religious Aphorisms* (London: J. Payne, 1753), 76.
2 John Knox, *The Works of John Knox*, ed. David Laing (Edinburgh, 1895), 6:619.
3 Charles Hodge, *What is Darwinism?* (New York: Charles Scribner's Sons, 1874), 177.
4 Charles Hodge, *Systematic Theology*, 3 vols. (Grand Rapids: Eerdmans, 1872, reprinted 1982), 1:570.

Chapter 30

1 Quoted in Iain Murray, *The Puritan Hope: Revival and the Interpretation of Prophecy* (Edinburgh: Banner of Truth, 1971), 140.
2 Stephen Neill, *A History of Christian Missions*, 2nd ed. (New York: Penguin, 1991), 226.
3 William Napier, *History of General Sir Charles Napier's Administration of Scinde* (London: Chapman and Hall, 1851), 35.
4 Quoted in Iain Murray, *The Puritan Hope*, 141.
5 Quoted in Richard France, "Henry Martyn," in *Five Pioneer Missionaries* (Edinburgh: Banner of Truth Trust, 1965), 266.
6 Ibid., 274.
7 Ibid., 296.
8 Quoted in Courtney Anderson, *To the Golden Shore: The Life of Adoniram Judson* (Judson Press, 1987), 193.
9 Edward Judson, *The Life of Adoniram Judson* (New York: Anson D.F. Randolph & Co., 1883), 157.
10 Ibid., 253.
11 James Paton, ed., *John G. Paton: Missionary to the New Hebrides: An Autobiography* (New York: Fleming Revell Co., 1898), 23.
12 Ibid., 34.
13 Ibid., 119.
14 Ibid., 90-91.
15 Ibid., 190-191.
16 Ibid., 260.
17 Ibid., 261.
18 Ibid., 127.
19 Westminster Larger Catechism, Q. 191
20 Quoted in Murray, *The Puritan Hope*, 101.
21 Andrew A. Bonar and Robert Murray M'Cheyne, *Narrative of a Mission of Inquiry to the Jews from the Church of Scotland in 1839* (Philadelphia: Presbyterian Board of Publication, 1845), 49.
22 Ibid., 132.
23 Ibid., 149.
24 Ibid., 513.

Chapter 31

1 Quoted in John B. Boles, *The Great Revival: Beginnings of the Bible Belt* (Lexington: University of Kentucky Press, 1996), 49.
2 Ibid., 93.
3 Quoted in Collin Hansen and John Woodbridge, *A God-Sized Vision: Revival Stories That Stretch and Stir* (Grand Rapids: Zondervan, 2010), 65.
4 Quoted in William Speer, *The Great Revival of 1800* (Philadelphia: Presbyterian Board of Publication, 1872), 85.
5 Quoted in Iain Murray, *Revival and Revivalism: The Making and Marring of American Evangelicalism, 1750-1858* (Edinburgh: Banner of Truth, 1994), 285.
6 Ibid., 289.
7 Melissa Steffan, "The Surprising Countries Most Missionaries Are Sent From and Go To," http://www.christianitytoday.com/gleanings/2013/july/missionaries-countries-sent-received-csgc-gordon-conwell.html
8 Tertullian, *Apology*, 50.
9 Iain Murray, *A Scottish Christian Heritage* (Edinburgh: Banner of Truth, 2006), 80.
10 Ibid., 89.
11 Dr. and Mrs. Howard Taylor, *Hudson Taylor in the Early Years: The Growth of a Soul* (Singapore: OMF International, 1998), 1:349.
12 Thomas Phillips, *The Welsh Revival: Its Origin and Development* (Edinburgh: Banner of Truth, 1989), 7.
13 Ibid., 9.
14 Ibid., 119ff.

Chapter 32

1 Woodrow Wilson, *The Constitutional Government of the United States* (New York: Columbia University Press, [1908] 1961), 54-57.
2 Quoted in Stephen J. Nichols, *J. Gresham Machen: A Guided Tour of His Life and Thought* (Phillipsburg, NJ: P&R, 2004), 87-88.
3 Harry Emerson Fosdick, "Shall the Fundamentalists Win?" May 21, 1922.
4 Quoted in Ned B. Stonehouse, *J. Gresham Machen: A Biographical Memoir* (Willow Grove, PA: The Committee for the Historian of the Orthodox Presbyterian Church, repr. 2004), 295.
5 J. Gresham Machen, *Christianity and Liberalism* (Grand Rapids, MI: Eerdmans, 1923, repr. 2009), 82.
6 Quoted in Stonehouse, 417.
7 Quoted in ibid., 418.
8 Quoted in ibid., 419.

Chapter 33

1 Achim Maseko, *Church Schism and Corruption* (Durban, South Africa: Lulu, 2008), 154.
2 Alexander N. Yakovlev, *A Century of Violence in Soviet Russia* (New Haven: Yale University Press, 2002), 165.
3 Dimitry Mustafin, *My Beloved Russia: A Story of God's Love for a Persecuted People* (Christian Focus, 2005), 15.
4 These figures are found in Matthew Heise, *The Gates of Hell: An Untold Story of Faith and Perseverance in the Soviet Union* (Bellingham, WA: Lexham Press, 2022), 11.
5 Quoted in ibid., 16.
6 Ibid., 22.
7 Ibid., 41.
8 Brother Andrew, *God's Smuggler* (New York: Signet, 1968), 112.
9 Ibid., 183.
10 Ibid., 148.
11 Richard Wurmbrand, *Tortured for Christ* (Bartlesville, OK: Living Sacrifice Book Company, 1967), 16.
12 Ibid., 31-32.
13 Ibid., 40.
14 Ibid., 43.
15 Ibid., 57.
16 Ibid., 74.
17 Ibid., 94.
18 Ibid., 90.

Chapter 34

1 Paul Berben, *Dachau: The Official History: 1933–1945* (London: Norfolk Press, 1975), 142.
2 *The Barmen Declaration*
3 Dietrich Bonhoeffer, *Life Together: The Classic Exploration of Christian Community* (New York: Harper, 1978), 112-113.
4 Eberhard Bethge, *Dietrich Bonhoeffer: A Biography* (Minneapolis: Fortress Press, 2000), 927.
5 Corrie Ten Boom, *The Hiding Place* (Grand Rapids: Chosen Books, 1984), 247-248.
6 The details of this account are drawn from Tim Townsend, *Mission to Nuremberg: An American Army Chaplain and the Trial of the Nazis* (New York: Harper, 2014).
7 Quoted in ibid., 174.
8 Quoted in ibid.
9 Quoted in ibid., 224.
10 Quoted in ibid., 236.
11 Quoted in ibid., 253.
12 Quoted in ibid., 260.
13 Quoted in ibid., 261.
14 Quoted in ibid., 264-265.
15 Quoted in ibid., 272.
16 Quoted in ibid., 273.
17 Quoted in ibid., 277.

Chapter 35

1 Nat Brandt, *Massacre in Shansi* (Syracuse: Syracuse University Press, 1994), 221.
2 Ibid., 222.
3 Ibid., 232.
4 Ibid.
5 Brother Yun, *The Heavenly Man: The Remarkable True Story of Chinese Christian Brother Yun* (Grand Rapids: Monarch Books, 2002), 76.
6 Ibid., 50.
7 Ibid., 52.
8 Ibid., 53.
9 William Blair and Bruce Hunt, *The Korean Pentecost and the Sufferings Which Followed* (Edinburgh: Banner of Truth, 2015), 86.
10 Ibid., 86-87.
11 Ibid., 176-184.
12 Timothy Kiho Park, "A Survey of the Korean Missionary Movement," *Journal of Asian Missions*, 4:1 (2002), 111.

Chapter 36

1 Quoted in Steven Lawson, *The Passionate Preaching of Martyn Lloyd-Jones* (Sanford, FL: Reformation Trust, 2016), 8.
2 Richard Vijgen Grantee and Bregtje van der Haak, "Pentecostalism: Massive Global Growth Under the Radar," *Pulitzer Center,* March 9, 2015, http://pulitzercenter.org/reporting/global-religion-evangelical-church-pentecostal.
3 Guy P. Duffield and Nathaniel M. Van Cleave, *Foundations of Pentecostal Theology* (Los Angeles: Foursquare Media, 1983), 347.
4 Philip Jenkins, *The Next Christendom: The Coming of Global Christianity* (New York: Oxford University Press, 2011), 3.
5 Art Swift, "In U.S., Belief in Creationist View of Humans at New Low," *Gallup,* May 22, 2017, http://news.gallup.com/poll/210956/belief-creationist-view-humans-new-low.aspx.
6 "Southern Baptists Lose Almost 1,000 Missionaries After Budget Cuts," *CBN News,* February 28, 2016, https://www1.cbn.com/cbnnews/us/2016/Southern-Baptists-Lose-Almost-1000-Missionaries-After-Budget-Cuts.
7 "Statistics," *About Missions,* http://www.aboutmissions.org/statistics.html.

Bibliography

Below is a list of works consulted or quoted in the research and writing of *How Jesus Built His Church*. These works may be consulted with benefit by the parent/teacher or student to learn more about the topics covered in this book. Books on this list may be acquired for additional learning or for essay development. However, in a few cases, books consulted in research are written from a perspective not consistent with biblical orthodoxy. The parent/teacher is advised to use Christian discernment in the use of these additional works.

Anderson, Courtney, *To the Golden Shore: The Life of Adoniram Judson* (Judson Press, 1987).
Anselm, *Proslogion.*
Beeke, Joel R. and Randall J. Pederson, *Meet the Puritans: With a Guide to Modern Reprints* (Reformation Heritage Books, 2007).
Benedict of Nursia, *Rule of Saint Benedict.*
Bethge, Eberhard, *Dietrich Bonhoeffer: A Biography* (Fortress Press, 2000).
Beveridge, Henry, and Jules Bonnet, ed., *John Calvin: Tracts and Letters*, 7 volumes (Banner of Truth, 2009).
Blair, William, and Bruce Hunt, *The Korean Pentecost and the Sufferings Which Followed* (Banner of Truth, 2015).
Boles, John B., *The Great Revival: Beginnings of the Bible Belt* (University of Kentucky Press, 1996).
Bonar, Andrew and Robert Murray M'Cheyne, *Narrative of a Mission of Inquiry to the Jews from the Church of Scotland in 1839* (Presbyterian Board of Publication, 1845).
Bonhoeffer, Dietrich, *Life Together: The Classic Exploration of Christian Community* (Harper, 1978).
Bradford, William, *Of Plymouth Plantation.*
Bromiley, Geoffrey, ed., *Zwingli and Bullinger* (The Westminster Press, 1953).
Brother Andrew, *God's Smuggler* (Signet, 1968).
Brother Yun, *The Heavenly Man: The Remarkable True Story of Chinese Christian Brother Yun* (Monarch Books, 2002).
Calvin, John, *Institutes of the Christian Religion.*
Clement of Alexandria, *The Instructor.*
Clement of Alexandria, *Exhortation to the Pagans.*
Dallimore, Arnold, *George Whitefield: The Life and Times of the Great Evangelist of the 18th Century Revival, Vol. 1* (Banner of Truth, 1970).
Dallimore, Arnold, *George Whitefield: The Life and Times of the Great Evangelist of the 18th Century Revival, Vol. 2* (Banner of Truth, 1980).
Dallimore, Arnold, *Spurgeon: A New Biography* (Banner of Truth, 1985).
Daniell, David, *William Tyndale: A Biography* (Yale University Press, 2001).
Davis, R.H.C., *A History of Medieval Europe: From Constantine to Saint Louis,* edited by R.I. Moore (Routledge, 2006)
Didascalia Apostolorum in English, ed. and trans. By Margaret Dunlop Gibson (Cambridge University Press, 2011).
Dillenberger, John, *John Calvin, Selections from His Writings* (Oxford University Press, 1975).
Duffield, Guy P., and Nathaniel M. Van Cleave, *Foundations of Pentecostal Theology* (Foursquare Media, 1983).
Eusebius, *The Church History,* trans. Paul L. Maier (Kregel, 2007).
Fairbairn, Donald, *The Global Church, The First Eight Centuries: From Pentecost Through the Rise of Islam* (Zondervan, 2021).
Ferguson, Everett, *Church History, Volume 1: From Christ to the Pre-Reformation* (Zondervan, 2013).
France, Richard, *Five Pioneer Missionaries* (Banner of Truth Trust, 1965).
Francis of Assisi, *Rule of St. Francis.*
Francis of Assisi, *Testament of St. Francis.*
Foxe, John, *Book of Martyrs.*
Fuller, Thomas, *Church History of Britain* (Thomas Tegg, 1842).
Gonzalez, Justo L., *The Story of Christianity, Vol. 1: The Early Church to the Dawn of the Reformation* (Harper, 2010).
Gonzalez, Justo L., *The Story of Christianity, Vol. 2: The Reformation to the Present Day* (Harper, 2010).
Gordon, Bruce, *Calvin* (Yale University Press, 2009).
Gordon, Bruce, *Zwingli: God's Armed Prophet* (Yale University Press, 2021).
Green, J.R., *A Short History of the English People, vol. 4* (Macmillan & Co., 1903).
Gregory of Nyssa, *Homilies on Ecclesiastes.*
Gregory the Great, *Register of the Epistles.*
Gregory the Great, *Pastoral Care.*
Hamer, Colin, *Thomas Cranmer* (Evangelical Press, 2012).
Hansen, Collin, and John Woodbridge, *A God-Sized Vision: Revival Stories That Stretch and Stir* (Zondervan, 2010).
Heise, Matthew, *The Gates of Hell: An Untold Story of Faith and Perseverance in the Early Soviet Union* (Lexham Press, 2022).
Hodge, Charles, *Systematic Theology,* 3 volumes (Eerdmans, 1872).
Hodge, Charles, *What is Darwinism?* (Charles Scribner's Sons, 1874).
Holmes, Michael W., *The Apostolic Fathers in English* (Baker Books, 2006).
Howie, John, *The Scots Worthies* (Oliphant, Anderson, & Ferrier, 1885).
Huss, John, *Letters of John Hus* (Hodder & Stoughton, 1904).
Jackson, Luke, *The Life of the Rev. Charles Wesley* (G. Lane & P.P. Sandford, 1842).
Jenkins, Philip, *The Next Christendom: The Coming of Global Christianity* (Oxford University Press, 2011).
Judson, Edward, *The Life of Adoniram Judson* (Anson D.F. Randolph & Co., 1883).
Knox, John, *History of the Reformation in Scotland.*
Kruger, Michael J., *Christianity at the Crossroads: How the Second Century Shaped the Future of the Church* (IVP, 2018).
Kuiper, B.K., *The Church in History* (Eerdmans, 1964).

Lahey, Stephen E, *John Wyclif* (Oxford University Press, 2009).
Laing, David, ed., *Works of John Knox*, 6 volumes (Bannatyne Club, 1846).
Lawson, Steven J., *The Bible Convictions of John Wycliffe* (Ligonier Ministries, 2021).
Lawson, Steven J., *The Daring Mission of William Tyndale* (Reformation Trust, 2014).
Lawson, Steven J., *The Expository Genius of John Calvin* (Reformation Trust, 2007).
Lawson, Steven J., *The Passionate Preaching of Martyn Lloyd-Jones* (Reformation Trust, 2016).
Leithart, Peter, *Defending Constantine: The Twilight of an Empire and the Dawn of Christendom* (IVP, 2010).
Machen, J. Gresham, *Christianity and Liberalism* (Eerdmans, 1923, repr. 2009).
Madigan, Kevin, *Medieval Christianity: A New History* (Yale University Press, 2015).
Markus, R.A., *Gregory the Great and His World* (Cambridge University Press, 1997).
M'Crie, Thomas, *The Story of the Scottish Church* (Blackie & Son, 1875).
McNeill, John T., *The History and Character of Calvinism* (Oxford University Press, 1967).
Metaxas, Eric, *Bonhoeffer: Pastor, Martyr, Prophet, Spy* (Thomas Nelson, 2010).
Metaxas, Eric, *Martin Luther: The Man Who Rediscovered God and Changed the World* (Viking, 2017).
Murray, Iain H., *Evangelicalism Divided: A Record of Crucial Change in the Years 1950 to 2000* (Banner of Truth, 2000).
Murray, Iain H., *The Puritan Hope: Revival and the Interpretation of Prophecy* (Banner of Truth, 1971).
Murray, Iain H., *Revival & Revivalism: The Making and Marring of American Evangelicalism, 1750-1858* (Banner of Truth, 1994).
Murray, Iain H., *A Scottish Christian Heritage* (Banner of Truth, 2006).
Mustafin, Dimitry, *My Beloved Russia: A Story of God's Love for a Persecuted People* (Christian Focus, 2005).
Napier, William, *History of General Sir Charles Napier's Administration of Scinde (Chapman and Hall, 1851).*
Needham, Nick, *2000 Years of Christ's Power, Vol. 1: The Age of the Early Church Fathers* (Christian Focus, 2016).
Needham, Nick, *2000 Years of Christ's Power, Vol. 2: The Middle Ages* (Christian Focus, 2016).
Needham, Nick, *2000 Years of Christ's Power, Vol. 3: Renaissance and Reformation* (Christian Focus, 2016).
Needham, Nick, *2000 Years of Christ's Power, Vol. 4: The Age of Religious Conflict* (Christian Focus, 2016).
Nichols, Stephen J., *J. Gresham Machen: A Guided Tour of His Life and Thought* (P&R, 2004).
Neill, Stephen, *A History of Christian Missions* (Penguin, 1991).
Parker, G.H.W., *The Morning Star: Wycliffe and the Dawn of the Reformation* (Wipf and Stock, 2006).
Paton, James, ed., *John G. Paton: Missionary to the New Hebrides: An Autobiography* (Fleming Revell & Co., 1898).
Philip, Robert, *The Life and Times of the Rev. George Whitefield* (J.R. & C. Childs, 1837).
Phillips, Thomas, *The Welsh Revival: Its Origin and Development* (Banner of Truth, 1989).
Russell, Thomas, ed., *The Works of the English Reformers: William Tyndale and John Frith,* 3 volumes (Ebenezer Palmer, 1831).
Schaff, David S., *John Huss: His Life, Teachings and Death After Five Hundred Years* (Charles Scribner's Sons, 1915).
Schaff, Philip, and David S. Schaff, *History of the Christian Church,* 8 volumes (Charles Scribner's Sons, 1910).
Schmidt, Alvin J. *How Christianity Changed the World* (Zondervan, 2004).
Selderhuis, Herman, *Martin Luther: A Spiritual Biography* (Crossway, 2017).
Simons, Menno, *The Complete Works of Menno Simons,* 2 volumes (John F. Funk, 1871).
Skidmore, Chris, *Edward VI: The Lost King of England* (St. Martin's Griffin, 2009).
Speer, William, *The Great Revival of 1800* (Presbyterian Board of Publication, 1872).
Spurgeon, Susannah, ed., *C.H. Spurgeon Autobiography*, 2 volumes (Banner of Truth, 1962).
Stonehouse, Ned B., *J. Gresham Machen: A Biographical Memoir* (Orthodox Presbyterian Church, 2004).
Swanson, Kevin, *Epoch: The Rise and Fall of the West* (Generations, 2021).
Swanson, Kevin, *Taking the World for Jesus: The Remarkable Story of the Greatest Commission* (Master Books/Generations, 2017).
Tacitus, Annals.
Taylor, Dr. and Mrs. Howard, *Hudson Taylor in the Early Years: The Growth of a Soul* (OMF International, 1998).
Ten Boom, Corrie, *The Hiding Place* (Chosen Books, 1984).
Tertullian, *Apology.*
Tertullian, *Against Marcion.*
Tertullian, *Prescription Against Heretics.*
Townsend, Tim, *Mission at Nuremberg: An American Army Chaplain and the Trial of the Nazis* (William Morrow, 2014).
Tracy, Joseph, *The Great Awakening: A History of the Revival of Religion in the Time of Whitefield and Edwards* (Banner of Truth, 1842, repr. 2019)
Tyerman, Luke, *The Life of the Rev. George Whitefield,* 2 volumes (Anson D.F. Randolph & Co., 1877).
Tyndale, William, *Tyndale's 1534 New Testament,* edited by David Daniell (Yale University Press, 1989).
Waldron, Samuel. *Baptist Roots in America* (Simpson, 1991).
Wesley, John, *Works of John Wesley,* 10 volumes (J.&J. Harper, 1827).
Whichcote, Benjamin, *Moral and Religious Aphorisms* (J. Payne, 1753).
White, James F., *A Brief History of Christian Worship* (Abingdon Press, 1993).
Whitefield, George, *George Whitefield's Journals* (Sovereign Grace Publishers, 2000).
Whitefield, George, *The Works of the Reverend George Whitefield,* vol. 1 (Edward & Charles Dilly, 1771).
Wilson, Derek, *The People's Bible: The Remarkable History of the King James Version* (Lion, 2011).
Wilson, Woodrow, *The Constitutional Government of the United States* (Columbia University Press, 1908).
Woodbridge, John D. and Frank A. James III, *Church History, Volume 2: From Pre-Reformation to the Present Day* (Zondervan, 2013).
Wurmbrand, Richard, *Tortured for Christ* (Voice of the Martyrs, 1967).
Zwemer, Samuel, *Raymond Lull: First Missionary to the Moslems* (Funk & Wagnalls, 1902).